Jesus, Son and Savior
A Catechesis on The Creed

Pope John Paul II

With a Foreword
by Rev. Paul E. Ritt, S.T.D.

Pauline
BOOKS & MEDIA
BOSTON

Library of Congress Cataloging in Publication Data

John Paul II, Pope, 1920-
    Jesus, Son, and Savior / Pope John Paul II.
       p. cm.
    Includes index.
    ISBN 0-8198-3959-0
      1. Jesus Christ—Papal documents. 2. Jesus Christ—Person
and offices—Papal documents. 3. Nicene creed—Papal documents. 5. Catholic Church—Doctrines—Papal documents.
I. Title.
BT202.J63   1996
232—dc20   96-38587
                                                   CIP

Reprinted with permission from *L'Osservatore Romano,* English
Edition.

Cover: *Raphael.* Detail from the Transfiguration. Pinacoteca,
      Vatican Museums, Vatican State.

Printed and published in the U.S.A. by Pauline Books & Media, 50
St. Paul's Avenue, Boston, MA 02130.

Pauline Books & Media is the publishing house of the Daughters of
St. Paul, an international congregation of women religious serving
the Church with the communications media.

1 2 3 4   99 98 97 96

Contents

The Miracles of Christ

The Church's Faith in Jesus Christ

The Mission of Christ

The Mystery of Redemption

Foreword

John Paul II has produced an impressive corpus of writings since he was elected Pope in 1978. At the heart of this vast collection of papal literature is a deep and sustained reflection on the person and work of Jesus Christ. Beginning with his first encyclical, *Redemptor Hominis* (1979), the present Pope has focused the contemporary Church's attention on the unique identity and saving mission of Jesus Christ, our Redeemer. Time after time, John Paul II has reminded his readers that by the Incarnation the Son of God united himself with every human being, thus elevating human nature to an incomparable dignity, and drawing the Body of Christ, the Church, into intimate communion with God. Indeed, the Holy Father has repeatedly described the aim of catechesis as putting people in communion with Jesus Christ, who alone can lead us to a share in the life of the triune God (cf. *Catechesi Tradendae* 15).

This volume contains a series of catecheses on Jesus Christ that the Pope delivered in his general audience addresses from 1986-1989. His talks constitute an extended papal commentary on the articles of the Apostles' and Nicene-Constantinopolitan Creeds in which the Church expresses faith in the Lord Jesus. Affirming the best instincts of Catholic theologians today, the Pope locates his Christology within anthropology and history. In other words, Christ-talk is all about the Word of God becoming flesh and dwelling among us in the setting of history.

John Paul II contextualizes his remarks on Christ with an initial explanation of the mystery of sin which surrounds, besets and alienates the human person. Because of sin, humanity and indeed all of creation cry out for the divine gift of redemption. The Pope then takes up the same penetrating question which Jesus posed to his disciples: "Who do you say that I am?" Tapping the content of his answer from what he calls "the perennial font of Sacred Tradition and Sacred Scripture," the Holy Father presents a portrait of Jesus the Redeemer, who saves us *from* sin and *for* love of one another. In the course of his answer to Jesus' famous question, John Paul II focuses on prominent biblical titles and the ancient conciliar description of Jesus Christ as "true God and true man."

In his running catechesis on the mystery of Christ, the Pope covers and clarifies several contemporary Christological issues, such as the relationship between the divinity and humanity of Christ, the nature and extent of Jesus' self-awareness, the proper interpretation of Christ's miracles, the significance of Jesus' suffering and death on the cross, and the historicity of the resurrection. The Pope concludes his reflections with an explanation of the lordship of Jesus Christ, who is the fulfillment of history and God's final Word on eternal life.

During his years as Bishop of Rome, John Paul II has taught the Church and the world about the life, death and resurrection of our Redeemer. This collection of instructions serves both as a compendium of his papal teaching on Christ and as an authentic companion to the Christological section (nn. 422-682) of the *Catechism of the Catholic Church.* Those who read these pages will find enlightenment for the mind, food for the soul, and motivation for Christian discipleship in the world.

Rev. Paul E. Ritt, S.T.D.
Professor of Systematic Theology
St. John's Seminary, Brighton, MA

THE MYSTERY OF SIN

Sin Involves the Deep Deformation of Creation

After the catecheses on God as One and Three, the provident Creator, Father and Lord of the universe, we open another series of catecheses on God as Savior.

The fundamental reference point for the present catecheses is also found in the formulas of faith, especially in the most ancient of these, which is called the Apostles' Creed, and by the one known as the Nicene-Constantinopolitan Creed. These are also the best known and most used creeds in the Church, the former especially in the prayer of Christians, and the latter in the liturgy. Both texts have a similar arrangement of their contents, which proceed from the articles that speak of God, the almighty Father, Creator of heaven and earth and of all that is visible and invisible, to the articles that speak of Jesus Christ.

The Apostles' Creed is concise: (I believe) "in Jesus Christ his (i.e., God's) only Son, our Lord, who was conceived by the Holy Spirit, born of the Virgin Mary..." etc.

The Nicene-Constantinopolitan Creed, on the other hand, notably amplifies the profession of faith in the divinity of Christ the Son of God: "Born of the Father before all ages...begotten, not created, of one substance with the Father," who—and this is the passage to the mystery of the incarnation of the Word—"for us men and for our salvation...came down from heaven; by the power of the Holy Spirit...was born of the Virgin Mary, and became man." At this point, both creeds present the components of the paschal mystery of Jesus Christ, and announce his second coming for the judgment.

Both creeds go on to profess faith in the Holy Spirit. We must therefore emphasize that their essential structure is trinitarian: Father—Son—Holy Spirit. At the same time, they contain the salient elements that constitute the action *ad extra* of the Most Holy Trinity. They speak first of the mystery of creation (by the Father as Creator) and then of the mysteries of redemption (by the Son as Redeemer), and of the mysteries of sanctification (by the Holy Spirit who makes holy).

The whole created cosmos

Thus, following the creeds, after the cycle of catecheses about the mystery of the creation—or better, about God as Creator of everything—we pass now to a cycle of catecheses that concern the mystery of redemption, or better, God as the Redeemer of man and of the world. These will be the catecheses about Jesus Christ (Christology). Although the work of redemption pertains to the God who is One and Three (like the work of creation), it was brought about in time by Jesus Christ, the Son of God who became man in order to save us.

Let us note at once that in this sphere of the mystery of redemption, Christology is located within anthropology and history. This is because the Son who is consubstantial with the Father and became man by the work of the Holy Spirit and was born of the Virgin Mary, entered the history of humanity in the context of the whole created cosmos. He became man "for us men *(propter nos homines)* and for our salvation *(et propter nostram salutem*)." The mystery of the Incarnation *(et incarnatus est)* is seen by the creed as part of the redemption. According to revelation and to the faith of the Church, it has therefore a salvific (soteriological) meaning.

For this reason, when the creeds locate the mystery of the salvific Incarnation within the setting of history, they touch on the reality of evil, and in the first place the evil of sin. For salvation means above all liberation from evil and, in particular, liberation from sin. However, it is obvious that the scope of this term (salvation) is not reduced to this but embraces the riches of the divine life that Christ has brought to humanity. According to revelation, sin is the principal and fundamental evil. It contains the rejection of God's will, of the truth and holiness of God and of his fatherly goodness, as they are already revealed in the work of creation, and above all in the creation of the rational and free beings who are made "in the image and likeness" of the Creator. It is precisely this "image and likeness" that is used against God, when the rational being of his own free will rejects the finality which God has established for the existence and life of the creature. Sin therefore contains a particularly deep deformation of the created good, especially in a being that, like man, is the image and likeness of God.

In its very root, the mystery of the redemption is joined to the reality of man's sin. It follows that when we explain the articles of the creed which speak of Jesus Christ, in whom and by whom God has accomplished salvation, we must confront the theme of sin in this systematic catechesis. Sin is the obscure reality diffused abroad in the world created by God. It lies at the root of all the evil in man, and, one can also say, in what is created. Only in this way can one fully understand the meaning of the fact that, according to revelation, the Son of God became man "for us men" and "for our salvation." The history of salvation presupposes de facto the existence of sin in the history of humanity, created by God. The salvation of which divine revelation speaks is first of all the liberation from the evil that is sin. This is the central truth of Christian soteriology—*"propter nos homines et propter nostram salutem descendit de coelis."*

Here we must say that, in consideration of the centrality of the truth about salvation in all of divine revelation—and, in other words, in consideration of the centrality of the mystery of redemption—the truth about sin also takes its place in the central nucleus of the Christian faith. Sin and redemption are correlative terms in the history of salvation. We must reflect first of all on the truth about sin, in order to give due meaning to the truth about the redemption wrought by Jesus Christ, which we profess in the creed. One could say that it is the interior logic of revelation and of faith that impels us to concern ourselves in these catecheses above all with sin.

We have been prepared for this in a certain measure by the cycle of catecheses on divine Providence. As the First Vatican Council teaches: "God conserves and directs by his providence all that he has created," and the Council quotes the Book of Wisdom: "reaching from one end to the other with might, and governing all things with goodness" (cf. Wis 8:1; *DS* 3003).

When it affirmed this universal care for the things which God conserves and guides with a powerful hand and the tenderness of a Father, this Council stated precisely that divine Providence embraces in a particular way all that the rational and free beings introduce into the work of creation. Now we know that this consists in acts of their faculties, which can be in conformity or in opposition to the divine will; this therefore includes sin.

As we see, the truth about divine Providence allows us to see sin also in a proper perspective; it is in this light that the creeds help us to reflect on it. In reality—let us say this right at the beginning of the first catechesis on sin—the creeds only touch on this theme. But precisely in this, they suggest that we examine sin from the perspective of the mystery of redemption, in soteriology. We can immediately go on to say that the truth about creation, and still more the truth about divine Providence, allows us to approach the problem of evil, and especially the problem of sin, with clarity of vision and precise terms. This is because of the revelation of the infinite goodness of God. The truth about redemption will make us profess, along with the Apostle, *"ubi abundavit delictum, super-abundavit gratia*—where sin increased, grace abounded all the more"* (Rom 5:20), because it will let us discover better the mysterious reconciliation in God of justice and mercy, which are the two dimensions of his goodness. We can already say that the reality of sin becomes, in the light of redemption, the occasion for a deeper knowledge of the mystery of God, of the God who is love (cf. 1 Jn 4:16).

Faith enters into an attentive dialogue with the many voices of philosophy, literature, and the great religions, which often speak of the roots of evil and sin, and frequently yearn for the light of redemption. It is precisely on this common ground that the Christian faith seeks to bring the truth and the grace of divine revelation, to the benefit of all.

General audience of August 27, 1986

Sin Involves the
Misuse of God's Gifts

Although the formulas of faith use few words when speaking of sin, the term and the concept of "sin" are found with greater frequency in Sacred Scripture. This proves that, while Sacred Scripture is the book of God and about God, it is also a great book about man. It takes him as he is, and as he experiences his existential condition. For sin belongs to man and to his history. It would be futile to attempt to overlook it or to give this obscure reality other names, or other interpretations, as has happened under the influence of the Enlightenment and of secularism. If sin is acknowledged as a reality, we recognize at the same time a profound bond between humanity and God. This is because the evil of sin does not appear in its true dimension outside this relationship between man and God, although it obviously continues to be present in human life and in history. Sin weighs down on man as an obscure and deadly reality. This happens all the more when it is not known, recognized and identified in its essence as denial of and opposition to God. Naturally the human person is the subject and agent of this choice. He can reject the dictates of his own conscience even without explicitly referring to God. But his insane and evil act acquires its full negative meaning only when it is seen against the background of man's relationship with God.

For this reason, Sacred Scripture describes the first sin in the context of the mystery of creation. In other words, the sin committed at the beginning of human history is presented against the background of creation, that is, of God's magnificent gift of existence. In the context of the visible world, man receives his existence as a gift—as the "image and likeness of God," a rational being, endowed with intellect and will. Within the context of God's creative gift we can best see the essence of the first sin—man's free choice made with a misuse of these faculties.

Obviously we are not speaking here of the beginning of history as scientific theories describe it, but of the "beginning" as it appears in the pages of Scripture. Scripture uncovers in this "beginning" the origin of the moral evil which humanity experiences, and identifies it as sin.

Friendship with God

The first narrative of the work of creation appears in Genesis 1:1-28, which is chronologically later than the narrative of Genesis 2:4-15. This first account underlines the original goodness of all that is created, and in particular the goodness of man, created by God as "male and female" (cf. Gen 1:27). It says several times in the description of creation, "God saw that it was good" (cf. Gen 1:12, 18, 21, 25). Finally, after the creation of man, it declares: "God saw what he had made, and behold it was very good" (Gen 1:31). The phrase indicates the goodness that belongs to such a being in accordance with the plan of the Creator, because it is a case of a created being in the image of God—rational and free.

This is the basis of the truth of faith which the Church

teaches about the original innocence of man, his original righteousness *(iustitia originalis)*. This is seen in the description
given in Genesis of the human person as he came from the
hands of God and lived in full intimacy with him (cf. Gen 2:8-
25). The Book of Ecclesiastes also says that "God made man
righteous" (Eccl 7:29). The Council of Trent taught that the
first Adam lost the holiness and righteousness in which he had
been established *(Primum hominem Adam...sanctitatem et
iustitiam, in qua constitutus fuerat, amisisse*: Decree on Original Sin, DS* 1511). This means that before sin, man possessed
sanctifying grace with all the supernatural gifts that make him
righteous before God. We may sum all this up by saying that
man was in friendship with God at the beginning.

In the light of the Bible, the state of man before sin
appears as a condition of original perfection. Genesis expresses this in a certain way by the image of "paradise" that it
offers us. We may ask what the source of this perfection was.
The answer is that it was found above all in friendship with
God by means of sanctifying grace, and in the other gifts that
in theological language are called preternatural, which were
lost through sin. Thanks to such divine gifts, man, who was
joined in friendship and harmony with his principle of being,
had and maintained in himself an interior equilibrium. He was
not worried about the prospect of decay and death. The "dominion" over the world, which God had given man from the
beginning, was realized first of all in man himself, as dominion
over himself. In this self-dominion and equilibrium he had the
"integrity" *(integritas)* of existence, in the sense that man was
intact and well-ordered in all his being. He was free from the
triple concupiscence that inclines him to the pleasures of the
senses, to coveting earthly goods, and to assert himself against
the dictates of reason.

Therefore there was also order in his relationship with
the other, in the communion and intimacy that make for happi-

ness—as in the initial relationship between man and woman,
Adam and Eve, the first couple and also the first nucleus of
human society. The brief sentence of Genesis seems very eloquent from this point of view: "Now both were naked, the man
and his wife, but they were not ashamed" (Gen 2:25).

The presence of original righteousness and perfection in
the human person, created in the image of God, as we know
from revelation, did not mean that man, as a creature endowed
with liberty like the other spiritual beings, was exempted from
the testing of his freedom right from the beginning! Revelation
shows us the state of original righteousness of man before sin,
in virtue of his friendship with God. The happiness of his
existence derived from this. That same revelation also tells of
the fundamental test that was reserved for man, and in which
he failed.

Genesis describes this test as the prohibition to eat the
fruit "of the tree of the knowledge of good and evil." The text
reads: "The Lord God gave this commandment to the man:
'You may eat of all the trees of the garden, but of the tree of
the knowledge of good and evil you must not eat, because on
the day you eat of it, you shall certainly die'" (Gen 2:16-17).

This means that from the very beginning the Creator
reveals himself to a rational and free being as the God of the
covenant and hence of friendship and joy, but also as the
source of good and therefore of the distinction between good
and evil in the moral sense. The tree of the knowledge of good
and evil recalls symbolically the absolute limit which man, as a
creature, must recognize and respect. Man depends on the
Creator and is subject to the laws by which the Creator has
established the order of the created world, the essential order
of existence *(ordo rerum)*. Man is also subject to the moral
norms which regulate the use of freedom. The primordial test
is therefore aimed at the person's free will, at his freedom.
Will man confirm the fundamental order of creation in his

conduct, and recognize the truth that he himself is created—
the truth of the dignity that belongs to him as the image of
God, but also the truth of his creaturely limitation?

Unfortunately, we know the results of the test—man
failed. Revelation tells us this, but it sets this sad news within
the context of the truth of the redemption, so that we can look
with confidence to our merciful Creator and Lord.

General audience of September 3, 1986

Original Sin Causes
a Fundamental Change in Mankind

The description of the first sin, which we find in the third chapter of Genesis, acquires a greater clarity in the context of creation and of the bestowal of gifts. By these gifts, God constituted man in the state of holiness and of original justice. This description hinges on the transgression of the divine command not to eat "of the fruit of the tree of the knowledge of good and evil." This is to be interpreted by taking into account the character of the ancient text and especially its literary form. However, while bearing in mind this scientific requirement in the study of the first book of Sacred Scripture, it cannot be denied that one sure element emerges from the detailed account of the sin. It describes a primordial event, that is, a fact, which according to revelation took place at the beginning of human history. For this reason it also presents another certain element, namely, the fundamental and decisive implication of that event for man's relationship with God, and consequently for the interior "situation" of man himself, for reciprocal relationships between people, and in general for man's relationship with the world.

Underlying the descriptive forms, the fact that really mat-

27

ters is of a moral nature and is imprinted in the very roots of the human spirit. It gives rise to a fundamental change in the human condition. Man is driven forth from the state of original justice and finds himself in a state of sinfulness *(status naturae lapsae)*. Sin exists in this state, which is also marked by an inclination to sin. From that moment, the whole history of humanity will be burdened by this state. In fact the first human being (man and woman) received sanctifying grace from God not only for himself, but as founder of the human family, for all his descendants. Therefore through sin which set man in conflict with God, he forfeited grace (he fell into disgrace) even in regard to the inheritance for his descendants. According to the Church's teaching based on revelation, the essence of original sin as the heritage of our progenitors consists in this privation of grace added to nature.

We shall understand better the nature of this inheritance by analyzing the account of the first sin as contained in the third chapter of Genesis. It begins with the conversation between the tempter, presented under the form of a serpent, and the woman. This is something completely new. Until then the Book of Genesis had not spoken of the existence in the created world of other intelligent and free beings, apart from the man and the woman. The description of creation in chapters 1 and 2 of Genesis concerns the world of "visible beings." The tempter belongs to the world of "invisible beings," purely spiritual, even though for the duration of this conversation he is presented by the Bible under a visible form. One must consider this first appearance of the evil spirit in the Bible in the context of all that we find on this subject in the books of the Old and New Testaments. (We have already done so in the previous catecheses.) Especially to be noted is the Book of Revelation (the last of Sacred Scripture) according to which "the great dragon was thrown down upon the earth—that ancient serpent [this is an explicit reference to Genesis 3], who is called the

Devil and Satan, the deceiver of the whole world" (Rev 12:9). Because he "deceives the whole world" he is also called elsewhere "the father of lies" (Jn 8:44).

The human sin at the beginning of history, the primordial sin of which we read in Genesis 3, occurred under the influence of this being. The "ancient serpent" tempted the woman: "Did God say, 'You shall not eat of any tree of the garden?'" She replied: "We may eat of the fruit of the trees of the garden; but God said, 'You shall not eat of the fruit of the tree which is in the midst of the garden, neither shall you touch it, lest you die.'" But the serpent said to the woman: "You shall not die. For God knows that when you eat of it your eyes will be opened, and you will be like God, knowing good and evil" (Gen 3:1-5).

It is not difficult to discern in this text the essential problems of human life hidden under an apparently simple form. To eat or not to eat the fruit of a certain tree may itself seem irrelevant. However, the tree "of the knowledge of good and evil" denotes the first principle of human life to which a fundamental problem is linked. The tempter knows this very well, for he says: "When you eat of it...you will be like God, knowing good and evil." The tree therefore signifies the insurmountable limit for man and for any creature, however perfect. The creature is always merely a creature, and not God. Certainly he cannot claim to be "like God," to "know good and evil" like God. God alone is the source of all being, God alone is absolute Truth and Goodness, according to which good and evil are measured and from which they receive their distinction. God alone is the eternal legislator, from whom every law in the created world derives, and in particular the law of human nature *(lex naturae)*. As a rational creature, man knows this law and should let himself be guided by it in his own conduct. He himself cannot pretend to establish the moral law, to decide himself what is good and what is bad, independently of the Creator, even against the Creator. Neither man nor any other creature can set himself in the place of God, claiming for himself the mastery of the moral order. This is contrary to creation's own ontological constitution which is reflected in the psychological-ethical sphere by the fundamental imperatives of conscience and therefore human conduct.

In the Genesis account, in the guise of an apparently irrelevant plot, we find man's fundamental problem linked to his very condition as a creature. Man as a rational being should let himself be guided by the "First Truth," which is moreover the truth of his very existence. Man cannot claim to substitute himself for this truth or to place himself on a par with it. If this principle is called into question, the foundation of the "justice" of the creature in regard to the Creator is shaken to the roots of human action. The tempter, "the father of lies," calls in question the state of original justice by insinuating doubt on the truth of the relationship with God. In yielding to the tempter, man commits a personal sin and causes the state of original sin in human nature.

As we see from the biblical account, human sin does not have its primary origin in the heart (and in the conscience) of man. It does not arise from his spontaneous initiative. It is in a certain sense the reflection and the consequence of the sin that had already occurred in the world of invisible beings. The tempter, "the ancient serpent," belongs to this world. Previously these beings endowed with knowledge and freedom had been "put to the test" so that they could make their choice commensurate with their purely spiritual nature. In them arose the "doubt" which, as recounted in the third chapter of Genesis, the tempter insinuates in our first parents. Already they had placed God in a state of suspicion and accusation—God who as Creator, is the sole source of the good granted to all creatures, and especially to spiritual creatures. They had contested the truth of existence, which demands the total subordination of the creature to the Creator. This truth was supplanted by an original pride, which led them to make their own spirit the principle and rule of freedom. They were the first who had claimed the power "to know good and evil like God." They had chosen themselves over God, instead of choosing themselves "in God," according to the demands of their existence as creatures, for "who is like God?" By yielding to the suggestion of the tempter, man became the slave and accomplice of the rebellious spirits!

According to Genesis 3, the words which the first man heard beside the "tree of the knowledge of good and evil" contain all the assault of evil that can arise in the free will of the creature in regard to him who, as Creator, is the source of all being and of all good—he who, being absolutely disinterested and authentically paternal love, is in his very essence the will to give! This gift of love meets with objection, contradiction and rejection. The creature who wishes to be "like God" concretely realizes the attitude expressed so well by St. Augustine: "love of self to the point of contempt of God" (cf. *De Civitate Dei,* XIV, 28; PL 41, 436). This is perhaps the most penetrating explanation possible of the concept of that sin at the beginning of history, which occurred through man's yielding to the devil's suggestion—*contemptus Dei,* rejection of God, contempt of God, hatred of everything connected with God or that comes from God.

Unfortunately it is not an isolated event at the dawn of history. How often is one confronted with facts, deeds, words and conditions of life in which the legacy of that first sin is evident!

Genesis places that sin in relation to Satan, and this truth about the "ancient serpent" is later confirmed in many other passages of the Bible. How is man's sin presented against this background? We read also in Genesis 3: "So when the woman saw that the tree was good for food, and that it was a delight to the eyes, and that the tree was to be desired to make one wise, she took of its fruit and ate; and she also gave some to her husband, and he ate" (Gen 3:6).

So detailed in its own way, what does this description reveal? It attests that the first man acted against the will of the Creator, under the influence of the tempter's assurance that "the fruits of this tree serve to acquire knowledge." It does not seem that man had fully accepted the totality of negation and hatred of God contained in the words of the "father of lies." Instead, he accepted the suggestion to avail himself of a created thing contrary to the prohibition of the Creator, thinking that he also—man—could be "like God, knowing good and evil."

According to St. Paul, man's first sin consisted especially in disobedience to God (cf. Rom 5:19). The analysis of Genesis 3 and the reflection on this marvelously profound text show how that "disobedience" can come about and in what direction it can develop in the human will. It can be said that the sin "at the beginning," described in Genesis 3, in a certain sense contains the original "model" of every sin of which man is capable.

General Audience of September 10, 1986

The Universality of Sin in Human History

We can summarize the content of the previous catechesis in the words of the Second Vatican Council: "Although he was made by God in a state of holiness, from the very onset of his history man abused his liberty...and sought to attain his goal apart from God" *(GS* 13). Essentially this analyzes the first sin in human history, which we have done on the basis of the third chapter of Genesis.

It was the sin of our first parents. But a sinful condition was connected with it which was passed on to all their descendants. This is called original sin. What does this mean? The term does not appear even once in Sacred Scripture. But against the background of the account in Genesis 3, the Bible describes in the subsequent chapters of Genesis, and also in other books, how sin "invaded" the whole world as a result of Adam's sin, by a kind of universal infection of all humanity.

Already in Genesis 4 we read what happened between the two elder sons of Adam and Eve. Cain killed his younger brother Abel (cf. Gen 4:3-15). We read in chapter six of the universal corruption resulting from sin: "The Lord saw that the wickedness of man was great on the earth, and that the thoughts of his heart were only evil" (Gen 6:5). Later: "God saw the earth, and behold, it was corrupt; for all flesh had corrupted their way upon the earth" (Gen 6:12). In this context, the Book of Genesis does not hesitate to say: "The Lord was sorry that he had made man on the earth, and it grieved him to his heart" (Gen 6:6). Likewise in the same book we see, in the account of the flood at the time of Noah, the consequence of that universal corruption resulting from sin (cf. Gen 7-9). Genesis mentions also the building of the tower of Babel (cf. Gen 11:1-9), which resulted—contrary to the intention of the builders—in the dispersal of peoples and the confusion of languages. This shows that no external sign, and similarly no merely human agreement, can bring about union among men if it is not rooted in God. We must note that, in the course of history, sin manifests itself not only as an action clearly directed "against" God, but at times it is also an attempt to act "independently of God," as if God did not exist. It is a pretense to ignore him, to do without him, and to exalt man's power instead. This is presumptuous beyond all limits. In this sense the tower of Babel can also serve as a warning to the people of today. For this reason I mentioned it in the Apostolic Exhortation *Reconciliatio et Paenitentia* (13-15).

Already so clear in Genesis, the witness to the general sinfulness of humanity is found in various ways in other parts of the Bible. In every case this universal condition of sinfulness is placed in relationship with the fact that man turns his back on God. St. Paul in the Letter to the Romans is particularly eloquent on this subject: "Since they did not see fit to acknowledge God, God gave them up to a base mind and to improper conduct. They were filled with all manner of wickedness, evil, covetousness, malice. Full of envy, murder, strife, deceit, malignity, they are gossips, slanderers, haters of God, insolent, haughty, boastful, inventors of evil, disobedient to parents, foolish, faithless, heartless, ruthless...because they exchanged the truth about God for a lie and worshipped and served the creature rather than the Creator, who is blessed for ever! Amen. For this reason God gave them up to dishonorable passions. Their women exchanged natural relations for unnatural, and the men likewise gave up natural relations with women and were consumed with passion for one another. Men committed shameless acts with men and received in their own persons the due penalty for their error.... Though they know God's decree that those who do such things deserve to die, they not only do them but approve those who practice them" (Rom 1:28-31; 25-27; 32).

A radical change of life

This precisely describes the "sinful situation" at the time of the Church's foundation, when St. Paul wrote and worked with the other apostles. Certainly many values could be appreciated in that world, but they were contaminated to a large extent by the multiple infiltrations of sin. Christianity faced up to that situation with courage and firmness. It succeeded in obtaining from its followers a radical change of life, the fruit of a conversion of heart, which later gave a characteristic stamp to the cultures and civilizations which were formed and developed under its influence. Even today large segments of the population enjoy its heritage, especially in certain nations.

A description similar to that in St. Paul's Letter to the Romans is found in the Constitution *Gaudium et Spes* of the Second Vatican Council. It is symptomatic of the times in which we live: "Whatever is opposed to life itself, such as any type of murder, genocide, abortion, euthanasia or willful self-destruction; whatever violates the integrity of the human person, such as mutilation, torments inflicted on body or mind, attempts to coerce the will itself; whatever insults human dignity, such as subhuman living conditions, arbitrary imprisonment, deportation, slavery, prostitution, the selling of women and children, as well as disgraceful working conditions, where men are treated as mere tools for profit, rather than as free and responsible persons; all these things and others of their like are infamies indeed. They poison human society, but they do more harm to those who practice them than those who suffer from the injury. Moreover, they are a supreme dishonor to the Creator" *(GS* 27).

This is not the moment to make a historical analysis or a statistical calculation to establish to what extent this conciliar text—among so many other denunciations by pastors of the Church, and also by Catholic and non-Catholic scholars and teachers—represents a description of the "sin situation" in the world of today. But it is certain that apart from the quantitative dimension, these facts sadly give evidence of that "infection" of human nature, as it appears in the Bible and is taught by the Church's Magisterium, as we shall see in the next catechesis.

For the moment, we shall make two observations. The first is that divine revelation and the Magisterium of the Church, its authentic interpreter, constantly and systematically speak of the presence and universality of sin in human history. The second is that this sinful situation, repeated from generation to generation, is perceptible "from outside" in history through the grave phenomena of moral sicknesses which are noticeable in personal and social life. But it becomes perhaps even more recognizable and striking if we direct our glance to the "interior" of man.

The same document of Vatican Council II says elsewhere: "What divine revelation makes known to us agrees with experience. Examining his heart, man finds that he has inclinations toward evil too, and is engulfed by manifold ills which cannot come from his good Creator. Often refusing to acknowledge God as his beginning, man has disrupted also his proper relationship to his own ultimate goal as well as his whole relationship toward himself and others and all created things" *(GS* 13).

These statements of the Church's Magisterium in our time contain not only the data of historical and spiritual experience, but also and above all a faithful reflection of the teaching repeated in many books of the Bible, beginning with that description in Genesis 3, which we have previously analyzed as a witness to the first sin in man's history on the earth. Here we shall recall only the anguished queries of Job: "Can mortal man be righteous before God? Can a man be pure before his maker?" (Job 4:17). "Who can bring clean things out of unclean?" (Job 4:4). "What is man, that he can be clean? Or he that is born of a woman, that he can be righteous?" (Job 15:14). There are other similar questions in the Book of Proverbs: "Who can say, 'I have made my heart clean, I am pure from my sin?'" (Prov 20:9).

In the Psalms the same cry rings out: "Enter not [O God] into judgment with your servant; for no man living is righteous before you" (Ps 143:2). "The wicked go astray from the womb; they err from their birth, speaking lies" (Ps 58:3). "Behold, I was brought forth in iniquity, and in sin did my mother conceive me" (Ps 51:5).

All these texts indicate a continuity of sentiment and thought in the Old Testament, and at least they pose the difficult problem of the universal situation of sin.

Sacred Scripture impels us to seek the root of sin in the interior of the human person, in his conscience, in his heart. This thought seems to be expressed in Psalm 51, which says that man was "conceived" in sin and cries out to God: "Create in me a clean heart, O God" (Ps 51:10). The Bible frequently states both the universality of sin and its hereditary character, which make it in a certain sense "congenital" in human nature. Thus in Psalm 14: "They have all gone astray, they are all alike corrupt; there is none that does good, no, not one" (Ps 14:3).

Jesus' words on the "hardness of hearts" can be understood in this biblical context (cf. Mt 19:8). St. Paul conceived
this "hardness of heart" principally as a moral weakness,
rather, as a kind of incapacity to do good. This is what he said:
"I am carnal, sold under sin. I do not understand my own
actions. For I do not do what I want, but I do the very thing I
hate..." (Rom 7:14-15). "I can will what is right, but I cannot
do it..." (Rom 7:18). "When I want to do right, evil lies close at
hand" (Rom 7:21). These words are linked by an interesting
analogy to those of the pagan poet: *Video meliora proboque,
deteriora sequor* (I see what is better and I approve, but I do
what is worse) (cf. Ovid, *Metamorph*, 7, 20). One of the more
disconcerting aspects of human experience emerges in both
cases (but also in so many others of spirituality and in the
whole field of literature). The revelation of original sin throws
some light on these.

The Church's teaching in our time, expressed in a particular way by the Second Vatican Council, reflects precisely
this revealed truth when it speaks of the "world...created and
sustained by its Maker's love...fallen indeed into the bondage
of sin" *(GS* 2). In the same Pastoral Constitution we read: "For
a monumental struggle against the powers of darkness pervades the whole history of man. The battle was joined from the
very origins of the world and will continue until the last day, as
the Lord has attested. Caught in this conflict, man is obliged to
wrestle constantly if he is to cling to what is good, nor can he
achieve his own integrity without great efforts and the help of
God's grace" *(GS* 37).

General Audience of September 17, 1986

The Church's Teaching on Original Sin

Thanks to the previous catechesis of the present series, we have before our eyes, on the one hand, the analysis of the first sin in human history according to the description contained in Genesis 3; on the other, we have an ample view of what divine revelation teaches on the universality and hereditary nature of sin. This truth is constantly proposed, over and over again, by the Church's Magisterium, even in our own time. Here we must refer to the documents of Vatican II, especially to the Constitution *Gaudium et Spes,* and with a special mention of the post-synodal Exhortation *Reconciliatio et Paenitentia* (1984).

The source of this teaching is above all the passage of the Book of Genesis, in which we see that man, tempted by the evil one ("when you eat of it...you will be like God, knowing good and evil"; Gen 3:5), "abused his liberty, setting himself against God and seeking to attain his goal apart from God" *(GS* 13). Then "the eyes of both were opened" (that is, of the man and of the woman), "and they knew that they were naked" (Gen 3:7). When the Lord God "called the man and said to him: 'where are you?' he replied: 'I was afraid because I was

naked, and I hid myself'" (Gen 3:9-10). This is a very significant reply. Man in the beginning (in the state of original
justice) spoke to the Creator with friendship and confidence in
the whole truth of his spiritual-corporeal being, created in
God's image. But now he has lost the basis of that friendship
and covenant. He has lost the grace of sharing in God's life—
the good of belonging to him in the holiness of the original
relationship of subordination and sonship. But sin has immediately made its presence felt in the existence and the whole
comportment of the man and the woman—shame for their
transgression, the consequent condition as sinners and therefore fear of God. Revelation and psychological analysis are
united in this page of the Bible to express man's "state" after
the fall.

Death is a consequence of sin

We have seen another truth emerge from the books of the
Old and New Testaments—a kind of "invasion" of sin in the
history of humanity. Sin has become the common lot of man,
his inheritance from his mother's womb. "In sin did my mother
conceive me," exclaimed the Psalmist in a moment of existential anguish, in which repentance is coupled with the
invocation of divine mercy (Ps 51). St. Paul frequently referred
to this same anguishing experience, as we saw in the previous
catechesis. He gave a theoretical formulation to this truth in
the Letter to the Romans: "All are under the power of sin"
(Rom 3:9). "Let every mouth be stopped, and let the whole
world be held accountable to God" (Rom 3:19). "We were by
nature children of wrath" (Eph 2:3). Biblical scholars comment that these are all allusions to human nature left to itself,
without the help of grace. They refer to nature as it is reduced
by the sin of our first parents, and thus to the condition of all
their descendants and heirs.

The biblical texts on the universality and hereditary nature of sin lead us to examine more directly the Catholic teaching on original sin. It is as though sin is "congenital" in nature in the state in which everyone receives it at the moment of conception from one's parents.

It concerns a truth transmitted implicitly in the Church's teaching from the beginning. It became the object of a formal declaration of the Magisterium in the fifteenth Synod of Carthage in 418 and the Synod of Orange in 529, principally against the errors of Pelagius (cf. *DS* 222-223; 371-372). Later, during the period of the Reformation, the Council of Trent solemnly formulated this truth in 1546 (cf. *DS* 1510-1516). The Tridentine decree on original sin expresses this truth in the precise form in which it is the object of faith and of the Church's teaching. We can refer to this decree for the essential content of Catholic dogma on this point.

Our first parents (the decree says: *Primum hominem Adam*), in the earthly paradise (and therefore in the state of original justice and perfection) sinned gravely, by transgressing the commandment of God. Because of their sin they lost sanctifying grace; likewise they lost also the holiness and justice in which they were "constituted" from the beginning, and they drew down on themselves the anger of God. The consequence of this sin was death as we now know it. One must recall here the words of the Lord in Genesis 2:17: "Of the tree of the knowledge of good and evil you shall not eat, for in the day that you eat of it you shall die." In the previous catecheses we spoke of the meaning of this prohibition. As a result of sin Satan was able to extend his "dominion" over man. The Tridentine decree speaks of "slavery under the dominion of him who has the power of death" (cf. *DS* 1511). Being under the "power" of Satan is described as "slavery."

It will be necessary to return to this aspect of the drama of the origins to examine the elements of "alienation" that sin brought with it. Meanwhile we note that the Tridentine decree refers to the "sin of Adam" inasmuch as it was our first parents' own personal sin (what the theologians call *peccatum originale originans*). But it does not fail to describe its fateful consequences in the history of the human race (the so-called *peccatum originale originatum*).

It is especially in regard to original sin in this second meaning that modern culture raises strong reservations. It cannot admit the idea of a hereditary sin, connected with the decision of a progenitor and not with that of the person concerned. It holds that such a view runs counter to the personalistic vision of man and to the demands which derive from full respect for his subjectivity.

However, the Church's teaching on original sin can be extremely valuable for modern people. Having rejected the data of faith in this matter, they can no longer understand the mysterious and distressing aspects of evil which they daily experience. They end up by wavering between a hasty and unjustified optimism and a radical pessimism bereft of hope.

In the next catechesis we shall pause to reflect on the message faith offers us on a theme so important for the individual and for the whole of humanity.

General audience of September 24, 1986

Consequences of Original Sin for All Humanity

The Council of Trent solemnly expressed the Church's faith concerning original sin. In the previous catechesis we considered that Council's teaching in regard to the personal sin of our first parents. Now we wish to reflect on what the Council said about the consequences of that sin for humanity.

In this regard the Tridentine decree states first of all: Adam's sin has passed to all his descendants, that is, to all men and women as descendants of our first parents, and their heirs, in human nature already deprived of God's friendship.

The Tridentine decree (cf. *DS* 1512) explicitly states that Adam's sin tainted not only himself but also all his descendants. Adam forfeited original justice and holiness not only for himself, but also "for us" *(nobis etiam)*.

Therefore he transmitted to the whole human race not only bodily death and other penalties (consequences of sin), but also sin itself as the death of the soul *(peccatum quod mors est animae)*.

Here the Council of Trent uses an observation of St. Paul in the Letter to the Romans. The Synod of Carthage had already referred to it, repeating a teaching already widespread in the Church.

Adam's sin transmitted by generation

In a modern translation the Pauline text reads as follows: "Therefore as sin came into the world through one man and death through sin, so death spread to all men because all men sinned" (Rom 5:12). In the original Greek we read: εφ ω παντεσ ημαρτον, an expression which was translated in the old Latin Vulgate as: *in quo omnes peccaverunt,* "in whom (a single man) all sinned." But what the Vulgate translates as "in whom," from the very beginning the Greeks clearly understood in the sense of "because" or "inasmuch." This sense is now generally accepted by modern translations. However, this diversity of interpretations of the expression εφ ω does not change the basic truth in St. Paul's text, namely, that Adam's sin (the sin of our first parents) had consequences for all humanity. Moreover, in the same chapter of the Letter to the Romans the Apostle wrote: "By one man's disobedience all became sinners" (Rom 5:19), and in the preceding verse: "One man's trespass led to condemnation for all men" (Rom 5:18). St. Paul connects the sinful situation of all humanity with the fault of Adam.

The Church's Magisterium refers to these statements of St. Paul just quoted, which enlighten our faith on the consequences of Adam's sin for all humanity. Catholic exegetes and theologians will always be guided by this teaching in evaluating, with the wisdom of faith, the explanations offered by science about the origins of the human race.

In particular, the words of Pope Paul VI to a symposium of theologians and scientists are valid and a stimulus for further research in this regard: "It is evident that the explanations of original sin given by some modern authors will appear to you as irreconcilable with genuine Catholic teaching. Such authors, starting from the unproved premise of polygenism, deny more or less clearly that the sin from which such a mass of evils has derived in humanity, was, above all, the disobedience of Adam 'the first man,' figure of that future one, which occurred at the beginning of history" (AAS, LVIII, 1966, 654). The Tridentine decree contains another statement: Adam's sin is transmitted to all his descendants by generation and not merely by way of bad example. The decree states: "This sin of Adam, which by origin is unique and transmitted by generation and not by way of imitation, is present in all as proper to each" *(DS* 1513).

Therefore original sin is transmitted by way of natural generation. This conviction of the Church is indicated also by the practice of infant baptism, to which the conciliar decree refers. Newborn infants are incapable of committing personal sin, yet in accordance with the Church's centuries-old tradition, they are baptized shortly after birth for the remission of sin. The decree states: "They are truly baptized for the remission of sin, so that what they contracted in generation may be cleansed by regeneration" *(DS* 1514).

Reference to the mystery of redemption

In this context it is evident that original sin in Adam's descendants does not have the character of personal guilt. It is the privation of sanctifying grace in a nature which has been diverted from its supernatural end through the fault of the first parents. It is a "sin of nature," only analogically comparable to "personal sin." In the state of original justice, before sin, sanctifying grace was like a supernatural "endowment" of human nature. The loss of grace is contained in the inner "logic" of sin, which is a rejection of the will of God, who bestows this gift. Sanctifying grace has ceased to constitute the supernatural enrichment of that nature which the first parents passed on to all their descendants in the state in which it existed when human generation began. Therefore man is conceived and born without sanctifying grace. It is precisely this "initial state" of man, linked to his origin, that constitutes the essence of original sin as a legacy (*peccatum originale originatum,* as it is usually called).

We cannot conclude this catechesis without emphasizing again what we said at the beginning of the present cycle, namely, that original sin must constantly be considered in reference to the mystery of the redemption carried out by Jesus Christ, the Son of God, who "for us men and for our salvation became man." This article of the creed on the salvific purpose of the Incarnation refers principally and fundamentally to original sin. Also the decree of the Council of Trent is entirely composed in reference to this finality, and is thus inserted into the teaching of the whole of Tradition. It has its point of departure in Sacred Scripture, and first of all in the so-called "proto-evangelium," namely, in the promise of a future conqueror of Satan and liberator of man. This already appeared in the Book of Genesis (3:15) and later in so many other texts, until the fuller expression of this truth given to us by St. Paul in the Letter to the Romans. According to the Apostle, Adam is "a type of the one who was to come" (Rom 5:14). "For if many died through one man's trespass, much more have the grace of God and the free gift in the grace of that one man Jesus Christ abounded for many" (Rom 5:15).

"For as by one man's disobedience many were made sinners, so by one man's obedience many will be made righteous" (Rom 5:19). "Then as one man's trespass led to condemnation for all men, so one man's act of righteousness leads to acquittal and life for all men" (Rom 5:18).

The Council of Trent refers especially to the Pauline text of the Letter to the Romans (5:12) as the cornerstone of its teaching, seeing in it the affirmation of the universality of sin, but also the universality of redemption. The Council has recourse also to the practice of infant baptism, and does so because of the close connection of original sin—the universal legacy received with nature from the first parents—with the truth of the universal redemption in Jesus Christ.

General audience of October 1, 1986

The State of Man in Fallen Nature

The profession of faith proclaimed by Paul VI in 1968 at the conclusion of the "Year of Faith," reproposes in its entirety the teaching of Sacred Scripture and Sacred Tradition on original sin. Let us listen to it once again:

"We believe that in Adam all have sinned, which means that the original offense committed by him caused human nature, common to all men, to fall to a state in which it bears the consequences of that offense, and which is not the state in which it was at first in our first parents, established as they were in holiness and justice, and in which man knew neither evil nor death. It is human nature so fallen, stripped of the grace that clothed it, injured in its own natural powers and subjected to the dominion of death, that is transmitted to all men, and it is in this sense that every man is born in sin. We therefore hold, with the Council of Trent, that original sin is transmitted with human nature 'not by imitation, but by propagation' and that it is thus 'proper to everyone.'"

"We believe that our Lord Jesus Christ, by the sacrifice of the cross, redeemed us from original sin and all the personal sins committed by each one of us, so that, in accordance with the word of the Apostle, 'where sin abounded, grace did more abound.'"

Following that, the profession of faith, also known as the *Credo of the People of God,* goes back, like the decree of the Council of Trent, to holy Baptism, and first of all to that of infants: "in order that, though born deprived of supernatural grace, they may be reborn 'of water and the Holy Spirit' to the divine life in Christ Jesus."

Light of redemption

As is evident, this text of Paul VI confirms that the whole of revealed doctrine on sin and in particular on original sin is always closely connected with the mystery of redemption. Let us seek to present it also in this way in these catecheses. Otherwise it would not be possible to understand fully the reality of sin in human history. St. Paul sets that out clearly in the Letter to the Romans to which the Council of Trent especially refers in the decree on original sin.

In the *Credo of the People of God,* Paul VI reproposed in the light of Christ the Redeemer all the elements of the doctrine on original sin contained in the Tridentine decree.

In regard to the sin of our first parents the *Credo of the People of God* speaks of "fallen human nature." For the proper understanding of this expression it is well to return to the description of the fall contained in Genesis, chapter three. It also contains God's punishment of Adam and Eve, under the anthropomorphic presentation of the divine interventions described by the Book of Genesis. According to the biblical narrative, after the sin the Lord says to the woman: "I will greatly multiply your pain in childbearing; in pain you shall bring forth children, yet your desire shall be for your husband, and he shall rule over you" (Gen 3:16).

"To the man [God] said: 'Because you have listened to

the voice of your wife, and have eaten of the tree of which I commanded you, "You shall not eat of it," cursed is the ground because of you; in toil shall you eat of it all the days of your life; thorns and thistles it shall bring forth to you; and you shall eat the plants of the field. In the sweat of your face you shall eat bread till you return to the ground, for out of it you were taken; you are dust, and to dust you shall return'" (Gen 3:17-19).

These strong and severe words refer to man's situation in the world as it appears in history. The biblical author does not hesitate to attribute it to God as a sentence of condemnation. It implies the "cursing of the ground"—visible creation has become rebellious and hostile. St. Paul says that as a result of man's sin "creation was subjected to futility," and for this reason also "the whole creation has been groaning in travail together until now" until it will be "set free from its bondage to decay" (cf. Rom 8:19-22).

This lack of balance of creation has its influence on the destiny of man in the visible world. The labor by which he acquires the means of sustenance is carried out "in the sweat of his face," and is linked with toil. The whole of human existence is characterized by toil and suffering and this begins already from birth, accompanied by the sufferings of the woman in labor, and of the child itself, who is unconscious of them but who wails and whimpers.

Finally the whole of human existence on earth is subject to the fear of death, which according to revelation is clearly connected with original sin. Sin itself is synonymous with spiritual death, because through sin man has lost sanctifying grace, the source of supernatural life. The sign and consequence of original sin is bodily death, such as it has been experienced since that time by all humanity. Man was created by God for immortality. Death appears as a tragic leap in the dark, and is the consequence of sin, as if by an immanent logic, but especially as the punishment of God. Such is the teaching of revelation and such is the faith of the Church. Without sin, the end of the earthly trial would not have been so dramatic.

Man was created by God also for happiness. In the context of earthly existence, this should have meant being free from many sufferings, at least in the sense of a possibility of exemption from them—*posse non mori.* As can be seen from the words attributed to God by Genesis (Gen 3:16-19), and from many other texts of the Bible and Tradition, with original sin this exemption ceased to be man's privilege. His life on earth was subjected to many sufferings and to the necessity of death.

The *Credo of the People of God* teaches that human nature after original sin is no longer in the "state at which it was at first in our first parents." It is "fallen" since it is deprived of sanctifying grace, and also of other gifts, which in the state of original justice constituted the perfection of this nature. Here we are dealing not only with immortality and exemption from many sufferings, gifts lost because of sin, but also with interior dispositions of the reason and will, that is, with habitual energies of the reason and will. As a consequence of original sin the whole man, body and soul, has been thrown into confusion—*secundum animam et corpus,* as the Council of Orange expressed it in 529. The Tridentine decree echoed this when it noted that man had undergone a change for the worse—*in deterius commutatum fuisse.*

As regards spiritual faculties this deterioration consists in a darkening of the intellect's capacity to know the truth, and in a weakening of free will. The will is weakened in the presence of the attractions of the goods perceived by the senses and is more exposed to the false images of good elaborated by reason under the influence of the passions. However, according to the Church's teaching, it is a case of a relative and not an absolute deterioration, not intrinsic to the human faculties. Even after original sin, man can know by his intellect the fundamental natural and religious truths, and the moral principles. He can also perform good works. One should therefore speak rather of a darkening of the intellect and of a weakening of the will, of "wounds" of the spiritual and sensitive faculties, and not of a loss of their essential capacities even in relation to the knowledge and love of God.

The Tridentine decree emphasizes this truth of the fundamental soundness of nature against the contrary thesis maintained by Luther (and taken up later by the Jansenists). The Council of Trent teaches that as a result of Adam's sin, man has not lost free will (can. 5: *Liberum arbitrium...non amissum et extinctum*). He can therefore perform acts which have an authentic moral value—good or evil. This is possible only by the freedom of the human will. But without Christ's help, fallen man is incapable of directing himself to the supernatural goods which constitute his total fulfillment and salvation.

In the condition in which nature finds itself after sin, and especially because man is more inclined to evil than to good, one speaks of a "spark of sin" *(fomes peccati),* from which human nature was free in the state of original perfection *(integritas).* This "spark of sin" is also called "concupiscence" *(concupiscentia)* by the Council of Trent, which adds that it also continues in man justified by Christ, therefore even after holy Baptism. The Tridentine decree clearly states that concupiscence in itself is not yet sin, but "it derives from sin and inclines to sin" (cf. *DS* 1515). As a consequence of original sin, concupiscence is the source of the inclination to various personal sins committed by people through the evil use of their faculties (these sins are called actual, to distinguish them from original sin). This inclination remains in man even after holy Baptism. In this sense everyone bears in himself the "spark" of sin.

Catholic doctrine defines and describes the state of fallen human nature in terms which we have explained on the basis of the data of Sacred Scripture and Tradition. It is clearly proposed in the Council of Trent and in the *Credo* of Paul VI. However, once again we note that, according to this doctrine based on revelation, human nature is not only "fallen" but also "redeemed" in Jesus Christ, so that "where sin increased, grace abounded all the more" (Rom 5:20). This is the real context in which original sin and its consequences must be considered.

General audience of October 8, 1986

Sin Breaks Man's Covenant with God

In the catecheses of the present series we have the truth about original sin continually before our eyes. At the same time we seek to view the reality of sin in the overall dimension of human history. Historical experience confirms in its own way what is expressed by revelation—sin is continually present in the life of every person. From the point of view of human knowledge it is present as moral evil, with which ethics (moral philosophy) is more directly concerned. But in their own way other branches of anthropological science of a more descriptive nature, such as psychology and sociology, are also concerned with it. One thing is certain—moral evil (as well as moral good) belongs to human experience—and this is the point of departure for all the other sciences that intend to study it as an object of experience.

At the same time, however, one must observe that, apart from revelation, we are not in a position to perceive fully or to express adequately the essence of sin (or of moral evil as sin). Only against the background of the relationship instituted with God through faith can the full reality of sin become understandable. In the light of this relationship let us seek to develop and deepen this understanding.

In the case of revelation and especially of Sacred Scripture, the truth which it contains about sin cannot be presented except by returning to the "beginning" itself. In a certain sense even "actual" sin, pertaining to the life of every person, becomes fully understandable in reference to that "beginning," to that sin of the first man. This is not only because what the Council of Trent calls "the spark of sin" *(fomes peccati),* the consequence of original sin, is the basis and source of personal sins in man, but also because that "first sin" of our first parents remains to a certain extent the "model" of every sin committed personally by man. The "first sin" was also in itself a personal sin; hence the individual elements of its "structure" are found in some way in every other human sin.

The Second Vatican Council recalls: "Although he was made by God in a state of holiness, from the very onset of his history man abused his liberty...and sought to attain his goal apart from God" *(GS* 13). In these words the Council treats of the sin of our first parents committed in the state of original justice. However, all the sins committed throughout history reflect those same essential elements, as a result of the moral weakness that the human race has inherited. Understood as a personal act of man, every sin contains a particular "abuse of freedom," that is, an evil use of freedom, of free will. As a created being, man abuses his free will when he uses it against the will of his Creator, when in his behavior "he lifts himself up against God," when he seeks "to attain his goal apart from God."

Every human sin repeats the essential elements, which from the very beginning constitute the moral evil of sin in the light of the revealed truth on God and man. They are presented in a degree of intensity different from that of the first sin, committed in the state of original justice. Committed after original sin, personal sins are conditioned by the state of inherited inclination to evil ("the spark or incitement of evil

desire"), in a certain sense already at the very point of departure. However, this situation of inherited weakness does not
cancel human freedom. Every actual (personal) sin is a real
abuse of freedom, contrary to the will of God. The degree of
this abuse may vary. The different degrees of guilt of the
sinner also depend on this. In this sense one must apply a
different measure for actual sins, when it is a question of
evaluating the degree of evil contained in them. From this, too,
derives the difference between "grave" sin and "venial" sin.
Grave sin is also "mortal" because it brings about the loss of
sanctifying grace in the one who commits it.

Sin as disobedience

Speaking about Adam's sin, St. Paul describes it as "disobedience" (cf. Rom 5:19). The same is valid for every actual
sin committed. Man sins by transgressing God's commandment, therefore he is "disobedient" to God as supreme
lawgiver. In the light of revelation this disobedience is at the
same time a breaking of the covenant with God. God, as we
know him from revelation, is the God of the covenant. Precisely as God of the covenant, he is lawgiver. He inserts his
law in the context of the covenant with man, making it a
fundamental condition of the covenant itself.

Thus it was in that original covenant, which, as we read
in Genesis (cf. Gen 2-3), was violated "in the beginning." This
appears still more clearly in the relationship of the Lord God
with Israel at the time of Moses. The covenant made with the
Chosen People at the foot of Mount Sinai (cf. Ex 24:3-8)
contains as its constitutive part the Commandments—the
Decalogue (cf. Ex 20; Dt 5). They constitute the fundamental
and inalienable principles of behavior of every person in regard to God and in regard to creatures, especially to human
beings.

According to St. Paul's teaching in his Letter to the Romans, these fundamental and inalienable principles of conduct, revealed in the context of the covenant of Sinai, are "written in the heart" of every human being, even independently of the revelation made to Israel. The Apostle wrote: "When Gentiles who have not the law do by nature what the law requires, they are a law to themselves, even though they do not have the law. They show that what the law requires is written on their hearts, while their conscience also bears witness and their conflicting thoughts accuse or perhaps excuse them" (Rom 2:14-15).

Reinforced by God with the revelation of the law in the context of the covenant, the moral order is already endowed with effectiveness in the law "written in the heart," even apart from the limits indicated by the Mosaic law and revelation. It can be said that it is inscribed in man's rational nature itself, as St. Thomas so very well explains when speaking of the "law of nature" (cf. *Summa Theol.*, I-II, q. 91, a 2; q. 94, aa. 5-6). The fulfillment of this law determines the moral value of human acts and insures their goodness. On the contrary, the transgression of the law "written in the heart," that is, in the rational nature of the human being, determines that human acts are evil. They are evil because they are opposed to the objective order of human nature and of the world, behind which stands God, its Creator.

In the light of the revealed law the nature of sin is set out in still greater relief. Man then possesses a greater awareness of transgressing a law explicitly and positively established by God. He is therefore aware of opposing God's will, and in this sense, of "disobeying." It is not merely a case of disobedience to an abstract principle of behavior, but to a principle in which the "personal" authority of God is formulated, to a principle in which God's wisdom and Providence are expressed. The whole moral law is laid down by God because of his solicitude for the true good of creation, and in particular for the good of the human person. It was precisely this good that was inscribed by God in the covenant which he made—both in the first covenant with Adam, and also in the covenant of Sinai through Moses, and finally, in the definitive covenant revealed in Christ and sealed in the blood of his redemption (cf. Mk 14:24; Mt 26:28; 1 Cor 11:25; Lk 22:20).

Viewed against this background, sin as "disobedience" to the law is more clearly revealed in its nature of disobedience to a personal God—to God as lawgiver, who at the same time is a loving Father. Already profoundly expressed in the Old Testament (cf. Hos 11:1-7), this message will find its fullest formulation in the parable of the prodigal son (cf. Lk 15:18-19, 21). In any event, disobedience to God, that is, opposition to his creative and salvific will, including man's desire "to attain his goal apart from God" *(GS* 13), is an "abuse of liberty" *(GS* 13).

Sin as disbelief

On the day before his passion, Jesus Christ spoke of the "sin" of which the Holy Spirit must "convince the world." He explained the essence of this sin in the words: "because they do not believe in me" (Jn 16:19). That "non-belief" in God is in a certain sense the first and fundamental form of sin, which man commits against the God of the covenant. This form of sin had already been manifested in original sin, spoken of in Genesis. The law given in the covenant of Sinai also refers to it, but in order to exclude it: "I am the Lord your God, who brought you out of the land of Egypt, out of the house of bondage. You shall have no other gods before me" (Ex 20:2-3). The words of Jesus in the cenacle and the whole of the Gospel and the New Testament also refer to it.

This disbelief, this lack of trust in God who is revealed as Creator, Father and Savior, indicate that man, by sinning, not only transgresses the commandment (the law), but really "lifts himself up against" God himself, "seeking to attain his goal apart from God" *(GS* 13). In this way we can find at the root of every actual sin the echo, distant perhaps, but nonetheless real, of those words which were at the basis of the first sin. The words of the tempter presented disobedience to God as a way of being like God; of knowing, like God, "good and evil."

However, as we have already said, even in actual sin, when it is a case of grave (mortal) sin, man chooses himself in opposition to God. He chooses the creature in place of the Creator, and he rejects the Father's love as did the prodigal son in the first phase of his foolish adventure. To a certain extent every human sin is an expression of that "mystery of iniquity" (2 Thess 2:7) which St. Augustine summarized in the words: *amor sui usque ad contemptum Dei*—love of self to the point of contempt of God *(De Civitate Dei,* XIV, 28, PL 41, 436).

General audience of October 29, 1986

The Sin of Man
and the "Sin of the World"

In this series of catecheses on sin, considered in the light of faith, the direct object of examination is actual (personal) sin. But this is always in reference to the first sin which has left its consequences in every descendant of Adam, and which is therefore called original sin. As a result of original sin human beings are born in a state of hereditary moral weakness. They easily follow the path of personal sin, if they do not correspond with the grace offered by God to humanity by means of Christ's redemption.

The Second Vatican Council noted this when it wrote, among other things: "As a result, all of human life, whether individual or collective, shows itself to be a dramatic struggle between good and evil, between light and darkness. Indeed, man finds that by himself he is incapable of battling the assaults of evil successfully.... But the Lord himself came to free and strengthen man, renewing him inwardly" (GS 13). All reflection on personal sin must be situated in this context of tensions and conflict linked to the condition of fallen human nature.

Personal sin has this essential characteristic, that it is always the responsible act of a definite person, an act incompatible with the moral law and therefore opposed to God's will. The Bible helps us to discover what is implied and involved in this act. Already in the Old Testament we find different expressions used to indicate the various moments or aspects of the reality of sin in the light of divine revelation. Thus sometimes it is simply called "evil" (in Hebrew, *"ra"*). One who commits sin does "what is evil in the sight of the Lord" (Dt 31:29). Therefore the sinner, also designated as "ungodly" *("raša")* is one who "forgets God" (cf. Ps 9:18), who "does not wish to know God" (cf. Job 21:14), and in whom there "is not the fear of God" (cf. Ps 36:2). The sinner does not "trust in the Lord" (cf. Ps 32:10), indeed, is one who "despises God" (cf. Ps 10:13), in the conviction that "the Lord does not see" (cf. Ps 94:7) and "he will not demand an account" (cf. Ps 10:4). Again, the sinner (the ungodly) is one who does not fear to oppress the just (cf. Ps 12:9), nor to "cause injustice to the widows and orphans" (cf. Ps 82:4; 94:6), nor even "to repay good with evil" (cf. Ps 109:2-5). In Sacred Scripture the opposite of the sinner is the just man *("sadîq")*. Sin is injustice in the broadest sense of the word.

This multifaceted injustice is also expressed by the term *"peša,"* which contains the idea of wrong done to another, to one whose rights have been violated by the sinful action. The same word, however, also signifies "rebellion" against superiors, which is all the more grave if directed against God, as we read in the prophets: "Sons have I reared and brought up, but they have rebelled against me" (Is 1:2; cf. also, e.g., Is 48:8-9; Ez 2:3).

Sin, therefore also signifies "injustice" (Hebrew *"awoñ,"* Greek *adikia, anomia).* At the same time this word, according to the Bible, underlines man's sinful state inasmuch as he is guilty of sin. Etymologically it signifies a "deviation from the right path" or "wrongness" or "deformation"—being really outside of justice! The consciousness of this state of injustice comes to the surface in Cain's remorseful confession: "My sin is too great to be pardoned!" (Gen 4:13); and in that other confession of the Psalmist: "For my iniquities have gone over my head; they weigh like a burden too heavy for me" (Ps 38:5). Guilt—injustice—implies a breaking with God, expressed by the term *"hata,"* which means, etymologically, a "defect with regard to someone." Hence, too, the Psalmist's awareness: "Against you, you alone have I sinned!" (Ps 51:4).

Furthermore, according to Sacred Scripture, sin is an offense against God, by its essential nature of "injustice." It is ingratitude for his benefits, even contempt for his most holy Person. "Why have you despised the word of the Lord, to do what is evil in his sight?"—the prophet Nathan asked David after his sin (cf. 2 Sam 12:9). Sin is also a stain and an impurity. Therefore Ezekiel speaks of "defilement" with sin (cf. Ez 14:11), especially with the sin of idolatry which the prophets frequently compare to "adultery" (cf. Hos 2:4, 6-7). Hence even the Psalmist asks: "Purge me with hyssop, and I shall be clean; wash me, and I shall be whiter than snow" (Ps 51:7).

In this same context the words of Jesus in the Gospel can be better understood: "What comes out of a person is what defiles him...out of the heart of man come evil thoughts, fornication, theft, murder, adultery, coveting, wickedness, deceit, licentiousness, envy, slander, pride, foolishness. All these things...defile a person" (Mk 7:20-23; cf. Mt 15:18-20). It should be noted that in New Testament lexicons there are not as many names for sin as in the Old Testament. It is named especially with the Greek word *"anomia"* (iniquity, injustice, opposition to the kingdom of God; cf. e.g., Mk 7:23; Mt 13:14; Mt 24:12; 1 Jn 3:4). It is also called *"amartia"* (error, defect) or *"ojeilhma"* (debt, e.g., "forgive us our debts..." i.e., sins) (Mt 6:12; Lk 11:4).

Sin is a conscious and free act

We have just heard Jesus' words describing sin as something coming "out of the heart," from within man. They emphasize the essential nature of sin. Originating within man, in his will, sin, by its very essence, is always an act of the person. It is a conscious and free act, in which man's free will is expressed. Only on the basis of this principle of freedom, and therefore of the fact of deliberation, can its moral value be established. Only for this reason can we judge it evil in the moral sense, just as we judge and approve as good an act in conformity with the objective moral norm, and ultimately with the will of God. Personal responsibility is verified only in what derives from free will. It is only in this sense that a person's free and conscious act—which is opposed to the moral norm (to God's will), to the law, to the commandment, and ultimately to conscience—constitutes a sin.

It is in this individual and personal sense that Sacred Scripture speaks of sin, since on principle it refers to a specific subject, to man who is its cause. Even when the expression "the sin of the world" appears in some passages, this personal meaning is not denied, at least as regards the causality and responsibility of sin. The "world" as such cannot be the cause of sin. It can be caused only by a rational and free being in the world, that is, by man (or in another realm of beings, also by a created pure spirit, namely an angel, as we have seen in previous catecheses).

The expression "the sin of the world" is found in St. John's Gospel: "Behold the Lamb of God, who takes away the sin of the world" (Jn 1:29). The liturgical formula says, "the sins of the world." In the First Letter of St. John another passage reads: "Do not love the world or the things in the world...for all that is in the world, the lust of the flesh and the lust of the eyes and the pride of life, is not of the Father, but is of the world" (1 Jn 2:15-16). And still more severely: "We know that we are of God, and the whole world is in the power of the evil one" (1 Jn 5:19).

How are we to understand these expressions about the

"sin of the world"? The passages quoted clearly indicate that here it is not a case of the "world" as a creation of God, but as a specific dimension, almost a spiritual space closed to God, in which evil arises on the basis of created freedom. This evil transferred into the "heart" of our first parents under the influence of the "ancient serpent" (cf. Gen 3 and Rev 12:9), that is, Satan, "the father of lies," has borne evil fruits from the beginning of human history. Original sin has left in its wake that "spark or incitement of evil desire," that is, the threefold concupiscence, which induces people to sin. In their turn the many personal sins that are committed form a kind of "environment of sin." This creates the conditions for new personal sins and in a certain way induces and attracts individuals to sin. Therefore "the sin of the world" is not to be identified with original sin, but it is, as it were, a synthesis or summing up of the consequences of original sin in the history of each generation and so in the whole history of humanity. From this it also follows that the various human initiatives, tendencies, achievements and institutions, even in those "ensembles" which constitute cultures and civilizations, bear a certain imprint of sin. In this sense one can perhaps speak of a sin of the structures as a kind of "infection" which is spread from human hearts into the environments in which they live and into the structures which support and condition their existence.

Sin has a social dimension

While preserving its essential character of a personal act, sin possesses at the same time a social dimension, of which I spoke in the *Post-Synodal Apostolic Exhortation on Reconciliation and Penance,* published in 1982. As I wrote in that document: "To speak of social sin means in the first place to recognize that, by virtue of a human solidarity which is as mysterious and intangible as it is real and concrete, each individual's sin in some way affects others. This is the other aspect of that solidarity which on the religious level is developed in the profound and magnificent mystery of the communion of saints, thanks to which it has been possible to say that 'every soul that rises above itself, raises up the world.' To this law of ascent there unfortunately corresponds the law of descent. Consequently one can speak of a communion of sin, whereby a soul that lowers itself through sin drags down with itself the Church and, in some way, the whole world" *(Reconciliatio et Paenitentia,* 16).

Then the Exhortation speaks of sins which particularly deserve to be described as "social sins"—a subject to which we shall return in the course of another series of catecheses.

It is sufficiently clear from what has been said that "social sin" is not the same thing as the biblical "sin of the world." However, one must recognize that to understand "the sin of the world" one must take into consideration not only the personal dimension of sin, but also the social. The Exhortation *Reconciliatio et Paenitentia* continues: "There is no sin, not even the most intimate and secret one, the most strictly individual one, that exclusively concerns the person committing it. With greater or lesser violence, with greater or lesser harm, every sin has repercussions on the entire ecclesial body and the whole human family. According to this first meaning of the term, every sin can undoubtedly be considered as social sin" *(RP* 16). At this point we can conclude with the observation that the social dimension of sin explains better why the world becomes that specific negative spiritual environment, to which Sacred Scripture alludes when it speaks of the "sin of the world."

General audience of November 5, 1986

Sin Alienates the Human Person

Our considerations regarding sin during this cycle of our catecheses keep leading us back to that first sin of which we read in Genesis. St. Paul speaks of it as the "disobedience" of the first Adam (cf. Rom 5:19), directly connected with the transgression of the Creator's commandment concerning "the tree of the knowledge of good and evil." A superficial reading of the text may give one the impression that prohibition regarded something insignificant ("You shall not eat of the fruit of the tree"). But a more profound analysis easily leads to the conviction that the apparently insignificant content of the prohibition symbolizes an absolutely fundamental matter. This is made apparent by the words of the tempter, who, in order to persuade man to act contrary to the Creator's prohibition, entices him with this incentive: "When you eat of it your eyes will be opened and you will be like God, knowing good and evil" (Gen 3:5).

In this light, it seems that one must understand that the purpose of that tree of knowledge and the prohibition to eat of its fruit was to remind man that he is not "like God"—he is only a creature! Yes, a creature of particular perfection, because he is made "in the image and likeness of God," but still only a creature. This was the fundamental truth of that being which is man. The commandment man received in the beginning included this truth, expressed in the form of an admonition—remember that you are a creature called to friendship with God, who alone is your Creator. Do not wish to be what you are not! Do not wish to be "like God." Act in accordance with what you are, and all the more willingly since this is already such an exalted status, that of being "the image and likeness of God." This distinguishes you from the other creatures of the visible world, placing you above them. But at the same time, the status of image and likeness of God obliges you to act in conformity with what you are. So be faithful to the covenant that God the Creator has made with you, a creature, from the beginning.

The words of the tempter recounted in Genesis 3 not only placed in doubt but radically "contested" this truth—and thus the primordial principle of man's conduct. In pronouncing those words of temptation, the "ancient serpent," as he is called in the Book of Revelation (cf. Rev 12:9), formulates for the first time a criterion of interpretation to which sinful man would later turn many times, in an attempt to affirm himself or even to create an ethics without God. That criterion states that God is "alienating" for man, so that, if he wants to be himself, man must discard God (cf. for example, Feuerbach, Marx, Nietzsche).

The word "alienation" presents diverse shades of meaning. In every case it indicates the "usurpation" of something which belongs to another. The tempter of Genesis 3 says for the first time that the Creator has "usurped" what belongs to the creature man! "Being like God" is to be considered a human attribute, which would exclude any sort of dependence on God. The rejection of all religion as incompatible with what man is logically derives from this metaphysical presupposition. In fact, atheist (or anti-theist) philosophies maintain that religion is a fundamental form of alienation, by means of which man divests himself, or allows himself to be deprived, of what pertains exclusively to his being as man. Even in creating the idea of God, man produces his own alienation, because he renounces what originally and principally belongs to him, in favor of the perfect and happy being imagined by him. Religion, in its turn, accentuates, preserves and fuels this state of self-deprivation in favor of a God of "idealistic" creation, and so is one of the principal factors of the "expropriation" of man, of his dignity and rights.

I would like to note here that this false theory—so contrary to the data of religious history and psychology—presents certain analogies with the biblical narration of the temptation and fall. It is significant that the tempter ("the ancient serpent") of Genesis 3 does not call in question the existence of God, nor does he even directly deny the reality of the creation: these truths were much too obvious in that historical age. Instead, the tempter—in his experience as a creature who has freely chosen to rebel—seeks already "in the beginning" to implant in man's conscience, as it were in "germinal" form, what constitutes the nucleus of the ideology of "alienation."

In so doing, he produces a radical inversion of the truth of creation in its deepest essence. In place of a God who generously bestows existence upon the world, in place of God the Creator, the words of the tempter in Genesis 3 present a God that is the "usurper" and "enemy" of creation, and especially of man. In reality, it is precisely man who is the recipient of a special divine endowment, having been created in the "image and likeness" of God. In this way, truth is expelled by untruth. It is turned into a lie, because it is manipulated by the "father of lies," as the Gospel calls him who carried out this deceit at the "beginning" of history: "He was a murderer from the beginning, because there is no truth in him. When he lies, he speaks according to his own nature, for he is a liar and the father of lies" (Jn 8:44).

This "lie" is found at the beginning of history as the root of sin in the world of created beings endowed with freedom in the image of the Creator. In seeking its source, the words of the great Augustine come to mind: *amor sui usque ad contemptum Dei* (love of self to the point of despising God: *De Civitate Dei*, XIV, 28, PL 41, 438). The primordial lie has its source in the hatred which is reflected in man's first sin. This permits one to understand better what St. Paul teaches when he describes Adam's sin as "disobedience" (cf. Rom 5:19). The Apostle does not speak of direct hatred of God, but of "disobedience," of opposition to the Creator's will. This will remain the principal characteristic of sin in the course of human history. Weighed down by this inheritance, the human will, rendered weak and prone to evil, will remain permanently exposed to the influence of the "father of lies." One notes it in the various epochs of history. In our own times it is witnessed to by the different kinds of negation of God, from agnosticism to atheism or even to anti-theism. In different ways there is stamped in it the idea of the "alienating" character of religion and morality, which finds in religion its own root, precisely as had been suggested at the beginning by the "father of lies."

But looking at things without prejudice, we must say in all frankness that in the light of revelation and of faith, the theory of alienation should be reversed. It is precisely sin and only sin which leads to man's alienation! It is precisely sin that from the very beginning led to man's being "disinherited" in a certain way of his own humanity. Sin robs man, in various ways, of the decisive element of his true dignity—that of the image and likeness of God. In a certain sense, every sin "lessens" this dignity. The more a man becomes a "slave of sin" (cf. Jn 8:34), so much the less does he enjoy the freedom of the children of God. He ceases to be master of himself as would be required by the structure of his being as a person, as a rational, free and responsible creature.

Sacred Scripture effectively underlines this concept of alienation by illustrating its threefold dimension: the alienation of the sinner from himself (cf. Ps 58:3—"The wicked go astray from the womb"), from God (cf. Ez 14:7: "he who separated himself from me"; Eph 4:18: "alienated from the life of God"), from the community (cf. Eph 2:12: "alienated from the commonwealth of Israel").

Sin, therefore, is not only "against God," but also against man. As the Second Vatican Council teaches: "Sin has diminished man, blocking his path to fulfillment" *(GS* 13). This truth has no need of proof by elaborate arguments. It suffices simply to observe it. Moreover, do not so many works of literature, the movies and the theater supply eloquent confirmation? In them man appears weakened, confused, deprived of an inner center, a relentless adversary both of himself and others, a slave of non-values, awaiting someone who never comes, as if to confirm the fact that once contact with the Absolute is lost, man ends up by losing himself also.

It suffices to refer to experience, whether to interior experience, or to historico-social experience in its various forms, to realize that sin is a dreadful "destructive force." It destroys with a deceptive and inexorable virulence the good of life among men and human societies. For this very reason one can rightly speak of "social sin" (cf. *Reconciliatio et Paenitentia,* 16). Granted however, that personal sin is always at the root of the social dimension of sin, one must first and foremost emphasize what sin destroys in every human being, its subject and cause, considered in the concrete as a person.

In this regard St. Thomas Aquinas's observation should be recalled. He says that to the extent that man as such becomes better by every morally good act he performs, so likewise by every morally evil act man as such becomes worse

(Summa Theol., cf. I-II, q. 55, a. 3; q. 63, a. 2). Sin destroys in man that good which is essentially human. In a certain sense it "robs" man of that good which is proper to him, it "usurps" man from himself. In this sense "whoever sins is the slave of sin," as Jesus stated in St. John's Gospel (8:34). This is precisely what is contained in the concept of "alienation." Sin, therefore, is the real "alienation" of the rational and free human being. It pertains to the rational being to pursue truth and to exist in the truth. In place of the truth concerning the good, sin introduces what is not true. Sin eliminates the real good in favor of an "apparent" good, which is not a real good, since the real good was eliminated to make way for the "false."

The alienation which occurs in sin touches the cognitive sphere, but through knowledge it affects the will. What then happens in the sphere of the will finds perhaps its most exact expression in St. Paul's Letter to the Romans: "I do not do the good I want, but the evil I do not want is what I do. Now if I do what I do not want, it is no longer I that do it, but sin which dwells in me.... When I want to do right, evil lies close at hand.... Wretched man that I am!" (Rom 7:19-20, 21, 24).

As is evident, man's real "alienation"—the alienation of a rational and free being made in the image of God—is nothing other than "the domination of sin" (Rom 3:9). Sacred Scripture forcefully emphasizes this aspect of sin. Sin is not only "against" God, it is at the same time "against" man.

If it is true that by its very logic and according to revelation, sin calls for adequate punishments, the first of these punishments is constituted by sin itself. Through sin man punishes himself! Sin contains its own immanent punishment. As someone has said, sin is already hell, as the privation of God!

"Is it I whom they provoke?" God asks through the prophet Jeremiah. "Is it not themselves, to their own confusion?" (Jer 7:19). "Your wickedness will chasten you, and your apostasy will reprove you" (Jer 2:19). The prophet Isaiah lamented: "We all fade like a leaf, and our iniquities, like the wind, take us away.... For you have hidden your face from us, and have delivered us into the hand of our iniquities" (Is 64:6-7). This "consignment (and self-consignment) of man into the hand of his iniquities" explains most eloquently the significance of sin as the alienation of the human person. However, the evil is not complete or at least not without a remedy, as long as man is aware of it, as long as he preserves the sense of sin. But when even this is lacking, the complete collapse of moral values is practically inevitable and there looms over man as a terrifying reality the risk of definitive perdition. For this reason the grave words of Pius XII (which have become almost proverbial) should always be remembered and meditated on with great attention: "The sin of the century is the loss of the sense of sin" (cf. *Discorsi e Radiomessaggi*, VIII, 1946, 288).

General audience of November 12, 1986

The Entire Human Race
Struggles Against the Forces of Evil

In the introduction to the Constitution *Gaudium et Spes* of the Second Vatican Council we read: "The Council focuses its attention on the world of men, the whole human family along with the sum of those realities in the midst of which it lives; that world which is the theater of man's history, and the heir of his energies, his tragedies and his triumphs; that world which the Christian sees as created and sustained by its Maker's love, fallen indeed into the bondage of sin, yet emancipated now by Christ, who was crucified and rose again to break the stranglehold of personified evil, so that the world might be fashioned anew according to God's design and reach its fulfillment" *(GS* 2).

It is the world we have before our eyes in these catecheses. As you know, they deal with the reality of evil, of sin, both in its beginning and throughout the whole history of the human family. In seeking to reconstruct a synthetic image of sin we make use of all that we learn of it from humanity's varied experience down the centuries. We do not forget, however, that sin in itself is a mystery of evil. Its historical beginning and successive development cannot be fully understood unless we refer to the mystery of God the Creator, and in particular to the Creator of the beings made in his own image and likeness. The words of Vatican II already quoted tell us that the mystery of evil and of sin, the "mystery of iniquity," cannot be understood without reference to the mystery of redemption, to the "paschal mystery" of Jesus Christ, as we noted from the first catechesis of this series. The most ancient creeds already expressed this "logic of faith."

From the first announcement of redemption which we find in Genesis, we are already introduced to this view of the truth about sin, constantly professed and proclaimed by the Church. After the transgression of the first commandment, on which God the Creator had established his most ancient covenant, Genesis presents us with the following dialogue: "But the Lord God called to the man and said to him 'Where are you?' And he said, 'I heard you in the garden, and I was afraid, because I was naked; and I hid myself.' He said, 'Who told you that you were naked? Have you eaten of the tree of which I commanded you not to eat?' The man said, 'The woman whom you gave to be with me, she gave me fruit of the tree, and I ate.' Then the Lord said to the woman, 'What is this that you have done?' The woman said, 'The serpent beguiled me and I ate'" (Gen 3:9-13).

"Then the Lord God said to the serpent, 'Because you have done this, cursed are you.... I will put enmity between you and the woman, and between your seed and her seed; he shall bruise your head, and you shall bruise his heel'" (Gen 3:14-15).

This passage of Genesis 3 fits in harmoniously in the "Yahwist" context of which it forms a part. It fits both in regard to style and the mode of presenting the truths which we already know from the examination of the tempter's words, and from the description of the first sin. Notwithstanding the appearances which the style of the biblical account may create, the essential truths are sufficiently clear in it. They can be understood in themselves, and still more in the context of all that is said on this subject in the entire Bible, from beginning to end, through the fuller sense of Sacred Scripture (*sensus plenior*).

Thus the passage of Genesis 3:9-15 (and also the continuation of this chapter) contains God's response to man's sin. It is a direct response to the first sin, and at the same time it is a response viewing in perspective the whole future history of humanity on earth until the end. A real continuity and at the same time a profound consistency in the truth revealed by God exists between Genesis and the Book of Revelation. To this harmonious consistency of revelation there corresponds "the logic of faith" on the part of the person who consciously believes. The truth about sin is included in the development of this logic.

According to Genesis 3:9-15, man's first sin is described, above all, as "disobedience," that is, opposition to the commandment which expressed the Creator's will. We have already seen that. Man (male and female) is responsible for this act, since Adam is completely aware and free in doing what he does. The same responsibility is found in every personal sin in the history of man, who acts for one purpose. In this regard it is significant that we are told by Genesis, that the Lord God asked both—first the man and then the woman—the motive of their behavior: "Why have you done this?" From this it follows that the essential significance of the act is in reference to this motive, that is, to the purpose of the act. The "why" of God's question signifies *for what motive?* But it also means *for what purpose?* Here the woman (together with the man) refers to the prompting of the tempter: "The serpent beguiled me." From this reply one must infer that the motive suggested by the serpent: "You will be like God," contributed in a decisive manner to the transgression of the Creator's prohibition, and gave an essential dimension to the first sin. This motive is not directly mentioned by God in his sentence of punishment. But it is undoubtedly present and dominates the whole historical and biblical scenario as a reminder of the gravity and stupidity of the pretension of opposing God or of substituting oneself for God. It indicates the most essential and profound dimension of original sin and of every sin which has its primary root therein.

It is significant and fitting that in the wake of the response to man's first sin, God should turn his attention to the tempter, "the ancient serpent" of which the author of the Book of Revelation will say that "he deceives the whole world" (cf. Rev 12:9: "the deceiver of the whole world"). According to Genesis, the Lord said to the serpent: "Because you have done this, cursed are you." The words of the curse addressed to the serpent concern him whom Christ will call "the father of lies" (cf. Jn 8:44). But at the same time, in that divine response to the first sin, the struggle is announced which will be waged throughout all of human history between "the father of lies" and the woman and her offspring.

The Second Vatican Council declared itself very clearly on this subject: "A monumental struggle against the powers of darkness pervades the whole history of man. The battle was joined from the very origins of the world and will continue until the last day.... Caught in this conflict, man is obliged to wrestle constantly if he is to cling to what is good, nor can he achieve his own integrity without great efforts and the help of God's grace" *(GS* 37).

"Man finds that by himself he is unable to overcome the assaults of evil successfully, so that everyone feels as though bound by chains." But to this strong expression the Council sets out in juxtaposition the truth about redemption with an affirmation of faith no less strong and decisive: "The Lord himself came to free and strengthen man, renewing him inwardly and casting out 'the prince of this world' (Jn 12:31), who held him in bondage of sin" *(GS* 13).

These observations of the Magisterium of the Church today repeat in a precise and homogeneous way the truth about sin and redemption, expressed initially in Genesis 3:15, and later in the whole of Sacred Scripture. Let us hear once again the words of *Gaudium et Spes:* "Although set by God in a state of rectitude, man...abused his freedom at the very start of history. He lifted himself up against God, and sought to attain his goal apart from him" *(GS* 13). Evidently it concerns a sin in the strict sense of the word, whether in the case of the first sin or in that of every other human sin. But the Council does not fail to recall that the first sin was committed by man "enticed by the evil one" *(GS* 13). As we read in the Book of Wisdom: "Through the devil's envy death entered the world, and those who belong to his party experience it" (Wis 2:24). It seems that in this case "death" signifies both the sin itself (that is to say, the death of the soul as the loss of divine life conferred by sanctifying grace), and also the death of the body deprived of the hope of the glorious resurrection. Man who transgressed the law regarding "the tree of the knowledge of good and evil," has been separated by the Lord God from the "tree of life" (Gen 3:22), in the perspective of his whole earthly history.

The Letter to the Ephesians describes this well: "For we are not contending against flesh and blood, but against the principalities, against the powers, against the world rulers of this present darkness, against the supernatural hosts of wickedness in the heavenly places" (6:12). But also the thought of the appalling reality of sin which weighs on the whole of history but particularly in our time, forces us back to the tremendous truth of those biblical and conciliar words on "the monumental struggle against the powers of darkness." But we should not forget that a light is shed on this mystery of the powers of evil from the very beginning which frees history from the nightmare of an inexorable condemnation—the announcement of the Savior.

General audience of December 10, 1986

The Protoevangelium of Salvation

In the fourth Eucharistic Prayer (Canon IV) the Church addresses God in the following words: "Father, we proclaim your greatness: all your actions show your wisdom and love. You formed man in your own likeness and set him over the whole world to serve you, his creator, and to rule over all creatures. Even when in disobedience he rejected your friendship you did not abandon him to the power of death...."

In harmony with the truth expressed in this prayer of the Church, we noted in the previous catechesis the complex content of the words of Genesis 3, which contain God's response to the first human sin. That text speaks of the combat against "the powers of evil" in which humanity has been involved from the beginning of its history. At the same time, however, it assures us that God does not abandon man to himself, he does not leave him "in the power of death," reduced to a "slave of sin" (cf. Rom 6:17). Accordingly, God tells the serpent who has tempted the woman: "I will make you enemies of each other; you and the woman, your offspring and her offspring. It will crush your head and you will strike its heel" (Gen 3:15).

These words of Genesis are called the *"Protoevan-*

gelium" or the first announcement of the Messiah Redeemer. They reveal God's salvific plan in regard to the human race which after original sin is found in the fallen state which we know. They indicate especially the central event in God's plan of salvation. It is the same event referred to in the fourth Eucharistic Prayer, already quoted, when we turn to God with this profession of faith: "Father, you so loved the world that in the fullness of time you sent your only Son to be our Savior. He was conceived through the power of the Holy Spirit, and born of the Virgin Mary, a man like us in all things but sin."

The statement of Genesis 3 is called the "Protoevangelium" because it has received its confirmation and fulfillment only in the revelation of the new covenant which is the Gospel of Christ. In the old covenant this announcement was constantly re-evoked in different ways, in the rites, symbolisms, prayers, prophecies, and in the history of Israel as the "people of God" reaching out toward a messianic goal. But it was always under the veil of the imperfect and provisional faith of the Old Testament. When the announcement will be fulfilled in Christ there will be the full revelation of the messianic and trinitarian content implicit in the monotheism of Israel. The New Testament will then lead to the discovery of the full meaning of the writings of the Old Testament, according to the famous saying of St. Augustine: "In the Old Testament the New lies hidden, and in the New the Old lies open" (cf. *Quaestiones in Heptateuchum,* II, 73).

The analysis of the "protoevangelium" informs us, by means of the announcement and promise contained in it, that God has not abandoned the human race to the power of sin and death. He wished to rescue and save it. He did so in his own way, according to the measure of his transcendent holiness, and at the same time according to a self-effacement such as only a God of love could display.

The words of the "protoevangelium" express this saving

self-effacement when they announce the struggle ("I will put
enmity") between him who represents "the powers of evil" and
the other whom Genesis calls "the offspring of the woman." It
is a struggle which will end with the victory of Christ! ("He
shall bruise your head.") However, this will be the victory
bought at the price of the sacrifice of the cross ("and you shall
bruise his heel.") The mystery of iniquity is dispelled by the
"mystery of mercy." It is precisely the sacrifice of the cross
that helps us to penetrate into the essence of sin, enabling us to
understand something of its dark mystery. In a particular way
St. Paul is our guide when he wrote in the Letter to the Romans: "As by one man's disobedience many were made
sinners, so by one man's obedience many will be made righteous" (Rom 5:18). "One man's act of righteousness leads to
acquittal and life for all men" (Rom 5:18).

In the "protoevangelium," in a certain sense, the Christ is
announced for the first time as "the new Adam" (cf. 1 Cor
15:45). Indeed, his victory over sin obtained through "obedience unto the death of the cross" (cf. Phil 2:8), will imply such
an abundance of pardon and of saving grace as to overcome
immeasurably the evil of the first sin and of all the sins of the
human race. St. Paul again writes: "If many died through one
man's trespass, much more have the grace of God and the free
gift in the grace of that one man Jesus Christ abounded for
many" (Rom 5:15).

Moreover, solely on the basis of the "protoevangelium,"
it can be deduced that in regard to the destiny of fallen man
(status naturae lapsae) there is already introduced the prospect
of future redemption *(status naturae redemptae)*.

The first response of the Lord God to man's sin, contained in Genesis 3, provides us from the beginning with a
knowledge of God as infinitely just and at the same time
infinitely merciful. From that first announcement he is manifested as that God who "so loved the world that he gave his

only Son" (Jn 3:16); who "sent his Son to be the expiation for our sins" (1 Jn 4:10); who "did not spare his own Son but gave him up for us all" (Rom 8:32).

Thus we have the certainty that God, who in his transcendent holiness abhors sin, justly punishes the sinner. But at the same time in his ineffable mercy he embraces him in his saving love. The "protoevangelium" already announced this saving victory of good over evil, which will be manifested in the Gospel through the paschal mystery of Christ crucified and risen.

It is to be noted that in the words of Genesis 3:15, "I will put enmity," the woman is placed in the first place in a certain sense: "I will put enmity between you and the woman." Not: "between you and the man," but precisely "between you and the woman." Commentators from the earliest times emphasize that we have here an important parallelism. The tempter—"the ancient serpent"—according to Genesis 3:4, first addressed the woman, and through her obtained his victory. In his turn the Lord God, in announcing the Redeemer, makes the woman the first "enemy" of the prince of darkness. In a certain sense, she should be the first beneficiary of the definitive covenant, in which the powers of evil will be overcome by the Messiah, her Son ("her offspring").

This—I repeat—is an extremely significant detail, if we bear in mind that in the history of the covenant God first of all addresses men (Noah, Abraham, Moses). In this case the precedence appears to belong to the woman, naturally in consideration of her descendant, Christ. Many Fathers and Doctors of the Church see in the woman announced in the "protoevangelium" the Mother of Christ, Mary. She is also the one who first shares in that victory over sin won by Christ. She is free from original sin and from every other sin, as emphasized by the Council of Trent in line with tradition (cf. *DS* 1516; 1572). As regards original sin in particular, Pius IX solemnly defined it by proclaiming the dogma of the Immaculate Conception (cf. *DS* 2803).

Not a few ancient Fathers, as the Second Vatican Council says (cf. LG 56), in their preaching present Mary, the Mother of Christ, as the new Eve (just as Christ is the new Adam, according to St. Paul). Mary takes the place and is the opposite of Eve, who is "the mother of all the living" (Gen 3:20), but also the cause, along with Adam, of the universal fall into sin. Mary is for all the "cause of salvation" by her obedience in cooperating with Christ in our redemption (cf. Irenaeus, *Adv. Haereses*, II, 22, 4).

The Council made a magnificent synthesis of this doctrine, but we shall now limit ourselves to quoting a text which can serve as the best seal on the catecheses on sin, which we have developed in the light of the ancient faith and hope in the advent of the Redeemer:

"The Father of mercies willed that the Incarnation should be preceded by the acceptance of her who was predestined to be the mother of his Son, so that just as a woman contributed to death, so also a woman should contribute to life. That is true in outstanding fashion of the mother of Jesus, who gave to the world him who is Life itself and who renews all things, and who was enriched by God with the gifts which befit such a role. It is no wonder therefore that the usage prevailed among the Fathers whereby they called the mother of God entirely holy and free from all stain of sin, as though fashioned by the Holy Spirit and formed as a new creature. Adorned from the first instant of her conception with the radiance of an entirely unique holiness, the Virgin of Nazareth is greeted, on God's command, by an angel messenger as 'full of grace,' and to the heavenly messenger she replies: 'Behold the handmaid of the Lord, be it done unto me according to your word.' Thus Mary, a daughter of Adam, consenting to the divine Word, became the mother of Jesus, the one and only Mediator. Embracing

God's salvific will with a full heart and impeded by no sin, she devoted herself totally as a handmaid of the Lord to the person and work of her Son, under him and with him, by the grace of almighty God, serving the mystery of redemption" *(LG* 56).

Thus in Mary and through Mary the situation of humanity and of the world has been reversed, and they have in some way have re-entered into the splendor of the morning of creation.

General audience of December 17, 1986

JESUS CHRIST, GOD AND MAN

The Identity of Christ

"Who do you say that I am?" (Mt 16:15).

In beginning the series of reflections on Jesus Christ, which are of fundamental importance for the faith and Christian life, we are faced with the same question which the Master addressed Peter and the disciples who were with him about two thousand years ago. The Gospel of Matthew, who was a witness, relates that in that decisive moment, "When Jesus came into the district of Caesarea Philippi, he asked his disciples, 'Who do men say that the Son of Man is?' And they said, 'Some say John the Baptist, others say Elijah and others Jeremiah or one of the prophets.' He said to them, 'But who do you say that I am?'" (Mt 16:13-15).

We know Peter's frank and impetuous response: "You are the Christ, the Son of the living God" (Mt 16:16). So that we may be able to formulate it not only in abstract terms, but as the expression of a living experience, the fruit of the gift of the Father (cf. Mt 26:17), each one of us must let himself be touched personally by the question: "And you, who do you say that I am? You who hear me spoken of, answer me. What do I really mean for you?" Peter's divine illumination and response

of faith came after a long period of living close to Jesus,
hearing his words and observing his life and ministry (cf. Mt
16:21-24).

In our case also, in order to make a more conscious
profession of faith in Jesus Christ, we must, like Peter, listen
attentively and carefully. We must follow in the school of the
first disciples who had become his witnesses and our teachers.
At the same time we must accept the experience and testimony
of no less than twenty centuries of history marked by the
Master's question and enriched by the immense chorus of
responses of the faithful of all times and places. Today, while
the Spirit, "the Lord and Giver of Life" impels us toward the
threshold of the third Christian millennium, we are called to
give with renewed joy the response which God inspires and
awaits from us, as if for a new birth of Jesus Christ in our
history.

Jesus' question about his identity shows the pedagogical
shrewdness of one who does not trust hasty responses. He
desires an answer matured over a sometimes lengthy period of
reflection and prayer, in the attentive and intense hearing of
the truth of the Christian faith as professed and practiced by
the Church.

We recognize that in the presence of Jesus we cannot be
satisfied with a merely human sympathy, however legitimate
and valuable. Nor is it sufficient to consider him solely as a
personage worthy of historical, theological, spiritual and social
interest, or as a source of artistic inspiration. In regard to
Christ we frequently see, even among Christians, the shadows
of ignorance, or more painfully still, those of misunderstanding, if not of downright unbelief. There is always the risk of
appealing to the "Gospel of Jesus" without really knowing its
grandeur and all-embracing nature, and without living in accordance with what we profess. How many reduce the Gospel
to their own measure and make for themselves a more conve-

nient Jesus. They deny his transcendent divinity, or dismiss his real, historical humanity. They even manipulate the integrity of his message, especially by not bearing in mind the sacrifice of the cross which dominates his life and doctrine, or the Church which he instituted as his "sacrament" in history.

Even these shadows stimulate us to search for the full truth about Jesus. We can take advantage of the many insights which, as once in the case of Peter, the Father has provided down the centuries concerning Jesus in the hearts of so many persons by the power of the Holy Spirit—the insights of witnesses faithful to the point of martyrdom; the insights of so many dedicated scholars seeking to fathom the mystery of Jesus by using intelligence enlightened by faith; the insights which in particular the Magisterium of the Church, guided by the charism of the Holy Spirit, has provided in the dogmatic definitions concerning Jesus Christ.

We recognize that an urge to discover who Jesus really is, is present in the uncertain and anxious search of many of our contemporaries. They are like Nicodemus who went "by night to find Jesus" (cf. Jn 3:2), or like Zacchaeus who climbed a tree to "see Jesus" (cf. Lk 19:4). The desire to help everyone discover Jesus, who came to heal the sick and save sinners (cf. Mk 2:17), urges me to carry out the demanding and moving task of presenting the figure of Jesus to the members of the Church and to every person of good will.

Perhaps you will recall that at the beginning of my pontificate I addressed to all the invitation to "throw open the doors to Christ" *(L'Osservatore Romano,* English edition, November 2, 1978, p. 1). Later, in the Exhortation *Catechesi Tradendae,* as the spokesman of the mind of the bishops of the Fourth Synod, I stated that "the primary and essential object of catechesis is...the 'mystery of Christ.' Catechizing is in a way to lead a person to study this mystery in all its dimensions...to reveal in the Person of Christ the whole of God's eternal design reaching fulfillment in that Person.... Only he can lead us to the love of the Father in the Spirit and make us share in the life of the Holy Trinity" *(CT* 5).

In this catechetical series we shall consider four central points: 1) Jesus in his historical reality and in his transcendent messianic character, son of Abraham, Son of Man and Son of God; 2) Jesus in his identity as true God and true man, in profound communion with the Father and animated by the power of the Holy Spirit as he is presented to us in the Gospel; 3) Jesus as seen by the eyes of the Church which with the assistance of the Holy Spirit has elucidated and investigated the data of revelation by giving us, especially in the ecumenical councils, precise formulations of the Christological faith; 4) finally, Jesus in his life and in his works, Jesus in his redemptive passion and in his glorification, Jesus in our midst and within us, in history and in his Church until the end of the world (cf. Mt. 28:20).

Authentic catechesis

It is indeed true that in the Church there are many ways of catechizing the People of God in regard to Jesus. Each one of them, however, if it is to be authentic, must draw its content from the perennial font of Sacred Tradition and of Sacred Scripture. These are interpreted in the light of the teaching of the Fathers and Doctors of the Church, of the liturgy, of the faith and piety of the people, in a word, of the living and operative Tradition of the Church under the action of the Holy Spirit, who, according to the Master's promise, "will guide you into all the truth, for he will not speak on his own authority, but whatever he hears he will speak, and he will declare to you the things that are to come" (Jn 16:13). We recognize this Tradition expressed and synthesized particularly in the teaching of the Sacred Councils, collected in the creeds of the faith and deepened by theological reflection faithful to revelation and the Magisterium of the Church.

What would be the use of a catechesis on Jesus if it did not have the authenticity and completeness of view with which the Church contemplates, prays and announces his mystery? On the other hand, a pedagogical wisdom is required which knows how to take account of the conditions and needs of those to be catechized. As I wrote in the above-quoted Exhortation *Catechesi Tradendae:* "Whatever be the level of his responsibility in the Church, every catechist must constantly endeavor to transmit by his teaching and behavior the teaching and life of Jesus" *(CT* 6).

We conclude this introductory reflection by recalling that Jesus, in a particularly difficult moment in the life of his first disciples when the cross appeared imminent and many abandoned him, addressed to those who remained with him another of those questions, so strong, so penetrating and inescapable: "Will you also go away?" Once again it was Peter who replied as the spokesman of his brethren: "Lord, to whom shall we go? You alone have the words of eternal life. We have believed and known that you are the Holy One of God" (Jn 6:66-69). May these catechetical reflections make us ever more ready to allow ourselves to be questioned by Jesus, capable of giving the right answer to his questions, and ready to share his life to the best of our ability.

General audience of January 7, 1987

Jesus Christ, Son of God and Savior

In last week's catechesis, following the earliest creeds of the Christian faith, we began a new cycle of reflections on Jesus Christ. The Apostles' Creed proclaims: "I believe...in Jesus Christ, his [God's] only Son." The Nicene-Constantinopolitan Creed, after having defined with still greater precision the divine origin of Jesus Christ as Son of God, continues with the declaration that this Son of God "for us men and for our salvation came down from heaven...and became man." As can be seen, the central nucleus of the Christian faith is constituted by the twofold truth that Jesus Christ is Son of God and Son of Man (the Christological truth), and that God the Father brought about the salvation of man in him, his Son and Savior of the world (the soteriological truth).

In treating of evil, and particularly of sin, in the previous reflections, we were preparing the way for the present series on Jesus Christ, the Savior. Salvation means liberation from evil, especially from sin. The revelation contained in Sacred Scripture, beginning with the Protoevangelium (Gen 3:15), opens us to the truth that only God can free us from sin and from all the present evil of human existence. While revealing himself as Creator of the world and its guiding Providence, God at the same time reveals himself as Savior, as the one who frees from evil, in particular from sin caused by the free will of the creature. This is the apex of the creative project put into effect by divine Providence, in which the world (cosmology), the human race (anthropology) and God the Savior (soteriology) are closely linked.

As the Second Vatican Council recalls, Christians believe that the world "has been created and sustained by the love of its maker, that it has been freed from the slavery of sin by Christ, who was crucified and rose again..." *(GS* 2).

Considered etymologically, the name "Jesus" means "Yahweh sets free," saves, helps. Before the Babylonian captivity it was expressed in the form "Jehosua," a theophoric name which contains the root of the most holy name of Yahweh. After the exile in Babylon it took the abbreviated form "Jeshua," which the Septuagint translation transcribed as "Jesoûs," from which comes the English "Jesus."

The name was quite widespread both at the time of the old covenant and of the new. For example, it is the same as the name Joshua, who after the death of Moses led the Israelites into the promised land: "He became, in accordance with his name, a great savior of God's elect...so that he might give Israel its inheritance" (Sir 46:1). Jesus, son of Sirach, was the compiler of the Book of Sirach (50:27). In the genealogy of the Savior contained in Luke's Gospel we find listed "Er, son of Jesus" (Lk 3:28-29). Among the collaborators of St. Paul there is a certain Jesus "who is called Justus" (cf. Col 4:11).

The name Jesus, however, never had that fullness of meaning which it would have in the case of Jesus of Nazareth and which would be revealed by the angel to Mary (cf. Lk 1:31 ff.) and to Joseph (cf. Mt 1:21). At the beginning of Jesus' public ministry his name was understood by the people in the usual meaning of that time.

"We have found him of whom Moses in the law and also the prophets wrote, Jesus of Nazareth, the son of Joseph." Thus Philip, one of the first disciples, said to Nathanael who replied: "Can anything good come out of Nazareth?" (Jn 1:45-46). This question indicates that Nazareth was not highly esteemed by the children of Israel. Notwithstanding this, Jesus was called a "Nazarene" (cf. Mt 2:23) or also "Jesus from Nazareth of Galilee" (cf. Mt 21:11), an expression which Pilate himself used in the inscription which he had placed on the cross: "Jesus of Nazareth, the king of the Jews" (Jn 19:19).

The people called Jesus "the Nazarene" from the name of the place where he resided with his family until he reached the age of thirty. We know, however, that Jesus' birthplace was not Nazareth but Bethlehem, a locality of Judea to the south of Jerusalem. The evangelists Luke and Matthew stated this. In particular, Luke noted that because of the census ordered by the Roman authorities, "Joseph went up from Galilee, from the city of Nazareth, to Judea, to the city of David, which is called Bethlehem...to be enrolled with Mary, his betrothed, who was with child. And while they were there, the time came for her to be delivered" (Lk 2:4-6).

Fulfillment of prophecy

As is the case with other biblical places, Bethlehem also assumes a prophetic value. Referring to the prophet Micah (cf. 5:1-3), Matthew recalled that this little town had been indicated as the birthplace of the Messiah: "And you, O Bethlehem, in the land of Judah, are by no means least among the rulers of Judah; for from you shall come a ruler who will govern my people Israel" (Mt 2:6). The prophet added "whose origin is from of old, from ancient days" (Mic 1).

The priests and scribes referred to this text when Herod consulted them in order to reply to the wise men from the East who had asked where the Messiah was to be born. The text of Matthew's Gospel which states: "Jesus was born in Bethlehem of Judea in the days of Herod the king" (Mt 2:1), refers back to the prophecy of Micah, to which is referred also the question in the fourth Gospel: "Has not the Scripture said that the Christ is descended from David, and comes from Bethlehem, the village where David was?" (Jn 7:42).

From this we conclude that Jesus is the name of a historical person who lived in Palestine. If it is correct to accept the historical credibility of figures such as Moses and Joshua, for still greater reason must we accept the historical existence of Jesus. The Gospels do not tell us about his life in detail because their primary purpose was not biographical. But the Gospels themselves, read with critical honesty, lead us to the conclusion that Jesus of Nazareth is a historical person who lived in a definite place and time. Also from the purely scientific point of view, surprise should be caused not by those who affirm but by those who deny the existence of Jesus, as was done by the mythological theories of the past and by some scholars even today.

As regards the exact date of Jesus' birth, experts do not agree. It is generally admitted that the monk, Dionysius Exiguus was inaccurate when in the year 533 he proposed to calculate years not from the foundation of Rome, but from the birth of Jesus Christ. Until some time ago it was held that it was a matter of a mistake of about four years, but the question is by no means settled.

In the tradition of the Israelite people the name "Jesus" has preserved its etymological meaning: "God sets free." According to tradition, the parents always named their children. But in the case of Jesus, son of Mary, the name was chosen and assigned from on high already before his birth, as indicated by the angel to Mary in the annunciation (cf. Lk 1:31) and to Joseph in a dream (cf. Mt 1:21). "He was called Jesus," the evangelist Luke emphasizes, because that was "the name given by the angel before he was conceived in the womb" (Lk 2:21).

According to the disposition of divine Providence, Jesus of Nazareth bears a name which alludes to salvation, "God sets free," because he is what in fact his name indicates, that is, the Savior. This is confirmed by some phrases in the so-called infancy Gospels of Luke: "For you is born...a Savior" (Lk 2:11), and of Matthew: "for he will save his people from their sins" (Mt 1:21). These expressions reflect the truth revealed and proclaimed by the whole of the New Testament. For example, the Apostle Paul wrote in the Letter to the Philippians: "Therefore God has highly exalted him and bestowed on him the name which is above every name, that at the name of Jesus every knee should bow...and every tongue confess that Jesus Christ is Lord *(Kyrios, Adonai)*, to the glory of God the Father" (Phil 2:9-11).

The reason for the exaltation of Jesus is found in the witness rendered to him by the apostles who courageously proclaimed: "There is salvation in no one else, for there is no other name under heaven given among men by which we must be saved" (Acts 4:12).

General audience of January 14, 1987

Jesus Christ, Conceived by the Power of the Holy Spirit and Born of the Virgin Mary

In the previous meeting our reflection was concentrated on the name "Jesus" which means "Savior." This same Jesus who lived for thirty years at Nazareth in Galilee, is the eternal Son of God "conceived by the power of the Holy Spirit and born of the Virgin Mary." That is proclaimed by the creeds of the faith, the Apostles' Creed and the Nicene-Constantinopolitan Creed. It was taught by the Fathers of the Church and the councils, according to which Jesus Christ, eternal Son of God, is "born in the world of his mother's substance" (Creed *Quicumque, DS* 76). The Church then professes and proclaims that Jesus Christ was conceived and born of a daughter of Adam, a descendant of Abraham and of David, the Virgin Mary.

St. Luke's Gospel states that Mary conceived the Son of God through the power of the Holy Spirit, not knowing man (cf. Lk 1:34 and Mt 1:18, 24-25). Mary was therefore a virgin before the birth of Jesus, and she remained a virgin in giving birth and after the birth. That is the truth presented by the New Testament texts, and which was expressed both by the Fifth Ecumenical Council at Constantinopole in 553, which spoke of

Mary as "ever virgin," and also by the Lateran Council in 649, which taught that "the mother of God...Mary...conceived (her Son) through the power of the Holy Spirit without human intervention, and in giving birth to him her virginity remained uncorrupted, and even after the birth her virginity remained intact" *(DS* 503).

Mary's consent

This faith is presented in the teaching of the apostles. For example, we read in the Letter of St. Paul to the Galatians: "When the time had fully come, God sent forth his Son, born of woman...so that we might receive adoption as sons" (Gal 4:4-5). The events linked to the conception and birth of Jesus are contained in the first chapters of Matthew and Luke, generally called "the infancy Gospel," and it is to them that we must refer.

Luke's text is particularly well known, because it is frequently read in the Eucharistic liturgy and used in the angelus prayer. This passage of Luke's Gospel describes the annunciation to Mary, which took place six months after the announcement of the future birth of John the Baptist (cf. Lk 1:5-25).

"The angel Gabriel was sent from God to a city of Galilee named Nazareth, to a virgin betrothed to a man whose name was Joseph, of the house of David; and the virgin's name was Mary" (Lk 1:26). The angel greeted her with the words, "Hail, Mary," which became the Church's prayer (the "angelic salutation"). Mary was disturbed by the angel's greeting: "She was greatly troubled at the saying and considered in her mind what sort of greeting this might be. And the angel said to her, 'Do not be afraid, Mary, for you have found favor with God. And behold, you will conceive in your womb and bear a son, and you shall call his name Jesus. He will be great, and will be called the Son of the Most High'.... Then Mary said to the angel: 'How can this be, since I have no husband?' And the angel said to her: 'The Holy Spirit will come upon you and the power of the Most High will overshadow you; therefore the child to be born will be called holy, the Son of God'" (Lk 1:29-35). In making the announcement, the angel presented as a "sign" the unhoped-for maternity of Elizabeth, a relative of Mary, who had conceived a son in her old age, and added: "With God nothing is impossible." Then Mary said: "Behold, I am the handmaid of the Lord; let it be done to me according to your word" (Lk 1:37-38).

This text of Luke's Gospel is the basis of the Church's teaching on the motherhood and virginity of Mary from whom Christ was born, made man by the power of the Spirit. The first moment of the mystery of the Incarnation of the Son of God is identified with the miraculous conception which took place by the power of the Holy Spirit when Mary uttered her "yes": "Be it done to me according to your word" (Lk 1:38).

Matthew's Gospel completes Luke's narrative by describing certain circumstances which preceded the birth of Jesus. We read: "Now the birth of Jesus Christ took place in this way. When his mother Mary had been betrothed to Joseph, before they came together she was found to be with child of the Holy Spirit; her husband Joseph, being a just man and unwilling to put her to shame, resolved to send her away quietly. But as he considered this, behold, an angel of the Lord appeared to him in a dream, saying 'Joseph, son of David, do not fear to take Mary your wife, for that which is conceived in her is of the Holy Spirit; she will bear a son, and you shall call his name Jesus, for he will save his people from their sins'" (Mt 1:18-21).

As is evident, both texts of the "infancy Gospel" agree on the fundamental facts. Jesus was conceived by the power of the Holy Spirit and was born of the Virgin Mary. They are complementary in clarifying the circumstances of this extraordinary happening; Luke in reference to Mary, Matthew in reference to Joseph.

To identify the source of the infancy narrative one must go back to St. Luke's remark: "Mary kept all these things, pondering them in her heart" (Lk 2:19). Luke states this twice—after the departure of the shepherds from Bethlehem and after the finding of Jesus in the temple (cf. Lk 2:51). The evangelist himself provides us with the elements to identify in the mother of Jesus one of the sources of the information used by him in writing "the infancy Gospel." Mary, who "kept these things in her heart" (cf. Lk 2:19), could bear witness, after Christ's death and resurrection, in regard to what concerned herself and her role as mother, precisely in the apostolic period when the New Testament texts were being written and when the early Christian tradition had its origin.

The Gospel witness to the virginal conception of Jesus on the part of Mary is of great theological importance. It constitutes a particular sign of the divine origin of Mary's Son. The fact that Jesus did not have an earthly father because he was generated "without human intervention" sets out clearly the truth that he is the Son of God, so much so that even when he assumed human nature his Father remained exclusively God.

The revelation of the intervention of the Holy Spirit in the conception of Jesus, indicates the beginning of the history of the man of the new "spiritual generation" which has a strictly supernatural character (cf. 1 Cor 15:45-49). In this way the Triune God "is communicated" to the creature through the Holy Spirit. It is the mystery to which the words of the Psalmist may be applied: "Send forth your Spirit, and they are created, and you renew the face of the earth" (Ps 104:30). In the economy of this self-communication of God to the creature, the virginal conception of Jesus through the power of the Holy Spirit is a central and culminating event. It initiates the "new creation." In this way God enters decisively into history to activate our supernatural destiny, or the predestination of all things in Christ. It is the definitive expression of God's salvific love for the human race, which we spoke about in the reflections on Providence.

A participation on the part of the creature always occurs in the realization of the plan of salvation. Thus Mary participated in a decisive way in the conception of Jesus through the power of the Holy Spirit. Enlightened interiorly by the angel's message about her vocation as mother and the preservation of her virginity, Mary expressed her will and her consent and agreed to become the humble instrument of the "power of the Most High." The action of the Holy Spirit ensured that in Mary, motherhood and virginity are simultaneously present in a way which, although incomprehensible to the human mind, enters fully within the scope of God's predilection and omnipotence. Isaiah's great prophecy is fulfilled in Mary: "A virgin shall conceive and bear a son" (7:14; cf. Mt 1:22-23). Her virginity, an Old Testament sign of poverty and availability to God's plan, became the sphere of the exceptional action of God who chose Mary to be the mother of the Messiah.

The exceptional character of Mary is seen also in the genealogies contained in Matthew and Luke. In accordance with Jewish custom Matthew's Gospel begins with the genealogy of Jesus (cf. Mt 1:2-17) and, starting from Abraham, lists the generations in the male line. Matthew is concerned to make evident, through the legal paternity of Joseph, the descent of Jesus from Abraham and David and, consequently, the legitimacy of his claim to Messiah. However, at the end of the list of ancestors we read: "Jacob was the father of Joseph, the husband of Mary, of whom Jesus was born, who is called Christ" (Mt 1:16). By emphasizing the motherhood of Mary, the evangelist implicitly underlines the truth of the virginal birth: Jesus, as man, did not have a human father.

According to Luke's Gospel the genealogy of Jesus (cf. Lk 3:23-38) is in ascending order. From Jesus through his ancestors it goes back to Adam. The evangelist wished to show the link between Jesus and the whole human race. As God's collaborator in giving human nature to his eternal Son, Mary was the instrument that linked Jesus with the whole of humanity.

General audience of January 28, 1987

Jesus Christ, Son of Israel, Chosen People of the Old Covenant

Of the two genealogies of Jesus mentioned in the previous reflection, that of Matthew's Gospel (cf. 1:1-17) is made out in a descending order, that is, it lists the ancestors of Jesus, son of Mary, beginning from Abraham. The other in St. Luke's Gospel, (cf. 3:23-38) is in ascending order, beginning with Jesus and going back to Adam.

While Luke's genealogy links Jesus with the whole of humanity, Matthew's genealogy makes evident the fact that he was of the offspring of Abraham. It is as a son of Israel, God's Chosen People in the old covenant, to which he directly belongs, that Jesus of Nazareth is fully a member of the great human family.

Jesus was born among this people; he grew up in their religion and culture. He was a true Israelite who thought and expressed himself in Aramaic according to the conceptual and linguistic categories of his contemporaries. He followed the customs and usages of his surroundings. As an Israelite he was a faithful heir of the old covenant.

St. Paul highlights this fact when in the Letter to the Romans he writes of his people: "They are Israelites, and to them belong the sonship, the glory, the covenant, the giving of the law, the worship, and the promises; to them belong the patriarchs, and of their race, according to the flesh, is the Christ" (Rom 9:4-5). In the Letter to the Galatians he recalls that Christ was "born under the law" (Gal 4:4).

Shortly after his birth Jesus was circumcised according to the ritual prescriptions of the Mosaic law, thus becoming officially a member of the people of the covenant: "At the end of eight days, when he was circumcised, he was called Jesus" (Lk 2:21).

The Infancy Gospel, however scarce in details concerning the first part of Jesus' life, mentions however that "his parents went to Jerusalem every year at the feast of the Passover" (Lk 2:41), an indication of their fidelity to the law and tradition of Israel. "When he [Jesus] was twelve years old, they went up according to custom" (Lk 2:42). "When they were returning, the boy Jesus stayed behind in Jerusalem, without his parents knowing it" (Lk 2:43). After searching for three days "they found him in the temple, sitting among the teachers, listening to them and asking them questions" (Lk 2:46). Superimposed on the joy of Mary and Joseph were his words which they did not understand: "How is it that you sought me? Did you not know that I must be in my Father's house?" (Lk 2:49).

Apart from this event, the whole period of the infancy and youth of Jesus is passed over in silence in the Gospel. It is the period of his "hidden life," summarized by Luke in two simple statements: Jesus "went down with them [Mary and Joseph] and came to Nazareth, and was obedient to them" (Lk 2:51); and "He progressed steadily in wisdom and age and grace before God and men" (Lk 2:52).

We learn from the Gospels that Jesus lived in his own family, in the house of Joseph, who took the place of a father in regard to Mary's son by assisting and protecting him and gradually training him in his own trade of carpenter. The people of the town of Nazareth regarded him as "the carpenter's son" (cf. Mt 13:55). When he began to teach, his fellow citizens asked with surprise: "Is not this the carpenter, the son of Mary?" (Mk 6:3). Besides his mother they mentioned also his "brothers" and his "sisters," that is, those members of his kin ("cousins"), who lived at Nazareth. It was they who, as the evangelist Mark mentions, sought to dissuade Jesus from his activity of teaching (cf. Mk 3:21). Evidently they did not find in him anything to justify the beginning of a new activity. They thought that Jesus was just like any other Israelite, and should remain such.

Jesus' public ministry began at the age of thirty when he held his first discourse at Nazareth: "He went to the synagogue, as his custom was, on the sabbath day. And he stood up to read; and there was handed to him the book of the prophet Isaiah..." (Lk 4:16-17). Jesus read the passage beginning with the words: "The Spirit of the Lord is upon me, because he has anointed me to preach good news to the poor..." (Lk 4:18). Jesus then turned to those present and announced: "Today this scripture has been fulfilled in your hearing" (Lk 4:21).

In his teaching, which began at Nazareth and extended to Galilee and to Judea as far as the capital, Jerusalem, Jesus made use of the rich religious tradition of Israel. He penetrated it with a new insight, revealed its key values and set out its prophetic perspectives. He did not hesitate to condemn deviations from the plan of the God of the covenant.

In this way he brought about, within the scope of the one and the same divine revelation, the transition from the "old" to the "new," not by abolishing the law but by bringing it to fulfillment (cf. Mt 5:17). It is with this thought that the Letter to the Hebrews opens: "In many and various ways God spoke of old to our fathers by the prophets; but in these last days he has spoken to us by a Son..." (Heb 1:1).

This transition from the "old" to the "new" characterizes

the whole teaching of the "prophet" of Nazareth. A particularly clear example is the Sermon on the Mount recorded in
Matthew's Gospel. Jesus says: "You have heard that it was
said to the men of old, 'You shall not kill....' But I say to you
that every one who is angry with his brother shall be liable to
judgment" (Mt 5:21-22). "You have heard that it was said,
'You shall not commit adultery.' But I say to you that everyone
who looks at a woman lustfully has already committed adultery with her in his heart" (Mt 5:27-28). "You have heard that
it was said, 'You shall love your neighbor and hate your enemy.' But I say to you, love your enemies and pray for those
who persecute you..." (Mt 5:43-44).

Teaching in this way, Jesus states at the same time:
"Think not that I have come to abolish the law and the prophets; I have come not to abolish them but to fulfill them" (Mt
5:17).

This "fulfillment" is a key word which refers not only to
the teaching of the truth revealed by God, but also to the whole
history of Israel, or of the people of which Jesus is a son. This
extraordinary history, guided from the very beginning by the
powerful hand of the God of the covenant, finds its fulfillment
in Jesus. The plan which the God of the covenant had inscribed
from the very beginning in this history, making it the history of
salvation, was ordered to the "fullness of time" (cf. Gal 4:4)
which is realized in Jesus Christ. The prophet of Nazareth did
not hesitate to speak of it from his very first discourse delivered in the synagogue of his own town.

Jesus' words recorded in John's Gospel are particularly
eloquent, when he said to his opponents: "Your father
Abraham rejoiced that he was to see my day..." and in the face
of their incredulity: "You are not yet fifty years old, and have
you seen Abraham?" Jesus again more explicitly asserted:
"Truly, truly, I say to you before Abraham was, I am" (cf. Jn
8:56-58). It is evident that Jesus affirmed not only that he is the

fulfillment of God's salvific plan, inscribed in the history of Israel from the time of Abraham, but that his existence precedes the time of Abraham, even to the point of identifying himself with "He who is" (cf. Ex 3:14). Precisely for this reason, he, Jesus Christ, is the fulfillment of the history of Israel, because he transcends this history by his mystery. Here, however, we touch another dimension of Christology that we shall deal with later.

For the present we shall conclude with a final reflection on the two genealogies recorded by the evangelists Matthew and Luke. From them it follows that Jesus is a true son of Israel and that, as such, he belongs to the whole human family. If therefore we see the prophecies of the Old Testament fulfilled in Jesus, a descendant of Abraham, in him, as the descendant of Adam, we can discern, following the teaching of St. Paul, the principle and kernel of the "recapitulation" of all humanity (cf. Eph 1:10).

General audience of February 4, 1987

Jesus Christ, Messiah King

At the beginning of his Gospel, the evangelist Matthew concludes his genealogy of Jesus, Son of Mary, with the words "Jesus who is called Christ" (Mt 1:16). The term "Christ" is the Greek equivalent of the Hebrew word "Messiah," which means "Anointed." Israel, God's chosen people, had lived for generations in expectation of the fulfillment of the promise of the Messiah, whose coming was prepared by the history of the covenant. The Messiah, that is, the "Anointed" sent by God, was to bring to fulfillment the call of the people of the covenant. Through revelation Israel was granted the privilege of knowing the truth about God himself and about his plan for salvation.

The name "Christ" was attributed to Jesus of Nazareth. This testifies to the fact that the apostles and the primitive Church recognized that the plans of the God of the covenant were realized in Christ, along with the expectations of Israel. Peter proclaimed this on the day of Pentecost when, inspired by the Holy Spirit, he spoke for the first time to the inhabitants of Jerusalem and to the pilgrims who had come up for the feast: "Let all the house of Israel therefore know assuredly that

God has made him both Lord and Christ, this Jesus whom you crucified" (Acts 2:36).

The Anointed one

Peter's discourse and Matthew's genealogy propose once again the rich content of the term "Messiah-Christ" which is found in the Old Testament and which we shall treat in the following reflections.

The word "Messiah," including the idea of anointing, can be understood only in connection with the anointing with oil which was used in Israel, and which passed from the old covenant to the new. In the history of the old covenant, this anointing was received by those called by God to the office and dignity of king, priest or prophet.

The truth about the Christ-Messiah must be understood in the biblical context of this threefold office, which in the old covenant was conferred on those who were destined to guide or to represent the people of God. In the present reflection we intend to dwell on the office and dignity of Christ as king.

When the angel Gabriel announced to the Virgin Mary that she had been chosen to be the Mother of the Savior, he spoke to her of the kingship of her son: "The Lord God will give to him the throne of his father David, and he will reign over the house of Jacob for ever; and of his kingdom there will be no end" (Lk 1:32-33).

These words seem to correspond to the promise made to King David: "When your days are fulfilled...I will raise up your offspring after you...and I will establish his kingdom. He shall build a house for my name, and I will establish the throne of his kingdom for ever. I will be his father, and he shall be my son" (2 Sam 7:12-14). It can be said that this promise was fulfilled to a certain extent in Solomon, the son and immediate successor of David. But the full meaning of the promise goes well beyond the confines of an earthly kingdom and regards not only a distant future, but even a reality that goes beyond history, time and space: "I will establish the throne of his kingdom for ever" (2 Sam 7:13).

In the annunciation, Jesus is presented as he in whom the ancient promise is fulfilled. In this way the truth about Christ the king is situated in the biblical tradition of the messianic king (the Messiah-King). In this form it is frequently found in the Gospels which speak to us of the mission of Jesus of Nazareth and transmit his teaching to us.

In this regard the attitude of Jesus himself is significant, for example, when Bartimaeus, the blind beggar, cried out to him for help: "Jesus, Son of David, have mercy on me!" (Mk 10:47). Although this title had never been attributed to him, Jesus accepted as addressed to himself the words spoken by Bartimaeus. If necessary, he was concerned to clarify their significance. Turning to the Pharisees he asked: "What do you think of the Christ? Whose son is he? They said to him, 'The son of David.' He said to them, 'How is it then that David, inspired by the Spirit, calls him Lord, saying, "The Lord said to my Lord, sit at my right hand, till I put your enemies under your feet?" (Ps 110:1). If David then calls him Lord, how is he his son?'" (Mt 22:42-45).

As can be seen, Jesus called attention to the limited and insufficient manner of understanding the Messiah solely on the basis of the tradition of Israel, linked to the royal inheritance of David. However, he did not reject this tradition. He fulfilled it in its full meaning, which had already appeared in the words spoken during the annunciation and would be manifested in his Pasch.

Another significant fact is mentioned by the evangelists Matthew (cf. 21:5) and John (cf. 12:15). On entering Jerusalem on the eve of his passion, Jesus fulfilled the prophecy of Zechariah, in which the tradition of the messianic king finds expression: "Rejoice greatly, O daughter of Zion! Shout aloud, O daughter of Jerusalem! Lo, your king comes to you; triumphant and victorious is he, humble and riding on an ass, on a colt, the foal of an ass" (Zech 9:9); "Tell the daughter of Zion, behold, your king is coming to you, humble, and mounted on an ass, on a colt, the foal of an ass" (Mt 21:5). Indeed, riding on an ass Jesus made his solemn entrance into Jerusalem, accompanied by the enthusiastic cries: "Hosanna to the Son of David" (cf. Mt 21:1-10). Notwithstanding the indignation of the Pharisees, Jesus accepted the messianic acclamation of the "little ones" (cf. Mt 21:16; Lk 19:40), knowing that every ambiguity about the title of Messiah would be dispelled by his glorification through the passion.

The understanding of the kingship as an earthly power will enter into crisis, but the tradition will emerge from it clarified, not canceled. In the days following Jesus' entry into Jerusalem it will be seen how the angel's words at the annunciation are to be understood: "The Lord God will give to him the throne of his father David, and he will reign over the house of Jacob for ever; and of his kingdom there will be no end." Jesus himself will explain the nature of his own kingship, and therefore the messianic truth, and how it is to be understood.

The decisive moment of this clarification was in Jesus' conversation with Pilate, recorded in John's Gospel. Since Jesus was accused before the Roman governor of claiming to be "king of the Jews," Pilate questioned him about this accusation which particularly interested the Roman authority. If Jesus really claimed to be "king of the Jews" and his followers recognized him as such, this could be a threat to the empire. So Pilate asked Jesus: "'Are you the King of the Jews?' Jesus answered, 'Do you say this of your own accord, or did others say it to you about me?'" Then he explained: "'My kingship is not of this world; if my kingship were of this world, my servants would fight, that I might not be handed over to the Jews;

but my kingship is not from this world.' Pilate said to him, 'So
you are a king?' Jesus answered, 'You say that I am a king. For
this I was born, and for this I have come into the world, to bear
witness to the truth. Everyone who is of the truth hears my
voice'" (cf. Jn 18:33-37). These unambiguous words of Jesus
contain the clear statement that the kingly character or office,
linked with the mission of the Christ-Messiah sent by God,
cannot be understood in a political sense as though it concerned an earthly power, not even in relation to the Chosen
People, Israel.

The sequel of Jesus' trial confirmed the existence of the
conflict between Christ's conception of himself as Messiah-
King and the earthly and political one that was common among
the people. Jesus was condemned to death on the charge that
"he claimed to be king." The inscription placed on the cross,
"Jesus of Nazareth, the King of the Jews" is a proof that for the
Roman authority this was his crime. The very Jews who para-
doxically aspired to the re-establishment of the kingdom of
David in the earthly sense, at the sight of Jesus scourged and
crowned with thorns, presented to them by Pilate with the
words, "Behold your king!" cried out, "Crucify him...we have
no king but Caesar" (Jn 19:15).

Against this background we can better understand the
meaning of the inscription placed on Christ's cross, not without reference to the definition which Jesus gave of himself
during the interrogation before the Roman procurator. Only in
that sense is the Christ-Messiah the king; only in that sense
does he fulfill the tradition of the messianic king, present in the
Old Testament and inscribed in the history of the people of the
old covenant.

Finally, on Calvary one last episode illumined the kingly
messiahship of Jesus. One of the criminals crucified with Jesus
manifested this truth in a penetrating way when he said,
"Jesus, remember me when you come in your kingly power"

(Lk 23:42). Jesus said to him, "Truly I say to you, today you will be with me in Paradise" (Lk 23:43). In this dialogue we find a final confirmation of the words which the angel had addressed to Mary in the annunciation: Jesus "will reign...and of his kingdom there shall be no end" (Lk 1:33).

General audience of February 11, 1987

Jesus Christ, Messiah Priest

The name "Christ" is, as we know, the Greek equivalent of the word "Messiah" and means "Anointed." Besides the royal character, which we treated in the previous reflection, it also includes, according to Old Testament tradition, the "priestly" character. As elements pertaining to the messianic mission, these two aspects, though differing among themselves, are nonetheless complementary. The figure of the Messiah outlined in the Old Testament embraces both elements by showing the profound unity of the royal and priestly mission.

This unity has its earliest expression as a prototype and an anticipation in Melchizedek, king of Salem, the mysterious figure in the Old Testament at the time of Abraham. We read of him in the Book of Genesis that in going out to meet Abraham, "He offered bread and wine; he was priest of God Most High. And he blessed him and said, 'Blessed be Abram by God Most High, maker of heaven and earth'" (Gen 14:18-19).

The figure of Melchizedek, king and priest, entered into the messianic tradition, as indicated especially by Psalm 110 (the messianic psalm) by antonomasia. In this Psalm, God-

Yahweh addresses "my Lord" (i.e., the Messiah) with the words: "'Sit at my right hand till I make your enemies your footstool.' The Lord sends forth from Zion your mighty scepter. Rule in the midst of your foes!" (Ps 110:1-2).

These expressions which leave no doubt about the royal character of the one addressed by Yahweh, are followed by the announcement: "The Lord has sworn and will not change his mind, 'You are a priest forever after the order of Melchizedek'" (Ps 110:4). As is evident, the one whom God-Yahweh addresses by inviting him to sit "at his right hand," will be simultaneously king and priest according to the order of Melchizedek.

Sacrifices of adoration and atonement

In the history of Israel the institution of the Old Testament priesthood traces its origin to Aaron, the brother of Moses, and it was hereditary in the tribe of Levi, one of the twelve tribes of Israel.

In this regard, it is significant that we read in the Book of Sirach: "(God) exalted Aaron, the brother of Moses...of the tribe of Levi. He made an everlasting covenant with him and gave him the priesthood of the people" (Sir 45:6-7). "[The Lord] chose him out of all the living to offer sacrifice to the lord, incense and a pleasing odor as a memorial portion, to make atonement for the people. In his commandments he gave him authority in statutes and judgments to teach Jacob the testimonies, and to enlighten Israel with his law" (Sir 45:16-17). From these texts we deduce that selection as a priest is for the purpose of worship, for the offering of sacrifices of adoration and atonement, and that worship in its turn is linked to teaching about God and his law.

In this same context the following words from the Book of Sirach are also significant: "For even [God's] covenant with

David...was an individual heritage through one son alone; but the heritage of Aaron is for all his descendants" (Sir 45:25).

According to this tradition, the priesthood is placed "alongside" the royal dignity. However, Jesus did not come from the priestly line, from the tribe of Levi, but from that of Judah. Hence it would seem that the priestly character of the Messiah does not become him. His contemporaries discover in him, above all, the teacher, the prophet, some even their "king," the heir of David. It would therefore be said that the tradition of Melchizedek, the king-priest is absent in Jesus.

It is, however, only an apparent absence. The paschal events revealed the true meaning of the "Messiah-King" and of the "king-priest after the order of Melchizedek" which— present in the Old Testament—found its fulfillment in the mission of Jesus of Nazareth. It is significant that during his trial before the Sanhedrin, Jesus replied to the high priest who asked him if he was "the Christ, the Son of God," by saying, "You have said so. But I tell you, hereafter you will see the Son of Man seated at the right hand of God..." (Mt 26:63-64). It is a clear reference to the messianic Psalm 110 which expresses the tradition of the king-priest.

It must be said, however, that the full manifestation of this truth is found only in the Letter to the Hebrews which treats of the relationship between the levitical priesthood and that of Christ. The author of the Letter to the Hebrews touches the theme of Melchizedek's priesthood in order to say that Jesus Christ fulfilled the messianic pre-announcement linked to that figure who by a higher predestination was inscribed in the mission of the people of God already from the time of Abraham.

We read of Christ who "being made perfect, became the source of eternal salvation to all who obey him, being designated by God a high priest after the order of Melchizedek" (Heb 5:9-10). Then, after recalling what was said about Melchizedek in the Book of Genesis (cf. Gen 14:18), the Letter to the Hebrews continues: "His name when translated means king of righteousness, and then he is also king of Salem, that is, king of peace. He is without father or mother or genealogy, and has neither beginning of days nor end of life, but resembling the Son of God he continues a priest for ever" (Heb 7:2-3).

Using the analogies of the ritual of worship, of the ark and of the sacrifices of the old covenant, the author of the Letter to the Hebrews presents Jesus Christ as the fulfillment of all the figures and promises of the Old Testament, ordained "to serve a copy and shadow of the heavenly sanctuary" (Heb 8:5). Christ, however, a merciful and faithful high priest (cf. Heb 2:17; 3:2-5), bears in himself a "priesthood that continues for ever" (Heb 7:24), having offered "himself without blemish to God" (Heb 9:14).

It is worthwhile quoting completely some particularly eloquent passages of this letter. Coming into the world, Jesus Christ says to God his Father: "Sacrifices and offerings you have not desired, but a body you have prepared for me. In burnt offerings and sin offerings you take no pleasure. Then I said, 'Behold, I have come to do your will, O God'" (Heb 10:5-7). "For it was fitting that we should have such a high priest" (Heb 7:26). "Therefore he had to be made like his brethren in every respect, so that he might become a merciful and faithful high priest in the service of God, to make expiation for the sins of the people" (Heb 2:17). We have then, "a high priest...who in every respect has been tempted as we are, yet without sinning," a high priest who is able "to sympathize with our weaknesses" (cf. Heb 4:15).

Further on we read that such a high priest "has no need, like the other high priests, to offer sacrifices daily, first for his own sins and then for those of the people; he did this once for all when he offered up himself" (Heb 7:27). Again, "when Christ appeared as a high priest of the good things that have come...he entered once for all into the Holy Place...taking his own blood, thus securing an eternal redemption" (Heb 9:11-12). Hence our certainty that "the blood of Christ who through the eternal Spirit offered himself without blemish to God, will purify our conscience from dead works to serve the living God" (Heb 9:14).

This explains why an everlasting saving power is attributed to Christ's priesthood whereby "he is able for all time to save those who draw near to God through him, since he always lives to make intercession for them" (Heb 7:25).

An eternal priesthood

Finally, we can note that the Letter to the Hebrews states clearly and convincingly that Jesus Christ has fulfilled with his whole life, and especially with the sacrifice of the cross, all that was written in the messianic tradition of divine revelation. His priesthood is situated in reference to the ritual service of the priests of the old covenant, which he surpasses as priest and victim. God's eternal design which provides for the institution of the priesthood in the history of the covenant is fulfilled in Christ.

According to the Letter to the Hebrews, the messianic task is symbolized by the figure of Melchizedek. There we read that by God's will "another priest arises in the likeness of Melchizedek, not according to a legal requirement concerning bodily descent but by the power of an indestructible life" (Heb 7:15). It is therefore an eternal priesthood (cf. Heb 7:3-24).

The Church, faithful guardian and interpreter of these and other texts contained in the New Testament, has reaffirmed over and over again the truth of the Messiah-priest, as witnessed, for example, by the Ecumenical Council of Ephesus (431), that of Trent (1562) and in our own time, the Second Vatican Council (1962-1965).

An evident witness of this truth is found in the Eucharistic sacrifice which by Christ's institution the Church offers every day under the species of bread and wine, "after the order of Melchizedek."

General audience of February 18, 1987

Jesus Christ, Messiah and Prophet

During the trial before Pilate, on being questioned whether he was a king, Jesus at first denied that he was a king in the earthly and political sense. Then on being asked a second time, he replied: "You say that I am a king. For this I was born, and for this I have come into the world, to bear witness to the truth" (Jn 18:37). This reply links the royal and priestly mission of the Messiah with the essential characteristic of the prophetic mission. The prophet is called and sent to bear witness to the truth. As a witness to the truth he speaks in God's name. In a certain sense he is the voice of God. Such was the mission of the prophets sent by God to Israel throughout the centuries. It is particularly in the figure of David, king and prophet, that the prophetic characteristic is united to the royal mission.

Service to God and people

The history of the prophets of the Old Testament clearly indicates that the task of proclaiming the truth by speaking in God's name is above all a service. It is a service both in relation to God who gives the mandate, and to the people to whom the prophet presents himself as God's envoy. Consequently the prophetic service is not only eminent and honorable, but also difficult and wearying. The vicissitudes of Jeremiah are an obvious example. He met with resistance, rejection and even persecution, in the measure in which the truth he proclaimed was unwelcome. Jesus himself referred several times to the sufferings undergone by the prophets, and personally experienced them in full measure.

These preliminary references to the ministerial character of the prophetic mission introduce us to the figure of the servant of God (*Ebed Yahweh*) which is found in Isaiah (precisely in the so-called "Deutero-Isaiah"). The messianic tradition of the old covenant finds a particularly rich and important expression in this figure, in whom the characteristics of prophet especially stand out. The servant of Yahweh unites in himself, in a certain way, the qualities of priest and king as well. The songs of the servant in Isaiah present an Old Testament synthesis on the Messiah, open to future developments. Although written so many centuries before Christ, they serve in a surprising manner to identify his figure, especially as regards the description of the suffering servant of Yahweh. The picture is so accurate and faithful that it would seem to be an account based on the events of Christ's passion.

One must observe that the term "servant," "servant of God," is widely used in the Old Testament. Many eminent personages are called or identified as "God's servants." For example, Abraham (cf. Gen 26:26), Jacob (cf. Gen 32:11), Moses, David, Solomon and the prophets. Sacred Scripture attributes this term even to certain pagan personages who played their part in the history of Israel; for example, Nebuchadnezzer (cf. Jer 25:8-9) and Cyrus (cf. Is 44:26). Finally, the whole of Israel as a people is called "servant of God" (cf. Is 41:8-9; 42:19; 44:21; 48:20), according to a linguistic usage whose echo we find in the Magnificat where Mary praises God because "he has helped his servant Israel" (Lk 1:54).

Concerning the songs of the servant in Isaiah, we note especially that they do not regard a collective entity, such as a people, but an individual person, whom the prophet distinguishes in a certain way from Israel-sinner: "Behold my servant whom I uphold," we read in the first song, "my chosen, in whom my soul delights; I have put my spirit upon him, he will bring forth justice to the nations. He will not cry or lift up his voice, or make it heard in the street; a bruised reed he will not break, and a dimly burning wick he will not quench.... He will not fail or be discouraged till he has established justice in the earth..." (Is 42:1-4). "I am the Lord...I have given you as a covenant to the people, a light to the nations, to open the eyes that are blind, to bring out the prisoners from the dungeon, from the prison those who sit in darkness" (Is 42:6-7).

The second song develops the same thought: "Listen to me, O coastlands, and hearken, you peoples from afar. The Lord called me from the womb, from the body of my mother he named my name. He made my mouth like a sharp sword, in the shadow of his hand he hid me; he made me a polished arrow, in his quiver he hid me away" (Is 49:1-2). "He says 'It is too light a thing that you should be my servant to raise up the tribes of Jacob.... I will give you as a light to the nations, that my salvation may reach to the end of the earth'" (Is 49:6). "The Lord God had given me the tongue of those who are taught, that I may know how to sustain with a word him that is weary" (Is 50:4). And again: "So shall he startle many nations, and because of him kings shall stand speechless" (Is 52:15). "The righteous one, my servant, shall make many to be accounted righteous; and he shall bear their iniquities" (Is 53:11).

These last texts, from the third and fourth songs, introduce us with striking realism to the figure of the suffering servant, to which we shall return later. All that Isaiah says seems to foretell in a surprising way all that was foretold by the holy old man Simeon at the very beginning of Jesus' life. Simeon greeted Jesus as "a light to enlighten the Gentiles" and at the same time "a sign of contradiction" (cf. Lk 2:32, 34). Already from the Book of Isaiah the figure of the Messiah emerges as a prophet who comes into the world to bear witness to the truth and, precisely because of this truth he will be rejected by his people, becoming by his death a cause of justification for "many."

The songs of the Servant of Yahweh are fully echoed in the New Testament from the beginning of Jesus' messianic activity. The description of the baptism in the Jordan allows one to establish a parallel with the texts of Isaiah. Matthew wrote: "When Jesus was baptized...the heavens were opened and he saw the Spirit of God descending like a dove, and alighting on him" (Mt 3:16); in Isaiah it was said: "I put my spirit upon him" (Is 42:1). The evangelist added, "and a voice from heaven said, 'This is my beloved son, with whom I am well pleased'" (Mt 3:17). In Isaiah God says to the servant, "my chosen, in whom my soul delights" (Is 42:1). John the Baptist pointed out Jesus approaching the Jordan with the words, "Behold the Lamb of God, who takes away the sin of the world!" (Jn 1:29). This exclamation summarizes the third and fourth songs of the suffering servant of Yahweh.

A similar relationship is found in the passage in which Luke recorded the first messianic words spoken by Jesus in the synagogue of Nazareth when he read the text of Isaiah: "The Spirit of the Lord is upon me, because he has anointed me to preach good news to the poor. He has sent me to proclaim release to the captives and recovery of sight to the blind, to set at liberty those who are oppressed, to proclaim the acceptable year of the Lord" (Lk 4:17-19). These are the words of the first song of the servant of Yahweh (cf. Is 42:1-7; also Is 61:1-2).

If we look at the life and ministry of Jesus, he appears to us as the servant of God, who brings salvation to the people, who heals them, who frees them from their iniquity, and who wishes to win them to himself not by force but by goodness. The Gospel, especially that of Matthew, frequently refers to the Book of Isaiah, whose prophetic announcement is fulfilled in Christ. For example, Matthew narrated that "when it was evening they brought to him many who were possessed with demons; and he cast out the spirits with a word, and healed all who were sick. This was to fulfill what was spoken by the prophet Isaiah, 'He took our infirmities and bore our diseases'" (Mt 8:16-17; cf. Is 53:4). And in another place: "Many followed him, and he healed them all.... This was to fulfill what was spoken by the prophet Isaiah: 'Behold my servant...'" (Mt 12:15-21). At this point the evangelist quoted a long passage from the first song of the servant of Yahweh.

As in the case of the Gospels, so also the Acts of the Apostles shows that the first generation of Christ's disciples, beginning with the apostles, was profoundly convinced that Jesus fulfilled all that the prophet Isaiah had foretold in his inspired songs: that Jesus is the chosen servant of God (cf. Acts 3:13; 3:26; 4:27; 4:30; 1 Pet 2:22-25), that he fulfills the mission of the servant of Yahweh and brings the new Law, that he is the light of the covenant for all nations (cf. Acts 13:46-47). This same conviction is found later in the *Didache,* in the *Martyrdom of St. Polycarp,* and in the *First Letter* of St. Clement of Rome.

One must add an item of great importance: Jesus spoke of himself as a servant, clearly alluding to Isaiah 53, when he said: "The Son of Man came not to be served but to serve, and to give his life as a ransom for many" (Mk 10:45; cf. Mt. 20:28). The same idea is expressed by the washing of the feet of the apostles (cf. Jn 13:3-4, 12-15).

The first song of the servant of Yahweh (cf. Is 42:1-7)

underlines the election of the servant and his prophetic mission of liberation, healing and of covenant for all people. Throughout the entire New Testament, besides the passages and allusions to the first song, the greater number of texts refers to the third and fourth songs (cf. Is 50:4-11; Is 52:13-53:12) on the suffering servant. It is the same idea which St. Paul summed up briefly in his Letter to the Philippians when he sang the praises of Christ "who, though he was in the form of God, did not count equality with God a thing to be grasped, but emptied himself, taking the form of a servant, being born in the likeness of men...he humbled himself and became obedient unto death" (Phil 2:6-8).

General audience of February 25, 1987

Jesus Christ, Fulfillment of
the Messianic Prophecies

We continue our Wednesday reflections, focusing on the way that Christ fulfilled the prophecies concerning the Messiah's sufferings and death. In the previous reflection we sought to indicate the more important aspects of the truth about the Messiah, such as it was foretold in the old covenant, and as it was inherited by the generation of Jesus of Nazareth's contemporaries who had entered a new stage of divine revelation. Those of that generation who followed Jesus did so because they were convinced that he fulfilled the truth about the Messiah, that he was the Messiah, the Christ. Andrew, the first of the apostles called by Jesus, informed his brother Simon about Jesus with the significant words, "We have found the Messiah (which means Christ)" (Jn 1:41).

But it must be recognized that such explicit observations are rather rare in the Gospels. This is due to the fact that Jesus did not wish to adapt his figure and his work to the image of the Messiah which was widespread in the Jewish society of those times, notwithstanding the amazement and admiration aroused by all that "he did and taught" (Acts 1:1).

On the banks of the Jordan, John the Baptist had indicated Jesus as "he who was to come" (cf. Jn 1:15, 30), having prophetically perceived in him "the Lamb of God" come to take away the sins of the world. John had foretold the "new baptism" which Jesus would confer in the power of the Spirit. Yet when he was in prison, John himself sent his disciples to ask Jesus, "Are you he who is to come, or shall we look for another?" (Mt 11:3).

Jesus did not leave John and his messengers without an answer: "Go and tell John what you have seen and heard: the blind receive their sight, the lame walk, lepers are cleansed, the deaf hear, the dead are raised up, and the poor have good news preached to them" (Lk 7:22). With this reply Jesus intended to confirm his messianic mission by referring in particular to the words of Isaiah (cf. Is 35:4-5; 61:1). He concluded: "Blessed is he who takes no offense at me" (Lk 7:23). These last words sound like a call, addressed directly to John, his heroic precursor, who had a different idea about the Messiah.

In his preaching, John had delineated the figure of the Messiah as that of a severe judge. In this sense he had spoken of the "wrath to come," of the "axe already laid to the foot of the trees" (cf. Lk 3:7-9), which would cut down every tree "that does not bear good fruit" (cf. Lk 3:9). Certainly Jesus would not hesitate—firmly and even with severity, when necessary—to deal with obstinacy and rebellion to the word of God. But he was above all the preacher of "good news to the poor," and by his works and miracles he revealed the saving will of God, the merciful Father.

Jesus' answer to John also presents another element which is interesting to note: Jesus avoided proclaiming himself openly as the Messiah. In the social context of the time that title was ambiguous, and people generally interpreted it in a political sense. Jesus preferred to refer to the witness offered by his works, desiring to persuade and to engender faith.

However, the Gospels also present particular cases, such as the conversation with the Samaritan woman, narrated in

John's Gospel. To the woman who said to him, "I know that
the Messiah is coming (he who is called Christ); when he
comes, he will show us all things." Jesus replied, "I who speak
to you am he" (Jn 4:25-26). According to the context of the conversation, Jesus convinced the Samaritan woman whom he had perceived as ready
to listen. On returning to the city, she hastened to tell the
people, "Come, see a man who told me all I ever did. Can this
be the Christ?" (Jn 4:28-29). Moved by her words, many Sa-
maritans went out to meet Jesus. They listened to him, and in
turn they concluded, "This is indeed the Savior of the world"
(Jn 4:42).

Among the inhabitants of Jerusalem, however, Jesus'
words and miracles gave rise to questions about his messiahship. Some excluded the possibility that he could be the
Messiah: "We know where this man comes from; but when the
Christ appears, no one will know where he comes from" (Jn.
7:27). But others said, "When the Christ appears, will he perform more signs than this man has done?" (Jn 7:31). "Can this
be the Son of David?" (Mt 12:23). The Sanhedrin also inter-
vened, decreeing that "if any one should confess him to be the
Christ, he was to be put out of the synagogue" (Jn 9:22).

We are thus in a position to understand the key significance of Jesus' conversation with the apostles near Caesarea
Philippi. "Jesus...asked his disciples, 'Who do men say that I
am?' And they told him, 'John the Baptist, and others say
Elijah; and others one of the prophets.' And he asked them,
'But who do you say that I am?' Peter answered him, 'You are
the Christ'" (Mk 8:27-29), that is, the Messiah (cf. also Mt
16:13-16; Lk 9:18-21).

According to Matthew's Gospel this reply gave Jesus the
occasion to announce Peter's primacy in the future Church (cf.
Mt 16:18). According to Mark, after Peter's reply, Jesus
charged the apostles "to tell no one about him" (Mk 8:30).

Thence we can deduce that Jesus not only did not proclaim that he was the Messiah, but he did not even wish the apostles to spread the truth about his identity at that time. In fact, he wished that his contemporaries should arrive at this conviction by observing his works and hearing his teaching. On the other hand, the fact that the apostles were convinced of what Peter had expressed in the name of all of them, saying "You are the Christ," proves that Jesus' works and words were a sufficient basis on which faith in him as Messiah could be founded and developed.

However, the following part of the conversation, which we read in the parallel texts of Mark and Matthew, is still more significant concerning Jesus' mind on his own messiahship (cf. Mk 8:31-33; Mt 15:21-23). As if in close connection with the apostles' profession of faith, Jesus "began to teach them that the Son of Man must suffer many things, and the chief priests and the scribes and be killed, and after three days rise again" (Mk 8:31). The evangelist Mark observed that "Jesus said this plainly" (Mk 8:32). Mark said that "Peter took him aside and began to rebuke him" (Mk 8:32). Matthew tells us that the rebuke was as follows: "God forbid, Lord! This shall never happen to you" (Mt 16:22). And then the Master's reaction: Jesus "rebuked Peter and said, 'Get behind me, Satan! For you are not on the side of God, but of men'" (Mk 8:33; cf. Mt 16:23).

In this rebuke of the Master, one can hear a distant echo of the temptation undergone by Jesus in the desert at the beginning of his messianic activity (cf. Lk 4:1-13), when Satan wished to dissuade him from fulfilling his Father's will to the end. Although they had professed their faith in Jesus' messianic mission: "You are the Christ," the apostles and Peter in particular could not completely free themselves from a too human and earthly idea of the Messiah, by admitting the prospect of a Messiah who would suffer and undergo death. Again, at the moment of the ascension they would ask him "will you restore the kingdom of Israel?" (cf. Acts 1:6).

Precisely when faced with this attitude Jesus reacted with great decision and severity. He knew that his messianic mission was that of the suffering servant of Yahweh, as described by Isaiah, and especially that which the prophet had said: "For he grew up before him like a young plant, and like a root out of dry ground; he had no form or comeliness.... He was despised and rejected by men; a man of sorrows, and acquainted with grief, and as one from whom men hide their faces he was despised; and we esteemed him not. Surely he has borne our griefs and carried our sorrows...he was wounded for our transgressions, he was bruised for our iniquities" (Is 53:2-5).

Jesus firmly defended this truth about the Messiah. He was resolved to fulfill it to the end, because it expressed the Father's salvific will: "The righteous one, my servant, shall make many to be accounted righteous" (Is 53:11). In this way he prepared himself and his friends for the event in which the "messianic mystery" would find its complete fulfillment: the Pasch of his death and resurrection.

General audience of March 4, 1987

Jesus Christ, Inauguration and Fulfillment of the Kingdom of God

"The time is fulfilled and the kingdom of God is at hand" (Mk 1:15). With these words Jesus of Nazareth began his messianic preaching. In Jesus the kingdom of God enters into the life and history of mankind, and it constitutes the fulfillment of the promises of salvation which Israel had received from the Lord.

Jesus was revealed as the Messiah, not because he aimed at a temporal and political dominion according to the mentality of his contemporaries, but because in his mission, which culminated in his passion, death and resurrection, "all the promises of God find their yes in him" (2 Cor 1:20).

In order to understand fully Jesus' mission one must recall the Old Testament message which proclaims the saving kingship of the Lord. In the canticle of Moses (cf. Ex 15:1-18) the Lord is acclaimed as "king" because he freed his people in a marvelous way and led them with power and love to communion with him and their brethren in the joy of freedom. Moreover, the ancient Psalm 29 bears witness to the same faith—the Lord is contemplated in the power of his kingship, which holds dominion over all created being and communicates energy, blessing and peace to his people (Ps 29:10). It is especially in the call of Isaiah that faith in the Lord as "king" appears completely permeated with the theme of salvation. The "king" whom the prophet contemplates with the eyes of faith "sitting upon a throne, high and lifted up" (Is 6:1), is God in the mystery of his transcendent holiness and merciful goodness whereby he is present to his people as the source of love which purifies, pardons and saves: "Holy, holy, holy is the Lord of hosts; the whole earth is full of his glory" (Is 6:3).

This faith in the saving kingship of the Lord prevented the monarchy from developing autonomously in the people of the covenant as was the case in other nations. The king was the chosen one, the Lord's anointed, and as such, he was the instrument by which God himself exercised his sovereignty over Israel (cf. 1 Sam 12:12-15). "The Lord reigns," the Psalms continually proclaim (cf. 5:3; 9:5; 29:10; 93:1; 97:1-4; 146:10).

A new covenant

In face of the sad experience of human limitations and of sin the prophets announced a new covenant, in which the Lord himself would be the saving and royal guide of his renewed people (cf. Jer 31:31-34; Ez 34:7-16; 36:24-28).

The expectation of a new David whom the Lord will raise up as the instrument of the exodus, of liberation and salvation arose in this context (cf. Ez 34:23-25; Jer 23:5-6). From this moment onward the figure of the Messiah will appear in intimate relationship with the inauguration of the full kingship of God.

After the exile, even though the institution of the monarchy ceased in Israel, there was a continuous growth of faith in the kingship which God exercises over his people and which will extend even to "the ends of the earth." The Psalms which sing of the Lord as king are the most significant witness to this hope (cf. Ps 96; 99).

This hope reaches it high point when the eye of faith,

looking beyond the time of human history, will see that only in the future eternity the kingdom of God will be established in all its power. Then, by means of the resurrection, the redeemed will be in full communion of life and love with the Lord (cf. Dan 7:9-10; 12:2-3).

Jesus referred to this hope of the Old Testament and proclaimed its fulfillment. The kingdom of God formed the central theme of his preaching, as the parables show particularly.

The parable of the sower (cf. Mt 13:3-8) proclaims that the kingdom of God is already at work in Jesus' preaching, and at the same time it directs one's gaze to the abundance of fruits which will constitute the superabundant richness of the kingdom at the end of time. The parable of the seed which grows of itself (cf. Mk 4:26-29) emphasizes that the kingdom is not a human work. It is solely a gift of God's love, which acts in the hearts of believers and guides human history to its definitive fulfillment in eternal communion with the Lord. The parable of the darnel in the midst of the wheat (cf. Mt 13:24-30) and that of the net cast into the sea (cf. Mt 13:47-52) show first of all the already active presence of God's salvation. Together with the children of the kingdom, however, the children of the evil one, the workers of iniquity are also present. The powers of evil shall be destroyed only at the end of time, and those who have accepted the kingdom shall be forever with the Lord. Finally, the parables of the hidden treasure and the pearl of great price (cf. Mt 13:44-46) express the supreme and absolute value of God's kingdom. Whoever understands its value is prepared to face any sacrifice and renunciation to enter the kingdom.

There is a wealth of profound enlightenment in Jesus' teaching. In its full and complete fulfillment, the kingdom of God is certainly of the future: "until the kingdom of God comes" (cf. Mk 9:1; Lk 22:18). The Lord's Prayer teaches us to pray for its coming: "thy kingdom come" (Mt 6:10).

At the same time, however, Jesus stated that the kingdom of God "has already come" (Mt 12:28); "it is in the midst of you" (Lk 17:21) by means of the preaching and works of Jesus. Moreover, from the whole of the New Testament it is evident that the Church, founded by Jesus, is the place where God's kingship is made present, in Christ, as the gift of salvation in faith, of new life in the Spirit, of communion in charity.

The intimate relationship between the kingdom and Jesus thus appears. It is so strong a relationship that the kingdom of God can also be called the "kingdom of Jesus" (Eph 5:5; 2 Pet 1:11), as indeed Jesus himself stated before Pilate by asserting that Jesus' "kingdom is not of this world" (Jn 18:36).

In this light we can understand the conditions indicated by Jesus for entrance into the kingdom. They can be summed up in the word "conversion." Through conversion the human person opens up to the gift of God (cf. Lk 12:32), who "calls you into his own kingdom and glory" (1 Thess 2:12); he welcomes the kingdom as a child (cf. Mk 10:15) and is prepared for whatever renunciation is required to enter it (cf. Lk 18:29; Mt 19:29; Mk 10:29).

The kingdom of God demands a profound or new "justice" (cf. Mt 5:20); it requires commitment in doing "God's will" (cf. Mt 7:21); it calls for the interior simplicity "of children" (cf. Mt 18:3; Mk 10:15); and it implies the overcoming of the obstacle constituted by riches (cf. Mk 10:23-24).

The Beatitudes proclaimed by Jesus (cf. Mt 5:3-12) could be called the *Magna Carta* of the kingdom of heaven which is given to the poor in spirit, to those who mourn, to the meek, to those who hunger and thirst for righteousness, to the merciful, to the pure in heart, to the peacemakers and to those who are persecuted for righteousness' sake. The Beatitudes do not only indicate the requirements of the kingdom. First of all they manifest the work that God accomplishes in us by making us similar to his Son (cf. Rom 8:29) and capable of having his sentiments (cf. Phil 2:5 ff.) of love and pardon (cf. Jn 13:34-35; Col 3:13).

Jesus' teaching on the kingdom of God is witnessed to by the Church of the New Testament, which has lived it in the joy of its paschal faith. It is the community of the "little ones" whom the Father "has delivered from the dominion of darkness and transferred to the kingdom of his beloved Son" (Col 1:13). It is the community of those who live "in Christ," allowing themselves to be guided by the Spirit in the way of peace (cf. Lk 1:79), and who strive to avoid the works of the "flesh," and not "to fall into temptation," well knowing that "those who do such things shall not inherit the kingdom of God" (Gal 5:21). The Church is the community of those who proclaim by their life and words the same message of Jesus: "The kingdom of God has come near to you" (Lk 10:9).

"As the centuries succeed one another, the Church constantly moves forward toward the fullness of divine truth until the words of God reach their complete fulfillment in her" *(DV* 8). The Church prays to the Father in every Eucharistic celebration that his kingdom may come. She lives in fervent expectation of the glorious coming of the Lord and Savior Jesus who will offer to the divine majesty "an eternal and boundless kingdom: a kingdom of truth and life, a kingdom of holiness and grace, a kingdom of justice, of love and of peace" (Preface of the Solemnity of Christ the King).

This expectation of the Lord is a constant source of confidence and strength. It stimulates the baptized, who have become partakers in Christ's royal dignity, to live every day "in the kingdom of the beloved Son," to bear witness to and proclaim the presence of the kingdom with the same works as Jesus (cf. Jn 14:12). The Council teaches that in virtue of this witness of faith, the world will be imbued with the spirit of Christ and attain more effectively its end in justice, charity and peace (cf. *LG* 36).

General audience of March 18, 1987

Jesus Christ, Messiah and Divine Wisdom

A rich tradition of wisdom literature permeates the Old Testament. On the human level, it manifests the thirst of every person to make sense of the various experiences of daily existence and to direct one's life in the most profitable and worthwhile way. From this point of view Israel did not depart from the forms of wisdom found in other cultures of antiquity. It elaborated its own wisdom of life which embraced the various sectors of existence: individual, family, social and political.

This search for wisdom, however, was never separated from faith in the Lord, the God of the Exodus. This was due to the fact that for the Chosen People, perfect wisdom is to be found in God alone. For this reason the "fear of the Lord," the religious and vital orientation toward him, was regarded as the "principle," the "foundation," the "school" of true wisdom (Prov 1:7; 9:10; 15:33).

Under the influence of the liturgical and prophetic tradition the wisdom theme was singularly enriched and came to permeate the whole of revelation. After the exile there was an ever clearer understanding that human wisdom is a reflection of the divine Wisdom which God "has poured forth upon all his works, upon every living thing according to his bounty" (Sir 1:9-10). The peak point of the gift of wisdom occurred with the revelation to the chosen people to whom the Lord made known his Word (cf. Dt 30:14). Indeed divine Wisdom, known in the fullest form of which man is capable, is revelation itself, the "Torah," "the book of the Most High's covenant" (Sir 24:23).

Personalized symbol

In this context divine Wisdom appears as God's mysterious design which is at the origin of creation and salvation. It is the light which illumines all, the word which reveals, the power of love which joins God with creation and with his people. Divine Wisdom is not an abstract doctrine but rather a person who comes from God and who was with God from the beginning (cf. Prov 8:22-31). He is his delight in the moment of creation of the world and of humanity, rejoicing always before him (Prov 8:22-31).

The Book of Sirach again takes up this theme and develops it by showing that divine Wisdom finds its resting place in Israel and is established in Zion (Sir 24:3-12). Thus it indicates that the faith of the chosen people is the most sublime way to enter into communion with the divine thought and plan. The ultimate Old Testament fruit of this in-depth examination is the Book of Wisdom written shortly before Christ's birth. It defines divine Wisdom as "a breath of the power of God, a reflection of eternal light, a spotless mirror of the working of God, and an image of his goodness" (Wis 7:25-27).

At this level of personalized symbol of the divine plan, wisdom is a figure of the intimacy of communion with God and of the demand for a personal response of love. Wisdom therefore appears as a spouse (cf. Prov 4:6-9), the companion of life (cf. Prov 6:22; 7:4). With the motivations of love she invites the human person to communion with the living God. This communion is described with the liturgical image of a banquet, "Come, eat of my bread and drink of the wine I have mixed" (Prov 9:5). It is an image which will be taken up again by apocalyptic prophecy to indicate the eternal communion with God when he himself will have eliminated death forever (Is 25:6-8).

In the light of this sapiential tradition we have a better understanding of the mystery of Jesus the Messiah. A prophetic text of Isaiah already speaks of the Spirit of the Lord which shall rest on the King-Messiah and describes his Spirit especially as "the spirit of wisdom and understanding" and finally as the "spirit of knowledge and the fear of the Lord" (Is 11:2).

Various texts of the New Testament present Jesus as full of divine Wisdom. St. Luke's infancy Gospel suggests the important significance of Jesus' presence among the doctors in the temple, where "all who heard him were amazed at his understanding" (Lk 2:47). Luke summarizes the hidden life at Nazareth in the words, "Jesus increased in wisdom and in stature, and in favor with God and man" (Lk 2:52).

During the years of Jesus' ministry his teaching occasioned surprise and amazement: "Many who heard him were astonished, saying, 'Where did this man get all this? What is the wisdom given to him?'" (Mk 6:2).

This wisdom which came from God conferred a special prestige on Jesus, "for he taught them as one who had authority, and not as their scribes" (Mt 7:29). Jesus presented himself as one who is "greater than Solomon" (Mt 12:42). Since Solomon is the ideal figure of the recipient of divine Wisdom, it follows that in these words Jesus appears explicitly as the true wisdom revealed to mankind.

With singular insight, the Apostle Paul affirmed this identification of Jesus with wisdom. He wrote that God "has made Christ our wisdom and also our justice, our sanctification, and our redemption" (1 Cor 1:30). Jesus, indeed, is the "wisdom which is not of this age...which God decreed before the ages for our glorification" (1 Cor 2:6-7). The wisdom of God is identified with the Lord of glory who was crucified. The cross and resurrection of Jesus reveal in all its splendor the merciful plan of God who loves and pardons the human person to the point of making him a new creature. Sacred Scripture speaks also of another wisdom which is not of God, the "wisdom of this age," the human attitude which refuses to be the agent of one's own salvation. In the eyes of such a person the cross is a folly and a weakness. But he who believes in Jesus, Messiah and Lord, experiences with the Apostle that "the foolishness of God is wiser than men, and the weakness of God is stronger than men" (1 Cor 1:25).

Christ is ever more profoundly contemplated as the true wisdom of God. Thus, with clear reference to the language of the sapiential books he is proclaimed as "the image of the invisible God," "the first-born of all creation," the one through whom all things were created and in whom they subsist (cf. Col 1:15-17). As Son of God, he is "the reflection of the glory of God and bears the very stamp of his nature, upholding the universe by his word of power" (Heb 1:3).

Faith in Jesus, the wisdom of God, leads to a "full knowledge" of the divine will "in all spiritual wisdom and understanding," and makes it possible to lead a life "worthy of the Lord, fully pleasing to him, bearing fruit in every good work and increasing in the knowledge of God" (Col 1:9-10).

The evangelist John, on his part, referring to the wisdom described in his intimacy with God, speaks of the Word who was in the beginning with God, and professes that "the Word was God" (Jn 1:1). The wisdom which the Old Testament had come to equate with the Word of God is now identified with Jesus, the Word who "became flesh and dwelt among us" (Jn

1:14). Just as wisdom, so also Jesus, the Word of God, invites us to the banquet of his word and of his body, because he is the "bread of life" (Jn 6:48), he gives the living water of the Spirit (Jn 4:10; 7:37-39), and he has "the words of eternal life" (Jn 6:68). In all this Jesus is truly "greater than Solomon" because he not only carries out fully wisdom's mission of showing and communicating the way, the truth and the life, but he himself is "the Way, the Truth and the Life" (Jn 14:6). He is the supreme revelation of God in the mystery of his fatherhood (Jn 1:18; 17:6).

This faith in Jesus, revealer of the Father, is the most sublime and consoling aspect of the Good News. This is the testimony that comes to us from the first Christian communities in which Jesus' hymn of praise to the Father continued to resound, blessing him because he was pleased to reveal "these things" to the little ones.

Throughout the centuries the Church has grown with this faith. "No one knows the Son except the Father, and no one knows the Father except the Son and anyone to whom the Son chooses to reveal him" (Mt 11:27). In the final analysis God, in revealing the Son to us through the Spirit, manifests to us his design, his wisdom and the riches of his grace "lavished on us with all wisdom and insight" (Eph 1:8).

General audience of April 22, 1987

Jesus Christ, Son of Man

Jesus Christ, Son of man and of God: this is the culminating theme of our reflections on the identity of the Messiah. It is the fundamental truth of the Christian revelation and of the faith: the humanity and divinity of Christ, on which we shall have to reflect more fully later. For the present we shall complete our analysis of the messianic titles already present in some way in the Old Testament, and we shall see in what sense Jesus attributes them to himself.

The prophet Daniel

As regards the title "Son of Man," it is significant that Jesus made frequent use of it when speaking of himself. The others called him "Son of God," as we shall see in the following reflection. He, however, defined himself as "Son of Man," whereas no one else called him this, except the deacon Stephen before his stoning (cf. Acts 7:56) and the author of the Book of Revelation in two texts (cf. Rev 1:13; 14:14).

The title "Son of Man" is from the Book of the Prophet Daniel in the Old Testament. The following is the text which describes a vision which the prophet had at night: "I saw visions in the night, and behold, with the clouds of heaven there came one like a Son of Man, and he came to the Ancient of Days and was presented before him. And to him was given dominion and glory and kingdom, that all peoples, nations, and languages should serve him; his dominion is an everlasting dominion, which shall not pass away, and his kingdom is one that shall not be destroyed" (Dan 7:13-14).

When the prophet seeks an explanation of this vision, he receives the following reply: "the saints of the Most High shall receive the kingdom, and possess the kingdom for ever, for ever and ever.... And the kingdom and the dominion and the greatness of the kingdoms under the whole heaven shall be given to the people of the saints of the Most High" (Dan 7:18-27). The text of Daniel concerns a single person and the people. We note immediately that that which refers to the person of the Son of Man is found in the angel's words in the annunciation to Mary, "He shall reign forever...and his kingdom shall have no end" (Lk 1:33).

When Jesus called himself "Son of Man," he used an expression deriving from the canonical tradition of the Old Testament and which is found also in the Jewish apocrypha. It must be noted, however, that the expression "Son of Man" (*ben-adam*) had become in the Aramaic of Jesus' time an expression to mean simply "man" (*bar ethas*). Therefore, in calling himself "Son of Man," Jesus was able to conceal as it were behind the veil of the common meaning of the term its messianic significance in prophetic teaching. It is not by chance, however, that though the statements about the Son of Man appear especially in the context of the earthly life and passion of Christ, they are also found in reference to his eschatological elevation.

Ezekiel's prophecy

In the context of the earthly life of Jesus of Nazareth we find texts such as: "Foxes have holes, and birds of the air have nests: but the Son of Man has nowhere to lay his head" (Mt 8:20); and also: "The Son of Man came eating and drinking, and they say, 'Behold, a glutton and a drunkard, a friend of tax collectors and sinners'" (Mt 11:19). On other occasions Jesus' words assume a character more strongly indicative of his power, such as when he said, "The Son of Man is lord even of the sabbath" (Mk 2:28). On the occasion of the cure of the paralytic who had been let down through an opening in the roof, Christ stated as it were in a challenging tone, "But that you may know that the Son of Man has authority on earth to forgive sins, I say to you—he said to the paralytic—rise, take up your pallet and go home" (Mk 2:10-11). Elsewhere Jesus stated, "For as Jonah became a sign to the men of Nineveh, so will the Son of Man be to his generation" (Lk 11:30). On another occasion there were the prophetic words shrouded in mystery: "The days are coming when you will desire to see one of the days of the Son of Man, and you will not see it" (Lk 17:22).

Some theologians note an interesting parallel between Ezekiel's prophecy and the statements of Jesus. The prophet wrote that God said to him: "Son of man, I send you to the people of Israel...who have rebelled against me.... You shall say to them, 'Thus says the Lord God'" (Ez 2:3-4). "Son of man, you dwell in the midst of a rebellious house, who have eyes to see, but see not, who have ears to hear, but hear not" (Ez 12:2). "And you, O son of man...shall set your face toward the siege of Jerusalem...and you shall prophesy against the city" (Ez 4:1-7). "Son of man, propound a riddle and speak an allegory to the house of Israel" (Ez 17:2).

Echoing the words of the Prophet, Jesus taught, "The Son of Man came to seek and to save the lost" (Lk 19:10). "For the Son of Man also came not to be served but to serve, and to give his life as a ransom for many" (Mk 1:45; cf. also Mt 20:29). The "Son of Man...when he comes in the glory of his Father," will be ashamed of whoever is ashamed of him and of his words (cf. Mk 8:38).

The identity of the Son of Man appears in the twofold aspect of representative of God, herald of the kingdom of God, and the prophet calling people to conversion. In addition, he is the representative of the people, one who shares their earthly condition and sufferings in order to redeem and save them according to the Father's plan. As he himself said when speaking to Nicodemus, "As Moses lifted up the serpent in the wilderness, so must the Son of Man be lifted up, that whoever believes in him may have eternal life" (Jn 3:14-15).

Jesus repeated this clear announcement of the passion: "And he began to teach them that the Son of Man must suffer many things, and be rejected by the elders and the chief priests and the scribes, and be killed, and after three days rise again" (Mk 8:31). No less than three times we find this forecast in Mark's Gospel (cf. 9:31; 10:33-34), and on each occasion Jesus spoke of himself as "Son of Man."

The humiliation of the cross

Before the tribunal of Caiaphas Jesus used the same term in reference to himself. In reply to the question, "Are you the Christ, the Son of the Blessed?" he answered, "I am; and you will see the Son of Man sitting at the right hand of the Power, and coming with the clouds of heaven" (Mk 14:62). These words echo Daniel's prophecy on the "Son of Man who comes with the clouds of heaven" (Dan 7:13) and Psalm 110 which sees the Lord seated on the right hand of God (cf. Ps 110:1).

Jesus repeatedly spoke of the lifting up of the "Son of Man," but he did not conceal from his hearers that this includes the humiliation of the cross. To the objections and incredulity of the people and of the disciples who well understood the tragic nature of his allusions and who even asked him, "How can you say that the Son of Man must be lifted up? Who is this Son of Man?" (Jn 12:34), Jesus replied: "When you have lifted up the Son of Man, then you will know that I am he and that I do nothing on my own authority but speak thus as the Father taught me" (Jn 8:28). Jesus asserted that his "lifting up" by means of the cross would constitute his glorification. A little later he added, "The hour has come for the Son of Man to be glorified" (Jn 12:23). It is significant that on the departure of Judas from the upper room, Jesus said, "Now is the Son of Man glorified, and in him God is glorified" (Jn 13:31).

This constitutes the content of life, passion, death and glory of which the prophet Daniel had offered a faint outline. Moreover, Jesus did not hesitate to apply to himself the character of eternal and unending kingship which Daniel had assigned to the work of the Son of Man, when in the prophecy of the end of the world he proclaimed, "Then they will see the Son of Man coming in clouds with great power and glory" (Mk 13:26; cf. Mt 24:30). It is in this eschatological perspective that the Church's work of evangelization must take place. Jesus let it be known, "You will not have gone through all the towns of Israel, before the Son of Man comes" (Mt 10:23). And he asked himself the question, "When the Son of Man comes, will he find faith on earth?" (Lk 18:8).

If as Son of Man Jesus fulfilled by his life, passion, death and resurrection the messianic plan outlined in the Old Testament, at the same time he took his place with that same name as a true man among men, as a son of a woman, Mary of Nazareth. By means of this woman, his mother, he the "Son of God," is simultaneously "Son of Man," true man as attested by the Letter to the Hebrews: "He has truly been made one of us, like us in all things except sin" (Heb 4:15; cf. *GS* 22).

General audience of April 29, 1987

Jesus Christ, Son of God

As we saw in the previous reflections, the name "Christ" in the language of the Old Testament meant "Messiah." Israel, the People of God of the old covenant, lived in expectation of the realization of the promise of the Messiah, which was fulfilled in Jesus of Nazareth. Therefore, from the very beginning Jesus was called Christ, the "Messiah," and was accepted as such by all who "received him" (Jn 1:17).

We have seen that, according to the old covenant tradition, the Messiah is king and this messianic king is also called Son of God. In the sphere of the Yahwist monotheism of the old covenant, this title has an exclusively analogical meaning, or even metaphorical. In those books it does not mean the Son generated by God, but one chosen by God and entrusted with a particular mission or ministry.

In this sense even the entire people is sometimes called son, as in Yahweh's words addressed to Moses: "You shall say to Pharaoh...Israel is my first born son...let my son go that he may serve me!" (Ex 4:22-23; cf. also Hos 11:1; Jer 31:9). If then the king is called "Son of God" in the old covenant, it is because in the Israelite theocracy he is a particular representative of God.

146

We see it, for instance, in Psalm 2, in relation to the enthronement of the king: "He said to me, 'You are my son, today I have begotten you'" (Ps 2:7). We also read in Psalm 88, "He (David) shall cry to me, 'You are my Father....' And I will make him the first-born, the highest of the kings of the earth" (Ps 89:26-27). Later the prophet Nathan will say in regard to the offspring of David, "I will be his father and he shall be my son. When he commits iniquity, I will chasten him..." (2 Sam 7:14).

However, in the Old Testament the analogical and metaphorical meaning of the expression Son of God seems to include another which remains obscure. Thus in Psalm 2 God says to the king, "You are my son, today I have begotten you" (Ps 2:7), and in Psalm 110, "Before the daystar like the dew, I have begotten you" (v. 3).

Awareness of a completely new reality

One must bear in mind this biblical-messianic background in order to realize that Jesus' way of acting and of expressing himself indicated the awareness of a completely new reality. Even though the Synoptic Gospels do not describe Jesus as Son of God (nor as Messiah), nevertheless in different ways he stated and made it understood that he is Son of God, and not in an analogical or metaphorical sense, but in the natural sense.

Indeed, he emphasized the exclusiveness of his relationship of Son of God. Never did he say of God, "our Father," but only "my Father," or else he made the distinction, "my Father, your Father." He did not hesitate to declare, "All things have been delivered to me by my Father" (Mt 11:27).

This exclusiveness of the relation of sonship to God is manifested particularly in prayer. Jesus addressed God as Father, using the Aramaic word Abba, which denotes the special closeness of a son to his father. On Jesus' lips it expresses his total surrender to the Father's will: "Abba, Father, all things are possible to you; remove this cup from me" (Mk 14:36).

On other occasions Jesus used the expression "your Father"; for example, "as your Father is merciful" (Lk 6:36); "your Father who is in heaven" (Mk 11:25). In this way he underlined the specific nature of his own relationship to the Father, while desiring that this divine Fatherhood should be communicated to others, as shown by the prayer "our Father" which Jesus taught his apostles and followers.

The truth about Christ as Son of God is the converging point of the whole New Testament. The Gospels, especially John's Gospel, and the writings of the apostles, particularly St. Paul's letters, provide us with explicit testimonies. In the present reflection we shall concentrate merely on some particularly significant statements. In a certain sense these open the way for the discovery of the truth about Christ as Son of God and bring us nearer to a correct understanding of his sonship.

It is important to note that Jesus' conviction of his divine sonship was confirmed by a voice from heaven during his baptism in the Jordan (cf. Mk 1:11) and on the mountain at the moment of the transfiguration (cf. Mk 9:7). The evangelists tell us that on both occasions the Father proclaimed Jesus to be "his beloved Son" (Mt. 3:17; Lk 3:22).

The apostles had a similar confirmation also from the unclean spirits who cried out against Jesus: "What have you to do with us, Jesus of Nazareth? Have you come to destroy us? I know who you are, the Holy One of God" (Mk 1:24). "What have you to do with me...Son of the Most High God?" (Mk 5:7).

Charge of blasphemy

When we consider the testimony of the apostles and others, Simon Peter's profession of faith near Caesarea Philippi merits particular attention: "You are the Christ, the Son of the living God" (Mt 16:16). It is to be noted that this profession was confirmed in an unusually solemn way by Jesus: "Blessed are you, Simon Bar-Jona! For flesh and blood has not revealed this to you, but my Father who is in heaven" (Mt 16:17).

This is not an isolated fact. In the same Gospel of Matthew we read that on seeing Jesus walking on Lake Gennesaret, calming the wind and saving Peter, the apostles worshipped the Master, saying, "Truly you are the Son of God" (Mt 14:33).

Therefore, what Jesus did and taught convinced the apostles that he was not only the Messiah, but also the true "Son of God." And Jesus confirmed that conviction.

It was precisely some statements made by Jesus that gave rise to the charge of blasphemy made against him. There were some particularly dramatic moments as narrated in John's Gospel where we read that the Jews "sought...to kill him, because he not only broke the sabbath but also called God his Father, making himself equal to God" (Jn 5:18).

The same problem was raised in the trial of Jesus before the Sanhedrin. The high priest Caiaphas said to him: "I adjure you by the living God, tell us if you are the Christ, the Son of God." To this Jesus replied quite simply, "You have said so," that is to say, "Yes, I am" (cf. Mt 26:63-64). Again in the trial before Pilate, although there was a different charge, namely, that he proclaimed himself king, the Jews nevertheless repeated the basic charge: "We have a law, and by that law he ought to die, because he has made himself the Son of God" (Jn 19:7).

Thus we can say that in the last analysis Jesus died on the cross for the truth about his divine sonship. Even though the inscription placed on the cross as an official declaration of his condemnation stated, "Jesus of Nazareth, King of the Jews," nevertheless St. Matthew observed that "those who passed by derided him, wagging their heads and saying... 'If you are the

Son of God, come down from the cross'" (Mt 27:39-40). And again: "He trusted in God; let God deliver him now, if he desires him; for he said, 'I am the Son of God!'" (Mt 27:43).

This truth is at the center of the event of Golgotha. Although it would be the object of the conviction, proclamation and testimony of the apostles, now it is the object of derision. However, even here, the Roman centurion watched over the agony of Jesus and heard the words which he addressed to the Father at the moment of death. The centurion, a pagan, gave a final surprising testimony to Christ's divine identity: "Truly this man was the Son of God!" (Mk 15:39).

The words of the Roman centurion on the fundamental truth of the Gospel and of the whole New Testament remind us of the angel's words to Mary at the annunciation, "Behold, you will conceive and bear a son, and you shall call his name Jesus. He will be great, and will be called the Son of the Most High" (Lk 1:31-32). When Mary asked, "How can this be?" the angel replied: "The Holy Spirit will come upon you, and the power of the Most High will overshadow you; therefore the child to be born will be called holy, the Son of God" (Lk 1:34-35).

Because Jesus was aware that he was Son of God in the real and natural sense of the word, he "called God his Father" (Jn 5:18). With the same conviction he did not hesitate to say to his adversaries and accusers: "Truly, truly, I say to you before Abraham was, I am" (Jn 8:58).

In this "I am" there is the truth of the divine sonship which precedes not only the time of Abraham, but all time and all created existence.

St. John will say at the end of his Gospel, "These (signs that Jesus did) have been written that you may believe that Jesus is the Christ, the Son of God, and that believing you may have life in his name" (Jn 20:31).

General audience of May 13, 1987

The Heart of the Gospel Witness

The cycle of reflections on Jesus Christ has gradually approached its center while remaining in constant relationship with the article of the creed: "I believe in Jesus Christ, the only Son of God." The previous reflections have prepared us for this central truth by showing first of all the messianic character of Jesus of Nazareth. Indeed, the promise of the Messiah—present in the whole revelation of the old covenant as the principal object of the expectations of Israel—finds its fulfillment in him who was accustomed to call himself Son of Man.

In the light of Jesus' words and deeds it becomes ever more clear that he is at the same time the true Son of God. This is a truth which a mentality rooted in a rigid religious monotheism found very difficult to accept. Such was the mentality of the Israelites at the time of Jesus. Our reflections on Jesus Christ now enter the very sphere of this truth which determines the essential newness of the Gospel and the entire originality of Christianity as a religion founded on faith in the Son of God made man for us.

The creeds concentrate on this fundamental truth concerning Jesus Christ. In the Apostles' Creed we profess: "I believe in God, the Father almighty and in Jesus Christ, his only Son." Only later does the Apostles' Creed emphasize the fact that the only-begotten Son of the Father is the same Jesus Christ as Son of Man, "who was conceived by the Holy Spirit, and born of the Virgin Mary." The Nicene-Constantinopolitan Creed expresses the same thing in slightly different words: "For us men and for our salvation he came down from heaven; by the power of the Holy Spirit he was born of the Virgin Mary, and became man." Previously in the same creed we find more fully expressed the truth of the divine sonship of Jesus Christ, Son of Man: "I believe in one God, the Father almighty...I believe in one Lord, Jesus Christ, the only Son of God, eternally begotten of the Father, God from God, Light from Light, true God from true God, begotten, not made, one in being with the Father. Through him all things were made." These last words set out still more clearly the unity in divinity of the Son with the Father, who is "the creator of heaven and earth, of all that is, seen and unseen."

The creeds express the Church's faith in a concise manner, but thanks to this very conciseness they stress the more essential truths; those which constitute, as it were, the very "marrow" of the Christian faith, the fullness and summit of God's self-revelation. And so, according to the expression of the author of the Letter to the Hebrews, God "spoke of old...in many and various ways," but last of all "he spoke" to humanity "through his Son" (cf. Heb 1:1-2). It is difficult not to recognize as indicated here the authentic fullness of revelation. God not only speaks of himself by means of men called to speak in his name. But in Jesus Christ, God himself speaking "through his Son" becomes the subject of the revelation. He himself speaks of himself. His word contains in itself God's self-revelation, a self-revelation in the strict and immediate sense.

This self-revelation of God constitutes the great newness and originality of the Gospel. In professing her faith with the words of the creeds, both the Apostles' Creed and the Nicene-Constantinopolitan Creed, the Church draws on the fullness of the Gospel witness and arrives at its essential depth.

In the light of this testimony she professes and bears witness to Jesus Christ as Son, who is "one in Being with the Father." The term "Son of God" could be, and has been, used in a wide sense, as is seen in some texts of the Old Testament such as Wisdom 2:18; Sirach 4:11; Psalm 82:6 and more clearly, 2 Samuel 7:14; Psalm 2:7; Psalm 110:3. The New Testament and especially the Gospels speak of Jesus Christ as Son of God in the strict and full sense. He is "begotten, not made," he is "of the same Being with the Father."

We shall now devote our attention to this central truth of the Christian faith by analyzing the testimony of the Gospel from this point of view. It is above all the Son's witness to the Father and, in particular, the witness of a relation of sonship which is proper to him and to him alone.

In fact, as significant as are the words of Jesus, "No one knows the Father except the Son and any one to whom the Son chooses to reveal him" (Mt 11:27), so likewise are the other words, "No one knows the Son except the Father" (Mt 11:27). Indeed it is the Father who reveals the Son. It is worth noting that in the same context we find Jesus' words, "I thank you, Father, Lord of heaven and earth, that you have hidden these things from the wise and understanding and revealed them to babes" (Mt 11:25; also Lk 20:21-22). The evangelist notes that these words are spoken by Jesus with a particular joy of heart: "rejoicing in the Holy Spirit" (cf. Lk 10:21).

The truth about Jesus Christ, Son of God, belongs therefore to the very essence of the Trinitarian revelation. In it and through it God reveals himself as Unity of the inscrutable Trinity, of the Father, Son and Holy Spirit.

Thus the ultimate source of the testimony which the Gospels (and the whole of the New Testament) give of Jesus Christ as Son of God, is the Father himself, the Father who knows the Son and himself in the Son. In revealing the Father, Jesus shares with us in a certain way the knowledge which the Father has of himself in his eternal, only-begotten Son. By means of this eternal sonship God is eternally Father.

Truly in a spirit of faith and joy, and moved with admiration we make our own the words of Jesus: All things have been delivered to you by the Father, O Jesus, Son of God, and no one knows the Son except the Father, nor the Father except the Son and anyone to whom you, O Son, choose to reveal him.

General audience of May 20, 1987

The Father Bears Witness to the Son

The Gospel—and the whole New Testament—bear witness to Jesus Christ as Son of God. This is a central truth of the Christian faith. Professing belief in Christ as Son "of the same substance" as the Father, the Church follows faithfully this Gospel witness. Jesus Christ is the Son of God in the strict and precise meaning of the word. He is therefore generated in God, and not created by God and subsequently accepted as adopted Son. This testimony of the Gospel (and of the whole New Testament) on which the faith of all Christians is based, finds its definitive source in God the Father who bears witness to Christ as his Son.

We already spoke about this in the previous reflection in referring to the texts of the Gospel according to Matthew and Luke. "No one knows the Son except the Father" (Mt 11:27); "No one knows who the Son is except the Father" (Lk 10:22).

This unique and fundamental testimony which flows from the eternal mystery of the Trinitarian life is particularly expressed in the Synoptic Gospels, first of all in the account of Jesus' baptism in the Jordan, and then in the account of Jesus' transfiguration on Mount Tabor. Both events deserve attentive consideration.

Mystery of trinitarian life

In Mark's Gospel we read, "In those days Jesus came from Nazareth of Galilee and was baptized by John in the Jordan. And when he came up out of the water, immediately he saw the heavens opened and the Spirit descending upon him like a dove; and a voice came from heaven, 'You are my beloved Son; with you I am well pleased'" (Mk 1:9-11). According to Matthew's account, the voice from heaven directs its words not directly to Jesus, but to those who were present at his baptism in the Jordan, "This is my beloved Son" (Mt 3:17). In Luke's text (cf. Lk 3:22) the tenor of the words is identical with that of Mark.

We are therefore witnesses of a trinitarian theophany. The voice from heaven, which addresses the Son in the second person, "You are" (Mark and Luke), or speaks of him in the third person, "This is" (Matthew), is the very voice of the Father, which in a certain sense presents his own Son to those who had come to the Jordan to hear John the Baptist. Indirectly he presents him to the whole of Israel. Jesus is he who comes in the power of the Holy Spirit, the anointed of the Holy Spirit, that is, the Messiah, the Christ. He is the Son with whom the Father is well pleased, the beloved Son. This predilection, this love, suggests the presence of the Holy Spirit in the trinitarian unity, even though in the theophany of the baptism in the Jordan this is not yet sufficiently clear.

The testimony contained in the voice from heaven occurred precisely at the beginning of the messianic mission of Jesus of Nazareth. It will be repeated at the moment which precedes the passion and the paschal event which concludes his entire mission—the moment of the transfiguration. Notwithstanding the similarity of the two theophanies, there is a clear difference, which derives mainly from the context of the narratives. At the baptism in the Jordan Jesus is proclaimed

Son of God before the entire people. The theophany of the transfiguration was made solely to some chosen persons; not even the apostles were introduced as a group, but only three of them, Peter, James and John. "(After six days)...Jesus took with him Peter and James and John, and led them up a high mountain by themselves; and he was transfigured before them."

This transfiguration was accompanied by the apparition of Elijah with Moses, and they were talking to Jesus. When the three apostles overcame their fright at such an event, they expressed the desire to prolong it and to continue gazing at it ("it is good for us to be here"). Then "a cloud overshadowed them, and a voice came out of the cloud, 'This is my beloved Son; listen to him'" (Mk 9:2-7). This is Mark's account. Similarly in Matthew, "This is my beloved Son with whom I am well pleased; listen to him" (Mt 17:5). In Luke, however, "This is my Son, my chosen; listen to him!" (Lk 9:35).

The event described by the Synoptics took place when Jesus had already made himself known to Israel through his signs (miracles), his deeds and his words. The Father's voice is as it were a confirmation from on high of that which was already maturing in the consciousness of the disciples. Jesus desired that on the basis of his signs and words, faith in his divine mission and sonship should be born in the consciousness of his hearers in virtue of the intimate revelation granted to them by the Father himself.

Depth of God's self-revelation

Particularly significant from this point of view was Jesus' reply to Peter after his profession of faith near Caesarea Philippi. On that occasion Peter said, "You are the Christ, the Son of the living God" (Mt 16:16). Jesus answered him, "Blessed are you, Simon Bar-Jona! For flesh and blood has not revealed this to you, but my Father who is in heaven" (Mt

16:17). One knows how important Simon Peter's profession
was. For it is essential to know that the profession of the truth
about the divine sonship of Jesus of Nazareth—"You are the
Christ (the Messiah), the Son of the living God"—comes from
the Father. Only the Father "knows the Son" (Mt 11:27), only
the Father knows "who the Son is" (Lk 10:22), and only the
Father can convey this knowledge to humanity. This is precisely what Christ says in his reply to Peter. The truth about
Christ's divine sonship uttered by the apostle, and first matured within him in his consciousness, comes from the depth of
God's self-revelation. In this moment all the analogical mean-
ings of the expression "Son of God," already known in the Old
Testament, are completely transcended. Christ is the Son of the
living God, the Son in the proper and essential meaning of this
word—he is "God from God."

Transfiguration

The voice which the three apostles hear during the transfiguration on the mountain (which later tradition identifies
with Mount Tabor) confirms the conviction expressed by
Simon Peter in the vicinity of Caesarea (according to Mt
16:16). In a certain sense it confirms "externally" what the
Father has already "revealed internally." If the Father now
confirms the interior revelation about Christ's divine sonship,
"This is my beloved Son, listen to him," it seems that he
wishes to prepare those who had already believed in him for
the events of the Passover which is drawing near, for his hu-
miliating death on the cross. It is significant that "as they were
coming down the mountain" Jesus commanded them, "Tell no
one the vision, until the Son of Man is raised from the dead"
(Mt 17:9, also Mk 9:9; and to a certain extent Lk 9:21). The
theophany on the mountain of the transfiguration of the Lord is
thus situated in relationship with Christ's paschal mystery.

Following this one can understand the significant passage of John's Gospel (12:20-28) which recounts a fact which occurred after the raising of Lazarus, when on the one hand admiration for Jesus increases, and on the other, the threats confronting him become more dangerous. Christ then speaks of the grain of wheat which must die in order to produce more fruit. Then he concludes significantly, "Now is my soul troubled. And what shall I say? 'Father, save me from this hour'? No, for this purpose I have come to this hour. Father, glorify your name. Then a voice came from heaven, 'I have glorified it and I will glorify it again'" (cf. Jn 12:27-28). This voice expresses the Father's reply which confirms Jesus' previous words, "The hour has come for the Son of Man to be glorified" (Jn 12:23).

The Son of Man who is approaching his paschal hour is precisely he of whom the voice from on high proclaimed at the baptism and the transfiguration, "My beloved Son in whom I am well pleased...the chosen...." This voice contains the witness of the Father to the Son. The author of the Second Letter of Peter, gathering together the personal testimony of the chief of the apostles, writes to strengthen the Christians in a moment of harsh persecution. "(Jesus Christ)...received honor and glory from God the Father and the voice was borne to him by the majestic glory, 'This is my beloved Son, with whom I am well pleased,' we heard this voice from heaven, for we were with him on the holy mountain" (2 Pet 1:16-18).

General audience of May 27, 1987

The Prologue of John's Gospel Synthesizes the Faith of the Apostolic Church

In the last catechesis we have shown, on the basis of the Synoptic Gospels, how faith in the divine sonship of Christ comes into being through the revelation of the Father in the awareness of his disciples and hearers, and first of all in the awareness of the apostles. The Father revealed his Son in Christ ("my Son") through the theophanies which took place at the baptism in the Jordan and then during the transfiguration on the mountain. It is above all the testimony of the Father himself that contributes to create the conviction that Jesus is the Son of God in the strict and full sense of this word, not merely in a metaphorical sense. We have also seen how the revelation of the truth about the divine sonship of Jesus reached the minds and the hearts of the apostles through the work of the Father, as is clear from the words of Jesus to Peter: "It was not flesh and blood that revealed this to you, but my Father who is in heaven" (Mt 16:17).

We must read the whole Gospel of John, and particularly its prologue (Jn 1:1-18), in the light of this faith in the divine sonship of Jesus, a faith which acquired much greater strength after the resurrection. It is a unique synthesis that expresses the faith of the apostolic Church—of that first generation of disciples to whom it was given to have contact with Christ, whether directly or through the apostles who spoke of what they had personally heard and seen. In these events they had discovered the fulfillment of all that the Old Testament had foretold about him. What had already been revealed beforehand, but in a certain sense was covered with a veil, now took on transparency and became clear and comprehensible in the light of what Jesus had done.

In this way, the Gospel of John (which was the last of the four Gospels to be written) is in a certain sense the most complete testimony about Christ as the Son of God, the Son who is consubstantial with the Father. The Holy Spirit, who had been promised by Jesus to the apostles, and who was to "teach them everything" (cf. Jn 14:26), truly permitted the evangelist "to search the depths of God" (cf. 1 Cor 2:10) and to express them in the inspired text of the prologue.

The first generation of disciples

"In the beginning was the Word, and the Word was with God, and the Word was God. He was in the beginning with God. Everything was made through him, and without him nothing was made of all that exists" (Jn 1:1-3). "And the Word became flesh and dwelt among us; and we saw his glory, glory as of the only-begotten of the Father, full of grace and truth" (Jn 1:14). "He was in the world and the world was made through him, yet the world did not recognize him. He came among his own people, but his own did not receive him" (Jn 1:10-11). "But to all who received him, he gave the power to become sons of God; to those who believe in his name, who were born, not of blood, nor of the will of the flesh, nor of the will of man, but of God" (Jn 1:12-13). "No one has ever seen God: it is the only-begotten Son, who is in the bosom of the Father, who has made him known" (Jn 1:18).

The prologue of John is certainly the key text that gives full expression to the truth about the divine sonship of Christ. He who "became flesh" in time, is the Word himself from all eternity. He is the only-begotten Son—God "who is in the bosom of the Father." He is the Son "of the same substance of the Father," he is "God from God." He receives the fullness of glory from the Father. He is the Word "through whom everything was made." Therefore everything that exists owes to him that "beginning" of which the Book of Genesis speaks (cf. Gen 1:1), the beginning of the work of creation. This same eternal Son, when he comes into the world as the "Word become flesh," brings with him for humanity the fullness "of grace and truth." He brings the fullness of truth because he gives teaching about the true God whom "no one has ever seen." And he brings the fullness of grace, because he gives to all those who receive him the power to be reborn of God. Alas, as the evangelist observes, "the world did not recognize him," and even though "he came among his own people," many "did not receive him."

The truth contained in the Johannine prologue is the same truth that we find in other books of the New Testament. Thus, for example, we read in the Letter to the Hebrews that God "in these days has spoken to us through the Son, whom he has constituted heir of all things, and through whom also he made the world. This Son, who is the reflection of his glory and the imprint of his substance, and upholds everything with the power of his word, after having accomplished the purification of sins, has taken his place at the right hand of the majesty in the highest heavens" (Heb 1:2-3).

Source in the Old Testament

Like the Letter to the Hebrews in its own way, the prologue of the Gospel of John expresses through biblical allusions the accomplishment in Christ of everything that was said in the old covenant, beginning with the Book of Genesis, through the law of Moses (cf. Jn 1:17) and the prophets, up to the sapiential books. The expression "the Word" (which "was with God in the beginning") corresponds to the Hebrew word *dabar.* Even though we find the term *logos* in Greek, nevertheless the source of the thought is primarily the Old Testament. Two dimensions are borrowed from the Old Testament at one and the same time: that of *hochma,* (wisdom), understood as God's plan for creation, and that of *dabar (logos),* understood as the realization of this plan. The use of the word *logos,* which had been taken over from Greek philosophy, in turn made it easier for minds formed by this philosophy to approach these truths.

Remaining for the present in the realm of the Old Testament, we read in Isaiah: "The word that goes forth from my mouth shall not return to me empty, without having done what I desire and without having carried out that for which I sent it" (Is 55:11). It is clear from this text that the biblical *dabar* (word) is not merely a word but is also a realization (act). One can say that there already appears in the books of the old covenant a certain personification of the word *(dabar, logos),* and likewise of wisdom *(sophia).*

Wisdom "is initiated into the knowledge of God, and chooses his works" (Wis 8:4), and in another passage: "With you is wisdom, who knows your works, and was present when you created the world; she knows what is pleasing to your eyes and what is fitting.... Send her from the holy heavens, for your glorious throne, so that she may assist me and stand by me in my work, so that I may know what is pleasing to you" (Wis 9:9-10).

Thus, we are very close to the first words of the prologue of John. The following words of the Book of Wisdom are even closer: "While a deep silence enveloped all things, and night was halfway through its course, your almighty word leaped down from your royal throne...into the midst of this land doomed to destruction, bearing your inexorable command like a naked sword" (Wis 18:14-15). Nevertheless, this word to which the sapiential books refer, this wisdom which is with God from the beginning, is considered in relationship to the created world which it orders and directs (cf. Prov 8:22-27). "The Word" in the Gospel of John, on the other hand, not only exists "in the beginning," but is revealed as turned wholly toward God *(pros ton theon)* and as being himself God. "The Word was God." He is the only-begotten Son, who "is in the bosom of the Father"—God the Son. He is in Person the pure expression of God, the "reflection of his glory" (cf. Heb 1:3), consubstantial with the Father.

Source of life and holiness

It is precisely this Son—the Word who becomes flesh— who receives testimony from John at the Jordan. In the prologue, we read about John the Baptist: "There came a man sent from God, whose name was John. He came as a witness, to give testimony to the light" (Jn 1:6-7). This light is none other than Christ—as the Word. We read further on in the prologue: "In him was life, and the life was the light of men" (Jn 1:4). This is "the true light, that gives light to every man" (Jn 1:9). The light that "shines in the darkness, but the dark- ness has not overcome it."

Accordingly, the prologue of the Gospel of John shows us that Jesus Christ is God, because he is the only-begotten Son of God the Father—the Word. He comes into the world as the source of life and of holiness. Truly, we are at the central and decisive point of our profession of faith here: "The Word became flesh and came to dwell among us."

General audience of June 3, 1987

Jesus Christ,
the Son Sent by the Father

In the previous reflection we dealt with the prologue of John's Gospel, when speaking of Christ as Logos, Word and Son of God. The prologue expresses beyond all doubt the essential nucleus of the truth about Jesus Christ, a truth which forms the central content of the self-revelation of the God of the new covenant, and as such is solemnly professed by the Church. It is faith in the Son of God, who is "one in being with the Father" as the eternal Word, eternally "begotten," "God from God and Light from Light," in no way created (or adopted). The prologue also reveals the truth about the divine pre-existence of Jesus Christ as the "only-begotten Son" who is "in the bosom of the Father." It sets out clearly the truth about the coming of God the Son into the world to carry out a special mission on the part of the Father—"the Word was made flesh and dwelt among us" (Jn 1:14). This mission *(missio Verbi)* has an essential importance in the divine plan of salvation. It contains the supreme and definitive implementation of God's salvific plan in regard to the world and the human race.

The whole New Testament expresses the truth of the sending of the Son by the Father. This truth is made concrete in the messianic mission of Jesus Christ. In this regard, of particular importance are the numerous texts of John's Gospel to which we must first of all refer. Speaking to his disciples and even to his adversaries, Jesus says, "I proceeded and came forth from God; I came not of my own accord, but he sent me" (Jn 8:16). "I bear witness to myself, and the Father who sent me bears witness to me" (Jn 18:18). "He who sent me is true, and him you do not know. I know him for I came from him, and he sent me" (Jn 7:28-29). "For the works which the Father has granted me to accomplish, these very works which I am doing, bear me witness that the Father has sent me" (Jn 5:36). "My food is to do the will of him who sent me, and to accomplish his work" (Jn 4:34).

The priestly prayer

As is seen in John's Gospel, Jesus often speaks of himself in the first person as one sent by the Father. In a special way, the same truth will emerge in the priestly prayer, where Jesus, recommending his disciples to the Father, emphasizes, "They...know in truth that I have come from you; and they have believed that you have sent me" (Jn 17:8). And continuing this prayer on the eve of his passion, Jesus says, "As you sent me into the world, so I have sent them into the world" (Jn 17:8). As though referring directly to the priestly prayer, the first words addressed to the disciples on the evening of the day of the resurrection are, "As the Father has sent me, even so I send you" (Jn 20:21).

If the truth about Jesus Christ as the Son sent by the Father is set out clearly especially in the Johannine texts, it is also contained in the Synoptic Gospels. There we see, for example, that Jesus said, "I must preach the kingdom to the other cities also; for I was sent for this purpose" (Lk 4:43). Of particular importance is the parable of the wicked tenant farmers. They badly treated the servants sent by the owner of the vineyard "to get from them some of the fruit of the vineyard," and they killed many of them. Finally, the owner of the vineyard decided to send to them his own son, "He had still one other, a beloved son; finally he sent him to them, saying, 'They will respect my son!' But those tenants said to one another, 'This is the heir; come, let us kill him, and the inheritance will be ours.' And they took him and killed him, and cast him out of the vineyard" (Mk 12:6-8). Commenting on this parable, Jesus recalls what was written in Psalm 118 about the stone rejected by the builders. It was this very stone that became the head of the corner (that is, the cornerstone) (cf. Ps 118:22).

The parable of the son sent to the tenants of the vineyard is recorded by all the Synoptics (cf. Mk 12:1-12; Mt 21:33-46; Lk 20:9-19). The truth about Jesus sent by the Father clearly emerges from this parable. Indeed, it emphasizes rather graphically the sacrificial and redemptive character of the mission. The Son is truly "he whom the Father consecrated and sent into the world" (Jn 10:36). Thus God not only "spoke to us by a Son...in these last days" (cf. Heb 1:1-2), but he has given for us this Son, in an act of incomprehensible love, by sending him into the world.

In these terms John's Gospel also speaks in a particularly moving way, "For God so loved the world that he gave his only Son, that, whoever believes in him should not perish but have eternal life" (Jn 3:16). And he adds, "God sent his only Son into the world, as the savior of the world." Elsewhere John writes, "God is love. In this the love of God was made manifest among us, that God sent his only Son into the world, so that we might live through him. In this is love, not that we loved God but that he loved us and sent his Son to be the expiation for our sins." Therefore he adds that in accepting Jesus, his Gospel, his death and resurrection, "we know and believe the love God has for us. God is love, and he who abides in love abides in God, and God abides in him" (cf. 1 Jn 4:8-16).

St. Paul expresses the same truth in the Letter to the Romans: "He (God) did not spare his own Son but gave him up for us all; will he not also give us all things with him?" (Rom 8:32). Christ was "given" for us, as we read in John 3:16; he was given in sacrifice "for us all" (Rom 8:32). The Father "has sent his Son to be the expiation for our sins" (1 Jn 4:10). The creed professes this same truth: "For us men and for our salvation (the Word of God) came down from heaven."

The truth about Jesus Christ, as the Son sent by the Father for the redemption of the world, for the salvation and liberation of those who were prisoners of sin (and therefore of the powers of darkness) constitutes the essential kernel of the Good News. Jesus Christ is the "only Son" (Jn 1:18), who, to carry out his messianic mission, "did not count equality with God a thing to be grasped, but emptied himself, taking the form of a servant, being born in the likeness of men...and became obedient unto death" (Phil 2:6-8). In this situation freely accepted by him as man, as the servant of the Lord, he proclaimed, "The Father is greater than I" (Jn 14:28) and again, "I always do what is pleasing to him" (Jn 8:29).

This very obedience to the Father, freely accepted, this submission to the Father, in opposition to the "disobedience" of the first Adam, remains the expression of the most profound union between Father and Son, a reflection of the trinitarian unity: "I do as the Father has commanded me, so that the world may know that I love the Father" (Jn 14:31). Indeed, this union of will for the salvation of man reveals definitively the truth about God in his intimate essence—love. At the same time it reveals the original source of the salvation of the world and humanity, the "life which is the light of men" (Jn 1:4).

General audience of June 24, 1987

Jesus' Awareness of His Unique Relationship to the Father

Jesus' self-revelation as the Son of God is given a unique expression in the term Abba, Father. Abba is an Aramaic word which is preserved in the Greek text of Mark's Gospel (14:36). It appears precisely when Jesus addressed his Father. Even though this word can be translated into every language, yet on the lips of Jesus of Nazareth one can better understand its unique meaning.

Abba expresses not only the traditional praise of God, "I bless you, Father, Lord of heaven and earth" (cf. Mt 11:25), but as used by Jesus it also indicates his awareness of the unique and exclusive relationship that exists between the Father and himself. It expresses the same reality to which Jesus alludes in such a simple and yet extraordinary way in the words preserved for us in the Gospels of Matthew (11:27) and Luke (10:22): "No one knows the Son except the Father, and no one knows the Father except the Son and any one to whom the Son chooses to reveal him." In other words, the term Abba not only manifests the mystery of the reciprocal bond between Father and Son, but summarizes in a certain way the whole truth about God's intimate life in the depths of the Trinity, that mutual knowledge of Father and Son which gives rise to the spiration of eternal Love.

The word Abba is taken from the vocabulary of family life and speaks of the personal communion between father and son, between the son who loves the father and is in turn loved by him. When Jesus used this word to speak of God, his hearers must have wondered and even been scandalized. An Israelite would not have used it even in prayer. Only one who regarded himself as Son of God in the proper sense of the word could have spoken thus of him and to him as Father—Abba, or my Father, Daddy, Papa!

A prophecy fulfilled in messianic times

A text of Jeremiah speaks of God wanting to be called Father, "I thought you would call me, 'My Father'" (Jer 3:19). It is as it were a prophecy that would be fulfilled in messianic times. It was fulfilled and surpassed by Jesus of Nazareth in speaking of himself in relation to the Father as he who "knows the Father," making use of the filial expression Abba. He constantly speaks of the Father, and invokes the Father as one having the right to address him simply with the name Abba— my Father.

All this was noted by the evangelists. Particularly in Mark's Gospel we read that during the prayer in Gethsemane Jesus exclaimed, "Abba, Father, all things are possible to you; remove this cup from me; yet not what I will, but what you will" (Mk 14:36). The parallel passage in Matthew reads, "my Father," that is, Abba, even though the Aramaic word is not literally quoted (cf. Mt 26:39-42). Even when the Gospel text says only "Father" (as in Lk 22:42, and also in another context, in Jn 12:27), the essential meaning is identical.

Jesus got his hearers to understand that when he used the word "God," and particularly the term "Father," he meant

"Abba—my Father." Thus even in his youth when he was barely twelve years old, he said to his parents who had sought him for three days, "Did you not know that I had to be in my Father's house?" (Lk 2:49). At the end of his life, in the priestly prayer which concludes his mission, he insists in asking God, "Father, the hour has come; glorify your Son that the Son may glorify you" (Jn 17:1). "Holy Father, keep them in your name, which you have given me" (Jn 17:11). "O righteous Father, the world has not known you, but I have known you" (Jn 17:25). Already in foretelling the end of the world, in the parable of the last judgment, he appears as the one who proclaims, "Come, O blessed of my Father" (Mt 25:34). Later, on the cross, his last words were "Father, into your hands I commend my spirit" (Lk 23:46). Finally, after the resurrection he told the disciples, "And behold, I send the promise of my Father upon you" (Lk 24:49).

Jesus Christ, who "knows the Father" so profoundly, came "to manifest his name to the men whom the Father had given him." (cf. Jn 17:6). An important moment of this revelation of the Father is the reply which he gave to his disciples when they asked him, "Teach us to pray" (cf. Lk 11:1). He then dictated to them the prayer which begins with the words "our Father" (Mt 6:9-13) or "Father" (Lk 11:2-4). Through the revelation of this prayer the disciples discover their special participation in the divine sonship, of which the Apostle John will say in the prologue of his Gospel, "To all who received him (that is, to all who received the Word who became flesh), Jesus gave power to become children of God" (Jn 1:12). Rightly therefore, according to his own instruction, do they pray, "Our Father."

Jesus however always drew a distinction between "my Father" and "your Father." Again, after the resurrection he said to Mary Magdalene, "Go to my brethren and say to them, I am ascending to my Father and your Father, to my God and your

God" (Jn 20:17). Moreover, it is to be noted that in no passage of the Gospel do we read that Jesus recommended his disciples to pray with the word Abba. That term refers exclusively to his personal relation of sonship with the Father. At the same time, however, the Abba of Jesus is in reality he who is also "our Father," as is clear from the prayer taught to his disciples. He is so by our participation or, better still, by our adoption, as the theologians teach following St. Paul who wrote to the Galatians: "God sent forth his Son...so that we might receive adoption as sons" (Gal 4:4-5; cf. *Summa Theol.*, III. q. 23, aa. 1, 2).

In this sense we are to understand the subsequent words of St. Paul in his Letter to the Galatians: "Because we are children, God has sent the Spirit of his Son into our hearts, saying, 'Abba, Father!'" (Gal 4:6), and also what he wrote in his Letter to the Romans: "You did not receive a spirit of slavery...but a spirit of adoption through which we cry out, 'Abba, Father!'" (Rom 8:15). When therefore as adoptive sons (adopted in Christ—"sons in the Son," says St. Paul—cf. Rom 8:29) we cry out to God "Father," "our Father," these words refer to the same God, to whom Jesus said with incomparable intimacy "Abba...my Father."

General audience of July 1, 1987

Jesus Christ, the Son
Intimately United with the Father

"Abba—my Father"—all that we said in the previous reflection enables us to penetrate more deeply the unique and exceptional relationship of the Son with the Father, which is expressed in the four Gospels and the whole New Testament. If more passages which stress this relationship are found in John's Gospel ("in the first person," one could say), yet the Synoptics contain the passage which seems to contain the key to this question: "No one knows the Son except the Father, and no one knows the Father except the Son and anyone to whom the Son chooses to reveal him" (Mt 11:27; Lk 10:22).

The Son, therefore, reveals the Father as he who knows him and had sent him as Son to speak to humanity through him in a further and definitive way (cf. Heb 1:7). Indeed, the Father has given for the salvation of the world precisely this only Son, so that in him and through him man might attain eternal life (cf. Jn 3:16).

Frequently, but especially during the Last Super, Jesus insisted on making known to his disciples that he is united to the Father by a special bond. "All that is mine is yours, and all that is yours is mine" (Jn 17:10), he prayed in his priestly prayer, as he took leave of the apostles before going to his passion. He then asked for unity for his present and future disciples in words which emphasize the relation of such union and communion with that which exists only between the Father and the Son. He asked "that all may be one as you, Father are in me, and I in you; that they also may be one in us, that the world may believe that you sent me. I have given them the glory you gave me that they may be one, as we are one—I living in them, you living in me—that their unity may be complete. So shall the world know that you sent me, and that you loved them as you love me" (Jn 17:21-23).

Praying for the unity of his disciples and witnesses, Jesus at the same time revealed what kind of unity and communion exists between himself and the Father; the Father is "in the Son" and the Son "in" the Father. Jesus explained it saying, "All that is mine is yours, and all that is yours is mine" (Jn 17:10). It is a relation of reciprocal possession in the unity of essence, and at the same time it is a relation of gift. In fact Jesus said, "Now they know that everything that you have given me is from you" (Jn 17:7).

The signs of attention, of wonderment and recollection with which the apostles heard these words of Jesus in the upper room at Jerusalem on the eve of the paschal events can be gleaned from John's Gospel. But the truth of the priestly prayer had already in a certain way been expressed publicly by him antecedently on the day of the feast of the Dedication of the Temple. In reply to the challenge, "If you are the Christ tell us openly" Jesus stated: "I told you and you do not believe. The works that I do in my Father's name, they bear witness to me." Later Jesus stated that those who hear him and believe, belong to his flock by virtue of a gift from the Father. "My sheep hear my voice and I know them.... My Father, who has given them to me, is greater than all, and no one is able to snatch them out of the Father's hand. I and the Father are one" (Jn 10:24-30).

In this case his adversaries' reaction is violent: "The Jews took up stones again to stone him." When Jesus asked them for which of the good works from the Father which he had performed did they wish to stone him, they replied: "For the blasphemy; because you, being a man, make yourself God." Jesus' reply is unambiguous: "If I am not doing the works of my Father, then do not believe me; but if I did them, even though you do not believe me, believe the works, that you may know and understand that the Father is in me and I am in the Father" (cf. Jn 10:31-38).

Let us note well the significance of this crucial point of the life and revelation of Christ. The truth about the particular bond, the special unity between the Son and the Father, met with the opposition of the Jews: "If you are the Son in the sense expressed by your words, then you, being a man, make yourself God. In such case you utter the greatest blasphemy." His hearers therefore understood the meaning of the words of Jesus of Nazareth. As Son of God he is "God from God"—"of the same being as the Father"—but for this very reason they did not accept his words. Indeed, they rejected them in the most firm and absolute way. Even though in the conflict of that moment they did not arrive at the point of stoning him (cf. Jn 10:39), nevertheless on the morrow of his priestly prayer in the cenacle Jesus will be put to death on the cross. And the Jews present at the execution will cry out, "If you are the Son of God, come down from the cross" (Mt 27:40), and they will mock him saying, "He trusted in God; let God deliver him now, if he desires him; for he said 'I am the Son of God'" (Mt 27:42-43).

Also on Calvary Jesus affirmed his unity with the Father. As we read in the Letter to the Hebrews, "Son though he was, he learned obedience from what he suffered" (Heb 5:8). But this "obedience unto death" (cf. Phil 2:8) was a further and definitive expression of the intimacy of his union with the

Father. According to the text of Mark, during the agony on the cross "Jesus cried out *'Eloi, Eloi, lama sabachthani?'* which means, 'My God, my God, why have you forsaken me?'" (Mk 15:34). This cry—even though the words reveal the feeling of abandonment experienced psychologically as a man suffering for us—was the expression of the most intimate union of the Son with the Father in the fulfillment of his command: "I have accomplished the work which you gave me to do" (cf. Jn 17:4). In that moment the unity of the Son with the Father was manifested with a definitive divine-human depth in the mystery of the world's redemption.

Again in the cenacle Jesus said to the apostles, "No one comes to the Father but by me. If you had known me, you would have known my Father also.... Philip said to him, 'Lord, show us the Father, and we shall be satisfied.' Jesus said to him, 'Have I been with you so long, and yet you do not know me, Philip?' He who sees me sees the Father.... Do you not believe that I am in the Father and the Father in me?'" (Jn 14:6-10).

"He who sees me sees the Father." The New Testament is completely marked by the light of this Gospel truth. The Son is the reflection of the Father's glory, he is "the very stamp of his nature" (Heb 1:3). He is the "image of the invisible God" (Col 1:15). He is the epiphany of God. When he became man, taking on "the form of a servant" and "becoming obedient unto death" (cf. Phil 2:7-8), at the same time he became for all those who accepted his teaching "the way"—the way to the Father, whereby he is "the truth and the life" (Jn 14:6).

In the difficult ascent to be conformed to the image of Christ, those who believe in him, as St. Paul says, "put on the new nature" and "are renewed through a full knowledge of God" (cf. Col 3:10) according to the image of him who is the model. This is the solid basis of Christian hope.

General audience of July 8, 1987

Jesus Christ, the Son
Who Lives for the Father

In the previous reflection we considered Jesus Christ as the Son intimately united to the Father. This union permitted and obliged him to say: "The Father is in me, and I am in the Father," not only in the confidential conversation in the upper room, but also in the public declaration made during the celebration of the Feast of Tabernacles (cf. Jn 7:28-29). Indeed, still more clearly Jesus went as far as to say "I and the Father are one" (Jn 10:30). These words were regarded as blasphemous and provoked a violent reaction among his hearers: "They took up stones to stone him" (cf. Jn 10:31). The Mosaic law prescribed the death penalty for blasphemy (cf. Dt 13:10-11).

It is important to recognize the existence of an organic link between the truth of this intimate union of the Son with the Father and the fact that Jesus the Son lives completely for the Father. We know that the whole life, the entire earthly existence of Jesus was constantly directed to the Father. It was given to the Father without reserve. While still only twelve years old, Jesus, son of Mary, had a precise awareness of his relationship with the Father. He adopted an attitude consistent with his interior certainty. Therefore in reply to the remonstrance of his mother, when together with Joseph she found him in the Temple after having sought him for three days, he said, "Did you not know I had to be in my Father's house?" (Lk 2:49).

In the present reflection also we refer especially to the fourth Gospel, because the awareness and attitude shown by Jesus already at the age of twelve are deeply rooted in his great farewell discourse. According to John, this was delivered during the Last Supper, at the end of Jesus' life, as he was about to complete his messianic mission. The evangelist John says that Jesus, "realizing that the hour had come...(was fully aware) that the Father had handed everything over to him and that he had come from God and was going to God" (Jn 13:3).

Referring in a certain way to the pre-existence of Jesus, the Letter to the Hebrews emphasizes the same truth when it states: "Wherefore, on coming into the world, Jesus said, 'Sacrifice and offering you did not desire, but a body you have prepared for me; holocausts and sin offerings you took no delight in. Then I said, "As is written of me in the book, I have come to do your will, O God"'" (Heb 10:5-7).

Close communion of the divine Persons

In the words and deeds of Jesus, to do the will of the Father means to live totally for the Father. "Just as the Father who has life sent me...I have life because of the Father" (Jn 6:57), Jesus said in the context of the announcement of the institution of the Eucharist. That the fulfillment of the Father's will was for Christ his very life is shown by the words which he himself addressed to his disciples after his meeting with the Samaritan woman: "My food is to do the will of him who sent me, and to accomplish his work" (Jn 4:34). Jesus lived by the will of the Father. This was his "food."

He lived in this way—totally directed to the Father—

because he had come forth from the Father and was going back to the Father, knowing that the Father had given everything over to him (cf. Jn 3:35). Letting himself be guided in everything by this knowledge, Jesus proclaimed before the children of Israel: "Yet I have testimony greater than John's [that is, than John the Baptist's testimony], namely, the works the Father has given me to accomplish. These very works which I perform testify on my behalf that the Father has sent me" (Jn 5:36). Again in the same context we read: "I solemnly assure you, the Son cannot do anything by himself—he can do only what he sees the Father doing. For whatever the Father does, the Son does likewise" (Jn 5:19). And he added: "Just as the Father raises the dead and grants life, so the Son grants life to those to whom he wishes" (Jn 5:21).

The passage of the Eucharistic discourse (from John 6) which we quoted above: "As the Father who has life sent me...I have life because of the Father" is sometimes translated: "I live through the Father" (Jn 6:57). The words of John 5 which we have just cited above harmonize with this second interpretation. Jesus lives "through the Father" in the sense that all that he does corresponds fully to the Father's will; it is that which the Father himself does. For this very reason the Son's human life, his activity and his earthly existence are completely directed to the Father—Jesus lives entirely through the Father—because in him the source of everything is his eternal unity with the Father. "I and the Father are one" (Jn 10:30). His works prove the close communion of the divine Persons. In them the same divinity is manifested as the unity of the Father and the Son—the truth of the Father and the Son—the truth that provoked so much opposition among his hearers.

As if foreseeing the further consequences of that opposition, Jesus said in another moment of his conflict with the Jews: "When you lift up the Son of Man, you will come to realize that I Am and that I do nothing by myself. I say only what the Father has taught me. The One who sent me is with me. He has not deserted me since I always do what pleases him" (Jn 8:27-29). Truly Jesus fulfilled the Father's will to the end. By Jesus' passion and death on the cross he confirmed that "he always does what pleases the Father." He fulfilled the salvific will for the redemption of the world, in which the Father and Son are united because they are eternally "one" (Jn 10:30). When dying on the cross, Jesus "cried out with a loud voice, 'Father into your hands I commend my spirit'" (cf. Lk 23:46). These final words of his testified that to the very end his whole earthly existence was directed to the Father. Living, as Son, "through the Father" he lived completely "for the Father."

And the Father, as he had predicted, did not desert him. The paschal mystery of the death and resurrection fulfilled the words: "when you lift up the Son of Man, you will come to realize that I Am." "I Am"—the very same words used once by the Lord, the living God, in reply to Moses' question about God's name (cf. Ex 3:13f.).

In the Letter to the Hebrews we read certain consoling expressions: "Therefore Jesus is always able to save those who approach God through him, since he forever lives to make intercession for them" (Heb 7:25). He who as Son "of the same being with the Father" lives "through the Father," has revealed the way of eternal salvation. Let us also take this way and proceed along it, participating in that life "for the Father," whose fullness lasts for ever in Christ.

General audience of July 15, 1987

The Son Addresses the Father in Prayer

Jesus Christ is the Son intimately united to the Father; the Son who lives completely for the Father (cf. Jn 6:57); the Son whose entire earthly existence is given to the Father without reserve. These themes developed in the preceding reflections are closely linked to that of Jesus' prayer. It is precisely in prayer that we find particularly expressed the fact that the Son is intimately united to the Father, that he has given himself to the Father, and is directed to him with his whole human existence. This means that the theme of Jesus' prayer is already contained implicitly in the previous themes so that it can rightly be said that Jesus of Nazareth "prayed always without losing heart" (cf. Lk 18:1). Prayer was the life of his soul, and his whole life was prayer. Human history knows of no other personage who was so fully—and in such a way—absorbed in prayer with God, as was Jesus of Nazareth, Son of Man, and at the same time Son of God, "one in Being with the Father."

The prayer of Jesus

There are passages in the Gospels which emphasize the prayer of Jesus, stating explicitly that "Jesus prayed." This occurred at different moments of the day and night and on various occasions. The following are some of them. "In the morning, long before dawn, he rose and went out to a lonely place, and there he prayed" (Mk 1:35). He did so not only at the beginning of the day (the morning prayer), but also during the day and in the evening, and especially at night. We read: "Great multitudes gathered to hear and to be healed of their infirmities. But he withdrew to the wilderness and prayed" (Lk 5:15-16). And again: "When he had dismissed the crowds he went up into the hills by himself to pray. When evening came, he was there alone" (Mt 14:23).

The evangelists stress the fact that prayer accompanied events of special importance in Christ's life. "When all the people were baptized, and when Jesus also had been baptized and was praying, the heavens were opened" (Lk 3:21). Then follows the description of the theophany which took place during the baptism of Jesus in the Jordan. Similarly prayer was the introduction to the theophany on the mountain of the transfiguration. "He took with him Peter and John and James, and went up the mountain to pray. And, as he was praying, the appearance of his countenance was altered" (Lk 9:28-29).

Prayer also constituted the preparation for important decisions and played a part at moments of great significance for Christ's messianic mission. Thus, at the commencement of his public ministry, he retired into the desert to fast and pray (cf. Mt 4:1-11, and parallel passages). Again, before the choice of the apostles, "Jesus went out into the hills to pray; and all night he continued in prayer to God. And when it was day he called his disciples, and chose from them twelve, whom he named apostles" (Lk 6:12-13). Likewise, before Peter's confession of faith near Caesarea Philippi we read: "Now it happened that as he was praying alone the disciples were with him, and he asked them, 'Who do the people say that I am?' And Peter answered, 'The Christ of God'" (Lk 9:18-20).

The prayer before the resurrection of Lazarus is profoundly touching. "And Jesus lifted up his eyes and said, 'Father, I thank you that you have heard me. I know that you always hear me, but I have said this on account of the people standing by, that they may believe that you sent me'" (Jn 11:41-42).

The prayer during the Last Supper (the so-called priestly prayer), should be quoted in full. We shall consider at least the passages not already quoted in the previous reflections. First, "Jesus lifted up his eyes to heaven and said, 'Father, the hour has come; glorify your Son that the Son may glorify you, since you have given him power over all flesh, to give eternal life to all whom you have given him'" (Jn 17:1-2). Jesus prayed for that which is the essential purpose of his mission, the glory of God and the salvation of humanity. Then he added, "This is eternal life, that they know you the only true God, and Jesus Christ whom you have sent. I glorified you on earth, having accomplished the work which you gave me to do; and now, Father, glorify me in your own presence with the glory which I had with you before the world was made" (Jn 17:3-5).

Synthesis of God's self-revelation in the Son

Continuing his prayer, the Son as it were gives an account to his Father of his earthly mission. "I have manifested your name to the men whom you gave me out of the world; they were yours, and you gave them to me, and they have kept your word. Now they know that everything that you have given me is from you" (Jn 17:6-7). Then he added, "I am praying for them; I am not praying for the world but for those whom you have given me, for they are yours" (Jn 17:9). They are those who have accepted Christ's word, those who have believed that the Father had sent him. Jesus prayed especially for those, because "they are in the world, and I am coming to you" (Jn

17:11). He prayed that "they may be one," that "none of them be lost" (and here the Master mentioned "the son of perdition"), that "they may have my joy fulfilled in themselves" (cf. Jn 17:13). In view of his departure, while his disciples will have to remain in the world and be exposed to hatred because "they are not of the world," just like their Master, Jesus prayed: "I do not ask you to take them out of the world but to guard them from the evil one" (Jn 17:15).

Still during the prayer in the cenacle Jesus asked on behalf of the disciples: "Sanctify them in the truth; your word is truth. As you sent me into the world, so I have sent them into the world. And for their sake I consecrate myself, that they also may be consecrated in truth" (Jn 17:17-19). Later Jesus includes in the same prayer the future generations of his disciples. He prayed especially for unity, so that "the world may know that you have sent me and have loved them even as you have loved me" (Jn 17:23). Toward the end of his prayer, Jesus returned to the principal thoughts mentioned previously, emphasizing still more their importance. In this context he asked for all those whom the Father "has given" him that "they may be with me where I am, to behold my glory which you have given me in your love for me before the foundation of the world" (Jn 17:14).

Truly Jesus' "priestly prayer" is the synthesis of God's self-revelation in the Son which is at the heart of the Gospels. The Son speaks to the Father in the name of that unity which exists between them. "You, Father, are in me and I in you" (Jn 17:21). At the same time he prays that the fruits of the salvific mission for which he came into the world may be spread among men and women. Thus he reveals the mystery of the Church, which arises from his salvific mission, and he prays for its future development in the midst of the world. He opens up the perspective of glory, to which all those who accept his word are called together with him.

In the prayers of the Last Supper Jesus speaks to the Father as his consubstantial Son, but in the prayer of Gethsemane, which follows shortly afterward, the fact that he is Son of Man is especially evident. "My heart is filled with sorrow to the point of death. Remain here and stay awake" (Mk 14:34), he said to his followers as he entered the Garden of Olives. Once alone, he fell to the ground and the words of his prayer reveal the depth of his suffering. He kept saying, "Abba (O Father), you have the power to do all things. Take this cup away from me. But let it be as you would have it, not as I" (Mk 14:36).

It seems that the Letter to the Hebrews refers particularly to this prayer in Gethsemane when it says, "In the days of his flesh, Jesus offered up prayers and supplications, with loud cries and tears, to him who was able to save him from death." And here the author of the Letter adds that "he was heard for his godly fear" (Heb 5:7). Yes, even the prayer of Gethsemane was heard, since in it also—together with the whole truth of the human attitude toward suffering—there is perceived above all Jesus' union with the Father in the will to redeem the world, which is at the origin of his salvific mission.

Certainly Jesus prayed on the various occasions determined by Israel's religious tradition and law, as when, at the age of twelve, he went up with his parents to the Temple of Jerusalem (cf. Lk 2:41 ff.); or when, as the evangelists tell us, he went "to the synagogue, as his custom was, on the sabbath day" (cf. Lk 4:16). However, what the Gospels tell us about Christ's personal prayer is worthy of special attention. The Church has never forgotten it and she finds in Christ's personal dialogue with the Father the source, the inspiration and the power of her own prayer. The mystery of the Son, who lives totally for the Father and in intimate union with him, is expressed in the most personal way in Jesus at prayer.

General audience of July 22, 1987

The Son Lives to Give
Thanks to the Father

Jesus' prayer as the Son who had "gone forth from the Father" expresses in a special way the fact that he "goes to the Father" (cf. Jn 16:28). "He goes," and he leads to the Father all those whom the Father "had given him" (cf. Jn 17). Besides, he leaves to all the enduring legacy of his filial prayer: "When you pray, say 'Our Father'" (Mt 6:9; cf. Lk 11:2). As is evident from this formula taught by Jesus, his prayer to the Father is characterized by some fundamental notes. It is a prayer full of praise, full of unlimited abandonment to the Father's will, and as regards us, full of supplication and of petition for pardon. In this context the prayer of thanksgiving is particularly included.

Jesus said, "Thank you, Father, Lord of heaven and earth, that you have hidden these things from the wise and understanding and revealed them to babes" (Mt 11:25). In saying "I thank you," Jesus wished to express gratitude for the gift of God's revelation, since "no one knows the Son except the Father, and no one knows the Father except the Son and any one to whom the Son chooses to reveal him" (Mt 11:27). The priestly prayer also (which we analyzed in the previous reflection), while having the character of a great petition which the Son addressed to the Father at the end of his earthly mission, is at the same time imbued with a profound sense of thanksgiving. It can even be said that thanksgiving constitutes the essential element not only of Christ's prayer, but also of his essential intimacy with the Father. At the center of all that Jesus does and says, there is the awareness of the gift. Everything is the gift of God, creator and Father; and an adequate response to the gift is gratitude and thanksgiving.

One must pay attention to the Gospel passages, especially those of St. John, where this thanksgiving is clearly underlined. Such is the prayer on the occasion of the resurrection of Lazarus: "Father, I thank you that you have heard me" (Jn 11:41). At the multiplication of the loaves (near Capernaum), "Jesus took the loaves, and when he had given thanks, he distributed them to those who were seated; so also the fish" (Jn 6:11). Finally, at the institution of the Eucharist, before pronouncing the words of institution over the bread and wine, Jesus "gave thanks" (Lk 22:17; cf. also Mk 14:23; Mt 26:27). This expression is used over the chalice of wine, while over the bread the text speaks of a blessing. However, according to the Old Testament, "to bless God" also means to give thanks, besides meaning "to praise God," "to thank the Lord."

Thanksgiving in the Old Testament

The prayer of thanksgiving continues the biblical tradition which is expressed especially in the psalms. "It is good to give thanks to the Lord, to sing praise to your name, Most High.... For you make me glad, O Lord, by your deeds; at the works of your hands I rejoice" (Ps 92:2, 5). "Give thanks to the Lord, for he is good, for his kindness endures forever! Thus let the redeemed of the Lord say.... Let them give thanks to the Lord for his kindness and his wondrous deeds to the children of men. Let them make thank offerings" (Ps 107: 1, 2, 21-22). "Give thanks to the Lord, for he is good, for his mercy endures

forever.... I will give thanks to you, for you have answered me
and have been my savior.... You are my God, and I give thanks
to you; O my God, I extol you" (Ps 118:1, 21, 28). "How shall
I make a return to the Lord for all the good he has done for
me?.... To you I will offer sacrifice of thanksgiving, and I will
call upon the name of the Lord" (Ps 116:12, 17). "I give you
thanks that I am fearfully, wonderfully made; wonderful are
your works. My soul also you knew full well" (Ps 139:14). "I
will extol you, O my God and king, and I will bless your name
forever and ever" (Ps 145:1).

In the Book of Sirach we read: "Bless the Lord for all he
has done! Proclaim the greatness of his name, loudly sing his
praises.... Sing out with joy as you proclaim: 'The works of
God are all good; in its own time every need is supplied'.... No
cause then to say, 'What is the purpose of this?' Everything is
chosen to satisfy a need" (Sir 39:14-16, 21). Sirach's exhortation "to bless the Lord" has a didactic tone.

Jesus accepted this legacy so significant for the Old Testament, and in the theme of blessing-confession-praise he
made the dimension of thanksgiving explicit. It may therefore
be said that the culmination of this biblical tradition is to be
found in the Last Supper, when Christ instituted the sacrament
of his body and blood on the day before offering this body and
blood in the sacrifice of the cross. As St. Paul wrote: "The
Lord Jesus on the night when he was betrayed took bread, and
when he had given thanks, he broke it and said, 'This is my
body which is for you. Do this in remembrance of me'" (1 Cor
11:23-24). Likewise the Synoptics, in their turn, speak of the
thanksgiving over the chalice: "Then he took a cup; and when
he had given thanks he gave it to them, and they all drank of it.
And he said to them, 'This is my blood of the covenant, which
is poured out for many'" (Mk 14:23-24; cf. Mt 26:27: Lk
22:17).

The Eucharist

The original Greek of the expression "gave thanks" is (from *"eucaristein"*)—from which comes "Eucharist." Thus the sacrifice of the body and blood instituted as the most blessed sacrament of the Church fulfilled and at the same time superseded those sacrifices of blessing and praise spoken of in the psalms. The Christian communities from the earliest times joined the celebration of the Eucharist to thanksgiving, as is shown by a text of the *Didache* (composed between the end of the first century and the beginning of the second, probably in Syria, perhaps even in Antioch).

"We thank you, our Father, for the holy life of David your servant, which you have made known to us through Jesus Christ your servant.

"We thank you, our Father, for the life and knowledge which you have made known to us through Jesus Christ your servant.

"We thank you, our Father, for your holy name, which you have made to dwell in our hearts, and for the knowledge, the faith and immortality which you have made known to us through Jesus Christ your servant" *(Didache* 9:2-3; 10:2).

The Church's hymn of thanksgiving which accompanies the Eucharist arises from her inmost heart, and indeed from the very heart of the Son, who lives to give thanks. It can rightly be said that her prayer, and indeed her whole earthly existence, became a revelation of this fundamental truth stated in the Letter of James: "Every good endowment and every perfect gift is from above, coming down from the Father of lights" (Jas 1:17). By living to give thanks, Christ, the Son of Man, the new Adam, radically vanquished sin which was conceived in the heart of the first Adam, under the influence of the "father of lies"(cf. Gen 3). The giving of thanks restores to man the awareness of the gift bestowed by God from the beginning, and at the same time expresses the readiness to reciprocate the gift—to give with all one's heart to God oneself and everything else. It is as it were a restitution, because everything has in him its beginning and source.

"Let us give thanks to the Lord our God." This is the invitation which the Church places at the center of the Eucharistic liturgy. This exhortation strongly echoes the thanksgiving by which the Son of God lived on earth. The voice of the people of God responds in unison with a humble and grand testimony: *Dignum et iustum est;* "it is right to give him thanks and praise."

General audience of July 29, 1987

Jesus Christ Comes in the Power of the Holy Spirit

"I came from the Father and have come into the world; again, I am leaving the world and going to the Father" (Jn 16:28). Jesus Christ is aware of his origin from the Father; he is the Son because he comes from the Father. This mission (*missio*) which is based on the eternal origin of Christ the Son from the Father, is rooted in him. Therefore in this mission the Father reveals the Son and bears witness to Christ as his Son, while the Son reveals the Father. No one "knows the Son except the Father, and no one knows the Father except the Son and any one to whom the Son chooses to reveal him" (Mt 11:27). The Son, who came from the Father, expresses and confirms his own sonship inasmuch as he reveals the Father before the world. He does so not only by the words of the Gospel, but also through his life, by the fact that he lives completely for the Father, and this to the sacrifice of his life on the cross.

This saving mission of the Son of God as man was carried out in the power of the Holy Spirit. Numerous passages of the Gospels and the whole of the New Testament bear witness to this. In the Old Testament the truth about the close relation-

ship between the Son's mission and the coming of the Holy
Spirit (which is also his "mission") was hidden, even if in a
certain way already announced. The words of Isaiah have a
particular intimation of it. Jesus referred to them at the beginning of his messianic activity at Nazareth. "The spirit of the
Lord is upon me; therefore he has anointed me. He has sent me
to bring glad tidings to the poor, to proclaim liberty to captives, recovery of sight to the blind and release to prisoners,
and to announce a year of favor from the Lord" (Lk 4:17-19;
cf. Is 61:1-2).

These words refer to the Messiah, a word which means
"consecrated with oil" (anointed), that is to say, he who comes
in the power of the Spirit of the Lord. Jesus stated before his
fellow townspeople that these words refer to himself: "Today
this Scripture has been fulfilled in your hearing" (cf. Lk 4:21).

This truth about the Messiah who comes in the power of
the Holy Spirit was confirmed during Jesus' baptism in the
Jordan at the beginning of his messianic activity. Particularly
striking is the text of John which records the words of the
Baptist: "I saw the Spirit descend like a dove from the sky, and
it came to rest on him. But I did not recognize him. The one
who sent me to baptize with water told me, 'When you see the
Spirit descend and rest on someone, it is he who is to baptize
with the Holy Spirit.' Now I have seen for myself and have
testified, 'This is God's chosen One'" (Jn 1:32-34).

Jesus, then, is the Son of God, he who "went forth from
the Father and came into the world" (cf. Jn 16:28) to bring the
Holy Spirit. He came "to baptize with the Holy Spirit" (cf. Mk
1:8), that is, to institute the new reality of being reborn from
God on the part of the children of Adam burdened with sin.
The coming of the Son of God into the world, his human
conception and virginal birth were the work of the Holy Spirit.
The Son of God was made man and was born of the Virgin
Mary through the work of the Holy Spirit, and in his power.

John's testimony to Jesus of Nazareth as Son of God is closely linked to the passage of Luke's Gospel where we read that at the annunciation the angel told Mary that she would "conceive and bear a son who shall be called Son of the Most High" (cf. Lk 1:31-32). She asked, "How can this be, since I have no husband?" She received the answer: "The Holy Spirit will come upon you and the power of the Most High will overshadow you, hence, the holy offspring to be born will be called Son of God" (Lk 1:34-35).

If therefore the going forth from the Father and coming into the world (cf. Jn 16:28) of the Son of God as man (the Son of Man), was done in the power of the Holy Spirit, this manifests the mystery of God's trinitarian life. This vivifying power of the Holy Spirit was confirmed from the very beginning of Jesus' messianic activity, as is clear from the Gospel texts (Mk 1:10; Mt 3:16; Lk 3:22; Jn 1:32-34).

The sanctifying presence of the Holy Spirit

Already in the infancy narrative, when it is said of Jesus that "the grace of God was upon him" (Lk 2:40), the sanctifying presence of the Holy Spirit is indirectly shown. However, it is from the moment of the baptism in the Jordan that the Gospels speak more explicitly of Christ's activity in the power of the Spirit. "The Spirit immediately drove him out into the wilderness," according to Mark (1:12). In the desert, after a forty days' fast, the Spirit of God permitted Jesus to be tempted by the devil, as a result of which he gained his first messianic victory (cf. Lk 4:1-14). Also during his public life, Jesus showed the same power of the Holy Spirit in dealing with those possessed by the devil. Jesus himself emphasized it with the words, "If it is by the Spirit of God that I cast out demons, then the kingdom of God has come upon you" (Mt 12:28). The conclusion of the whole messianic struggle against the forces of evil was the paschal event—the death on the cross and the resurrection of him who came from the Father in the power of the Holy Spirit.

Likewise, after the ascension, Jesus remained for his disciples he whom "God anointed with the Holy Spirit and with power" (Acts 10:38). They recalled that thanks to this power, the people, hearkening to Jesus' teaching, praised God and said, "A great prophet has arisen among us and God has visited his people" (Lk 7:16). "No man ever spoke like this man" (Jn 7:46). They testified that by virtue of this power, Jesus "performed mighty works and wonders and signs" (Acts 2:22), and so "all the crowd sought to touch him, for power came forth from him and healed them all" (Lk 6:19). In all that Jesus of Nazareth, the Son of Man, did and taught, the words of the prophet Isaiah (cf. 42:1) about the Messiah were fulfilled: "Behold my servant whom I have chosen, my beloved with whom I am well pleased. I will put my Spirit upon him" (Mt 12:18).

This power of the Holy Spirit is manifested to the very depths in Christ's redemptive sacrifice and in his resurrection. Truly Jesus is the Son of God whom the Father anointed and sent into the world (cf. Jn 10:36). In obedience to the will of the Father, he offered himself to God through the Spirit as a spotless victim, and this victim purifies our conscience from dead works to serve the living God (cf. Heb 9:14). The same Holy Spirit—as the Apostle Paul testifies—"has raised Jesus from the dead" (Rom 8:11). Through this "rising from the dead" Jesus Christ received the fullness of messianic power, and was definitively revealed by the Holy Spirit as Son of God with power—"designated Son of God in power according to the Spirit of holiness by his resurrection from the dead" (Rom 1:4).

Therefore Jesus Christ, the Son of God, came into the world by the work of the Holy Spirit, and as Son of Man he fulfilled completely his messianic mission in the power of the Holy Spirit. But if Jesus Christ acted through this power during the whole of his saving activity and finally in the passion and resurrection, then it is the Holy Spirit himself who reveals that Jesus is the Son of God. Thus today, thanks to the Holy Spirit, the divinity of the Son, Jesus of Nazareth, shines before the world. With this in mind St. Paul writes: "No one can say, 'Jesus is Lord,' except in the Holy Spirit" (1 Cor 12:3).

General audience of August 5, 1987

Jesus Christ Brings the Holy Spirit to the Church and Humanity

Jesus Christ the Son of God, who was sent into the world by the Father, became man by the power of the Holy Spirit in the womb of Mary, the Virgin of Nazareth. As man, he fulfilled his messianic mission unto the cross and the resurrection, in the power of the Holy Spirit.

In reference to this truth (which was the theme of the previous reflection), one should recall the text of St. Irenaeus where he wrote: "The Holy Spirit descended on the Son of God who became the Son of Man, becoming accustomed together with him to dwell in the human race, to replace in men and women the works of God, by fulfilling in them the Father's will, and transforming their decay of old age into newness of Christ" *(Adv. Haer.* III, 17, 1).

It is a very significant passage which repeats in other words what we have learned from the New Testament, namely, that the Son of God became man by the power of the Holy Spirit, and in his power he carried out his messianic mission. Thus he prepared the sending and descent into human souls of his Spirit who "searches the depths of God" (cf. 1 Cor 2:10), to renew and consolidate his presence and sanctifying action in human life. That expression of Irenaeus is interesting in which he says that the Holy Spirit, working in the Son of Man, "became accustomed together with him to dwell in the human race."

We read in John's Gospel that "on the last day of the feast, the great day, Jesus stood up and proclaimed, 'If any one thirst, let him come to me and drink. He who believes in me, as the Scripture has said, out of his heart shall flow rivers of living water.' Now this he said about the Spirit, which those who believed in him were to receive; for as yet the Spirit had not been given, because Jesus was not yet glorified" (Jn 7:37-39). Jesus announced the coming of the Holy Spirit by the use of the metaphor of "living water," because it is "the Spirit that gives life" (Jn 6:63). The disciples will receive this Spirit from Jesus himself in due course, when Jesus will be glorified. The evangelist has in mind the paschal glorification through the cross and resurrection.

When this time—namely, Jesus' hour—was already near, during the discourse in the upper room, Christ resumed his announcement and several times promised the apostles the coming of the Holy Spirit as the new Counselor (Paraclete).

He told them, "When the Counselor comes, whom I shall send you from the Father, the Spirit of truth, who proceeds from the Father, he will bear witness to me" (Jn 15:26).

Jesus then concluded, "If I do not go away, the Counselor will not come to you; but if I go, I will send him to you. And when he comes, he will convince the world of sin and of righteousness and of judgment" (Jn 16:7-8).

The texts quoted contain very fully the revelation of the truth about the Holy Spirit, who proceeds from the Father and the Son. (I dealt at length with this subject in the Encyclical *Dominum et Vivificantem*). To sum up, when speaking to the apostles in the cenacle on the eve of his passion, Jesus linked his departure already close at hand with the coming of the Holy Spirit. For Jesus it is a causal connection—he must go

away by means of the cross and resurrection, so that the Spirit
of truth can descend on the apostles and the entire Church as
the Counselor. The Father will then send the Spirit "in the
name of the Son." He will send him in the power of the
mystery of redemption, which is to be carried out through this
Son, Jesus Christ. Therefore it is right to say, as Jesus did, that
the Son himself will also send the Spirit. "The Counselor
whom I shall send to you from the Father" (Jn 15:26).

On the day of his resurrection, Jesus fulfilled this promise to the apostles, which he had made on the eve of his
passion and death. John's Gospel narrates that when Jesus
appeared to the disciples who were still hiding in the upper
room, he greeted them, and while they were dumbfounded by
the extraordinary event: "He breathed on them, and said to
them, 'Receive the Holy Spirit. If you forgive the sins of any,
they are forgiven; if you retain the sins of any, they are retained'" (Jn 20:22-23).

In John's text there is a theological emphasis which it is
well to underline—the risen Christ is he who appears to the
apostles and brings them the Holy Spirit, and in a certain sense
gives him to them in the signs of his death on the cross. "He
showed them his hands and his side" (Jn 20:20). Since the
Spirit is "the Spirit who gives life" (Jn 6:63), the apostles
receive together with the Holy Spirit the capacity and power to
forgive sins.

That which happened in such a striking way on the day of
the resurrection, was in a certain way spread by the other
evangelists over the following days. During that time, Jesus
continued to prepare the apostles for the great moment when,
by virtue of his departure, the Holy Spirit will descend upon
them definitively, in such a way that his coming will be manifested to the world. That will also be the moment of the birth
of the Church. "You shall receive power when the Holy Spirit
has come upon you; and you shall be my witnesses in Jerusa-

lem and in all Judea and Samaria and to the end of the earth"
(Acts 1:8). This promise, referring directly to the coming of
the Paraclete, was fulfilled on the day of Pentecost.

To sum up, we can say that Jesus Christ is he who comes
from the Father as the eternal Son; he who went forth from the
Father, becoming man by the power of the Holy Spirit. After
having fulfilled his messianic mission as Son of Man by the
power of the Holy Spirit, "he goes to the Father" (cf. Jn 14:12).
Going there as Redeemer of the world, he gives to his disciples
and sends down upon the Church in all ages the same Spirit, in
whose power he acted as man. In this way Jesus Christ, as he
who "goes to the Father," leads to the Father all those who will
follow Jesus in the course of the centuries by means of the
Holy Spirit.

"Being exalted at the right hand of God, and having
received from the Father the promise of the Holy Spirit, [Jesus
Christ] has poured out this which you see and hear" (Acts
2:33), the Apostle Peter proclaimed on the day of Pentecost.
The Apostle Paul wrote: "Because you are sons, God has sent
the Spirit of his Son into our hearts, crying, 'Abba! Father!'"
(Gal 4:6). The Holy Spirit who "comes from the Father" (cf. Jn
15:26), is at the same time the Spirit of Jesus Christ—the Spirit
of the Son.

According to the fourth Gospel, John the Baptist proclaimed that God gave Christ the Holy Spirit "without
measure." St. Thomas Aquinas explains in his limpid commentary that the prophets received the Spirit "according to
measure," and therefore they prophesied "partially." Christ,
however, possesses the Holy Spirit without measure—both as
God, inasmuch as the Father, by means of the eternal generation, grants him to be the common principle with the Father of
the procession of the Spirit in an uncreated way; and as man,
because through the fullness of grace, God has filled him with
the Holy Spirit, so that he may pour him out on every believer

(cf. *Super Evang. S. Ioannis Lectura,* c. III, 1, 6, nn. 541-544).
The Angelic Doctor refers to the text of John (Jn 3:34): "For
he whom God has sent utters the words of God who gives to
him the Spirit without measure" (according to the translation
proposed by distinguished biblical scholars).

Truly we can exclaim with profound emotion, together
with John the evangelist, "From his fullness we have all received" (Jn 1:16); truly we have become partakers in the
divine life in the Holy Spirit.

On this world of the children of the first Adam, destined
to die, we see rising up in power the Christ, the "last Adam,"
who has become a "life-giving Spirit" (1 Cor 15:45).

General audience of August 12, 1987

Jesus Christ Reveals the Trinity

The core of the catecheses concerning Jesus Christ rests on the central theme of revelation—Jesus Christ, the man born of the Virgin Mary, is the Son of God. The Gospels and the other books of the New Testament pinpoint this fundamental Christian truth, which we have sought in the preceding catecheses to illustrate by investigating its various aspects. This testimony of the Gospels is reflected in the Church's solemn teaching in the Councils, which is expressed in the creeds (first of all the Nicene-Constantinopolitan). Likewise, it is also expressed in the Church's constant ordinary teaching, in the liturgy, in prayer and the spiritual life which she promotes and directs.

The truth concerning Jesus Christ, Son of God, constitutes the self-revelation of God, the keynote of the doctrine which unveils the inexpressible mystery of one God in the Blessed Trinity. According to the Letter to the Hebrews, when God, "in our own time...has spoken to us through his Son" (Heb 1:2), he revealed the reality of his personal life—that life wherein he remains an absolute unity in the divinity, while at the same time it is the Trinity, the divine communion of the three Persons. The Son, "who came from the Father and

entered the world" (cf. Jn 16:28) testified directly to this communion. The Son alone testified, none other. The Old
Testament, when God "spoke through the prophets" (Heb 1:1),
knew nothing of this personal mystery of God. Undoubtedly,
certain elements of the Old Testament revelation constituted a
preparation for what we have in the Gospels. Nevertheless,
only the Son was capable of introducing us to this mystery.
Since "no one has seen God," no one knew the mystery of his
inner life. The Son alone knew it. "It is only the Son, who is
nearest to the Father's heart, who has made him known" (Jn
1:18).

Gospel events and words referring to the Trinity

In the course of the preceding catecheses it was possible to
consider the principal aspects of this revelation, thereby affording us the opportunity to contemplate with complete clarity the
truth about the divine sonship of Jesus Christ. As we now
conclude this cycle of meditations, it is helpful to recall some of
the salient events in which we find revealed the mystery of the
Father and of the Holy Spirit, together with the truth concerning the divine sonship of the Son of Man—the Son of Mary.

The first in chronological order is the moment of the
annunciation at Nazareth. According to the angel, he who
would be born of the Virgin is the Son of the Most High, the
Son of God. In these words God is revealed as Father, and the
Son of God is presented as the person who would be born
through the work of the Holy Spirit. "The Holy Spirit will
come upon you" (Lk 1:35). Thus, the annunciation narrative
contains the Trinitarian mystery—Father, Son and Holy Spirit.

This mystery is also present in the theophany during the
baptism of Jesus in the Jordan, when the Father by means of a
voice from above, testified to the Son as being "the beloved."
The voice was accompanied by the Spirit "descending like a

dove and coming down on him" (Mt 3:16). This theophany is not unlike a "visual" confirmation of the words of the prophet Isaiah, to which Jesus referred at Nazareth as he began his messianic activity. "The Spirit of the Lord has been given to me, for he has anointed me; he has sent me" (Lk 4:18; cf. Is 61:1).

In the development of his mission we find the words which Jesus himself used to introduce his listeners to the mystery of the divine Trinity. In particular there is that joyous declaration noted in Matthew's Gospel (cf. 11:25-27) as also in St. Luke (cf. 10:21-22). We refer to it as joyous since we read in the text of St. Luke: "It was then that, filled with joy by the Holy Spirit" (Lk 10:21), Jesus said, "I bless you, Father, Lord of heaven and of earth, for hiding these things from the learned and the clever and revealing them to mere children. Yes, Father, for this is what it has pleased you to do. Everything has been entrusted to me by my Father; and no one knows the Son except the Father, just as no one knows the Father except the Son and those to whom the Son wishes to reveal him" (Mt 11:25-27).

In consequence of this "exultation of Jesus in the Holy Spirit" we are introduced into the "profundity of God"—into those profound depths which the Spirit alone can plumb—that inner unity of the life of God, that inscrutable communion of Persons.

The words used by Matthew and Luke harmonize perfectly with the various affirmations of Jesus which we find in the Gospel of St. John, as we have already seen in our preceding catecheses. Supreme among such affirmations is that assertion of Jesus which pinpoints his unity with the Father: "The Father and I are one" (Jn 10:30). This concept is repeated and developed in the priestly prayer (cf. Jn 17), and especially throughout the discourse of Jesus in the upper room as he prepared his apostles for his departure that would take place in the course of the paschal events.

It is precisely here, in the light of this departure, that Jesus pronounced in a definitive manner, those words which reveal the mystery of the Holy Spirit and his relationship to the Father and the Son. Christ who said, "I am in the Father and the Father is in me" also announced to the apostles the coming of the Holy Spirit whom he asserted is "the Spirit of truth who proceeds from the Father" (Jn 15:26). Jesus added that he will "pray to the Father" that this Spirit of truth be conferred on the disciples so that he will remain with them forever as "Consoler" (cf. Jn 14:16). He assured the apostles that "the Father will send the Spirit in my name" (cf. Jn 14:26), and "he will be my witness" (cf. Jn 15:26). All this will be verified, Jesus concluded, following his departure during the paschal events, through the passion and resurrection: "If I do go I will send him to you" (Jn 16:7).

The Consoler, the Spirit of Truth

"On that day you will know that I am in the Father" Jesus declared yet again, implying that through the work of the Holy Spirit the mystery of the unity of the Father and the Son will be fully clarified. "I in the Father—and the Father in me." Such a mystery can be fully illustrated only by the "Spirit who scrutinizes the hidden things of God" (cf. 1 Cor 2:10), where, in the communion of Persons the unity of the divine life of God is constituted. In this way also the mystery of the Incarnation of the Son in relation to the believers and the Church is illuminated by the work of the Holy Spirit. Jesus stated: "On the day (when the apostles will receive the Spirit of truth), you will know (not only) that I am in the Father (but also that) you (are) in me and I am in you" (Jn 14:20). For this reason the Incarnation is the foundation of our divine sonship through Christ; it is the basis of the mystery of the Church as the body of Christ.

It is important to point out that the Incarnation, even if it refers directly to the Son, is the work of the One and Triune God (cf. Fourth Lateran Council). This is already testified by the message of the annunciation (cf. Lk 1:26-38). Furthermore, by his teaching, Jesus has proposed for our consideration "vistas closed to human reason" (as we read in *Gaudium et Spes,* 24)—those of the inner life of the one God in the Trinity of the Father, Son and Holy Spirit. Finally, having fulfilled his messianic mission, in departing from his apostles on the fortieth day after the resurrection, Jesus completed in every detail that which he had announced. "As the Father has sent me I also send you" (Jn 20:21). He told them: "Go, therefore, make disciples of all the nations; baptize them in the name of the Father and of the Son and of the Holy Spirit" (Mt 28:19). In these concluding words of the Gospel prior to the beginning of the Church's evangelizing mission in the world, Jesus Christ gave her the supreme truth of his revelation—the indivisible unity of the Trinity.

From that time forward the Church has raised her voice in adoration and amazement, but always with profound emotion, in unison with John the evangelist at the conclusion of the prologue of the Fourth Gospel: "No one has ever seen God; it is the only Son, who is nearest to the Father's heart, who has made him known" (Jn 1:18).

General audience of August 19, 1987

Jesus Christ,
True God and True Man

"I believe in Jesus Christ, his (God the Father's) only Son, our Lord; who was conceived of the Holy Spirit and born of the Virgin Mary." The catechetical cycle which we have been studying makes constant reference to the truth expressed by the Apostle's Creed that we have just quoted. These words present Christ as true God—Son of the Father—and at the same time as true man, son of the Virgin Mary. The preceding catecheses offered the opportunity of examining this fundamental truth of faith. Our present study intends to deepen our understanding of the essential elements of such a truth. We must seek to penetrate the significance of the statement "true God and true man." This is a reality that is revealed for our consideration through the self-revelation of God in Jesus Christ. Admitting that such a truth—similar to every other revealed truth—can be justly apprehended only by faith, we are conscious that we are dealing with *rationabile obsequium fidei*—the rational deference due to faith. To strengthen such faith our future catecheses will concentrate on the mystery of the God-Man.

In earlier talks we noted that Jesus Christ often spoke of himself as the Son of Man (cf. Mt 16:28; Mk 2:28). Such a title referred to the messianic tradition of the Old Testament, while at the same time it served the purpose of teaching the faith, which Jesus intentionally wished to do. He desired that his disciples and listeners would be able to discover by themselves the Son of Man was also the true Son of God. This is especially evident in the profession of faith made by St. Peter in the region of Caesarea Philippi, to which we have already referred in the preceding catecheses. Jesus challenged the apostles by his questions. When Peter explicitly recognized Jesus' divine identity, the Lord confirmed this testimony, calling him "blessed, because neither flesh nor blood" had revealed this to him, "but the Father" (cf. Mt 16:17). It is the Father who testifies to the Son, because he alone knows the Son (cf. Mt 11:27).

However, notwithstanding the discretion used by Jesus in applying the pedagogical principle referred to above, the truth concerning the divine sonship gradually became more apparent, in the light of what he said and especially of what he did. Nevertheless, for some this constituted the object of faith, while for others it was a source of contradiction and accusation. This was openly manifest during the trial before the Sanhedrin. We read in St. Mark's Gospel: "The High Priest...put this question to Jesus: 'Are you the Christ, the Son of the Blessed One?' 'I am,' said Jesus, 'and you will see the Son of Man seated at the right hand of the Power and coming with the clouds of heaven'" (14:61-62). In the Gospel of St. Luke the question was formulated in these terms: "'So you are the Son of God, then?' He answered, 'It is you who say I am'" (22:70).

The reaction of those present was unanimous. "He has blasphemed!... You have just heard the blasphemy.... He deserves to die" (Mt 26:65-66). Such an accusation was the fruit of a material interpretation of the old law.

The Book of Leviticus is explicit: "The one who blasphemes the name of Yahweh must die; the whole community must stone him" (24:16). In the presence of the official representatives of the Old Testament, Jesus of Nazareth declared that he is the true Son of God, and in so doing—according to their conviction—he blasphemed. Because of this "he must die," and the sentence was carried out even though not with stoning in accordance with the Old Testament, but by crucifixion in obedience to the Roman legislation. To refer to himself as the "Son of God" was to declare himself God (cf. Jn 10:33), and it was this that aroused the radical protest on the part of the custodians of the Old Testament monotheism.

That which was eventually accomplished in the legal action undertaken against Jesus had been threatened beforehand, as the Gospels indicate, especially that of John. We read there that on several occasions his listeners wanted to stone Jesus, when they considered his statements blasphemous. An example of this concerns Jesus' words in the context of the Good Shepherd (cf. Jn 10:27, 29), and the conclusion he arrived at on that occasion: "I and the Father are one" (Jn 10:30). The Gospel narrative continues: "The Jews fetched stones to stone him, so Jesus said to them, 'I have done many good works for you to see, works from my Father; for which of these are you stoning me?' The Jews answered him, 'We are not stoning you for doing a good work but for blasphemy. You are only a man and you claim to be God'" (Jn 10:31-33).

There was a similar reaction to Jesus' other words, "Before Abraham was, I Am" (Jn 8:58). In this instance Jesus was confronted by a question that is also an accusation: "Who are you claiming to be?" (Jn 8:53), and the reply to such a query involved the possibility of being stoned (cf. Jn 8:59).

It is clearly evident that, although he referred to himself especially as the "Son of Man," at the same time the whole context of what he did and taught testified that he was the Son of God in the literal sense of the term. He was one with the Father and consequently, as the Father is God, similarly he too is God. The unambiguous substance of such testimony is doubly evident. First, he was recognized and accepted by certain persons. "Many believed in him" (cf., for example, Jn 8:30). Second, and more strikingly, he encountered in others a radical opposition, even to being accused of blasphemy with its implied threat of the punishment reserved for blasphemers in accordance with the law of the Old Testament.

Significance of "I Am"

In the context of our discussion, the affirmation of Christ—I Am—is particularly significant. The occasions when he used these words indicate that he referred to the reply given by God himself, when Moses asked God's name: "I Am who I Am...this is what you must say to the sons of Israel, I Am has sent me to you" (Ex 3:14). Christ used the same expression "I Am," in significant contexts, such as that in which he said concerning Abraham, "Before Abraham was, I Am," and not only this. Thus, for example, "If you do not believe that I Am you shall die in your sins" (Jn 8:24). And again, "When you have lifted up the Son of Man, then you will know that I Am he" (Jn 8:28); and finally, "I tell you this now, before it happens, so that when it does happen you may know that I Am he" (Jn 13:19).

This expression, "I Am" is found in other contexts in the Synoptic Gospels (such as Mt 28:20; Lk 24:39); but in the quotations used above, the use of the name of God as found in the Book of Exodus is clearly unequivocal and resolute. Christ speaks of his paschal "elevation" on the cross and subsequent resurrection, "Then you will know that I Am." In reality he is saying that it will then be clearly evident that I am the person to whom the name of God belongs. By this expression Jesus proclaimed that he is true God. Prior to the passion he prayed thus to the Father, "all I have is yours and all you have is mine" (Jn 17:10), which amounts to saying, "The Father and I are one" (Jn 10:30).

In the presence of Christ, the Word of God Incarnate, let us unite ourselves with Peter and repeat in a similar transport of faith, "You are the Christ, the Son of the living God" (Mt 16:16).

General audience of August 26, 1987

Jesus Christ, the Eternal Word of God the Father

In the preceding catechesis we paid particular attention to those statements in which Christ, speaking of himself, used the expression, "I Am." The context in which these words appear, especially in John's Gospel, encourages us to conclude that in using such a phrase, Jesus referred to the name by which the God of the Old Testament designated himself to Moses when God entrusted to Moses the mission to which he had been called: "I Am who I Am...tell the sons of Israel, 'I Am has sent me to you'" (Ex 3:14).

Jesus spoke of himself in a similar vein during the discussion concerning Abraham: "Before Abraham was, I Am" (Jn 8:58). This expression allows us to conclude that the Son of Man gave witness to his divine pre-existence, and this is not an isolated statement.

More than once Jesus spoke of the mystery of his person. The most synthetic of these comments about himself would seem to be, "I came from the Father and have come into the world and now I leave the world to go to the Father" (Jn 16:28). These words were addressed by Jesus to the apostles in his farewell discourse on the eve of the paschal events. These words clearly say that before he came into the world Christ "was" with the Father as a Son. They indicate, as a consequence, his pre-existence in God. Jesus unambiguously stated that his earthly existence cannot be separated from his pre-existence in God. Without that, his personal reality cannot be correctly understood.

There are many similar expressions. When Jesus referred to his coming into the world from the Father, his words usually denoted his divine pre-existence. This is especially clear in the Gospel of John. In the presence of Pilate Jesus stated: "I was born for this; I came into the world for this, to bear witness to the truth" (Jn 18:37). Perhaps it is not without significance that Pilate later asked him: "Where are you from?" (Jn 19:9). Earlier in the text we had read: "My testimony is still valid because I know where I came from and where I am going" (Jn 8:14). In that nocturnal conversation with Nicodemus, the question, "where are you from?" receives a special response: "No one has gone up to heaven except the one who came down from heaven" (Jn 3:13). This "coming down" from heaven, from the Father, indicates the divine pre-existence of Christ in relation to his "departure" as well: "What if you see the Son of Man ascend to where he was before?" Jesus asked in the context of the Eucharistic discourse in the neighborhood of Capernaum (cf. Jn 6:2).

Divine pre-existence

The entire earthly existence of Jesus as Messiah originates from that "before" and is united with it as a fundamental dimension which testifies to the Son as "one" with the Father. In this context, how eloquent are the words of the priestly prayer in the upper room, "I have glorified you on earth and finished the work that you gave me to do. Now, Father, it is time for you to glorify me with that glory I had with you before the world began" (Jn 17:4-5).

Similarly, the Synoptic Gospels speak in many instances of the coming of the Son of Man for the salvation of the world (cf. e.g., Lk 19:10; Mk 10:45; Mt 20:28). Nevertheless, the texts noted by St. John speak unequivocally about the pre-existence of Christ.

The prologue of St. John's Gospel contains the most comprehensive synthesis of this truth. It can be affirmed that in the text the truth of the divine pre-existence of the Son of Man is given a more explicit delineation that, in a certain sense, is more definitive. "In the beginning was the Word, and the Word was God. He was with God in the beginning. Through him all things came to be; not one thing had its being but through him. All that came to be had its life in him and that life was the light of men, a light that shines in the darkness, a light that the darkness could not overpower" (Jn 1:1-5).

In these statements, the evangelist confirms that which Jesus declared about himself: "I came from the Father and have come into the world" (Jn 16:28), or when he prayed to his Father to glorify him with the glory that he had with him before the world began (cf. Jn 17:5). At the same time there is a strict correlation between the pre-existence of the Son in the Father with the revelation of the trinitarian mystery of God. The Son is the eternal Word, he is "God from God"; he is of the same substance of the Father (as is expressed by the Council of Nicaea in the creed). That council's formula reflects exactly the prologue of John. "The Word was with God and the Word was God." To acknowledge the pre-existence of Christ in the Father is tantamount to recognizing the divinity. Eternity appertains to the substance of the divinity, just as it likewise pertains to the substance of the Father. It is this that is referred to when discussing the eternal pre-existence in the Father.

In revealing the truth concerning the Word, the prologue of John constitutes the definitive complement of what the Old Testament had already said regarding wisdom. For example we read: "From eternity in the beginning he created me and for eternity I shall remain" (Sir 24:9); "My creator made me pitch my tent and he said to me, 'Pitch your tent in Jacob'" (Sir 24:8). The wisdom referred to in the Old Testament is a creature that at the same time has attributes that enthrone it above all creation. "Although alone she can do all; herself unchanging she makes all things new" (Wis 7:27). The truth about the Word contained in the prologue of John reconfirms, in a certain sense, the revelation concerning the wisdom evident in the Old Testament. At the same time it surpasses it in a definitive manner. The Word is not merely, "with God" but "is God." Coming into this world, the Word "came into his own domain," since "the world had its being through him" (cf. Jn 1:10-11). He came "unto his own," because "he is the true light that enlightens every man" (cf. Jn 1:9). The self-revelation of God in Jesus Christ consists in this coming into the world by the Word, who is the eternal Son.

"The Word was made flesh and he lived among us and we saw his glory, the glory that is his as the only Son of the Father, full of grace and truth" (Jn 1:14). Let us repeat it once more—the prologue of John is the eternal echo of the words uttered by Jesus: "I have come from the Father and come into the world" (Jn 16:28). It also echoes his sentiments when he prayed to his eternal Father to glorify him with that glory he had before the creation of the world (cf. Jn 17:5). The evangelist is contemplating the Old Testament revelation concerning wisdom and simultaneously visualizes the entire paschal event—that departure through the cross and resurrection in which the truth about Christ, Son of Man and true God, is rendered crystal clear to those who were eyewitnesses of those events.

In strict relationship with the revelation of the Word, that is, with the divine pre-existence of Christ, one also finds confirmation of the truth about Emmanuel. This word—which literally signifies "God with us"—expresses a particular and personal presence of God in the world. Christ's "I Am" manifests exactly such a presence, as pre-announced by Isaiah (cf. 7:14), which the Gospel of Matthew (cf. Mt. 1:23) repeats following the prophet, and is confirmed in the prologue of John: "The Word was made flesh and came to dwell among us" (Jn 1:14). The language of the evangelists is indeed multiform but the truth expressed is identical. In the Synoptic Gospels Jesus pronounces his "I am with you" in moments of special tension (such as Mt 14:17; Mk 6:50; Jn 6:20), when he calmed the tempest, as also in the perspective of the Church's apostolic mission: "Behold I am with you all days even to the end of the world" (Mt 28:20).

Christ's statement, "I have come from the Father and have come into the world" (Jn 16:28) contains a salvific and soteriological significance. All the evangelists manifest this phenomenon. The prologue of John expresses it in these words: "To all who did accept him (the Word), he gave power to become children of God," that is, the possibility of being generated by God (cf. Jn 1:12-13).

This is the central truth of all Christian soteriology that finds an organic unity with the revealed reality of the God-Man. God became man so that man could truly participate in the life of God—so that, indeed, in a certain sense, he could become God. The Fathers of the Church had a clear consciousness of this fact. It is sufficient to recall St. Irenaeus who, in his exhortations to imitate Christ, the only sure teacher, declared: "Through the immense love he bore, he became what we are, thereby affording us the opportunity of becoming what he is" (cf. *Adv. Haer.*, V. Praef. PG 7, 1120).

This truth opens up for us unlimited horizons among which we locate and pinpoint the concrete expression of our Christian life, in the light of faith in Christ, Son of God, the Word of the Father.

General audience of September 2, 1987

Jesus Claimed the Divine Attributes for Himself

The series of reflections on Jesus Christ is centered on the revealed reality of the God-Man. Jesus Christ is true God and true man. It is the reality which is logically expressed in the truth of the indivisible unity of the person of Christ. We cannot treat of this truth in a disjointed manner or, still less, by separating one aspect from the other. However, we must seek to indicate here, in the first place, what is shown by the divinity, and then that which is shown by the humanity of the one Christ. This is because of the analytical and progressive nature of human knowledge, and partly also because of the way in which this truth is proposed in the very source of revelation—above all, in Sacred Scripture.

Jesus Christ is true God. He is God the Son consubstantial with the Father (and with the Holy Spirit). The expression "I Am" which Jesus Christ used in regard to his own person, echoes the name by which God identified himself to Moses (cf. Ex 3:14). Since Christ applied to himself the same "I Am" (cf. Jn 13:19), it must be recalled that this name defines God not only as the Absolute (Existence *in se* of Being *per se*), but also as the one who entered into a covenant with Abraham and his descendants, and who by virtue of the covenant sent Moses to free Israel (the descendants of Abraham) from the bondage of Egypt. Hence the expression "I Am" refers also to God's saving power, denoting the God of the covenant who is with man (as with Israel) to save him. Indirectly it refers to Emmanuel (cf. Is 7:14), "God with us."

Christ's use of the phrase "I Am" (especially in John's Gospel) should be understood in the same way. Undoubtedly it indicates the divine pre-existence of the Word-Son (this was spoken of in the pervious reflection). But at the same time it recalls the fulfillment of Isaiah's prophecy concerning Emmanuel, "God with us." "I Am" therefore also signified "I am with you," both in John's Gospel and in the Synoptics (cf. Mt 28:20). "I came from the Father and have come into the world" (Jn 16:28) "to seek and save the lost" (Lk 19:10). The truth about salvation (soteriology) already contained in the Old Testament in the revelation of God's name is confirmed and fully expressed by God's self-revelation in Jesus Christ. Precisely in this sense "the Son of Man" is true God. The Son is one in being with the Father, and he has willed to be with us to save us.

We should have these preliminary considerations constantly in mind when we seek to obtain from the Gospel all that is revealed by the divinity of Christ. Here are some important Gospel passages in this connection. In the first place, we consider the Master's last conversation with the apostles on the eve of his passion, when he spoke of his "Father's house" to which he would go to prepare a place for them (cf. Jn 14:1-3). When Thomas asked him the way, Jesus replied, "I am the way, and the truth, and the life." Jesus is the way because no one comes to the Father except through Jesus (cf. Jn 14:6). Indeed, he who sees him, sees the Father (cf. Jn 14:9). "Do you not believe that I am in the Father and the Father in me?" (Jn 14:10).

It is easy enough to realize that in this context, Christ's proclaiming of himself as "truth" and "life" is equivalent to claiming for himself the attributes proper to the divine Being—Being-Truth, Being-Life.

On the morrow Jesus would say to Pilate, "For this I was born, and for this I have come into the world, to bear witness to the truth" (Jn 18:37). Witness to the truth can be borne by man, but "to be the truth" is an exclusively divine attribute. When Jesus, as true man, bears witness to the truth, this witness has its source in the fact that he himself "is the truth" in the subsisting truth of God: "I am...the truth." Therefore he can also say that he is "the light of the world," so that whoever follows him "will not walk in darkness, but will have the light of life" (cf. Jn 8:12).

Likewise, this applies also to the other saying of Jesus, "I am...the life" (Jn 14:6). Man, who is a creature, can have life; he can also give it, just as Christ gives his life for the salvation of the world (cf. Mk 10:45 and parallel passages). When Jesus spoke of giving his life, he spoke as true man. But he "is the life" because he is true God. He himself said so before raising Lazarus from the dead, when he said to Martha, the sister of the dead man, "I am the resurrection and the life" (Jn 11:25). In the resurrection he will confirm definitively that his life as Son of Man is not subject to death, because he is the Life, and therefore he is God. Being the Life, he can share it with others. "He who believes in me, though he die, yet shall he live" (Jn 11:25). In the Eucharist Christ can also become "the bread of life" (cf. Jn 6:35, 48), "the living bread which came down from heaven" (Jn 6:51). Even in this sense Christ compared himself to the vine who gives life to the branches grafted into him (cf. Jn 15:1), that is to say, all those who form part of his Mystical Body.

To these obvious expressions concerning the mystery of divinity hidden in the "Son of Man," we can add some others where the same concept is expressed in images pertaining to the Old Testament, especially to the prophets, which Jesus applied to himself. For instance, there is the image of the shepherd. The parable of the good shepherd is well known. In it Jesus speaks of himself and of his mission of salvation. "I am the good shepherd. The good shepherd lays down his life for the sheep" (Jn 10:11). We read in the Book of Ezekiel: "For thus says the Lord God, behold, I, I myself will search for my sheep, and will seek them out.... I myself will lead my sheep to pasture.... I will seek the lost, and I will bring back the strayed, and I will bind up the crippled and I will strengthen the weak.... I will feed them in justice" (cf. 11, 15-16). "You are my sheep, the sheep of my pasture, and I am your God" (Ex 34:31). A similar image is found also in Jeremiah (cf. 23:3).

Speaking of himself as the good shepherd, Christ indicated his redemptive mission ("I lay down my life for the sheep"). At the same time, addressing his hearers who knew the prophecies of Ezekiel and Jeremiah, he indicated clearly enough his identity with him who in the Old Testament had spoken of himself as a solicitous shepherd, declaring: "I am your God" (Ez 34:31).

In the teaching of the prophets the God of the old covenant presented himself also as the bridegroom of Israel, his people. "For your maker is your husband, the Lord of hosts is his name; and the Holy One of Israel is your Redeemer" (Is 54:5; cf. Hos 2:21-22). In his teaching Jesus frequently referred to this image (cf. Mk 2:19-20 and par.; Mt 25:1-12; Lk 12:36; also Jn 3:27-28). It will be subsequently developed by St. Paul who in his letters presents Christ as the bridegroom of his Church (cf. Eph 5:25-29).

All these expressions, and other similar ones used by Jesus in his teaching acquire their full meaning if we reread them in the context of what he did and said. They constitute the thematic units which, in this series of reflections, must be constantly linked to the ensemble of meditations on the Man-God.

Christ is true God and true man. "I Am" as the name of

God indicates the divine essence whose properties or attributes are: the truth, the light, the life, and also that which is expressed by the images of the good shepherd and the bridegroom. He who said of himself, "I Am who I Am!" (Ez 3:14) presents himself also as the God of the covenant, as the Creator and likewise Redeemer, as Emmanuel—God who saves. All this is confirmed and realized in the Incarnation of Jesus Christ.

General audience of September 9, 1987

Jesus Christ
Has the Power to Judge

God is the judge of the living and the dead—the final judge, the judge of everyone. Already in the catechesis preceding the descent of the Holy Spirit on the pagans St. Peter proclaimed concerning Christ: "He is the one set apart by God as judge of the living and the dead." This divine power (*exousia*) is, according to Christ's teaching, connected with the Son of Man. The well-known text in St. Matthew's Gospel on the last judgment begins with the words, "When the Son of Man comes in his glory, escorted by all the angels of heaven, he will sit upon his royal throne, and all the nations will be assembled before him. Then he will separate them into two groups, as a shepherd separates sheep from goats" (Mt 25:31-33). The text then speaks of the unfolding of the process and foretells the sentence—that of approbation: "Come, you have my Father's blessing! Inherit the kingdom prepared for you from the creation of the world" (Mt 25:34); and that of condemnation, "Out of my sight, you condemned, into that everlasting fire prepared for the devil and his angels" (Mt 25:41).

Linked with the power to grant life

Jesus Christ, who is Son of Man, is at the same time truly God because he has the divine power to judge human works and consciences, and this power is definitive and universal. He himself explained why he has this power, saying, "The Father himself judges no one, but has assigned all judgment to the Son, so that all men may honor the Son just as they honor the Father" (Jn 5:22-23).

This power is linked by Jesus with the power to grant life. "Just as the Father raises the dead and grants life, so the Son grants life to those to whom he wishes" (Jn 5:21). "Just as the Father possesses life in himself, so has he granted it to the Son to have life in himself. The Father has given over to him power to pass judgment because he is Son of Man" (Jn 5:26-27). Therefore, according to this assertion of Jesus, the divine power to judge has been linked to Christ's mission as Savior, as Redeemer of the world. Judgment itself belongs to the work of salvation, to the order of salvation; it is a definitive salvific act. The scope of the judgment is the full participation in the divine life as the final gift made to man—the definitive fulfillment of his eternal vocation. At the same time the power of judging is linked with the external revelation of the Father's glory in his Son as Redeemer of mankind. "The Son of Man will come with his Father's glory...and he will repay each one according to his conduct" (Mt 16:27). From the very beginning the order of justice has been inscribed in the order of grace. The final judgment is to be the definitive confirmation of this bond. Jesus said clearly that "the saints will shine like the sun in their Father's kingdom" (Mt 13:43). But he no less clearly announced the rejection of those who have done evil (cf. Mt 7:23). As is evident from the parable of the talents (Mt 25:14-30), the measure of judgment will be the cooperation with the gift received from God, cooperation with grace or its rejection.

The divine power to judge each and every person belongs to the Son of Man. The classical text of Matthew's Gospel emphasizes the fact that Christ exercises this power not only as God the Son, but also as man. He exercises it—and pronounces sentence—in the name of solidarity with every person, who receives from others either good or evil. "I was hungry and you gave me food" (Mt 25:35), or "I was hungry and you gave me no food" (Mt 25:42). The works of charity in regard to one's neighbor are a fundamental element of the judgment. Christ identifies himself precisely with this neighbor. "As often as you did it for one of my least brothers, you did it for me" (Mt 25:40); "As often as you neglected to do it to one of these least ones, you neglected to do it to me" (Mt 25:45).

According to this text of Matthew we shall all be judged according to love. But there is no doubt that we shall all be judged also on our faith. "Whoever acknowledges me before men—the Son of Man will acknowledge him before the angels of God" (Lk 12:8). "If anyone is ashamed of me and my doctrine, the Son of Man will be ashamed of him when he comes with the holy angels in his Father's glory" (Lk 9:26; cf. also Mk 8:38).

We learn from the Gospel this truth—which is one of the fundamental truths of faith—that God is judge of all humanity in a universal and definitive way, and that this power has been assigned by the Father to the Son (cf. Jn 5:22) in close relationship with his mission of salvation. Jesus attested this during his nighttime conversation with Nicodemus: "God did not send his Son into the world to condemn the world, but that the world might be saved through him" (Jn 3:17).

If it is true, as we learn especially from the Synoptics, that Christ is judge in the eschatological sense, it is also true that the divine power to judge is linked to God's salvific will, which is manifested in the whole messianic mission of Christ.

This is especially underlined by John, "For judgment I came into this world, that those who do not see may see, and that those who see may become blind" (Jn 9:39). "If anyone hears my words and does not keep them, I am not the one to condemn him, for I did not come to condemn the world but to save it" (Jn 12:47).

Without doubt, Christ is and presents himself especially as Savior. He does not regard it as his mission to condemn people according to merely human principles (cf. Jn 8:15). He is, first of all, the one who teaches the way of salvation, and not the accuser of the guilty. "Do not imagine that I will be your accuser before the Father; the one to accuse you is Moses...for it was about me that he wrote" (Jn 5:45-46). In what then does the judgment consist? Jesus replied, "The judgment of condemnation is this—the light came into the world, but men loved darkness rather than light, because their deeds were wicked" (Jn 3:19).

It must therefore be said that, in the presence of this light which is God revealed in Christ, in the presence of this truth, each one is judged by one's own deeds. The will to save humanity on God's part is definitively manifested in Christ's word and work, in the entire Gospel up to the paschal mystery of the cross and resurrection. It becomes at the same time the deepest foundation, so to say, the central criterion of the judgment of human works and consciences. Especially in this sense "the Father...has assigned all judgment to the Son" (Jn 5:22), offering in him to everyone the possibility of salvation.

In this same sense man is already condemned, when he rejects the possibility offered him. "Whoever believes in him avoids condemnation, but whoever does not believe is already condemned" (Jn 3:18). Not to believe means precisely to reject the salvation offered to man in Christ ("He did not believe in the name of God's only Son"; Jn 3:18). It is the same truth foreshadowed in the prophecy of the ancient Simeon reported in Luke's Gospel when he announced of Christ: "He is destined to be "the downfall and the rise of many in Israel" (Lk 2:34). The same can be said of the reference to the "stone rejected by the builders" (cf. Lk 20:17-18).

It is a certitude of faith that "the Father...has assigned all judgment to the Son" (Jn 5:22). Now then, if the divine power to judge belongs to Christ, it is a sign that he—the Son of Man—is true God, because judgment belongs to God alone. Since this power of judgment is deeply united to the will to save, as is seen from the Gospel, it is a new revelation of the God of the covenant, who comes to mankind as Emmanuel, to liberate people from the slavery of evil. It is the Christian revelation of the God who is Love.

This corrects the too human way of viewing God's judgment as a cold act of justice or some kind of revenge. In actual fact, this term, judgment, which is clearly of biblical derivation, is the last link in the chain of God's love for all of us. God judges because he loves and in view of love. The judgment which the Father entrusts to Christ is according to the measure of the Father's love and of our liberty.

General audience of September 30, 1987

Jesus Christ
Has the Power to Forgive Sins

Linked to the divine power of judgment about which we spoke in the previous reflection, Jesus Christ claimed the power of forgiving sins. The evangelists inform us of that, especially John. We have seen that the divine power of judging each and every person—underlined especially in the apocalyptic description of the last judgment—is profoundly connected with the divine will to save humanity in Christ and through Christ. The first step in putting the plan of salvation into effect is the remission of sins.

It may be said that the revealed truth of the power of judgment has its continuation in all that the Gospel says about the power to forgive sins. This power belongs to God alone. If Jesus Christ—the Son of Man—has that power, it means that he is God, according to what he himself said, "I and the Father are one" (Jn 10:30). From the beginning of his messianic mission, Jesus not only proclaimed the necessity of conversion ("Be converted and believe the Gospel"; Mk 1:15) and taught that the Father is ready to pardon repentant sinners, but he himself forgave sins.

The power which Jesus professed to possess by claiming it for his personal self without any hesitation is seen with greater clarity precisely in such moments. For example, he stated that, "The Son of Man has power on earth to forgive sins" (Mk 2:10). He said it to the scribes who were present at Capernaum when a paralyzed man was brought to him to be healed. The evangelist Mark tells us that those who accompanied the paralytic had gone so far as to open the roof and let down before Jesus the pallet on which the sick man lay. On seeing their faith, Jesus said to the paralyzed man, "My son, your sins are forgiven" (Mk 2:5). Some of the scribes were sitting there asking themselves, "Why does this man speak thus? It is blasphemy! Who can forgive sins except God alone?" (2:7). Jesus was immediately aware of their reasoning, though they kept it to themselves, and he said to them, "Why do you harbor these thoughts? Which is easier to say to the paralytic, 'Your sins are forgiven,' or to say, 'Rise, take up your pallet and walk?' But that you may know that the Son of Man has authority on earth to forgive sins, (he said to the paralytic), 'I command you, rise, take up your pallet and go home.' The people who saw the miracle were amazed, and they praised God saying, 'We never saw anything like this'" (2:8-12).

The amazement aroused by that extraordinary cure is understandable, as well as the feeling of fear or awe. According to Matthew, fear seized the crowd in the presence of the manifestation of that power of healing granted by God to men (cf. Mt 9:8) or, as Luke put it, on account of the "extraordinary things" seen that day (5:26). But for those who reflect on what took place, the miraculous cure is seen as the confirmation of the truth proclaimed by Jesus and perceived and opposed by the scribes, "The Son of Man has power on earth to forgive sins."

Jesus' claim aroused opposition and scandal

Jesus' precise statement about his power to forgive sins on earth should also be noted. He already exercised this power during his historical life, while he moved about as Son of Man in the towns and roads of Palestine, and not merely at the eschatological judgment, after the glorification of his humanity. Already on earth Jesus is "God with us," the God-Man who forgives sins. It is likewise to be noted that in all cases in which Jesus spoke of forgiveness of sins, those present manifested opposition and were scandalized. This was so in the case of the woman who was a sinner, who went to the Master while he was seated at table in the Pharisee's house. Jesus said to the woman, "Your sins are forgiven" (Lk 7:48). The reaction of the others seated at table was significant. They began to say among themselves, "Who is this, who even forgives sins?" (Lk 7:49).

Also in the case of the woman caught in adultery and brought before Jesus by the scribes and Pharisees in order to force him to give judgment on the basis of the Mosaic law, we find some significant details recorded by the evangelist John. Jesus' first reply to the woman's accusers, "Let him who is without sin among you be the first to throw a stone at her," gives us a perception of his realistic understanding of the human condition, beginning with that of his questioners who began to drift away one by one. We note also Jesus' profound humanity in his treatment of the unfortunate woman, of whose sins he certainly disapproved, for he said to her, "Go and do not sin again." But he did not crush her under the weight of a condemnation without appeal.

In Jesus' words we can discern the reaffirmation of this power to forgive sins and therefore of the transcendency of his divine identity. When he asked the woman, "Has no one condemned you?" she replied, "No one, Lord." He declared, "Neither do I condemn you; go and do not sin again" (8:10 f.). Those words, "neither do I" vibrate with the power of the judgment and forgiveness which the Word has in common with the Father and which he exercises in his human Incarnation for the salvation of each one of us.

In this context of the whole mystery of salvation and of the forgiveness of sins, what matters most is that we love Jesus with our whole soul—he who comes to us as the eternal will of love and of forgiveness. Christ himself teaches us this when, seated at table with the Pharisees and seeing them surprised by the fact that he accepted the marks of veneration on the part of the woman who was a sinner, he recounted to them the parable of the two debtors. One owed the money-lender five hundred coins, the other fifty. Since neither was able to repay, the money-lender wrote off both debts. "Which of the two," Jesus asked, "was more grateful to him?" Simon replied, "He, I presume, to whom he remitted the larger sum." Jesus said to him, "You are right.... You see this woman?... Her many sins are forgiven because of her great love. But he who is forgiven little, loves little" (cf. Lk 7:42-47).

The complex psychology of the relationship between the creditor and the debtor, between the love which obtains pardon and the pardon which engenders new love, between the rigorous measure of giving and possessing and the generosity of the grateful heart which tends to give without measure, is condensed in these words of Jesus. They invite us to adopt the right attitude in the presence of the God-Man who exercises his divine power of forgiving sins for our salvation.

Since we are all in debt to God, Jesus included in the prayer taught to his disciples and passed on by them to all believers, that fundamental request to the Father, "Forgive us our debts" (Mt 6:12), which in Luke's version reads, "Forgive us our sins" (Lk 11:4). Once again he wished to teach us that only God can forgive sins (cf. Mk 2:7). At the same time, however, Jesus exercised this divine power in virtue of that other truth also taught by him, namely, that the Father has not only "given all judgment to the Son" (Jn 5:22), but has also conferred on him the power to forgive sins. Evidently it is not a case of a simple "ministry" entrusted to a mere man who carries it out by divine command. The significance of the words with which Jesus claimed the power to forgive sins—and in fact forgave them in so many cases narrated by the Gospels—is more forceful and more telling for the minds of Christ's hearers. They charged him with claiming to be God and accused him of blasphemy with such fury as to lead eventually to his death on the cross.

Jesus entrusted the ministry of forgiving sins to the apostles (and their successors) when he appeared to them after the resurrection, "Receive the Holy Spirit. If you forgive the sins of any, they are forgiven" (Jn 20:22 ff.). As Son of Man who is personally identified with the Son of God, Jesus forgave sins by his own power, communicated to him by the Father in the mystery of the trinitarian communion and of the hypostatic union. As Son of Man who in his human nature suffered and died for our salvation, Jesus expiated our sins and obtained for us their remission from God One and Three. As Son of Man who in his messianic mission must prolong his saving action until the end of time, Jesus conferred on the apostles the power to forgive sins to help mankind to live in harmony of faith and action with that eternal will of the Father "who is rich in mercy" (Eph 2:4).

Our entire hope of salvation rests on this infinite mercy of the Father, on the sacrifice of Christ, Son of God and Son of Man, who died for us, and on the work of the Holy Spirit who, through the ministry of the Church, continually carries out in the world the "forgiveness of sins" (cf. Encyclical *Dominum et Vivificantem*).

General audience of October 7, 1987

Jesus Christ, the Divine Lawgiver

In the Gospels we find another fact which demonstrates Jesus' awareness of his possession of divine power, and the conviction of the evangelists and the first Christian community about this authority. The Synoptics agree in saying that Jesus' hearers were astonished at his teaching, "for he taught them as one having authority, and not as the scribes" (Mk 1:22; and Mt 7:29; Lk 4:32). This is a valuable item of information which Mark gives us at the beginning of his Gospel. It is a witness to us that the people immediately recognized the difference between Christ's teaching and that of the Israelite scribes, not only in manner but also in substance. The scribes based their teaching on the text of the Mosaic Law of which they were the interpreters and glossators. Jesus did not at all follow the method of a teacher or commentator of the old law, but he conducted himself as a lawgiver and, in the last analysis, as one who had authority over the law. It is to be noted that the hearers well knew that it was a matter of divine law, given by Moses in virtue of a power which God himself had granted him as his representative and mediator with the people of Israel.

The evangelists and the first Christian community who reflected on that remark of the hearers about Jesus' teaching, had a better realization of its full significance, because they could set it alongside Christ's entire later ministry. For the Synoptics and their readers the passage from the affirmation of a power over the Mosaic law and the entire Old Testament to the affirmation of a divine authority in Christ was therefore a logical step. It was not merely the authority of a divine envoy or legate as in the case of Moses. In claiming the power to complete and interpret authoritatively or even to propose the law of God in a new way, Christ showed his awareness of being "equal to God" (cf. Phil 2:6).

That the power claimed by Christ over the law implies divine authority is shown by the fact that he did not create another law by abolishing the old one. "Do not think that I have come to abolish the law or the prophets. I have come not to abolish but to fulfill" (Mt 5:17). It is clear that God could not abolish the law which he himself had given. He can, however, as Jesus Christ did, make clear its full significance. He explained its correct meaning, and corrected false interpretations and arbitrary applications, to which the people and even their teachers and rulers had subjected it, yielding to the weaknesses and limitations of the human condition.

For this reason Jesus announced, proclaimed and called for a righteousness surpassing that of the scribes and Pharisees (cf. Mt 5:20)—the righteousness which God himself proposed and demanded by the faithful observance of the law for the sake of the kingdom of heaven. The Son of Man acted as a God who re-establishes what God had willed and laid down once for all.

Speaking of the law of God, he proclaimed in particular, "Amen, I say to you, until heaven and earth pass away, not the smallest letter or the smallest part of a letter will pass from the law, until all things have taken place" (Mt 5:18). It is a drastic

statement with which Jesus intended to affirm both the sub-
stantial immutability of the Mosaic law, and the messianic
fulfillment which it receives in his word. It is a question of a
fullness of the old law. Teaching "as one having authority"
over the law, he indicated that it is manifested especially in the
love of God and of one's neighbor. "The whole law and the
prophets depend on these two commandments" (Mt 22:40). It
is a case of a fulfillment corresponding to the spirit of the law,
which already appears from the letter of the Old Testament.
Jesus took that up, synthesized and propounded it with the
authority of one who is Lord also of the law. The precepts of
love and also of faith engendering hope in the messianic work,
which he added to the old law by making explicit its content
and by developing its hidden virtualities, are also a fulfillment.

His life was a model of this fulfillment. Jesus could say
to his disciples not only and not merely, "Follow my law," but,
"Follow me, imitate me, walk in the light which comes from me."

Evangelical spirit of charity and sincerity

As recorded by Matthew, the Sermon on the Mount is the
place in the New Testament where one sees the power over the
law (which Israel had received from God as the foundation of
the covenant) clearly affirmed and decisively exercised by
Jesus. It is there, after having declared the perpetual validity of
the law and the duty to observe it (Mt 5:18-19), that Jesus went
on to affirm the necessity of a righteousness surpassing that of
the scribes and Pharisees, or of an observance of the law
animated by the new evangelical spirit of charity and sincerity.

The concrete examples are known. The first consists in
the victory over anger, resentment and ill will, which easily
nestle in the human heart, even with the outward observance of
the Mosaic precepts, among which is that of not killing. "You
have heard that it was said to your ancestors, 'You shall not

kill; and whoever kills will be liable to judgment.' But I say to you, whoever is angry with his brother will be liable to judgment" (Mt 5:21-22). The same holds good in the case of one who has offended another with hurtful words, mockery and derision. It is the condemnation of all yielding to the instinct of aversion, which is potentially an act of injury and even of killing, at least spiritually, because it violates the economy of love in human relationships and causes harm to others. Jesus set out the law of charity which purifies and re-orders man in the most intimate feelings and movements of his spirit. Fidelity to this law is required by Jesus as an indispensable condition of religious practice itself. "Therefore, if you bring your gift to the altar, and there recall that your brother has anything against you, leave your gift there at the altar. Go first and be reconciled with your brother, and then come and offer your gift" (Mt 5:23-24). Since it is a matter of a law of love, it is even irrelevant who it is that has in his heart something against another. The love preached by Jesus equalizes and unifies all in willing what is good, in establishing or re-establishing harmony in relations with one's neighbors, and even in cases of judicial contentions and proceedings (cf. Mt 5:25).

Another example of bringing the law to perfection is that concerning the sixth commandment of the Decalogue in which Moses prohibited adultery. In hyperbolic and even paradoxical language suited to rivet the attention and shake the state of mind of his hearers, Jesus announced, "You have heard what was said, 'You shall not commit adultery'; but I say to you..." (Mt 5:27). He went on to also condemn impure looks and desires, while recommending flight from occasions of sin, the courage of mortification, the subordination of all acts and behavior to the demands of the salvation of the soul and of the whole person (cf. Mt 5:29-30).

To this case there is linked in a certain way another which Jesus took up immediately. "It was also said, 'Whoever divorces his wife must give her a bill of divorce.' But I say to you...." He declared as no longer valid the concession made by the old law to the people of Israel "because of the hardness of their hearts" (cf. Mt 19:8), by prohibiting even this form of the violation of the law of love in harmony with the re-establishment of the indissolubility of marriage (cf. Mt 19:9).

Similarly Jesus opposed to the ancient prohibition of perjury the precept of not swearing at all (cf. Mt 5:33-38). The reason which emerges sufficiently clearly is once again based on love. One should not be disbelieving or distrustful of one's neighbor when he is habitually candid and sincere. Rather, one should follow this fundamental law of speech and action, "Let your 'yes' mean 'yes' and your 'no' mean 'no.' Anything more is from the evil one" (Mt 5:37).

Again, "You have heard that it was said, 'An eye for an eye and a tooth for a tooth.' But I say to you, offer no resistance to one who is evil..." (Mt 5:38-39). With metaphorical language Jesus teaches us to turn the other cheek, to hand over not only the tunic but also the cloak, not to respond with violence to the vexations of others, and above all, "Give to the one who asks of you, and do not turn your back on one who wants to borrow" (Mt 5:42). This is a radical exclusion of the law of retaliation in the personal life of Jesus' disciples—whatever be the right of society to defend its members from evildoers and to punish those guilty of violating the rights of citizens and of the state itself.

Then he teaches the ultimate step in the process of bringing to perfection, that in which all the others find their dynamic center, "You have heard that it was said, 'You shall love your neighbor and hate your enemy.' But I say to you, love your enemies and pray for those who persecute you, that you may be children of your heavenly Father, for he makes his sun rise on the bad and the good, and causes rain to fall on the just and the unjust..." (Mt 5:43-45). In opposition to the common interpretation of the old law which identified the neighbor with the Israelite, and indeed with the pious Israelite, Jesus set out the authentic interpretation of God's commandment. He added to it the religious dimension of reference to the clement and merciful heavenly Father who does good to all and is therefore the supreme exemplar of universal love.

Jesus concluded, "Be perfect, just as your heavenly Father is perfect" (Mt 5:48). He asked of his followers the perfection of love. Love is the synthesis of the new law he brought. This love will enable man to overcome in his relations with others the classical opposition of friend-enemy. It will tend from within hearts to transform into corresponding forms of social, political and even institutionalized solidarity. Thus the irradiation of Jesus' new commandment will be very widespread in history.

At this point we are anxious above all to point out that in the important passages of the Sermon on the Mount, the contraposition is repeated, "You have heard that it was said.... But I say to you." This was not to abolish the divine law of the old covenant, but to indicate its perfect fulfillment, according to the sense intended by God the lawgiver. Jesus illumined this with a new light and explained it in all its value to achieve a new life, and as the generating principle of a new history. He did so by claiming for himself an authority identical with that of God the lawgiver. It can be said that in that expression repeated six times, "I say to you," there resounds the echo of God's self-definition, which Jesus also attributes to himself, "I Am" (cf. Gen 8:58).

Finally we must recall the reply given by Jesus to the Pharisees who rebuked his disciples for plucking the ears of corn from the fields to eat them on the sabbath, thereby transgressing the Mosaic law. Jesus began by citing the example of David and his companions who did not hesitate to eat the "bread of offering" when they were hungry, and that of the priests who did not observe the law of the sabbath rest because they had to carry out their functions in the Temple. Then he concluded with two peremptory affirmations, unheard of for the Pharisees, "I say to you, something greater than the Temple is here...." and "The Son of Man is Lord even of the sabbath" (Mt 12:6-8; cf. Mk 2:27-28). They are statements which clearly reveal Jesus' consciousness of his divine authority. His definition of himself as "one greater than the Temple" was a clear enough allusion to his divine transcendence. Then in proclaiming himself "Lord of the sabbath," or of a law given by God himself to Israel, he was openly proclaiming his own authority as head of the messianic kingdom and promulgator of the new law. So it was not a case of mere derogations from the Mosaic law, allowed also by the rabbis in very restricted cases, but of a re-integration, a complement and a renewal which Jesus announced as everlasting, "Heaven and earth will pass away but my words will not pass away" (Mt 24:35). What comes from God is eternal, just as God is eternal.

General audience of October 14, 1987

Have Faith in God
and Have Faith in Me

The ensemble of the facts analyzed in the previous re-flection provides eloquent and convincing proof of the consciousness of his own divinity shown by Jesus when he claimed for himself the name of God, the divine attributes, the power of final judgment on the deeds of all humanity, the power to forgive sins and the power over the law of God itself. They are all aspects of the one truth strongly affirmed by him, that of being true God, one with the Father. It is what he said openly to the Jews when speaking to them in the Temple on the feast of the Dedication, "The Father and I are one" (Jn 10:30). However, in attributing to himself what is proper to God, Jesus spoke of himself as Son of Man. He did this both because of his unity of person as man and as God, and to follow the pedagogy chosen to lead the disciples gradually, as though taking them by the hand, to the mysterious heights and depths of his truth. As "Son of Man" he did not hesitate to ask, "Have faith in God and have faith in me" (Jn 14:1).

The development of the whole discourse in chapters 14-17 of John, and especially Jesus' replies to Thomas and Philip, prove that when he asked them to believe in him, it was not merely a question of faith in the Messiah as the anointed one sent by God. It concerned faith in the Son who is one in being with the Father. "Have faith in God and have faith in me" (Jn 14:1).

These words must be examined in the context of Jesus' conversation with the apostles at the Last Supper, recorded by John. Jesus told the apostles that he was going to prepare a place for them in his Father's house (cf. Jn 14:2-3). When Thomas asked the way to that house, to that new kingdom, Jesus replied that he is the way, the truth and life (cf. Jn 14:6). When Philip asked that the disciples be shown the Father, Jesus replied with absolute clarity, "Whoever has seen me has seen the Father. How can you say, 'Show us the Father?' Do you not believe that I am in the Father and the Father is in me? The words that I speak to you I do not speak on my own. The Father who dwells in me is doing his works. Believe me that I am in the Father and the Father is in me, or else believe because of the works themselves" (Jn 14:9-1).

One cannot escape the grip which this statement of Jesus has on human intelligence unless one begins from an *a priori* prejudice against the divine. To those who admit the Father and sincerely seek him, Jesus showed himself and said, "Behold, the Father is in me!"

If motives of credibility were needed, Jesus appealed to his works, to all that he did before the eyes of the disciples and the whole people. These were holy and frequently miraculous works which served as a confirmation of his truth. For this reason he is worthy of belief. Jesus said so not only in the circle of the apostles, but also before the entire people. We read that on the day following his triumphal entry into Jerusalem, the large crowd who had come for the paschal celebrations were discussing the figure of the Christ, and generally they did not believe in Jesus, "although he had performed so many signs in their presence" (Jn 12:37). At a certain point "Jesus cried out, 'Whoever believes in me believes not only in me but also in the one who sent me, and whoever sees me sees the one who sent me'" (Jn 12:44). It can therefore be said that Jesus Christ identified himself with God as the object of the faith asked of and proposed to his followers. He explained to them, "What I say, I say as the Father told me" (Jn 12:50). This is an obvious allusion to the eternal utterance whereby the Father generates the Word-Son in the trinitarian life.

This faith, linked to the works and words of Jesus, becomes a logical consequence for those who honestly listen to Jesus, observe his works and reflect on his words. But it is also the presupposition and indispensable condition which Jesus demands of those who wish to become his disciples or benefit from his divine power.

Significant in this regard is what Jesus said to the father of the epileptic youth, possessed from infancy by a mute spirit which raged in him in a frightening way. The poor father begged Jesus, "If you can do anything, have compassion on us and help us." Jesus replied, "'If you can!' Everything is possible to one who has faith." Then the boy's father cried out, "I do believe, help my unbelief!" (Mk 9:22-23). Jesus performed the cure and freed the unfortunate youth. However, he desired from the boy's father an opening of his soul in faith. That is what has been given to Jesus in the course of the centuries by so many humble and afflicted creatures who, like the father of the epileptic youth, have turned to him to ask his help in temporal and especially in spiritual needs.

However, when people, whatever their social and cultural tradition, resisted through pride or incredulity, Jesus chastised this attitude of theirs by not admitting them to the benefits of his divine power. What we read of the people of Nazareth is significant and striking. Jesus had returned there after beginning his ministry and working his first miracles. They were not only amazed by his teaching and his works, but they were even "scandalized by him." In other words, they spoke of him and treated him with suspicion and hostility, as one who was unwelcome.

"Jesus said to them, 'A prophet is not without honor except in his native place, and among his own kin and in his own house.' So he was not able to perform any mighty deed there, apart from curing a few sick people by laying his hands on them. He was amazed at their lack of faith" (Mk 6:4-6). Miracles are signs of Jesus' divine power. When there is an obstinate blindness in recognizing such power, a miracle loses its raison d'être. Moreover, when the disciples asked Jesus after the curing of the epileptic why they, who had received power from him, could not cast out the demon, he told them, "Because of your little faith. Amen, I say to you, if you have faith the size of a mustard seed, you will say to this mountain, 'Move from here to there,' and it will move. Nothing will be impossible for you" (Mt 17:19-20). The language is symbolic and exaggerated, but Jesus used it to inculcate in his followers the necessity and power of faith.

Jesus emphasized this after the miraculous cure of the man born blind. When Jesus met him he asked him, "'Do you believe in the Son of Man?' He answered and said, 'Who is he, sir, that I may believe in him?' Jesus said to him, 'You have seen him and the one speaking to you is he.' He said, 'I do believe, Lord,' and he worshipped him" (Jn 9:35-38). It was the act of faith of a humble man, the image of all humble people who seek God (cf. Dt 29:3; Is 6:9 f.; Jer 5:21; Ez 12:2). He obtained the grace not only of physical sight but also of spiritual vision, because he recognized the Son of Man. He was not like the self-sufficient ones who trust only in their own lights and reject the light which comes from on high, and consequently condemn themselves to blindness before Christ and God.

The decisive importance of faith appears even more clearly in the dialogue between Jesus and Martha before the tomb of Lazarus. "Jesus said to her, 'Your brother will rise.' Martha said to him, 'I know he will rise, in the resurrection on the last day.' Jesus told her, 'I am the resurrection and the life; whoever believes in me, even if he dies, will live, and everyone who lives and believes in me will never die. Do you believe this?' She said to him, 'Yes, Lord, I have come to believe that you are the Messiah, the Son of God, the one who is coming into the world'" (Jn 11:23-27). Jesus raised Lazarus from the dead as a sign of Jesus' own divine power not only to raise the dead, because he is the Lord of life, but also to conquer death—he who is the resurrection and the life, as he said to Martha.

Jesus' teaching on faith as a condition of his saving action is summed up and confirmed in his nighttime conversation with Nicodemus, a Jewish leader who was well disposed to him and ready to recognize him as a "teacher come from God" (cf. Jn 3:12).

Jesus spoke to him at length about the new life and, eventually, about the new economy of salvation based on faith in the "Son of Man who must be lifted up, so that everyone who believes in him, might not perish but might have eternal life" (Jn 3:15-16). Therefore faith in Christ is a constitutive condition of salvation, of eternal life. It is faith in the only-begotten Son—one in being with the Father—in whom the Father's love is manifested. "For God did not send his Son into the world to condemn the world, but that the world might be saved through him" (Jn 3:17). The judgment is implicit in the choice of accepting or rejecting faith in Christ. "Whoever believes in him will not be condemned, but whoever does not believe has already been condemned, because he has not believed in the name of the only Son of God" (Jn 3:18).

When speaking to Nicodemus, Jesus indicated in the paschal mystery the central point of the faith which saves: "The Son of Man must be lifted up on the cross, so that everyone who believes in him may have eternal life" (Jn 3:14-15). This can also be called the critical point of faith in Christ. The cross was the definitive test of faith for Christ's apostles and disciples. In the presence of that lifting up one should have been overwhelmed, as partly happened. But the fact that he "rose on the third day" enabled them to emerge victoriously from the final test. Also Thomas, who was the last to overcome the paschal test of faith, burst out into that stupendous profession of faith during his meeting with the risen one, "My Lord and my God!" (Jn 20:28). As in the case of Peter at Caesarea Philippi (cf. Mt 16:16), so likewise Thomas in this paschal meeting burst out with the cry of faith which comes from the Father—Jesus crucified and risen is "Lord and God."

Immediately after recording this profession of faith and Jesus' response which proclaimed blessed those "who have not seen and yet believe" (Jn 20:29), John offers a first conclusion of his Gospel: "Jesus did many other signs in the presence of his disciples that are not written in this book. But these are written that you may believe that Jesus is the Messiah, the Son of God, and that through this belief you may have life in his name" (Jn 20:30-31).

Therefore all that Jesus did and taught, all that the apostles preached and bore witness to and that the evangelists wrote, all that the Church preserves and repeats of their teaching, should be at the service of faith, so that, by believing, one might attain salvation. Salvation—and therefore eternal life— is linked to Jesus Christ's messianic mission from which derives the whole "logic" and "economy" of the Christian faith. John himself proclaimed it from the prologue of his Gospel: "To those who did accept him, (the Word) gave the power to become children of God, to those who believe in his name" (Jn 1:12).

General audience of October 21, 1987

Whoever Loses His Life for My Sake and that of the Gospel Will Save It

In our search for the Gospel signs revealing Christ's consciousness of his divinity, we emphasized in the previous reflection his appeal to his disciples to have faith in him. "Have faith in God and have faith also in me" (Jn 14:1) is a request which only God could make. Jesus demanded this faith when he manifested his divine power which transcends all natural powers, for example, in the raising of Lazarus from the dead (cf. Jn 11:38-44). He demanded it also in the test of faith in the saving power of the cross, as he stated right from his conversation with Nicodemus (cf. Jn 3:14-15). This faith is faith in his divinity, "Whoever has seen me has seen the Father" (Jn 14:9).

Faith concerns an invisible reality which is beyond sense experience and surpasses the limits of the human intellect itself *(argumentum non apparentium,* "the evidence of things not seen," cf. Heb 11:1). As St. Paul wrote, it refers to "what eye has not seen, and ear has not heard, and what has not entered the human heart," but what God has prepared for those who love him (cf. 1 Cor 2:9). Jesus demanded such a faith when on the day before his death on the cross—ignominious from a human standpoint—he told the apostles that he was going to prepare a place for them in his Father's house (cf. Jn 14:2).

These mysterious things, this invisible reality, is identified with the infinite Goodness of God, eternal Love, supremely worthy of being loved above everything. Therefore, together with the request for faith Jesus placed the commandment of the love of God "above all things." It had already been laid down in the Old Testament, but Jesus repeated and corroborated it in a new spirit. It is true that in replying to the query, "What is the greatest commandment of the law?" Jesus quoted the words of the Mosaic law. "You shall love the Lord, your God, with all your heart, with all your soul, and with all your mind" (Mt 22:37; cf. Dt 6:5). But the full meaning which the commandment assumed on the lips of Jesus appears from the reference to other elements in the context in which he moved and taught. Without doubt he wished to inculcate that only God can and must be loved above all created things; and only in relationship to God can there be in man a demand of a love above all things. Only God, by virtue of this demand of radical and total love, can call a person to follow him without reserve or limitation, and in an indivisible way, as we read in the Old Testament, "The Lord, your God, shall you follow...his commandment shall you observe...you shall serve him and hold fast to him alone" (Dt 13:5). Only God "is good" in the absolute sense (cf. Mk 10:18; also Mt 19:17). Only he "is love" (1 Jn 4:16) by essence and definition. But here we have an element which appears new and surprising in the life and teaching of Christ.

Jesus calls us to follow him personally. This call, it may be said, is at the very heart of the Gospel. On the one hand Jesus issues this call; on the other, the evangelists speak of the people who follow him, and indeed, of some who leave everything to follow him.

We think of all those calls of which the evangelists tell us. "One of the disciples said to him, 'Lord, let me go first and bury my father.' But Jesus answered him, 'Follow me, and let the dead bury their dead'" (Mt 8:21-22). This is a drastic way of saying: leave everything, immediately, for me. This is Matthew's account. Luke adds the apostolic connotation of this call, "You go and proclaim the kingdom of God" (Lk 9:60). On another occasion he found Matthew sitting at the customs post, and he said to him with a certain insistence, as Matthew himself recorded later, "'Follow me.' And he got up and followed him" (Mt 9:9; cf. Mk 2:13-14).

Frequently, to follow Jesus means not only to leave one's occupation and to sever one's bonds with the world, but also to renounce the condition of prosperity one may enjoy, and indeed to give one's goods to the poor. Not all are prepared to take this radical step. The rich young man was not prepared to do so, even though he had observed the law from his youth and was perhaps seeking seriously a way of perfection. But "on hearing this [that is, Jesus' invitation], he went away sad for he had many possessions" (Mt 19:22; cf. Mk 10:22). Others, however, not only accept this "Follow me," but, like Philip of Bethsaida, feel the need to communicate to others their conviction of having found the Messiah (cf. Jn 1:43 ff.). Simon himself, at his very first meeting, heard the words, "You will be called Cephas (which is translated Peter)" (Jn 1:42). John the evangelist noted that Jesus "fixed his gaze on him." That intense look contained the strongest and most captivating "Follow me." But it seems that Jesus, given the altogether special vocation of Peter (and perhaps also his natural temperament) wished to allow his capacity to weigh and accept that invitation mature gradually. For Peter, the literal "Follow me" will come after the washing of the feet at the Last Supper (cf. Jn 13:36), and later, in a definitive way, after the resurrection, on the shore of Lake Tiberias (cf. Jn 21:19).

Doubtlessly, Peter and the other apostles—except Judas—understood and accepted the call to follow Jesus as a total donation of self and of their belongings to the cause of the proclamation of the kingdom of God. They themselves later reminded Jesus, through the mouth of Peter, "We have given up everything and followed you" (Mt 19:27). Luke's account is more precise: "all our possessions" (Lk 18:28). Jesus himself seemed to desire to specify what these possessions were when he said to Peter, "Amen, I say to you, there is no one who has given up house or wife or brothers or parents or children for the sake of the kingdom of God, who will not receive an overabundant return in this present age and eternal life in the age to come" (Lk 18:29-30).

Matthew's version also mentions leaving sisters, mother, and lands "for the sake of my name." He who does so, Jesus promised, "will receive a hundred times more, and will inherit eternal life" (Mt 19:29).

Mark's account is more specific about leaving all things "for my sake and for the sake of the Gospel," and also about the reward. "He will receive a hundred times more now in this present age—houses and brothers and sisters and mothers and children and lands, with persecutions, and eternal life in the age to come" (Mk 10:29-30).

Without concerning ourselves for the moment with the figurative language used by Jesus, we may ask: who is he who issues the call to follow him, and promises to those who follow him such great rewards, even eternal life? Can an ordinary human being promise so much, and be believed and followed, and have such a hold not only on those happy disciples but also on thousands and millions of people throughout the centuries?

Those disciples well remembered the authority with which Jesus called them to follow him. He did not hesitate to ask of them a radical dedication, expressed in terms which could appear paradoxical. For example, he said that he had come to bring "not peace but a sword," that is, to create separations and divisions in families in order to follow him. Then he said, "Whoever loves father or mother more than me is not worthy of me, and whoever loves son or daughter more than me is not worthy of me; and whoever does not take up his cross and follow after me is not worthy of me" (Mt 10:37-38). Luke formulates it even more strongly and almost severely: "If anyone comes to me without hating [a Hebraism, which means: if he does not separate from] his father and mother, wife and children, brothers and sisters, and even his own life, he cannot be my disciple" (Lk 14:26).

Faced with these expressions of Jesus one cannot but reflect on the nobility and difficulty of the Christian vocation. Undoubtedly the concrete forms of the following of Christ are graduated by himself according to the conditions, possibilities, missions and charisms of persons and classes. Jesus' words, as he himself said, are "spirit and life" (cf. Jn 6:63). And one cannot presume to materialize them in an identical manner for everyone. But according to St. Thomas Aquinas, the Gospel request for heroic renunciations, such as those of the evangelical counsels of poverty, chastity and self-denial in order to follow Jesus, commits everyone *secundum praeparationem animi* (cf. *Summa Theol.,* II-II, 184, 7 ad 1). That is, it means to be ready in spirit to carry out what is required, should one be called upon to do so. The same can be said of the oblation of self in martyrdom rather than deny the faith and the following of Christ. The counsels therefore imply for everyone an interior detachment, a donation of self to Christ, without which there is no true evangelical spirit.

From the Gospel itself it is clear that there are particular vocations dependent upon Christ's choice, such as that of the apostles and of many disciples indicated clearly enough by Mark, "He went up the mountain and summoned those whom he wanted and they came to him" (Mk 3:13-14). According to

John, Jesus himself said to the apostles in the final discourse, "It was not you who chose me, but I who chose you..." (Jn 15:16).

It does not appear that he definitively condemned those who did not consent to follow him on a path of total dedication to the cause of the Gospel (cf. the case of the rich young man in Mk 10:17-27). There is something more perfect which calls for the free generosity of the individual. It is certain, however, that the call to Christian faith and love is universal and of obligation—faith in the word of Jesus, love of God above all things and love of one's neighbor as oneself. "He who does not love a brother whom he has seen, cannot love God whom he has not seen" (1 Jn 4:20).

In establishing the need of the response to the call to follow him, Jesus concealed from no one that to follow him involves sacrifice, sometimes also the supreme sacrifice. He said to his disciples, "If any one would come after me, let him deny himself and take up his cross and follow me. For whoever would save his life will lose it; and whoever loses his life for my sake will save it" (Mt 16:24-25).

Mark stresses that together with the disciples Jesus had also called together the crowd, and to all he spoke of the denial required of those who wish to follow him, of the taking up of the cross and of the loss of life "for my sake and that of the Gospel" (Mk 8:34-35). And Jesus said this after having spoken of his proximate passion and death (cf. Mk 8:31-32).

At the same time, however, Jesus proclaimed blessed those who are persecuted "on account of the Son of Man" (Lk 6:22). "Rejoice and be glad, for your reward will be great in heaven" (Mt 5:12).

Once again we ask ourselves: who is this who authoritatively calls to follow him; foretells hatred, insults and persecutions of every kind (cf. Lk 6:22); and promises a reward in heaven? Only the Son of God could speak in such a manner. It was in this sense that the apostles and disciples understood him, and they transmitted to us his revelation and his message. In this sense we, too, wish to understand him, repeating to him with the Apostle Thomas, "My Lord and my God."

General audience of October 29, 1987

I Confer a Kingdom on You

Let us run through again the themes of the reflections on Jesus the Son of Man, which at the same time reveal him as the true Son of God. "I and the Father are one" (Jn 10:30). We have seen that he referred to himself the divine name and attributes; he spoke of his divine pre-existence in union with the Father (and with the Holy Spirit, as we shall explain in a further series of reflections); he claimed for himself power over the law which Israel had received from God through Moses in the old covenant. That claim was made especially in the Sermon on the Mount (cf. Mt 5); and together with this power, he claimed also the power to forgive sins (cf. Mk 2:1-12 and parallel passages; Lk 7:48; Jn 8:11), and to pronounce the final judgment on the consciences and works of all humanity (cf. Mt 25:31-46; Jn 5:27-29). Finally, he taught as one having authority and he called for faith in his word; he invited people to follow him even unto death, and promised eternal life as a reward. At this point we have at our disposal all the elements and all the reasons for affirming that Jesus Christ has revealed himself as the one who establishes God's kingdom in the history of humanity.

The revelation of God's kingdom had already been prepared in the Old Testament. It happened particularly in the second phase of the history of Israel as narrated in the words of the prophets and the Psalms, following the exile and the other painful experiences of the Chosen People. We recall especially the songs of the Psalmists to God who is king of all the earth, who "reigns over the peoples" (Ps 47: 8-9); and the exultant recognition, "Your kingdom is a kingdom for all ages, and your dominion endures through all generations" (Ps 145:13). In his turn the prophet Daniel speaks of the kingdom of God "which shall never be destroyed...rather, it shall break in pieces all these kingdoms, and put an end to them, and it shall stand forever." This kingdom which the "God of heaven" will set up (i.e., the kingdom of heaven), will remain under the dominion of God himself and "shall never be delivered to another people" (cf. Dan 2:44).

Structure of the kingdom of God

Entering into this tradition and sharing this concept of the old covenant, Jesus of Nazareth proclaimed this kingdom from the beginning of his Messianic mission. "The time is fulfilled, and the kingdom of God is at hand" (Mk 1:15). In this way he took up one of the constant motifs of Israel's expectation, but he gave a new direction to the eschatological hope which took shape in the final phase of the Old Testament. He did so by proclaiming that it had its initial fulfillment already here on earth, since God is the Lord of history. Certainly, his kingdom is projected toward a final fulfillment beyond time, but it begins to be realized already here on earth and in a certain sense it develops within history. In this perspective Jesus announced and revealed that the time of the ancient promises, expectations and hopes "is fulfilled," and that the kingdom of God "is at hand"—it is already present in his own Person.

Jesus Christ, indeed, not only taught about the kingdom of God, making it the central point of his teaching, but he established this kingdom in the history of Israel and of all humanity. This reveals his divine power, his sovereignty in regard to all in time and space that bears the signs of the primordial creation and of the call to be "new creatures" (cf. 2 Cor 5:17; Gal 6:15). Through Christ and in Christ all that is transient and ephemeral has been conquered, and he has established for ever the true value of the human person and of everything created.

It is a unique and eternal power which Jesus Christ—crucified and risen—claimed for himself at the end of his earthly mission when he said to the apostles, "All power in heaven and on earth has been given to me." By virtue of this power of his he ordered them, "Go, therefore, and make disciples of all nations, baptizing them in the name of the Father, and of the Son, and of the Holy Spirit, teaching them to observe all that I have commanded you. And behold, I am with you always, until the end of the age" (Mt 28:18-20).

Before reaching this definitive act in the proclamation and revelation of the divine sovereignty of the Son of Man, Jesus frequently announced that the kingdom of God has come into the world. Indeed, in the conflict with his adversaries who did not hesitate to ascribe Jesus' works to a demonic power, he refuted them with an argument that ends with the statement, "If it is by the finger of God that I drive out demons, then the kingdom of God has come upon you" (Lk 11:20). Therefore in him and through him the spiritual space of the divine dominion gains substance. The kingdom of God enters into the history of Israel and of all humanity. Jesus is in a position to reveal it and to show that he has the power to decide its realization. He shows it by freeing from demons—the whole psychological and spiritual space is reconquered for God.

Moreover, the definitive mandate given to the apostles by

Christ crucified and risen (cf. Mt 28:18-20), was prepared by him under every aspect. The key moment of the preparation was the calling of the apostles. "He appointed twelve that they might be with him and he might send them forth to preach and to have authority to drive out demons" (Mk 3:14-15). Among the Twelve, Simon Peter received a special power in regard to the kingdom. "And so I say to you, you are Peter, and upon this rock I will build my church, and the gates of the netherworld shall not prevail against it. I will give you the keys to the kingdom of heaven. Whatever you bind on earth shall be bound in heaven; and whatever you loose on earth shall be loosed in heaven" (Mt 16:18-19). He who spoke in this way showed that he was convinced to possess the kingdom, to hold its supreme sovereignty, and to be able to entrust the keys to his representative and vicar. He did this just as, and to a still greater degree than, an earthly king would do in the case of his lieutenant or prime minister.

This evident conviction of Jesus explains why, during his ministry, he spoke of his present and future work as of a new kingdom introduced into human history, not only as a truth announced but as a living reality. It develops, grows and ferments the entire human batch of dough, as we read in the parable of the leaven (cf. Mt 13:33; Lk 13:21). This and the other parables of the kingdom (cf. especially Mt 13), attest that this is the central idea of Jesus, and also the substance of his messianic work which he willed to be prolonged in history, even after his return to the Father, and this by means of a visible structure whose head is Peter (cf. Mt 16:18-19).

The establishment of this structure of the kingdom of God coincides with its transmission by Christ to his chosen apostles, "I confer (Latin, *dispono*; translated by some as "I convey") a kingdom on you, just as my Father has conferred one on me" (Lk 22:29). The transmission of the kingdom is at the same time a mission: "As you sent me into the world, so I send them into the world" (Jn 17:18). Appearing to the apostles after the resurrection, Jesus will again say, "As the Father has sent me, so I send you.... Receive the Holy Spirit. Whose sins you forgive are forgiven them, and whose sins you retain are retained" (Jn 2:21-23).

We should note well that in Jesus' mind, in his messianic work and in his mandate to the apostles, the inauguration of the kingdom in this world is closely connected with his power to conquer sin, to cancel Satan's power in the world and in every human being. It is therefore linked to the paschal mystery, to the cross and resurrection of Christ *(Agnus Dei qui tollit peccata mundi...)*, and as such it is built into the historical mission of the apostles and of their successors. The establishment of the kingdom of God has its foundation in the reconciliation of humanity with God, carried out in Christ and through Christ in the paschal mystery (cf. 2 Cor 5:19; Eph 2:13-18; Col 1:19-20).

The purpose of the vocation and mission of the apostles—and therefore of the Church—in the world is to establish God's kingdom in human history (cf. Mk 16:15; Mt 28:19-20). Jesus was well aware that this mission, like his own messianic mission, would encounter and provoke great opposition. From the days when he sent forth the apostles in the first experiments of collaborating with himself, he warned them, "Behold, I send you out as sheep in the midst of wolves; so be wise as serpents and innocent as doves" (Mt 10:16).

Matthew's Gospel also condenses what Jesus would say later about the fate of his missionaries (Mt 10:17-25). He returned to this theme in one of his last polemical discourses with the "scribes and Pharisees," by confirming, "Behold, I send to you prophets and wisemen and scribes; some of them you will kill and crucify, some of them you will scourge in your synagogues and pursue from town to town... (Mt 23:34). It was a fate which had already befallen the prophets and other personages of the old covenant to whom the text refers (cf. Mt 23:35). But Jesus gave his followers the assurance that his work and theirs would endure—the gates of the netherworld shall not prevail against it.

Despite the opposition and contradiction it would meet with throughout the course of history, the kingdom of God would be established once for all in the world by the power of God himself through the Gospel and the paschal mystery of the Son. It would always bear not only the signs of his passion and death, but also the seal of his divine power, radiant in the resurrection. History would demonstrate it. But the certainty of the apostles and of all believers is founded on the revelation of the divine power of Christ, historical, eschatological and eternal, about whom the Second Vatican Council taught, "Christ, becoming obedient even unto death and because of this exalted by the Father (cf. Phil 2:8-9), entered into the glory of his kingdom. To him all things are made subject until he subjects himself and all created things to the Father that God may be all in all (cf. 1 Cor 15:27-28)" *(LG* 36).

General audience of November 4, 1987

THE MIRACLES OF CHRIST

The Fact and Significance of Christ's Miracles

On the day of Pentecost, after receiving the light and power of the Holy Spirit, Peter bore clear and courageous witness to Christ crucified and risen. "Men of Israel," he proclaimed, "hear these words: Jesus of Nazareth, a man attested to you by God with mighty works and wonders and signs...you crucified...and killed. But God raised him up, releasing him from the pangs of death" (Acts 2:22-24).

This testimony includes a synthesis of the whole messianic activity of Jesus of Nazareth, whom God had commended by "mighty deeds, wonders and signs." It also constitutes an outline of the first Christian catechesis, which is offered to us by the head of the apostolic college, Peter.

After nearly two thousand years the present successor of Peter, in developing his reflections on Jesus Christ, must now deal with the content of that first apostolic catechesis on the day of Pentecost. Until now we have spoken of the Son of Man, who by his teaching made it known that he was the true Son of God, that he and the Father "are one" (cf. Jn 10:30). His word was accompanied by "mighty works, wonders and signs." These deeds accompanied the words, not only following them by way of confirming their authenticity, but frequently preceding them, as the Acts of the Apostles gives us to understand when speaking "of all that Jesus did and taught from the beginning" (Acts 1:1). It was those same works and particularly "the marvels and signs" that testified that "the kingdom of God was at hand" (cf. Mk 1:15), that with Jesus it had entered into the earthly history of humanity and was eager to enter into every human spirit. At the same time they were a witness that he who performed them was truly the Son of God. For this reason it is necessary to link these present reflections on Christ's mighty deeds and signs with the previous ones on his divine sonship.

Eyewitness testimonies to Christ

Before proceeding step by step in analyzing the significance of these "wonders and signs" (as Peter had specifically defined them on the day of Pentecost), one must note that they (the wonders and signs) certainly pertain to the integral content of the Gospels as eyewitness testimonies to Christ. It is not possible to exclude the mighty deeds from the Gospel text and context. The analysis not only of the text but also of the context speaks in favor of their "historical" character. It attests that they are facts which actually happened, and that they were really performed by Christ. Whoever approaches the matter with intellectual honesty and scientific expertise cannot dispose of them in a few words as simply later inventions.

In this regard it is well to observe that these facts are not only attested to and narrated by the apostles and disciples of Jesus, but in many cases they are admitted by his opponents. For example, it is significant that they did not deny the reality of the miracles performed by Jesus, but they attributed them to the power of Satan. For they said, "He is possessed by Beelzebul, and by the prince of demons he drives out demons"

(Mk 3:22; cf. also Mt 8:32; 12:24; Lk 11:14-15). But Jesus clearly pointed out the contradiction in these remarks. He said, "If Satan has risen up against himself and is divided, he cannot stand, but is coming to an end" (Mk 3:26). But the most important thing for us at the moment is the fact that even Jesus' opponents could not deny his "mighty deeds, wonders and signs" as reality—as facts which had actually taken place.

It is also a notable fact that his opponents watched Jesus to see whether he would heal on the sabbath, and thus they would be in position to accuse him of transgressing the Old Testament law. This was stated in the case of the man with the withered hand (cf. Mk 3:1-2).

Also to be considered is Jesus' reply, not to his opponents, but to the messengers sent by John the Baptist to ask Jesus, "Are you the one who is to come, or should we look for another?" (Mt 11:3). Jesus replied, "Go and tell John what you hear and see: the blind regain their sight, the lame walk, lepers are cleansed, the deaf hear, the dead are raised and the poor have the good news proclaimed to them" (Mt 11:4-5; cf. also Lk 7:22). Jesus' reply refers to Isaiah's prophecy about the future Messiah (cf. Is 35:5-6), which could undoubtedly be understood in the sense of a renewal and of a spiritual healing of Israel and of humanity. But in the Gospel context, in the mouth of Jesus, it indicates facts commonly known and which the Baptist's disciples can report to him as signs of Christ's messiahship.

All the evangelists record the facts to which Peter referred on the day of Pentecost, "mighty deeds, wonders and signs" (cf. Acts 2:22). The Synoptics narrate many individual events, but at times they also use generalized expressions. For example, Mark's Gospel states, "He cured many who were sick with various diseases, and he drove out many demons" (1:34). Likewise Matthew and Luke state, "...curing every disease and illness among the people" (Mt 4:23); "...power came forth from him and healed them all" (Lk 6:19). These expressions give us to understand the great number of miracles performed by Jesus. In John's Gospel we do not find such expressions, but rather the detailed description of seven events which the evangelist calls "signs" (and not miracles). Thereby he wished to indicate the most essential element of those facts, namely, the revelation of God's action in Jesus. The word "miracle" indicates rather the extraordinary aspect of those events in the eyes of those who saw them or who heard them spoken of.

However, before concluding his Gospel, John also considered it important to mention that "Jesus did many other signs in the presence of his disciples that are not written in this book" (Jn 20:30). He then gave the reason for the choice he had made. "These are written that you may believe that Jesus is the Messiah, the Son of God, and that through this belief you may have life in his name" (Jn 20:31). This is the aim of both the Synoptics and the Fourth Gospel—to show by means of the miracles the truth of the Son of God and to lead to the faith which is the beginning of salvation.

When on the day of Pentecost the Apostle Peter bore witness to the entire mission of Jesus of Nazareth, attested to by God with "mighty deeds, wonders and signs," he could not but recall that the same Jesus was crucified and risen (cf. Acts 2:22-24). He thus indicated the paschal event in which is offered the most complete sign of God's saving and redemptive action in human history. One might say that this sign encloses the "anti-miracle" of the death on the cross and the "miracle" of the resurrection (miracle of miracles) which are rooted in a single mystery. In it the human person can read to the very depths God's self-revelation in Jesus Christ, and by adhering to it by faith enter on the way of salvation.

General audience of November 11, 1987

I Say to You, Arise!

If we examine attentively "the mighty works and wonders and signs" spoken of by the Apostle Peter on Pentecost day in Jerusalem and provided by God as a proof of the credibility of Jesus Christ's mission, we note that in performing these "miraculous signs," Jesus acted in his own name. He was conscious of his divine power and at the same time of his intimate union with the Father. Once again and always we are in the presence of the mystery of the "Son of Man—Son of God," whose identity transcends all limits of the human condition (although belonging to it by his own free choice), and all possibility of human achievement and even of knowledge.

A glance at some individual events recorded by the evangelists enables us to take note of that mysterious presence in whose name Jesus Christ performed his miracles. For example, Jesus responded to the entreaties of the leper who begged him, "If you will, you can cure me!" In his human nature, moved with compassion, Jesus gave a word of command which, in such a case, is proper to God and not to a mere human being: "'I do will it. Be made clean!' The leprosy left him immediately, and he was made clean" (cf. Mk 1:40-42). Similarly in the case of the paralytic who was let down through an opening made in the roof of the house, Jesus said, "I say to you, rise, pick up your mat, and go home" (cf. Mk 2:1-12).

Again, in the case of Jairus' daughter we read that "he (Jesus) took the child by the hand, and said to her, *'Talitha koum,'* which means, 'Little girl, I say to you, arise!' The girl arose immediately and walked around" (Mk 5:41-42). In the case of the young man of Naim who had died, Jesus said, "'Young man, I tell you, arise!' The dead man sat up and began to speak" (Lk 7:14-15).

In so many of these episodes we see appearing from Jesus' words the expression of a will and a power to which he interiorly appealed and which he expressed, one might say, with the greatest naturalness. It was as though the power to give people health, healing and even to bring the dead back to life, belonged to his own mysterious condition.

The raising of Lazarus described in detail by St. John is especially noteworthy. We read, "Jesus looked upward and said; 'Father, I thank you for having heard me. I know that you always hear me, but I have said this for the sake of the crowd, that they may believe that you sent me.' Having said this, he called loudly, 'Lazarus, come out!' And the dead man came out" (Jn 11:41-44). In the precise description of this event, John emphasized that Jesus raised his friend Lazarus from the dead by Jesus' own power and in close union with the Father. Here we find a clear confirmation of Jesus' words, "My Father is working still and I am working" (Jn 5:17). Moreover, it could be said that we have here an anticipated demonstration of what Jesus will say in the upper room during his Last Supper conversation with the apostles concerning his relations with the Father, and, indeed, concerning his identity in being with the Father.

The Gospels show by various miracles-signs that the divine power at work in Jesus Christ extends beyond the human world and is revealed as a power of dominion also over the forces of nature. The calming of the tempest is significant. "Meanwhile a great storm of wind arose." The terrified fishermen-apostles awoke Jesus who was asleep in the stern. He "woke up, rebuked the wind, and said to the sea, 'Quiet! Be still!' The wind ceased and there was great calm...[the apostles] were filled with great awe and said to one another, 'Who then is this whom even wind and sea obey?'" (cf. Mk 4:37-41).

This series of events included the miraculous catches of fish which took place at Jesus' command *(in verbo tuo)* after previous attempts had failed (cf. Lk 5:4-6; Jn 21:3-6). The same can also be said, as regards the structure of the event, of the "first sign" performed at Cana in Galilee, when Jesus ordered the servants to fill the jars with water and then to bring "the water changed into wine" to the headwaiter (cf. Jn 2:7-9). As in the miraculous catches of fish, so likewise at Cana of Galilee, people played their part—the fishermen-apostles in one case, and the servants at the marriage feast in the other. But it is clear that the extraordinary effect of the action did not come from them, but from him who had given them the order to act and who worked with his mysterious divine power. This is confirmed by the reaction of the apostles, and especially of Peter who, after the miraculous catch of fish, "fell at the knees of Jesus and said, 'Depart from me, Lord, for I am a sinful man'" (Lk 5:8). It is one of the many cases of emotional feeling which assumes the form of reverential awe or even of fear, both in the apostles as in the case of Simon Peter, and also in the people when they feel touched by the wing of the divine mystery.

On a day after the ascension, those who witnessed "the wonders and signs...done through the apostles" (cf. Acts 2:43), were seized by a similar "awe." According to Acts, the people "carried the sick out into the streets and laid them on cots and mats so that when Peter came by, at least his shadow might fall on one or another of them" (Acts 5:15). However, these "wonders and signs" which accompanied the beginnings of the apostolic Church were done by the apostles not in their own name, but in the name of Jesus Christ, and were therefore a further proof of his divine power. One is impressed by Peter's reply and command to the crippled man who had asked him for an alms near the gate of the Temple of Jerusalem: "'I have neither silver nor gold, but what I do have I give you. In the name of Jesus Christ of Nazareth, walk.' And he took him by the right hand and raised him up; and immediately his feet and ankles were made strong" (Acts 3:6-7). One recalls also what Peter said to the paralyzed man named Aeneas, "'Jesus Christ hears you. Get up and make your bed.' And he got up at once" (Acts 9:34).

Also the other prince of the apostles, Paul, when recalling in the Letter to the Romans all that he had done as "minister of Christ among the pagans," hastened to add that his sole merit is to be found in that ministry. "For I will not dare to speak of anything except what Christ has accomplished through me to lead the Gentiles to obedience by word and deed, by the power of signs and wonders, by the power of the Spirit" (15:18-19).

In the early period of the Church and especially in the evangelization of the world carried out by the apostles, those "mighty works, wonders and signs" abounded, as Jesus himself had promised them (cf. Acts 2:22). But it can be said that they have always been repeated throughout salvation history, especially in decisive moments for putting God's plan into effect. Thus it was in the Old Testament in regard to the Exodus of Israel from the bondage of Egypt and the journey to the promised land under the leadership of Moses. With the Incarnation of the Son of God "the fullness of time had come" (cf. Gal 4:4). Those miraculous signs of the divine action then took on a new value and a new efficacy through the divine authority of Christ and through the reference to his name—and therefore to his truth, promise, command and glory—with which they were performed by the apostles and by so many saints in the Church. Miracles happen even today, and in each of them the face of the "Son of Man–Son of God" is outlined, and we see an affirmation of a gift of grace and salvation.

General audience of November 18, 1987

Miraculous Signs
Reveal Christ's Power

A text from St. Augustine offers us the key for interpreting Christ's miracles as signs of his saving power. "The fact that he became man for us contributed more to our salvation than the miracles he performed among us; and his healing of the evils of the soul is more important than the curing of the illnesses of the body which is doomed to death" (Augustine, *In Io. Ev. Tr.* 17, 1). For the salvation of the soul and the redemption of the whole world Jesus performed miracles of the corporeal order also. Hence the theme of the present reflection is as follows—by means of the "mighty deeds, wonders and signs" which he performed, Jesus Christ manifested his power to save the human race from the evil which threatens the immortal soul and the vocation to union with God.

This is revealed particularly in the healing of the paralytic of Capernaum. Since those who carried him were unable to enter by the door into the house where Jesus was teaching, they lowered the sick man through an opening in the roof so that he found himself at the feet of the Master. "Jesus, on seeing their faith, said to the paralytic, 'Son, your sins are forgiven.'" These words aroused among some of those present the suspicion of blasphemy, "This man is blaspheming! Who but God can forgive sins?" As though in response to those who had entertained these thoughts, Jesus said to those present, "Which is easier, to say to the paralytic, 'Your sins are forgiven,' or to say, 'Rise, pick up your mat and walk'? But that you may know that the Son of Man has authority to forgive sins on earth—he said to the paralytic—'I say to you, rise, pick up your mat, and go home.' He rose, picked up his mat at once, and went away in the sight of everyone" (cf. Mk 2:1-12; likewise Mt 9:1-8; Lk 5:18-26, "he went home glorifying God" Lk 5:25).

Power to forgive sins

Jesus himself explained in this case that the miracle of curing the paralytic was a sign of the saving power whereby he forgives sins. Jesus performed this sign to show that he had come as Savior of the world. His principal task was to free mankind from spiritual evil, the evil that separates man from God and impedes salvation in God. That evil is sin.

With the same key one can explain that special category of Christ's miracles, the driving out of demons. According to Mark's Gospel, Jesus ordered, "Unclean spirit, come out of the man!" when Jesus met the man in the territory of the Gerasenes who had an unclean spirit (Mk 5:8). On that occasion we witness an unusual conversation. When that unclean spirit felt threatened by Christ, he cried out against Jesus, "'What have you to do with me, Jesus, Son of the Most High God? I adjure you by God, do not torment me!' Jesus asked him, 'What is your name?' He replied, 'Legion is my name. There are many of us'" (cf. Mk 5:7-9). We are therefore on the margin of an obscure world involving physical and psychical factors which undoubtedly play their part in causing pathological conditions. The demonic reality is inserted into that world.

Variously represented and described in human language, the demonic world is radically hostile to God and therefore to man and to Christ who had come to free him from the power of evil. But in spite of himself, in that clash with the other presence, even the unclean spirit burst out into that admission coming from a perverse but lucid intelligence, "Son of the Most High God."

In Mark's Gospel we also find the description of the event usually described as the cure of the epileptic. The symptoms narrated by the evangelist are characteristic of this disease ("foaming at the mouth, grinding his teeth, and becoming rigid"). However the father of the epileptic presented his son to Jesus, describing the boy as one possessed by an evil spirit. The spirit would throw him into fits of convulsions and cast him down on the ground. The unfortunate youth would then roll about foaming at the mouth. It is indeed possible that in such a state of illness the evil one might insinuate himself and play a part. But even admitting that it was a case of epilepsy from which Jesus cured the youth reputed by his father as possessed by a devil, it is significant that Jesus effected the cure by ordering the "mute and deaf spirit" to "Come out of him and never enter him again" (cf. Mk 9:17-18). It is a reaffirmation of his mission and of his power to radically free the human person from spiritual evil.

Jesus made his mission clearly known—to free humanity from evil and first of all from sin, spiritual evil. This mission implies and explains his struggle with the evil spirit who is the prime author of evil in human history. As we read in the Gospels, Jesus repeatedly declared that this is the meaning of his work and of that of his apostles. We read in Luke: "I have observed Satan fall like lightning from the sky. Behold, I have given you the power to tread...upon the full force of the enemy and nothing will harm you" (Lk 10:18-19). According to Mark, after having appointed the Twelve, Jesus sent them forth "to preach and to have authority to drive out demons" (Mk 3:14-15). According to Luke the seventy-two disciples, after returning from their first mission, reported to Jesus, "Lord, even the demons are subject to us because of your name" (Lk 10:17).

This manifested the power of the Son of Man over sin and over the author of sin. Even the demons are subject to the name of Jesus, which means Savior. However, his saving power will have its definitive fulfillment in the sacrifice of the cross. The cross will mark the complete victory over Satan and sin. This is the Father's plan which his only-begotten Son fulfilled by becoming man, to conquer in weakness and to attain the glory of the resurrection and of life by means of the humiliation of the cross. The divine power shines forth even in this paradox, that power which can rightly be called the "power of the cross."

Even the victory over death, the dramatic consequence of sin, forms part of this power and belongs to the mission of the Savior of the world, manifested by "mighty deeds, wonders and signs." The victory over sin and over death marks the way of the messianic mission of Jesus from Nazareth to Calvary. Among the signs which particularly mark his journey toward the victory over death, the cases of people raised from the dead stand out. "The dead are raised" (Mt 11:5) was the answer Jesus gave to the messengers of John the Baptist (cf. Mt 11:3) when they questioned him whether he was the Messiah. Among the various dead people raised to life by Jesus, the case of Lazarus of Bethany merits special attention. His resurrection was a prelude to the cross and resurrection of Christ, which achieved the definitive victory over sin and death.

The evangelist John has left us a detailed description of this event. For us, let it suffice to refer to the final moment. Jesus asked that the stone which closed the tomb be removed ("Take away the stone"). The dead man's sister Martha observed that her brother had been dead for four days and that there would be a stench. Nevertheless Jesus cried out with a loud voice, "Lazarus, come out!" "And the dead man came out," the evangelist tells us (cf. Jn 11:38-43). This fact caused many of those present to believe in Jesus. Others, however, went to the representatives of the Sanhedrin to report the event. The chief priests and the Pharisees were alarmed, thinking of the possible reaction of the Roman occupying power ("the Romans will come and take away both our land and our nation," Jn 11:45-48). At that very moment Caiphas' famous words broke the silence of the Sanhedrin, "You know nothing, nor do you consider that it is better for you that one man should die instead of the people, so that the whole nation may not perish." The evangelist notes, "He did not say this on his own, but since he was high priest for that year, he prophesied." What was the nature of the prophecy? John gives us the Christian understanding of those words. "Jesus was to die for the nation, and not only for the nation, but also to gather into one the dispersed children of God" (cf. Jn 11:49-52).

As is evident, John's description of the resurrection of Lazarus also contains the essential indications regarding the salvific significance of this miracle. They are definitive indications, because it was then that the Sanhedrin decided to put Jesus to death (cf. Jn 11:53). It will be the redemptive death "for the nation" and "to gather into one the dispersed children of God," for the salvation of the world. But Jesus has already said that his death would become the definitive victory over death. On the occasion of the resurrection of Lazarus he assured Martha, "I am the resurrection and the life; whoever believes in me, even if he dies, shall live, and everyone who lives and believes in me shall never die" (Jn 11:25-26).

At the end of our reflection we turn once more to the text of St. Augustine, "If we consider now the deeds worked by Our Lord and Savior Jesus Christ, we see that the eyes of the blind, miraculously opened, were closed by death, and the limbs of the paralyzed, miraculously restored, were again immobilized in death. All that was temporarily cured in the mortal body, was in the end undone; but the soul that believed passed to eternal life. With this infirm man the Lord wished to give a great sign to the soul that would have believed, for the remission of whose sins he had come, and whose weaknesses he had healed by the humiliation of himself" (Augustine, *In Io, Ev. Tr.,* 17, 1).

Yes, all the "mighty deeds, wonders and signs" of Christ are for the purpose of revealing him as Messiah, as Son of God, for the revelation of him who alone has the power to free mankind from sin and from death, of him who is truly the Savior of the world.

General audience of November 25, 1987

Christ's Miracles—Salvific Signs

There is no doubt about the fact that in the Gospels Christ's miracles are presented as signs of the kingdom of God which has entered the history of mankind and of the world. "If I drive out demons by the Spirit of God, then the kingdom of God has come upon you," Jesus said (Mt 12:28). Whatever may be said or has been said on the subject of miracles (and this was answered by the Christian apologists), it is certain that one cannot separate from the authentic Gospel context the "mighty deeds, wonders and signs" attributed to Jesus, and even to his apostles and disciples "working in his name." In the apostolic preaching from which the Gospels principally derive, the early Christians heard the testimony of eyewitnesses about those extraordinary events which had occurred in the recent past and could therefore be checked under the critical-historical aspect. For that reason they were not surprised that they were included in the Gospel. Regardless of the objections of later times, one thing emerges as certain from the genuine sources of Christ's life and teaching. The apostles, the evangelists, and the whole primitive Church saw in each of those miracles the supreme power of Christ over nature and its laws. He who reveals God as Father, Creator and Lord of creation, when performing miracles by his own power, reveals himself as Son, one in being with the Father and equal to him in lordship over creation.

Some miracles, however, present other aspects which complement the basic significance of proof of the divine power of the Son of Man in the order of the economy of salvation.

Speaking of the first sign performed at Cana of Galilee, the evangelist John observed that by means of that sign Jesus "manifested his glory and his disciples believed in him" (Jn 2:11). The miracle therefore has a finality of faith, but it took place during a wedding feast. One may therefore say that, at least in the evangelist's intention, the "sign" serves to emphasize the whole divine economy of the covenant and of grace which is frequently expressed in the image of marriage in the books of the Old and New Testaments. The miracle at Cana of Galilee could therefore be related to the parable of the wedding feast which a king had prepared for his son, and with the eschatological kingdom of heaven which is similar to such a banquet (cf. Mt 22:2). Jesus' first miracle could be understood as a sign of this kingdom, especially since "Jesus' hour," that is, the hour of his passion and glorification, had not yet arrived (Jn 2:4; cf. 7:30; 8:20; 12:23-27; 13:1; 17:1). That "hour" was to be prepared by the preaching of the "Gospel of the kingdom" (cf. Mt 4:23; 9:35). The miracle obtained through Mary's intercession can be considered as a sign and a symbolic announcement of what was about to happen.

The miracle of the multiplication of the loaves which took place near Capernaum can be understood much more clearly as a sign of the economy of salvation. John linked it to the discourse held by Jesus the following day. He insisted on the necessity of acquiring through "faith in him who has sent me" (Jn 6:29), the food that does not perish. He spoke of himself as the true bread which "gives life to the world" (cf. Jn

6:33), and indeed as the one who gives his flesh "for the life of the world" (cf. Jn 6:51). The pre-announcement of the salvific passion and death is clear, not without reference to and preparation for the Eucharist which was to be instituted on the day before his passion, as the sacrament-bread of eternal life (cf. Jn 6:52-58).

The calming of the storm on the Lake of Genesareth can be understood as a sign of the constant presence of Christ in the barque of the Church, which is frequently exposed to the fury of the wind during stormy periods in the course of history. Awakened by the disciples, Jesus rebuked the wind and the sea and there was a great calm. Then he said to them, "Why are you terrified? Do you not yet have faith?" (Mk 4:40). In this, as in other events, one perceives Jesus' will to inculcate in the apostles and disciples faith in his operative and protective presence. This is true even in the most tempestuous periods of history in which the human spirit might possibly be tempted by a doubt about Jesus' divine assistance. Christian preaching and spirituality frequently interpret the miracle as a sign of Jesus' presence and a guarantee of trust in him on the part of Christians and of the Church.

Going toward his disciples walking on the water, Jesus offered them another sign of his presence, and gave an assurance of a constant watchfulness over his disciples and the Church. "Take courage, it is I, do not be afraid!" Jesus said to the apostles who had thought he was a ghost (cf. Mk 6:49-50; cf. also Mt 14:26-27; Jn 6:16-21). Mark notes the apostles' astonishment "because they had not understood the incident of the loaves and their hearts were hardened" (Mk 6:52). Matthew recounts Peter's question and his desire to get out of the boat and walk on the water toward Jesus. Matthew records Peter's fear and his cry for help when he saw that he was beginning to sink. Jesus saved him but rebuked him gently, "O you of little faith, why did you doubt?" (Mt 14:31). Matthew also adds that "those who were in the boat did him homage, saying, 'Truly, you are the Son of God'" (Mt 14:33).

The miraculous catches of fish are, for the apostles and the Church, the signs of the fruitfulness of their mission if they remain deeply united to Christ's saving power (cf. Lk 5:4-10; Jn 21:3-6). Indeed Luke includes in the narrative the fact that Peter threw himself at the knees of Jesus exclaiming, "Depart from me, Lord, for I am a sinful man" (Lk 5:8). Jesus replied, "Do not be afraid; from now on you will be catching men" (Lk 5:10). John in his turn follows up the catch of fish after the resurrection with Christ's command to Peter, "Feed my lambs, feed my sheep" (cf. Jn 21:15-17). It is a significant association.

So it can be said that Christ's miracles are a manifestation of the divine omnipotence in regard to creation, which is revealed in his messianic power over people and things. At the same time, they are signs which reveal the divine work of salvation. This is the economy of salvation which is introduced with Christ, is realized definitively in human history, and is thus inscribed in this visible world which is also a divine work. The people—like the apostles on the lake—seeing Christ's miracles ask themselves, "Who is this whom even the wind and the sea obey?" (Mt 4:41). Through these signs they are prepared to welcome the salvation offered to humanity by God in his Son.

This is the essential scope of all the miracles and signs wrought by Christ in the presence of his contemporaries, and of those miracles which, in the course of history, would be performed by his apostles and disciples in reference to the saving power of his name: "In the name of Jesus Christ of Nazareth, walk!" (Acts 3:6).

General audience of December 2, 1987

Christ's Miracles
Manifest Salvific Love

Christ's miracles recorded in the Gospels are signs of the divine omnipotence and of the salvific power of the Son of Man. They also reveal God's love for humanity—particularly for those who suffer, who are in need, who implore healing, pardon and compassion. They are therefore signs of the merciful love proclaimed in the Old and New Testaments (cf. Encyclical *Dives in Misericordia*). Especially the reading of the Gospel makes us understand and almost feel that Jesus' miracles have their source in God's loving and merciful heart which lives and beats in his human heart. Jesus performs them to overcome every kind of evil existing in the world: physical evil, moral evil which is sin, and finally him who is "the father of sin" in human history, namely, Satan.

The miracles are therefore "for man." In harmony with the redemptive finality of his mission, they are works of Jesus which re-established the good where evil had lurked, producing disorder and confusion. Those who accepted them and who were present at them were aware of this fact, so much so that, according to Mark, "they were exceedingly astonished and said, 'He has done all things well. He makes the deaf hear and the mute speak'" (Mk 7:37).

An attentive study of the Gospel texts reveal that no other motive than love for humanity, merciful love, explains the "mighty deeds and signs" of the Son of Man. In the Old Testament, Elijah made use of "fire from heaven" to confirm his power as a prophet and to punish incredulity (cf. 2 Kgs 1:10). When the Apostles James and John sought to induce Jesus to punish with "fire from heaven" a Samaritan village which had refused them hospitality, he definitely forbade them to make such a request. The evangelist mentions categorically that "he turned and rebuked them" (Lk 9:55). (Many codices including the Vulgate add, "You do not know of what manner of spirit you are; for the Son of Man came not to destroy men's lives but to save them.") Jesus never worked a miracle to punish anyone, not even the guilty.

The detail connected with Jesus' arrest in the garden of Gethsemane is significant in this regard. Peter was ready to defend his Master with the sword, and he even "struck the high priest's servant and cut off his right ear. The servant's name was Malchus" (Jn 18:10). But Jesus forbade Peter to use the sword. Indeed, Jesus "touched the servant's ear and healed him" (Lk 22:51). It is a further proof that Jesus did not perform miracles for his own defense. He told his followers that he could call upon his Father for "more than twelve legions of angels" (cf. Mt 26:53) to save him from the enemies who surrounded him. All that he does, even in working miracles, is done in close union with the Father. He does it for the sake of the kingdom of God and of the salvation of mankind. He does it for love.

Thus, at the beginning of his messianic mission, Jesus rejected the devil's suggestions to do "mighty works," for instance, to change stones into loaves of bread (cf. Mt 4:3-4). The power of the Messiah was granted to Jesus not for ostentatious display or vainglory. He who came "to bear witness to the truth" (Jn 18:37), who indeed is "the truth" (cf. Jn 14:6) always worked in absolute conformity with his salvific mission. All his "wonders and signs" expressed this conformity in the framework of the messianic mystery of God which was, as it were, concealed in the nature of a Son of Man, as is shown by the Gospels, especially that of Mark. The miracles nearly always radiated the divine power which the disciples and people sometimes grasped, to the extent that they recognized and exalted Christ as "Son of God." One likewise discovers in them the goodness, sincerity and simplicity which are the most visible qualities of the "Son of Man."

One notes Jesus' great simplicity in the very way he performed the miracles, as well as his humility, tact and delicacy of gesture. This is brought home to us by the words which accompanied the raising of the daughter of Jairus: "The child is not dead but asleep" (Mk 5:39), as if he wished to cloak the significance of what he was about to do. And then "he gave strict orders that no one should know this" (Mk 5:43). He did the same in other cases, for example, after the curing of the deaf mute (Mk 7:36), and after Peter's profession of faith (Mk 8:29-30).

In his healing of the deaf mute it is significant that Jesus took him off by himself "away from the crowd." There "looking up to heaven, he groaned." This "groan" seems to be a sign of compassion and, at the same time, a prayer. The word *ephphatha* (Be opened!) had the effect of "opening the ears" and removing "the speech impediment" of the deaf mute (cf. 7:33-35).

If Jesus performed some of his miracles on the sabbath, he did so not to violate the sacred character of the day dedicated to God, but to demonstrate that this holy day is marked in a particular way by God's salvific work. "My Father is at work until now, so I am at work" (Jn 5:17). This work is for the good of humanity. Therefore it is not contrary to the holiness of the sabbath, but underlines it: "The sabbath was made for man, and not man for the sabbath! Therefore the Son of Man is lord even of the sabbath" (Mk 2:27-28).

If we accept the Gospel account of Jesus' miracles—and there is no reason not to accept it other than prejudice against the supernatural—one cannot call into doubt a unique logic which links together all those signs and demonstrates their derivation from God's salvific economy. They serve to reveal his love for us, that merciful love which overcomes evil with good, as is shown by the very presence and action of Jesus Christ in the world. Inasmuch as they are inserted into this economy, the "wonders and signs" are an object of our faith in the plan of God's salvation and in the mystery of redemption effected by Christ.

As facts, the miracles belong to evangelical history, and the accounts contained in the Gospels are as reliable as, and even more so than, those contained in other historical works. It is clear that the real obstacle to their acceptance as facts of history and of faith is the anti-supernatural prejudice already referred to. It is a prejudice of those who would limit God's power or restrict it to the natural order of things, as though God were to subject himself to his own laws. But this concept clashes with the most elementary philosophical and theological idea of God—infinite, subsisting and omnipotent Being—who has no limits except in regard to non-existence and therefore the absurd.

One spontaneously notes that this infinity in being and power is also infinity in love. This is demonstrated by the miracles inserted into the economy of the Incarnation and redemption, as "signs" of the merciful love with which God sent his Son into the world "for us men and for our salvation," generous with us even unto death. *Sic dilexit!* (cf. Jn 3:16).

To such a great love let there not be lacking the generous response of our gratitude, expressed in the consistent witness of our lives.

General audience of December 9, 1987

Miracles Are a Call to Faith

To confirm his messianic mission and the coming of the kingdom of God, Jesus wrought "wonders and signs" which were directed and closely linked to the call of faith. In relation to the miracle, this call has two forms. Faith precedes the miracle and indeed is a condition for its accomplishment. Faith is also an effect of the miracle, because it engenders faith in the souls of those who are its recipients or witnesses.

It is known that faith is a human response to the word of divine revelation. The miracle is organically linked with this word of God the revealer. It is a "sign" of his presence and action—a particularly striking sign. All this is a sufficient explanation of the particular link which exists between Christ's "miracles-signs" and faith, a link so clearly outlined in the Gospels.

The Gospels contain a long series of texts in which the call to faith appears as an indispensable and systematic factor of Christ's miracles.

To head the list one must mention the pages concerning the Mother of Christ: how she acted at Cana of Galilee, how she acted earlier, and especially, at the moment of the annunciation. Precisely here we find the culminating point of her adherence to the faith, which will find its confirmation in Elizabeth's words during the visitation: "Blessed are you who believed that what was spoken to you by the Lord would be fulfilled" (Lk 1:45). Yes, Mary believed as none other, being convinced that "nothing is impossible for God" (cf. Lk 1:37).

At Cana of Galilee her faith anticipated, in a certain sense, the hour of Christ's self-revelation. Through her intercession he performed that first miracle-sign, thanks to which Jesus' disciples "believed in him" (Jn 2:11). The Second Vatican Council teaches that Mary constantly precedes the People of God on the pathways of the faith (cf. *LG* 58 and 63; Encyclical *Redemptoris Mater,* 5-6). We can say that the first foundation of this assertion is already found in the Gospel which gives an account of the "miracles-signs" in Mary and through Mary in regard to the call to faith.

This call is repeated many times. When Jairus, one of the officials of the synagogue, came to ask for his daughter's restoration to life, Jesus said to him, "Do not be afraid; just have faith" (and he said "do not be afraid" because some had advised Jairus not to bother Jesus) (Mk 5:36).

When the father of the epileptic asked for his son's cure, he said, "But if you can do anything...help us." Jesus replied, "'If you can!' Everything is possible to one who has faith." Then comes the fine act of faith in Christ by this sorely tried man, "I do believe, help my unbelief!" (cf. Mk 9:22-24).

Finally we recall the well-known conversation of Jesus with Mary before the raising of Lazarus, "I am the resurrection and the life.... Do you believe this.... Yes, Lord, I believe..." (cf. Jn 11:25-27).

The same link between the "miracle-sign" and faith is confirmed in the opposite sense by other facts of a negative kind. Let us recall some of them. In Mark's Gospel we read that Jesus of Nazareth "could not perform any mighty deed there, apart from curing a few sick people by laying his hands on them. He was amazed by their lack of faith" (Mk 6:5-6).

We know the gentle rebuke that Jesus once addressed to Peter, "Man of little faith, why did you doubt?" This occurred when Peter began by setting out courageously on the waves to go to Jesus. Then, because of the strong wind, he became afraid and began to sink (cf. Mk 14:29-31).

More than once Jesus emphasized that the miracle he worked is linked to faith. "Your faith has saved you," he said to the woman who had been suffering hemorrhages for twelve years and who came up behind him, touched the hem of his garment and was healed (cf. Mt 9:20-22; and also Lk 8:48; Mk 5:34).

Jesus spoke similar words when he healed the blind Bartimaeus who was seated by the roadside leading from Jericho. On hearing that Jesus was passing by, Bartimaeus cried out insistently, "Jesus, son of David, have pity on me" (cf. Mk 10:46-52). According to Mark, Jesus replied, "Go your way; your faith has saved you." Luke is more precise: "Have sight; your faith has saved you" (Lk 18:42).

Jesus made a similar statement to the Samaritan cured of leprosy (cf. Lk 17:19).

Two other blind men besought Jesus for the restoration of their sight. Jesus asked them, "'Do you believe that I can do this?' 'Yes, Lord,' they said. Then Jesus touched their eyes and said to them, 'Let it be done for you according to your faith'" (Mt 9:28-29).

Particularly touching is the case of the Canaanite woman who kept on asking Jesus to help her daughter who was "cruelly tormented by a demon." When she prostrated herself before Jesus to beg his assistance, he replied, "It is not right to take the food of the children and throw it to the dogs." (This was a reference to the ethnic diversity between the Israelites and the people of Canaan, which Jesus, Son of David, could not ignore in his ordinary behavior. But he referred to it from a methodological viewpoint in order to arouse faith.) Then the woman intuitively made an unusual act of faith and humility. She said, "Please, Lord, for even the dogs eat the scraps that fall from the table of their masters." Because of these words, so humble, courteous, and trusting, Jesus replied, "O woman, great is your faith! Let it be done for you as you wish" (cf. Mt 15:21-28).

It is an event difficult to forget, especially if one thinks of the numerous "Canaanites" of every time, country, color and social condition, who stretch out their hands to ask for understanding and help in their needs!

We should note that the gospel narrative continually stresses the fact that when Jesus "sees their faith," he works the miracle. This is clearly stated in the case of the paralytic who was lowered at his feet through an opening in the roof (cf. Mk 2:5; Mt 9:2; Lk 5:20). However, the same may be said in so many other cases recounted by the evangelists. The element of faith is indispensable. But once that is verified, Jesus' heart is prompt to hear the requests of those in need who turn to him for assistance through his divine power.

Once again we observe, as we said at the beginning, that the miracle is a sign of God's power and love which save all men and women in Christ. For this very reason, however, it is at the same time a call to faith. It should lead to belief, both the one for whom the miracle is worked and the witnesses of the miracle.

This holds good for the apostles themselves, from the very first sign Jesus performed at Cana of Galilee; it was then that they "believed in him" (Jn 2:11). Later when he miraculously multiplied the loaves in the vicinity of Capernaum, an event linked with the preannouncement of the Eucharist, the evangelist notes that "from that moment many of his disciples returned to their former way of life and no longer accompanied him," since they were unable to accept what appeared to them "a hard saying." Jesus then asked the Twelve, "Do you also want to leave?" Peter answered, "Master, to whom shall we go? You have the words of eternal life. We have come to believe and are convinced that you are the Holy One of God" (cf. Jn 6:66-69). The principle of faith is therefore fundamental in the relationship with Christ, both as a condition for obtaining the miracle and as the purpose for which it is performed. This is set out clearly at the end of John's Gospel, where we read, "Jesus did many other signs in the presence of his disciples that are not written in this book. But these are written that you may believe that Jesus is the Messiah, the Son of God, and that through this belief you may have life in his name" (Jn 20:30-31).

General audience of December 16, 1987

Miracles Manifest
the Supernatural Order

Speaking of the miracles which Jesus performed during his earthly ministry, St. Augustine, in an interesting text, interprets them as signs of God's saving power and love and as incentives to raise our minds to the kingdom of heavenly things. "The miracles worked by our Lord Jesus Christ," St. Augustine writes, "are divine works which raise the human mind above visible things to understand what is divine" *(In Io. Ev. Tr.,* 24, 1,).

Connected with this thought is the reaffirmation of the close link of Jesus' "miracles-signs" with the call to faith. These miracles demonstrate the existence of the supernatural order, which is the object of faith. Those who observed them and particularly those who experienced them were made aware as if by the touch of a hand that the natural order does not exhaust the whole of reality. The universe in which we live is not limited merely to the range of things accessible to the senses and even to the intellect itself conditioned by sense knowledge. The miracle is a sign that this order is surpassed by the "power from on high," and is therefore also subject to it. This "power from on high" (cf. Lk 24:49), namely, God himself, is above the entire natural order. It directs this order and at the same time it makes known that—through this order and superior to it—human destiny is the kingdom of God. Christ's miracles are signs of this kingdom.

Miracles are not opposed to the forces and laws of nature. They merely imply a certain empirical suspension of their ordinary function and not their annulment. Indeed, the miracles described in the Gospel indicate the existence of a Power superior to the forces and laws of nature, but which at the same time operates according to the demands of nature itself, even though surpassing its actual normal capacity. Is not this what happens, for example, in every miraculous cure? The potentiality of the forces of nature is actuated by divine intervention which extends this potential beyond the sphere of its normal capacity of action. This does not annul or frustrate the causality which God has communicated to created things, nor does it violate the natural laws established by God himself and inscribed in the structure of creation. But it exalts and in a certain way ennobles the capacity to operate or even to receive the effects of the operation of another, as happens precisely in the cures described by the Gospel.

The truth about creation is the first and fundamental truth of our faith. It is not, however, the only one nor the supreme one. Faith teaches us that the work of creation is contained within the ambit of God's plan which, according to his intention, goes well beyond the limits of creation itself. Creation—particularly the human creature called into existence in the visible world—is open to an eternal destiny, which is fully revealed in Jesus Christ. Even in Christ the work of creation is completed by the work of salvation. Salvation means a new creation (cf. 2 Cor 5:17; Gal 6:15), a creation according to the measure of the Creator's original design. Salvation means a re-establishment of what God had made and which in human history had suffered the disorder and "corruption" following upon sin.

Christ's miracles enter into the project of the "new creation" and are therefore linked to the order of salvation. They are the salvific signs which call to conversion and to faith, and in this way, to the renewal of the world that is subject to "corruption" (cf. Rom 8:19-21).

Therefore they do not stop at the ontological order of creation (*creatio*), which indeed they touch and set right, but they enter into the soteriological order of the new creation *(re-creatio totius universi)*, of which they are the factors and to which they bear witness as "signs."

The soteriological order is rooted in the Incarnation. The "miracles-signs" of which the Gospels speak also have their foundation in the same reality of the God-Man. This reality-mystery embraces and surpasses all the miraculous happenings connected with Christ's messianic mission. It may be said that the Incarnation is the "miracle of miracles," the radical and permanent "miracle" of the new order of creation. God's entrance into the dimension of creation is effected in the reality of the Incarnation in a unique way. To the eyes of faith it becomes a sign incomparably superior to all the other miraculous signs of the divine presence and action in the world. All these other signs are rooted in the reality of the Incarnation; they radiate its power of attraction and bear witness to it. They repeat to believers what is written by the evangelist John at the end of the prologue on the Incarnation, "We saw his glory, the glory as of the Father's only Son, full of grace and truth" (Jn 1:14).

The Incarnation is the fundamental sign to which are linked all the signs bearing witness to the disciples and to humanity that "the kingdom of God has come" (cf. Lk 11:20). Still, there is an ultimate and definitive sign, to which Jesus alluded when quoting the prophet Jonah: "Just as Jonah was in the belly of the whale three days and three nights, so will the Son of Man be in the heart of the earth three days and three nights" (Mt 12:40). It is the sign of the resurrection.

Jesus prepared the apostles for this definitive sign, but he did so gradually and tactfully, recommending them to be discreet "until a certain time." There is a particularly clear reference after the transfiguration on the mountain: "As they were coming down from the mountain, he charged them not to relate what they had seen to anyone, except when the Son of Man had risen from the dead" (Mk 9:9). One may ask the reason for this gradualness. To this one may reply that Jesus well knew how complicated the situation might become if the apostles and the other disciples had begun to discuss the resurrection. They were not yet sufficiently prepared to understand it, as appears from the comment of the evangelist himself in regard to the recommendation just quoted: "They kept the matter to themselves, questioning what rising from the dead meant" (Mk 9:10). Besides, it can be said that the resurrection from the dead, although enunciated and announced, was at the summit of the messianic secret. Jesus wished to maintain secrecy throughout the entire course of his life and mission, until the moment of the final fulfillment and revelation which were verified precisely with the "miracle of miracles," the resurrection, which, according to St. Paul, is the foundation of our faith (cf. 1 Cor 15:12-19).

After the resurrection, ascension and pentecost, the "miracles-signs" performed by Christ were continued by the apostles, and later by the saints from generation to generation. The Acts of the Apostles offer us numerous testimonies concerning miracles worked "in the name of Jesus Christ" by Peter (cf. Acts 3:1-8; 5:15; 9:32-41), Stephen (Acts 6:8) and Paul (e.g., Acts 14:8-10). We also see it in the lives of the saints, the history of the Church and in particular, the processes for the canonization of the Servants of God. These constitute a documentation which, when submitted to the most searching examination of historical criticism and of medical science, confirms the existence of the "power from on high" which operates in the natural order and surpasses it. It is a question of miraculous signs carried out from apostolic times until the present day. Their essential purpose is to indicate that the human person is destined and called to the kingdom of God. These signs therefore confirm in different ages and in the most varied circumstances the truth of the Gospel, and demonstrate the saving power of Christ who does not cease to call people (through the Church) on the path of faith. This saving power of the God-Man is manifested also when the "miracles-signs" are performed through the intercession of individuals, of saints, of devout people—just as the first sign at Cana of Galilee was worked through the intercession of the mother of Christ.

General audience of January 13, 1988

THE CHURCH'S FAITH
IN JESUS CHRIST

Jesus Christ Is True Man

The mystery of Jesus Christ as true God and true man is central to our faith and is the key truth of our Christological reflections. We propose to seek the basis of this truth in Sacred Scripture, especially in the Gospels, and in Christian Tradition.

We have already seen that in the Gospels Jesus Christ revealed himself as God the Son, especially when he said, "I and the Father are one" (Jn 10:30); when he referred to himself the name of God, "I Am" (cf. Jn 8:58), and the divine attributes; and when he claimed that "all power has been given (him) in heaven and on earth" (Mt 28:18). This includes the power to pronounce final judgment on all people; the power over the law (cf. Mt 5:22, 28, 32, 34, 39, 44) which comes from God and derives its binding force from him; and finally the power to forgive sins (cf. Jn 20:22-23). Since he received from the Father the power to pronounce the final judgment on the world (cf. Jn 5:22), Jesus came into the world "to seek and to save what was lost" (Lk 19:10).

To confirm his divine power over creation, Jesus worked miracles which are signs that the kingdom of God has come into the world together with him.

However, this Jesus who, by means of what he did and taught, bore witness to himself as Son of God, at the same time revealed himself as true man. The entire New Testament, and in particular the Gospels testify unequivocally to this truth of which Jesus was most clearly conscious. The apostles and evangelists also recognized it and transmitted it without the slightest shadow of doubt. In the present reflection we will collect and outline at least briefly the Gospel data on this truth, always in connection with what we have previously said about Christ as true God.

This way of presenting the true humanity of the Son of God is absolutely essential today, given the widespread tendency to regard Jesus as only a man, an unusual extraordinary man, but always and merely a man. This tendency characteristic of modern times is in a certain way the antithesis of the Docetism of the early centuries of Christianity. According to the Docetists, Jesus Christ only appeared to be a man; he had the appearance of a man, but he was solely God.

Faced with these opposite tendencies, the Church firmly professes and proclaims the truth that Christ is the God-Man, true God and true man. He is the one divine Person of the Word in two natures, divine and human, as the catechism teaches. It is a profound mystery of our faith, faceted with so many lights.

Biblical references to Christ's humanity

The Bible has many clear texts on Christ's true humanity. We should like to list them, in order to explain them in later reflections.

The Incarnation is the point of departure. "The Word became flesh," as we profess in the creed. This truth is more strikingly expressed in the prologue of John's Gospel: "And the Word became flesh and made his dwelling among us" (Jn

1:14). The Greek word for flesh is *sarx,* which denotes man as he actually is, with his body, and therefore its insecurity, its weakness, and in a certain sense its transitoriness ("All flesh is grass," as we read in the Book of Isaiah 40:6).

Jesus Christ is truly a man in this sense. He took flesh and a human nature from his mother Mary, the Virgin of Nazareth. If St. Ignatius of Antioch calls Jesus *sarkophoros (Ad Smyrn.,* 5), this is a delicate indication of his human birth of a woman, who gave him human flesh. St. Paul had said that "God sent his Son, born of a woman" (Gal 4:4).

The evangelist Luke spoke of this birth of a woman when he described the events of the night of Bethlehem: "While they were there, the time came for her to have her child, and she gave birth to her first-born son. She wrapped him in swaddling clothes and laid him in a manger" (Lk 2:6-7). The same evangelist tells us that on the eighth day after Jesus' birth, the child was circumcised and was "given the name Jesus" (Lk 2:21). On the fortieth day he was presented as the firstborn in the Temple of Jerusalem, according to the Mosaic law (cf. Lk 2:22-24).

Moreover, like every child, "he grew and became strong, filled with wisdom" (Lk 2:40). "Jesus advanced in wisdom and age and favor before God and man" (Lk 2:52).

We see him as an adult, as he is more frequently presented in the Gospels. As true man, a man of flesh, Jesus experienced fatigue, hunger and thirst. We read, "He fasted for forty days and forty nights, and afterward he was hungry" (Mt 4:2). And elsewhere, "Jesus, tired from his journey, sat down there at the well.... A woman of Samaria came to draw water. Jesus said to her, 'Give me to drink'" (Jn 4:6-7).

Jesus had a body subject to fatigue and suffering, a mortal body, a body that finally underwent the torture of martyrdom through the scourging, crowning with thorns, and eventually crucifixion. During the terrible agony when dying on the cross, Jesus uttered the words, "I thirst" (Jn 19:28). These words contain a final, sorrowful and moving expression of the truth of his humanity.

Only a true man could have suffered as Jesus suffered on Golgotha. Only a true man could have died as Jesus truly died. This death was observed by many eyewitnesses, not merely from among his friends and disciples. St. John's Gospel tells us that the soldiers "came to Jesus, and seeing that he was already dead, did not break his legs, but one soldier thrust his lance into his side, and immediately blood and water flowed out" (19:33-34).

"He was born of the Virgin Mary, suffered under Pontius Pilate, was crucified, died and was buried." In these words of the Apostles' Creed, the Church professes the truth of Jesus' birth and death. The truth of the resurrection is attested to immediately afterward in the words, "the third day he rose again from the dead."

The resurrection confirms in a new way that Jesus is truly man. The Word was born in time "by becoming flesh," and in the resurrection he returned to life in his own human body. Only a true man could suffer and die on the cross, and only a true man could rise from the dead. To rise again means to return to life in the body. Although transformed, endowed with new qualities and powers, and also glorified (as at Christ's ascension and in the future resurrection of the dead), it is a truly human body. The risen Christ made contact with the apostles; they saw him, looked at him and touched the wounds which remained after the crucifixion. He not only spoke to them and stayed with them, but he also accepted some of their food. "They gave him a piece of baked fish; he took it and ate it in front of them" (Lk 24:42-43). Finally, it was in this body, risen and glorified, but always the body of a true man, that Christ ascended into heaven, to sit "at the right hand of the Father."

Therefore, he is true God and true man, not a man merely in appearance, not a phantasm, but a true man. This is how the apostles and the group of believers of the early Church knew him. This is the testimony that they passed on to us.

We note that there is no opposition in Christ between what is divine and what is human. If man, from the very beginning, was made in the image and likeness of God (cf. Gen 1:27; 5:1), and therefore what is human can also manifest what is divine, how much more so could this be verified in Christ. He revealed his divinity through his humanity, through a genuinely human life. His humanity served to reveal his divinity—his Person of the Word-Son.

At the same time, as God the Son, he was not on that account "less man." To reveal himself as God, he was not obliged to be "less" man. Indeed, by this very fact he was "fully" man, for in assuming human nature in the unity of the divine Person of the Word, he achieved the fullness of human perfection. This is an anthropological dimension of Christology to which we must return later.

General audience of January 27, 1988

Like Us in All Things Except Sin

Jesus Christ is true man. We wish to continue the previous reflection on this theme, which is a fundamental truth of our faith. This faith is based on the word of Christ himself, confirmed by the witness of the apostles and disciples. It was transmitted from generation to generation in the Church's teaching: "We believe...true God and true man...not a phantasm, but the one and only Son of God" (Council of Lyons II, *DS* 852).

More recently the same doctrine was recalled by the Second Vatican Council, which emphasized the new relationship which the Word, on taking flesh and becoming man like us, has initiated with every human being. "By his Incarnation the Son of God has united himself in some fashion with every man. He worked with human hands, he thought with a human mind, acted by human choice and loved with a human heart. Born of the Virgin Mary, he has truly been made one of us, like us in all things except sin" *(GS* 22).

In the previous reflection we sought to show Christ's likeness to us, which derives from the fact that he is true man. "The Word made flesh"; flesh (*sarx*) indicates man precisely as a corporeal being (*sarkikos*), who comes into being through being born of a woman (cf. Gal 4:4). In his corporeal nature Jesus of Nazareth, like every man, experienced fatigue, hunger and thirst. His body was vulnerable, subject to suffering, and sensitive to physical pain. It was precisely in this flesh (*sarx*) that he was subjected to dreadful tortures and was eventually crucified. "He was crucified, died and was buried."

The conciliar text quoted above completes this picture still more when it says: "He worked with human hands, he thought with a human mind, acted by human choice and loved with a human heart" *(GS* 22).

Jesus' psychological life

Today we shall pay particular attention to this last statement which brings us to the heart of Jesus' psychological life. He truly experienced human feelings of joy, sadness, anger, wonder and love. For example, we read that "Jesus rejoiced in the Holy Spirit" (Lk 10:21). He wept over Jerusalem. "He saw the city and wept over it, saying, 'If this day you only knew what makes for peace'" (Lk 19:41-42). He also wept after the death of his friend Lazarus. "When Jesus saw [Mary] weeping and the Jews who had come with her weeping, he became perturbed and deeply troubled, and said, 'Where have you laid him?' They said to him, 'Sir, come and see.' And Jesus wept" (Jn 11:33-35).

His feelings of sorrow were especially intense in the Garden of Gethsemane. We read: "He took with him Peter, James and John and began to be troubled and distressed. Then Jesus said to them, 'My soul is sorrowful even to death'" (Mk 14:33-34; cf. also Mt 26:37). In Luke we read: "He was in such agony and he prayed so fervently that his sweat became like drops of blood falling on the ground" (Lk 22:44). This was a fact of the psycho-physical order which once again attests to Jesus' true humanity.

We read also of Jesus' anger. When on the sabbath he cured the man with the withered hand, Jesus first of all asked those present, "'Is it lawful to do good on the sabbath rather than to do evil?' But they remained silent. Looking around at them with anger and grieved at their hardness of heart, he said to the man, 'Stretch out your hand.' He stretched it out and his hand was restored" (Mk 3:4-5).

Similarly in the case of the buyers and sellers who were driven out of the Temple, Matthew writes: "He drove out all those engaged in selling and buying there. He overturned the tables of the money changers and the seats of those who were selling doves. And he said to them, 'It is written: "My house shall be a house of prayer," but you have made it a den of thieves'" (Mt 21:12-13; cf. Mk 11:15).

Elsewhere we read that Jesus "was amazed." "He was amazed at their lack of faith" (Mk 6:6). Or he was moved to admiration, as when he said, "Notice how the flowers grow...not even Solomon in all his splendor was dressed like one of them" (Lk 12:27). He also admired the faith of the Canaanite woman: "O woman, great is your faith!" (Mt 15:28).

Above all, the Gospels show that Jesus was a person who loved. We read that during his conversation with the young man who had come to ask him what he ought to do in order to enter the kingdom of heaven, "Jesus, looking at him, loved him" (Mk 10:21). The evangelist John writes that "Jesus loved Martha and her sister and Lazarus" (Jn 11:5), and John called himself "the disciple...whom Jesus loved" (Jn 13:23).

Jesus loved children. "And people were bringing children to him that he might touch them.... He embraced them and blessed them, placing his hands on them" (Mk 10:13-16). When he proclaimed the commandment of love, he referred to the love with which he himself loved. "This is my commandment: love one another as I love you" (Jn 15:12).

Christ's passion, especially the agony on the cross, constitutes the zenith of the love with which Jesus, "having loved his own who were in the world, loved them unto the end" (Jn 13:1). "Greater love has no man than this, that he lay down his life for his friends" (Jn 15:13). At the same time this is also the nadir of the sorrow and abandonment which he experienced during his earthly life. The words *"Eloi, Eloi, lema sabactani.... My God, my God, why have you forsaken me?"* (Mk 15:34) will forever remain a piercing expression of this abandonment. They are words which Jesus took from Psalm 22 (verse 2), and they express the excruciating agony of his soul and body, including the mysterious sensation of being momentarily abandoned by God. It was the most dramatically agonizing moment of the whole passion!

Jesus therefore became truly similar to men, by assuming the condition of a servant, as the letter to the Philippians expresses it (cf. 2:7). However, the Letter to the Hebrews, speaking of him as "high priest of the good things that have come to be" (Heb 9:11), confirms and clarifies that this is not a "priest who is unable to sympathize with our weaknesses, but one who has been similarly tested in every way, yet without sin" (cf. Heb 4:15). Truly he "knew not sin," even though St. Paul will say that "for our sake God made him to be sin who did not know sin, so that in him we might become the righteousness of God" (2 Cor 5:21).

The same Jesus could issue the challenge, "Can any of you charge me with sin?" (Jn 8:46). The faith of the Church is expressed as follows: "He was conceived, born and died without sin." This was proclaimed, in harmony with the whole of Tradition, by the Council of Florence (Decree for the Jacobites, *DS* 1347). Jesus "was conceived, was born and died without sin." He is the truly just and holy man.

We repeat with the New Testament, with the creed, and with Vatican Council II that Jesus Christ "has truly been made one of us, like us in all things except sin." It is precisely thanks to this likeness that "Christ, the final Adam, by the revelation of the mystery of the Father and his love, fully reveals man to man himself and makes his supreme calling clear" *(GS* 22).

Through this observation, Vatican Council II gives yet again the answer to the fundamental question which forms the title of St. Anselm's celebrated treatise, *Cur Deus homo?* It is a question of the intellect that explores the mystery of God the Son, who became true man "for us men and for our salvation," as we profess in the Nicene-Constantinopolitan Creed.

Christ has fully revealed man to himself precisely by the fact that "he knew not sin," for sin does not enrich man. Quite the contrary—it cheapens him, it diminishes him and it deprives him of the fullness which is his due (cf. *GS* 13). The rescue and the salvation of fallen man is the fundamental reason for the Incarnation.

General audience of February 3, 1988

Jesus, a Man in Solidarity with All Humanity

Jesus Christ, true man, is "like us in all things but sin," as we saw in our previous reflection. Sin is essentially excluded in him who, being true man, is also true God *(verus homo, not merus homo)*.

Christ's whole earthly life and the entire unfolding of his mission bear witness to the truth of his absolute impeccability. He himself issued the challenge: "Can any of you charge me with sin?" (Jn 8:46). A man without sin, during his whole life Jesus Christ was engaged in a struggle against sin, beginning with Satan who is the father of lies in human history "from the beginning" (cf. Jn 8:44). This struggle began on the threshold of Jesus' messianic mission, in the moment of the temptation (cf. Mk 1:13; Mt 4:1-11; Lk 4:1-13). It reached its apex in the cross and resurrection. It is a struggle which ends in victory.

This struggle against sin and its roots did not alienate Jesus from people. On the contrary, it brought him closer to them, to every individual. During his earthly life Jesus was accustomed to show himself particularly close to those who were regarded by others as sinners. We see it in many texts of the Gospel.

Under this aspect the comparison which Jesus made between himself and John the Baptist is important. He said, "John came neither eating nor drinking, and they said, 'Look, he is a glutton and a drunkard, a friend of tax collectors and sinners'" (Mt 11:18-19). The polemical character of these words is evident in regard to those who first of all criticized John the Baptist, a solitary prophet and severe ascetic who baptized at the Jordan. Then they criticized Jesus because he moved about and worked among the people. However, these words also reveal the truth of Jesus' mode of being, of feeling and of behavior in regard to sinners.

He was criticized for being a friend of public sinners and tax collectors, who lived by extortion and were regarded as non-observers of the law (cf. Mt 5:46; 9:11; 18:17). Jesus did not absolutely reject this judgment. Its truth is confirmed by many episodes recorded in the Gospels, though without any suggestion of Jesus turning a blind eye or remaining silent. There is the case of Zacchaeus, the chief tax collector of Jericho. Jesus invited himself to his home. Jesus told him, "Zacchaeus, come down quickly, for today I must stay at your house." Being small in stature, Zacchaeus had climbed a tree to get a better view of Jesus who was passing by. The tax collector came down full of joy and offered Jesus the hospitality of his home. He heard Jesus say to him, "Today salvation has come to this house because this man too is a descendant of Abraham. For the Son of Man has come to seek and to save what was lost" (cf. Lk 19:1-10). This text highlights not only Jesus' familiarity with tax collectors and sinners, but also the reason why he sought their company: their salvation.

A similar event is linked to the name of Levi, son of Alphaeus. This was all the more significant inasmuch as this man, whom Jesus had seen "seated at the customs post," was called to become one of the apostles. "Follow me," Jesus said to him. And he got up and followed him. He is listed among the Twelve under the name of Matthew, and we know that he is the author of one of the Gospels. The evangelist Mark tells us that Jesus "was at table in his house," and that "many tax collectors and sinners sat with Jesus and his disciples" (cf. Mk 2:13-15). In this case also "some scribes who were Pharisees" remonstrated with his disciples. But Jesus said to them, "Those who are well do not need a physician, but the sick do. I did not come to call the righteous but sinners" (Mk 2:17).

To be seated at table with others—including "tax collectors and sinners"—is a way of being human which one notes in Jesus from the very beginning of his messianic activity. One of the first occasions on which he manifested his messianic power was at the marriage feast of Cana in Galilee, at which he was present together with his mother and disciples (cf. Jn 2:1-12). Later, moreover, Jesus was accustomed to accept invitations to table, not merely from the tax collectors, but also from the Pharisees, who were his fiercest adversaries. For example, we read in Luke, "A Pharisee invited him to dine with him, and he entered the Pharisee's house and reclined at table" (Lk 7:36).

During this meal, something happened that throws a new light on Jesus' attitude to poor humanity, comprising so many sinners whom the presumed righteous people despise and condemn. A woman known in the city as a sinner was among those present. Weeping, she kissed Jesus' feet and anointed them with ointment. A discussion began between Jesus and his host, during which Jesus showed that an essential link exists between forgiveness of sins and love inspired by faith. "Her many sins have been forgiven, for she loved much.... Then he said to her, 'Your sins are forgiven...your faith has saved you; go in peace'" (cf. Lk 7:36-50).

This is not the only case of its kind. There is another dramatic case, that of a woman caught in adultery (cf. Jn 8:1-11). This event also, like the previous one, explains in what sense Jesus was "a friend of tax collectors and sinners." He said to the woman, "Go, and do not sin again." He who was "like us in all things but sin," was shown to be close to sinners in order to free them from sin. However, he aimed at this messianic purpose in a completely new way compared with the severity reserved for sinners by those who judged them on the basis of the Old Law. Jesus worked in the spirit of a great love for every human person, on the basis of the profound solidarity which he had for those created in the image and likeness of God (cf. Gen 1:27; 5:1).

What is this solidarity? It is the manifestation of the love which has its source in God himself. The Son of God came into the world to reveal this love. He already revealed it by the fact that he himself became man, one of us. This union with us on the part of Jesus Christ, true man, is the fundamental expression of his solidarity with every human person. It speaks eloquently of the love with which God himself has loved each and every person. Love is confirmed here in an entirely special way—one who loves seeks to share everything with the beloved. It is precisely for this reason that the Son of God became man. Isaiah had prophesied of him, "Yet it was our infirmities that he bore, our sufferings that he endured" (cf. Mt 8:17; Is 53:4). Jesus thus shared the same existential condition with every son and daughter of the human race. In this he also revealed the existential dignity of each and every human person. The Incarnation is an ineffable "re-evaluation" of the human person and of humanity!

This "love-solidarity" stands out in the entire earthly life and mission of the Son of Man, especially in regard to those who suffer under the weight of misery, whether physical or moral. At the end of his journey there will be the "giving of his life as a ransom for many" (cf. Mk 10:45), the redemptive sacrifice of the cross. However, on the way leading to this supreme sacrifice, Jesus' entire earthly life manifested his solidarity with mankind. He summed this up in his own words:

"The Son of Man came not to be served but to serve, and to give his life as a ransom for many" (Mk 10:45). He was a child like every human child. He worked with his hands alongside Joseph of Nazareth, just as all people work (cf. Encyclical *Laborem Exercens* 26). He was a son of Israel; he shared in the culture, tradition, hope and suffering of his people. He, too, experienced what often happens in the life of those called to some mission: misunderstanding and betrayal by one of those whom he himself had chosen as his apostles to continue his work. For this he experienced a profound sorrow (cf. Jn 13:21).

When the moment drew near in which he was "to give his life as a ransom for many" (Mt 20:28), Jesus voluntarily offered himself (cf. Jn 10:18), thus consummating the mystery of his solidarity in the sacrifice. The Roman governor found no other words to describe him before his assembled accusers except "Behold the man!" (Jn 19:5).

Pilate was unaware of the mystery but not insensitive to the attraction which issued from Jesus even in that moment. His words tell us everything about Christ's human reality. Jesus is the man; a true man who, like us in all things but sin, became a victim for sin and entered into solidarity with all, even to death on a cross.

General audience of February 10, 1988

Jesus Christ Emptied Himself

"Behold the man!" (Jn 19:5). In last week's reflection we recalled these words of Pilate when he presented Jesus to the high priests and guards, after having had him scourged and before pronouncing the definitive sentence of death on a cross. Jesus is the symbol of suffering humanity, covered with wounds, crowned with thorns, clothed in purple, mocked and smitten by the soldiers and already close to death.

"Behold the man!" This expression contains in a certain sense the whole truth about Christ, true man; about him who "is like us in all things but sin"; about him who "has united himself in some fashion with every man" (cf. *GS* 22). They called him the "friend of tax collectors and sinners." Precisely as a victim for sin, Jesus entered into solidarity with all humanity including "sinners," even to death on a cross. Precisely in this condition of victim to which Jesus was reduced, a final aspect of his humanity stands out. This aspect must be accepted and profoundly meditated on in the light of the mystery of his self-emptying *(kenosis).* According to St. Paul, "though he was in the form of God, [Jesus] did not regard equality with God something to be grasped. Rather, he emptied himself, taking the form of a slave, coming in human likeness; and found human in appearance, he humbled himself, becoming obedient to death, even death on a cross" (Phil 2:6-8).

This text from the Letter to the Philippians introduces us into the mystery of Christ's *kenosis*. To express this mystery the apostle uses first of all the words "emptied himself," which refers especially to the reality of the Incarnation. "The Word became flesh" (Jn 1:14). God the Son assumed human nature, humanity, and became true man, while remaining God! The truth about Christ as man must always be considered in relation to God the Son. This permanent reference itself is indicated by St. Paul's text. "He emptied himself" does not in any way mean that he ceased to be God; that would be absurd! It means rather, as the apostle perceptively expressed it, that "he did not deem equality with God something to be grasped," but "though he was in the form of God" *(in forma Dei),* as the true Son of God, he assumed a human nature deprived of glory, subject to suffering and death, in which he could live in obedience to the Father, even to the ultimate sacrifice.

In this context, his becoming like man involved a voluntary renunciation, which extended even to the privileges he could have enjoyed as man. He assumed "the form of a slave." He did not wish to belong to the powerful; he wished to be as one who serves. "The Son of Man did not come to be served but to serve" (Mk 10:45).

We see in the Gospels that Christ's earthly life was marked by poverty from the very beginning. This was clearly set out in the account of his birth, when the evangelist Luke observed that "there was no room for them [Mary and Joseph] in the inn," and that Jesus was born in a stable and laid in a manger (cf. Lk 2:7). From Matthew we learn that already in the first months of Jesus' life, he experienced the lot of a refugee (cf. Mt 2:13-15). His hidden life at Nazareth was lived in extremely modest conditions; the head of the family was a carpenter (cf. Mt 13:55) and Jesus himself worked with his putative father (Mk 6:3). When he began his teaching, his situation continued to be one of extreme poverty, as he himself bore witness to in a certain way by referring to the precarious conditions of life imposed by his ministry of evangelization. "Foxes have dens and birds of the sky have nests, but the Son of Man has nowhere to rest his head" (Lk 9:58).

From its beginning, Jesus' messianic mission encountered opposition and misunderstanding, despite the signs which he worked. He was observed and persecuted by those who had power and influence over the people. Finally, he was accused, condemned and put to death on a cross, the most infamous of all forms of capital punishment. It was applied only for crimes of extreme gravity, especially to those people who were not Roman citizens, and to slaves. For this reason also it can be said with the Apostle that Christ literally took "the form of a slave" (Phil 2:7).

In this self-emptying which profoundly characterizes the truth about Christ, true man, we can say that it re-establishes it and restores it. When we read that the Son "did not regard equality with God something to be grasped," we cannot but see in these words an allusion to the first and original temptation to which Adam and Eve yielded in the beginning: "You will become (that is, you will be) like God, knowing good and evil" (Gen 3:5). They yielded to the temptation to be like God, even though they were only creatures. He who is God the Son "did not regard equality with God something to be grasped." In becoming man, "he emptied himself" and by that choice he restored all human beings, however poor and deprived, to their original dignity.

To express this mystery of Christ's *kenosis* St. Paul also used another phrase: "He humbled himself." He used this expression in the context of the reality of the redemption. He wrote that Jesus Christ "humbled himself, becoming obedient to death, even death on a cross" (Phil 2:8). Here Christ's *kenosis* is described in its definitive dimension. From the human point of view it is the dimension of the self-emptying by means of his passion and cruel death. From the divine point of view, it is the redemption effected by the merciful love of the Father through the Son, who freely obeyed out of love for the Father and to save humanity. In that moment there was a new beginning of God's glory in human history, the glory of Christ, his Son made man. The Pauline text says, "Because of this, God greatly exalted him and bestowed on him the name which is above every name" (Phil 2:9).

Commenting on this text of the Letter to the Philippians, St. Athanasius says, "This expression, 'has exalted him,' does not imply that the nature of the Word was exalted. The latter has been and always will be equal to God. It indicates, however, the exaltation of human nature. These words, therefore, were uttered only after the Incarnation of the Word, so that it would be clear that terms such as humbled and exalted refer solely to the human dimension. In fact, only what is humble can be exalted" (Athanasius, *Adversus Arianos Oratio* I, 41). Here we shall add merely that the whole of human nature, all humanity, humiliated in the painful condition to which it has been reduced by sin, finds the source of its new glory in the exaltation of Christ the man.

We cannot conclude without a final remark about the fact that Jesus generally referred to himself as "Son of Man" (e.g., Mk 2:10, 28; 14:62; Mt 8:20; 16:27; Lk 9:22; 11:30; Jn 1:51; 8:28; 13:31; etc.). According to the meaning of the common language of the time, this expression could also indicate that he is true man just like all other human beings, and undoubtedly it refers to his real humanity.

However, the strictly biblical meaning, even in this case, must be established by bearing in mind the historical context deriving from the tradition of Israel. This was expressed and influenced by Daniel's prophecy which gave rise to the formulation of a messianic concept (cf. Dan 7:13-14). In this context, "Son of Man" did not signify merely a common man belonging to the human race. Rather, it refers to a personage who would receive from God a universal dominion, transcending history, in the eschatological era.

On the lips of Jesus and in the Gospel texts, the expression is fraught with a full meaning that embraces the divine and human, heaven and earth, history and eschatology. Jesus himself gave us to understand this when, testifying before Caiaphas that he is the Son of God, he emphatically predicted, "From now on you will see 'the Son of Man seated at the right hand of the Power' and 'coming on the clouds of heaven'" (Mt 26:64). The power and glory of God is therefore immanent in the Son of Man. We are once again face to face with the unique Man-God, true man and true God. This reflection brings us back continually to him so that we may believe, and that believing, we may pray and adore.

General audience of February 17, 1988

The Formulation of the Church's Faith in Christ

Faith is the human response to divine revelation. The catechesis on Jesus Christ which we are developing in the current series of reflections refers to the creeds, especially the Apostles' Creed and the Nicene-Constantinopolitan Creed. Through them the Church expresses and professes the faith which from the beginning was formulated within her as a response to God's revelation in Jesus Christ. Throughout this series of reflections, we have had recourse to the word of revelation to extract the truth revealed in it about Christ himself. Jesus of Nazareth is the Messiah announced in the old covenant. The Messiah, the Christ—true man (the Son of Man)—is in his own person Son of God, true God. This truth about him emerges from the ensemble of his words and deeds, which culminate definitively in the paschal event of his death on the cross and his resurrection.

This living complex of the data of God's self-revelation in Jesus Christ meets with the response of faith, first on the part of those who were the direct witnesses of the Messiah's life and teaching, those who have seen and heard and have touched with their hands the corporeal reality of the Word of

life (cf. 1 Jn 1:1), and later in the generations of believers in
Christ who followed in succession in the community of the
Church. How was the Church's faith in Jesus Christ first
formed? We wish to devote the following reflections to this
problem. We shall especially seek to see how this faith was
formed and expressed at the very beginning of the Church, in
the course of the first centuries. They had a particular importance for the formation of the Church's faith, because they
represent the first development of the living Tradition which
comes from the apostles.

All the written testimonies on this subject date from after
Christ's ascension into heaven. Certainly they reflect firsthand
knowledge of the definitive events of Christ's death on the
cross and resurrection. At the same time, however, those written testimonies cover the whole of Jesus' life and activity,
beginning with his birth and infancy. Moreover, those documents provide evidence that the faith of the apostles and that of
the earliest Church community was already formed in the
prepaschal stage of Christ's life and ministry, and was manifested with definitive power after Pentecost.

A particularly significant expression of this fact is found
in Peter's reply to the question which Jesus one day asked the
apostles in the neighborhood of Caesarea Philippi, "Who do
people say that the Son of Man is?" He later asked, "Who do
you say that I am?" (Mt 16:13, 15). Peter replied, "You are the
Christ (i.e., the Messiah), the Son of the living God" (Mt
16:16). This is the reply recorded by Matthew. The other
Synoptics speak of the Christ (cf. Mk 8:29) or of the Christ of
God (cf. Lk 9:20). These expressions correspond to John's
words, "You are the Holy One of God" (Jn 6:69). The reply in
Matthew is more complete: Jesus of Nazareth is the Christ,
that is, the Messiah, the Son of God.

The same expression of this original faith of the Church
is found in the first words of Mark's Gospel, "The beginning

of the Gospel of Jesus Christ, the Son of God" (Mk 1:1). It is well known that the evangelist was closely linked to Peter. Later we find the same faith in the entire teaching of the Apostle Paul, who from the time of his conversion "proclaimed in the synagogues that Jesus is the Son of God" (Acts 9:20). Later in many of his letters he expressed the same faith in different ways (cf. Gal 4:4; Rom 1:3-4; Col 1:15-18; Phil 2:6-11; also Heb 1:1-4). It can therefore be said that the princes of the apostles, Peter and Paul, stand at the origin of this faith of the Church.

Moreover, the Apostle John, author of the last Gospel, concluded it with the famous words in which he stated that it was written "that you may believe that Jesus is the Messiah, the Son of God, and that through this belief you may have life in his name" (Jn 20:31). "Whoever acknowledges that Jesus is the Son of God, God remains in him and he in God" (1 Jn 4:15). His authoritative voice informs us what was believed and professed about Jesus Christ in the primitive Church.

Jesus of Nazareth is the Son of God. This is the fundamental truth of faith in Christ (the Messiah), held by the apostles on the basis of their Master's words and deeds in the prepaschal period. After the resurrection, the faith was more deeply consolidated and expressed in the written testimonies.

It is a significant fact that the confession, "Truly this was the Son of God" (Mt 27:54) was uttered at the foot of the cross by the Roman centurion who was a pagan (cf. Mk 15:39). In that supreme hour what a mystery of grace and of divine inspiration was at work in the minds of both Israelites and pagans.

After the resurrection one of the apostles, Thomas, made a confession which referred still more directly to the divinity of Christ. He who was unwilling to believe in the resurrection, on seeing the risen one before him, exclaimed, "My Lord and my God!" (Jn 20:28). In this exclamation not only is the "my God" significant, but also the "my Lord." For already in the

Old Testament tradition, "Lord" *(kyrios)* also meant "God." In fact, every time we meet in the Bible the unnamaeble proper name of God, Yahweh, it is substituted with *Adonai,* equivalent to "my Lord." Therefore for Thomas also, Christ is "Lord," that is, God.

In the light of these multiple apostolic testimonies, the words spoken by Peter on the day of Pentecost to the crowd gathered around the apostles acquire their full meaning, "God has made him both Lord and Messiah, this Jesus whom you crucified" (Acts 2:36). In other words, Jesus of Nazareth, true man, who as such suffered death on a cross, is not only the expected Messiah, but also "the Lord" *(kyrios),* and therefore true God.

"Jesus is Lord...the Lord...the Lord Jesus." This confession resounded on the lips of the first martyr Stephen while he was being stoned to death (cf. Acts 7:59-60). It is a confession which appears frequently in Paul's preaching, as is evident from many passages of his letters (cf. 1 Cor 12:3; Rom 10:9; 1 Cor 16:22-23; 8:6; 10:21; 1 Thess 1:8; 4:15; 2 Cor 3:18).

In the First Letter to the Corinthians (12:3) the Apostle stated; "Jesus is Lord," and no one can say this "except by the Holy Spirit." Previously Peter, after his confession of faith at Caesarea, heard Jesus say to him, "Flesh and blood has not revealed this to you, but my heavenly Father" (Mt 16:17). Jesus had already observed, "No one knows the Son except the Father..." (cf. Mt 11:27). Only the Spirit of Truth can bear him adequate witness (cf. Jn 15:26).

We can therefore say that at the beginning of the Church, faith in Christ was expressed in the words, "Son of God" and "Lord" (that is, *kyrios-adonai*). It is faith in the divinity of the Son of Man. In this full sense, he and only he is the "Savior," namely, the author and giver of salvation which God alone has power to grant. This salvation consists not only in liberation from sin, but also in the gift of a new life, of a participation in the life of God himself. In this sense "there is salvation in none other," according to the words of the Apostle Peter in his initial preaching (Acts 4:12).

The same faith is found in many other texts of apostolic times, as in Acts (e.g., 5:31; 13:23); in the Pauline letters (Rom 10:9-13; Eph 5:23; Phil 3:20 f.; 1 Tim 1:1; 2:3-4; 4:10; 2 Tim 1:10; Titus 1:3 f.; 2:13; 3:6), in Peter's letters (1 Pet 1:11; 2 Pet 2:20; 3:18), of John (1 Jn 4:14), and also Jude (25). There is also a place for it in the infancy Gospel (cf. Mt 1:21; Lk 2:11).

We can conclude that Jesus of Nazareth, who habitually called himself "Son of Man," is the Christ (the Messiah), that he is the Son of God, the Lord *(kyrios),* the Savior. This is the faith of the apostles upon which the Church has been built from the beginning.

The Church has guarded this faith with the greatest love and veneration. She has transmitted it to new generations of disciples and followers of Christ under the direction of the Spirit of Truth. She has taught and defended this truth, seeking in every age not only to safeguard in its integrity its essential, revealed content, but also to investigate it constantly and to expound it according to the needs and possibilities of people. This is the task that she has been called upon to carry out until the time of the final coming of her Savior and Lord.

General audience of March 2, 1988

Conciliar Definitions About Christ

"We believe...in one Lord Jesus Christ, Son of God, the only begotten of the Father, that is, of the Being of the Father, God from God, light from light, true God from true God, begotten not created, one in Being with the Father, through him all things were made, both in heaven and on earth. For us men and for our salvation he came down from heaven; he became incarnate; he was made man; he suffered death and rose again on the third day; he ascended into heaven and will come to judge the living and the dead" (cf. *DS* 125).

This is the text of the definition in which the Council of Nicaea (325) expressed the Church's faith in Jesus Christ: true God and true man, God the Son, one in Being with the Eternal Father, and true man, with a nature like ours. This conciliar text was adopted almost literally in the profession of faith which the Church repeats in the liturgy and on other solemn occasions, in the version of the Nicene-Constantinopolitan Creed (381; cf. *DS* 150). The whole series of our reflections is based on this.

The text of the Council's dogmatic definition reproduces the essential elements of the biblical Christology which we have reviewed in the previous reflections of this series. From the very beginning they constituted the content of the living faith of the Church in apostolic times, as we saw in the previous reflection. Following the witness of the apostles, the Church believed and professed from the beginning that Jesus of Nazareth, son of Mary and therefore true man, crucified and risen, is the Son of God, the Lord *(kyrios),* the only Savior of the world, given to humanity in the "fullness of time" (cf. Gal 4:4).

From the beginning the Church guarded this faith and transmitted it to successive Christian generations. She taught and defended it, seeking—under the guidance of the Spirit of Truth—to study it in depth and to expound its essential content contained in the data of revelation. The Council of Nicaea (325) was a milestone on this path of knowledge and formulation of dogma. It was an important and solemn event which from then on indicated to all of Christ's followers the way of the true faith, long before the divisions of Christianity which occurred later. This Council was held shortly after the Church (in 313) had acquired freedom of action in public life throughout the Roman Empire. This indicates the will to remain in the one faith of the apostles when new ways of expansion were opening up to Christianity.

In that era, the Council's definition reflects not only the truth about Jesus Christ inherited from the apostles and fixed in the books of the New Testament, but also the teaching of the Fathers of the post-apostolic period. This was also the period of the persecutions and of the catacombs. For us it is a pleasant duty to name here at least the first two Fathers who, with their teaching joined to holiness of life, decisively contributed to handing on the Church's tradition and permanent patrimony. We mean St. Ignatius of Antioch, given as prey to the wild beasts at Rome in 107 or 106, and St. Irenaeus of Lyons, who was martyred, probably in 202. Both were bishops and pastors of their churches. Of St. Irenaeus we wish to recall here that in teaching that Christ is "true man and true God," he wrote: "How could people attain salvation if God had not accomplished their salvation on earth? Or how could man have gone to God, if God had not come to man?" *(Adv. Haer.,* IV, 33, 4). This is a soteriological argument, as is obvious, which in its turn found expression in the definition of the Council of Nicaea.

This text of St. Irenaeus is taken from his work *Adversus Haereses.* Its purpose was to defend the Christian truth against the errors of heretics who, in that case, were the Ebionites. The apostolic Fathers in their teaching often had to defend the authentic revealed truth in the face of errors which were continually presenting themselves in different guises. Arius was famous at the beginning of the fourth century. He originated a heresy which was named after him, Arianism. According to Arius, Jesus Christ is not God; even though existing before his birth from Mary, he was created in time. The Council of Nicaea rejected this error of Arius, and in so doing, it expounded and formulated the true doctrine of the Church's faith which we quoted at the beginning of this reflection. Affirming that Christ, as the only-begotten Son of God, is of one Being with the Father, the Council expressed, in a formula suited to the Greek culture of the time, the truth which we find in the whole of the New Testament. We know that Jesus spoke of himself as being one with the Father ("I and the Father are one," Jn 10:30). He asserted it before his hearers who, on this account, wished to stone him as a blasphemer (cf. Jn 10:31). He affirmed it again during his trial before the Sanhedrin, and this resulted in his condemnation to death. A more detailed list of the biblical passages on this theme is found in the previous reflection. From all these taken together it clearly follows that in speaking of Christ as the Son of God, "one in Being with the Father," eternally "begotten not made," the Council of Nicaea merely confirmed a precise truth contained in divine revelation, one which has become a truth of the Church's faith, a basic truth of all Christianity.

When it was defined by the Council, everything was already mature in the Church's thought and awareness for such a definition. It can equally be said that the definition does not cease to be relevant today in the face of tendencies, both old and new, to see Christ merely as a man, however extraordinary, but not as God. To admit or support them would destroy the Christological dogma and, at the same time, it would imply the annulment of the entire Christian soteriology. If Christ is not true God, he does not transmit divine life to humanity. Therefore he is not the Savior of humanity in the sense set out by revelation and Tradition. If this truth of the Church's faith is denied, the entire edifice of Christian dogma collapses. The integral logic of the faith and Christian life is nullified, because the keystone of the whole construction is eliminated.

However, we must immediately add that by confirming this truth in a solemn and definitive way in the Council of Nicaea, the Church has simultaneously maintained, taught and defended the truth about the true humanity of Christ. Even this truth had become the object of erroneous opinions and heretical theories. In particular, we must mention here Docetism. This theory denied Christ's human nature, holding that he did not have a real body, but only an appearance of human flesh. The Docetists held that God could not have been really born of a woman, nor could he really have died on the cross. From this position of theirs it follows that, in the whole sphere of the Incarnation and redemption, we are dealing merely with an illusory body. This is in open opposition to the revelation contained in the various texts of the New Testament, among which are those of St. John, "Jesus Christ has come in the flesh" (1 Jn 4:2); "The Word was made flesh" (Jn 1:14); and of St. Paul, according to whom Christ in the flesh became "obedient to death, even to death on a cross" (Phil 2:8).

According to the Church's faith derived from revelation, Jesus Christ was true man; for this very reason his human body was animated by a truly human soul. The testimony of the apostles and evangelists is unambiguous on this point. The teaching of the primitive Church corresponds to it, as does that of the first ecclesiastical writers, such as Tertullian. He wrote, "In Christ...we find soul and body, that is, a human soul and a human body" *(De carne Christi,* 13, 4). However, there were contrary opinions even on this point, in particular, those of Apollinaris, Bishop of Laodicea (born about 310 at Laodicea in Syria, and died about 390), and of his followers (who were therefore known as Apollinarists). According to them Christ did not have a real human soul, because its place was taken by the Word of God. It is clear that they also denied Christ's true humanity.

Pope Damasus I (366-384) in a letter to the bishops of the East dated around 374, pointed out and at the same time rejected the errors of both Arius and of Apollinaris, "These (i.e., the Arians) posit in the Son of God an imperfect divinity, while the others (i.e., the Apollinarists) falsely affirm that the humanity of the Son of Man is incomplete. If the Son of God did not become fully man, then God's work is imperfect and our salvation is imperfect, because the whole man has not been saved! We, who know that we have been saved in the fullness of the human being, profess according to the faith of the Catholic Church that God in the fullness of his being has assumed human nature in its fullness."

This letter of Damasus, written fifty years after Nicaea, was directed principally against the Apollinarists (cf. *DS* 146).

A few years later the First Council of Constantinople (381) condemned all the heresies of the time, including Arianism and Apollinarism. It thereby confirmed what Pope Damasus I had declared about Christ's humanity, which has by nature a real human soul (and therefore a real human intellect and free will) (cf. *DS* 146, 149, 151).

The Council of Nicaea explained the Incarnation with a soteriological argument, teaching that the Son, one in Being with the Father, was made man "for us men and for our salvation." This found a new expression in the defense of the integral truth about Christ, both against Arianism and Apollinarism, made by Pope Damasus and by the Council of Constantinople. In particular, in regard to those who denied the true humanity of the Son of God, that soteriological argument was presented in a new way: in order that the whole man could be saved, the entire (perfect) humanity had to be assumed in the unity of the Son: *"quod non est assumptum, non est sanatum"* (cf. St. Gregory Nazianzen, *Ep.,* 101 *ad Cledon.*).

The Council of Chalcedon (451), in again condemning Apollinarism, completed the Nicene Creed in a certain sense by proclaiming Christ "perfect in his divinity and perfect in his humanity, true God and true man, (composed) of a rational soul and body, of the same Being with the Father by his divinity, and of the same being with us by his humanity, 'like to us in all things except sin' (cf. Heb 4:15), begotten of the Father before time began according to his divinity, and in these last times begotten for us and for our salvation of Mary, Virgin and Mother of God, according to his humanity, one and the same Christ the Lord only-begotten..." (Creed of Chalcedon, *DS* 301).

As can be seen, the careful elaboration of the Christological dogma carried out by the Fathers and the councils always brings us back to the mystery of the one Christ. He is the Word who became incarnate for our salvation, as it is made known to us by revelation, so that believing in him and loving him, we may be saved and have life (cf. Jn 20:31).

General audience of March 9, 1988

The Church's Belief in Jesus Christ According to the Conciliar Definitions

The great Christological councils of Nicaea and Constantinople formulated the fundamental truth of our faith, firmly established in the creed, namely, that Jesus Christ is true God and true man, one in Being with the Father as regards his divinity, of the same nature as us as regards his humanity. After the conciliar explanations about the revealed truth concerning Christ's true divinity and true humanity, the question arose about the correct understanding of the unity of this Christ, who is at the same time fully God and fully man.

The question regarded the essential content of the mystery of the Incarnation, and therefore of Christ's human conception and birth from the Virgin Mary. As far back as the third century it was usual to call her *Theotokos,* (Mother of God), an expression found, among other places, in the oldest Marian prayer, the *Sub tuum praesidium,* "We fly to thy protection, O Holy Mother of God...." It is an antiphon frequently recited by the Church even to the present day. The most ancient text in which it occurs is on a papyrus found in Egypt, and can be dated to the period between the third and fourth century.

This invocation Theotokos, however, was challenged at the beginning of the fifth century by Nestorius and his followers. He held that Mary can be called only Mother of Christ and not Mother of God. This position was linked to the attitude of Nestorius to the problem of the unity of Christ. According to Nestorius, the divinity and humanity were not united, as in a single personal subject, in the earthly being which began to exist in the womb of the Virgin Mary from the moment of the annunciation. In opposition to Arianism which presented the Son of God as inferior to the Father, and to Docetism which reduced Christ's humanity to a mere appearance, Nestorius spoke of a special presence of God in Christ's humanity, as in a holy being, as in a temple. He said that there subsisted in Christ a duality, not only of nature, but also of person, the divine and the human. Being the mother of the Christ-Man, the Virgin Mary could not be regarded as, nor called, the Mother of God.

In opposition to the Nestorian thesis, the Council of Ephesus (431) confirmed the unity of Christ as derived from revelation and as had been believed and affirmed by Christian tradition—sancti patres—(cf. *DS* 250-266). The Council defined that Christ is the same eternal Word, God from God, who as Son is generated from eternity by the Father, and according to the flesh was born in time from the Virgin Mary. Therefore, since Christ is only one being, Mary has every right to the title "Mother of God," as had already been expressed for a long time in Christian prayer and in the thought of the Fathers (cf. *DS* 251).

The doctrine of the Council of Ephesus was later formulated in the so-called "Creed of union" (433) which put an end to the remaining post-conciliar controversies in the following words: "We confess that Our Lord Jesus Christ, only-begotten Son of God, perfect God and perfect man, composed of a rational soul and a body, conceived by the Father before time began as regards his divinity, is the same who in these last times, for us and for our salvation, was born of the Virgin Mary as regards his humanity. He who is of one being with the Father according to the divinity, is of one being also with us according to the humanity; in fact, there has been effected the union of the two natures (human and divine). Therefore we confess that the Blessed Virgin is Mother of God, because the Divine Word has become incarnate and was made man, and through his conception (in Mary) has united to himself the temple which he took from her" *(DS* 272). This is a stupendous concept of the humanity-temple truly assumed by the Word in the unity of person in Mary's womb!

The document known as the "formula of union" was the result of further interchanges between Bishop John of Antioch and St. Cyril of Alexandria, who for this reason received the congratulations of Pope St. Sixtus III (432-440). The text already spoke of the union of the two natures in the same and unique subject, Jesus Christ. Since new controversies had arisen, especially because of Eutyches and the Monophysites who held for the unification and mixture, as it were, of the two natures in the one Christ, the Council of Chalcedon met some years later (451). In agreement with the teaching of Pope St. Leo the Great (440-461), it introduced the term "person" for a greater clarification of the subject of this union of natures. It was a further milestone in the journey of Christological dogma.

In formulating its dogmatic definition, the Council of Chalcedon repeated that of Nicaea and Constantinople, and made its own the doctrine of St. Cyril at Ephesus, and that contained in the "letter to Flavian from the prelate Leo, the most blessed and most holy archbishop of the very great and very ancient city of Rome...in harmony with the confession of the great Peter...and for us a firm pillar" (cf. *DS* 300). Finally it stated with precision, "Following therefore, the Holy Fathers, we unanimously teach and confess one and the same Son, our Lord Jesus Christ...one and the same Christ—only-begotten Lord. He exists in two natures without mixture, change, division or separation. The union does not suppress the difference between the natures. The proper quality of each remains, and comes together with the other in one single person and hypostasis. He is not divided or separated into two persons, but is one and the same Son, only-begotten, God, Word and Lord Jesus Christ, as the prophets, first of all, and then Jesus Christ himself taught us about him, and as the creed of the Fathers has transmitted to us" (cf. *DS* 301-302).

It was a clear and forceful synthesis of faith in the mystery of Christ, received from Sacred Scripture and from sacred Tradition, which used the rational concepts and expressions "nature" and "person," pertaining to the current language. In this way they were raised to the dignity of philosophical and theological terminology, as happened especially after that conciliar definition. The Council, however, adopted those concepts and terms from the current language, without reference to a particular philosophical system. One must also note the concern of the Council Fathers for precision in the choice of words. In the Greek text the word prosopon corresponding to "person," indicated rather man's external, phenomenological side (literally, the theater mask). Therefore the Fathers used, alongside this word, another term, hypostasis, which indicates the ontological specificity of the person.

We too should renew our profession of faith in Christ, our Savior, in the words of that venerated formula used by countless generations of Christians who drew from it light and strength for a witness driven at times to the supreme test of martyrdom.

General audience of March 16, 1988

persona - "sound through" theater mask

The Council of Chalcedon and the Monothelite Heresy

In these reflections we are considering the ancient conciliar definitions which contributed to the formulation of the Church's faith. The Council of Chalcedon (451) made a decisive contribution to this formulation with its solemn definition that in Jesus Christ there are two natures, human and divine, which are united (without mixture) in the one personal subject which is the divine Person of God the Word. Because of the term hypostasis it is usual to speak of the hypostatic union. The same Person of the Word-Son is eternally begotten from the Father as regards his divinity; however, as regards his humanity, he was conceived and born in time of the Virgin Mary. The definition of Chalcedon therefore reaffirms, develops and explains what the Church taught in the previous Councils and what was witnessed to by the Fathers, for example, by Irenaeus who spoke of "one and the same Christ" (cf. *Adv. Haer.* III, 17, 4).

With the doctrine concerning the divine Person of the Word-Son who assumed human nature and thereby entered the world of human persons, the Council emphasized the dignity of the person and the relations existing between various persons. It can be said that it called attention to the reality and dignity of the individual human being who is the unmistakable subject of existence, life, and therefore of duties and rights. How can one not see in this the point of departure for a new history of thought and life? Therefore, the Incarnation of the Son of God is the foundation, source and model of two realities: a new supernatural order of existence for all men and women who draw from that mystery the grace that sanctifies and saves them, and of a Christian anthropology which views each man and woman as a person, placed at the center of society and of the entire world.

Council of Chalcedon

We return to the Council of Chalcedon to say that it confirmed the traditional teaching on the two natures in Christ in opposition to the Monophysite doctrine (monophysis—one nature) propagated after that council. By clarifying that the union of the two natures takes place in one Person, the Council of Chalcedon still more fully set out in relief the duality of these natures, as we saw in the text of the definition previously quoted: "We teach...that one and the same Christ, the only-begotten Son and Lord must be recognized as subsisting in two natures without mixture, change, division or separation. The union does not suppress the difference between the natures; indeed, the proper quality of each remains" (DS 302). This means that the human nature is in no way "absorbed" by the divine nature. Because of his divine nature Christ is "one in Being with the Father according to his divinity"; because of his human nature he is "one in being with us according to his humanity."

Hence Jesus Christ is true God and true man. On the other hand the duality of natures does not in any way affect the unity of Christ, which arises from the perfect unity of the divine Person.

According to the logic of the Christological dogma, the result of the duality of nature in Christ is a duality of will and activity, while safeguarding the unity of the person. This truth was defined in 681 by the Third Council of Constantinople (Sixth Ecumenical Council)—as also in the Lateran Council of 649 (cf. *DS* 500)—against the errors of the Monothelites, who held that Christ had only one will.

The Council condemned "the heresy of a single will and a single activity in two natures...of Christ," which deprived Christ of an essential part of his humanity. "Following the five holy ecumenical councils, and the saints and excellent fathers," and in accord with them it defined and proclaimed that in Christ there are "two natural wills and two natural activities...two natural wills which are not opposed to each other...but such that the human will follows, without opposition or reluctance, or rather, that it is subject to, his divine and omnipotent will...according to what he himself said: 'I have come down from heaven, not to do my own will, but the will of him who sent me' (Jn 6:38)" (cf. *DS* 556).

Human consciousness of Christ

This is the teaching of the early councils. They set out clearly both the divinity and the humanity of Christ. He is by nature a true man, capable of human action, human knowledge, human acts of will, and human consciousness, and also capable of human suffering, patience, obedience, passion and death. Only by virtue of his being completely human can we understand and explain the texts about the obedience of Christ unto death (cf. Phil 2:8; Rom 5:19; Heb 5:8), and above all, his prayer in Gethsemane: "Not my will, but yours be done" (Lk 22:42; cf. Mk 14:36). However, it is likewise true that Jesus' human will and human activity belong to the divine person of the Son; it was precisely in Gethsemane that he said, "Abba,

Father" (Mk 14:36). He is fully aware of his divinity, as is
revealed, for example, when he said, "Before Abraham came
to be, I Am" (Jn 8:58), and in the other Gospel passages which
we mentioned at the appropriate time. As true man, Jesus
certainly possesses a specifically human consciousness, which
we continually discover in the Gospels. At the same time,
however, his human consciousness belongs to that divine "I,"
so that he can say, "The Father and I are one" (Jn 10:30).
There is no Gospel text which indicates that Christ spoke of
himself as a human person, even when he frequently referred
to himself as "Son of Man." This term is rich with meaning.
Under the veil of the biblical and messianic expression, it
seems to imply that he who applies it to himself belongs to a
different and higher order than that of ordinary mortals as far
as the reality of his "I" is concerned. It is a term which bears
witness to his intimate awareness of his own divine identity.

St. Leo the Great

At the conclusion of our exposition of the Christology of
the great councils we can appreciate the full wealth of meaning
of the passage in Pope St. Leo the Great's *Letter to Bishop
Flavian of Constantinople (Tomus Leonis,* June 13, 449). It
was, as it were, an introduction to the Council of Chalcedon,
and summed up the Christological dogma of the ancient
Church: "The Son of God, coming down from his heavenly
abode without ceasing to share in the glory of the Father,
entered this lower world, born after a new order, by a new
mode of birth.... He who is true God, is also true man. There is
no unreality in this unity since the humility of the manhood
and the majesty of the deity exist in reciprocity. For just as
God does not change by his merciful condescension (whereby
he became man), so likewise man is not swallowed up by the
(divine) dignity. Each of the two natures performs its proper

functions in communion with the other, the Word doing what is proper to the Word, and the flesh doing what is proper to it. The one is resplendent with miracles, the other submits to insults. Just as the Word does not forfeit equality of glory with the Father, so the flesh does not desert the nature of our kind...." After referring to the many Gospel texts which constitute the basis of his doctrine, St. Leo concludes: "It does not pertain to the same nature to say, 'I and the Father are one' (Jn 10:30), and to say 'The Father is greater than I' (Jn 14:28). Although in the Lord Jesus Christ there is one single person of God and man, yet the source of the contumely which both share is distinct from the source of the glory which they also share. From our nature he has a humanity inferior to the Father; from the Father he possesses divinity equal to that of the Father" (cf. *DS* 294-295).

While appearing difficult, these formulations of the Christological dogma contain and reveal the mystery of the Word made flesh, announced in the prologue of St. John's Gospel. In the presence of this mystery we feel the need to prostrate ourselves in adoration in the company of those eminent spirits who have honored it also with their investigations and reflections for our benefit and that of the whole Church.

General audience of March 23, 1988

The Christological Definitions and the Church's Faith Today

Summarizing the Christological teaching of the ecumenical councils and of the Fathers, we perceived in the previous reflections the effort of the human mind to penetrate the mystery of the God-Man. We can discern therein the truth about the human and divine natures, their duality and union in the person of the Word, the properties and faculties of human nature and their perfect harmony and subordination to the dominion of the divine "I." The councils expressed that deepened understanding in concepts and terms taken from the current language. This was the natural expression of the common way of knowing and reasoning prior to the conceptualization introduced by any philosophical or theological school. Research, reflection and an attempt to perfect the mode of expression were not lacking in the Fathers. Nor would they be lacking in successive ages of the Church when the concepts and terms used in Christology—especially that of "person"—would be elucidated and clarified in a manner of incalculable value even for the progress of human thought. However, their meaning, when used to express revealed truth, was not connected with, nor conditioned by, particular authors or schools. It was that which could be gathered from the ordinary language of the lettered and even of the unlettered of every age, as can be seen from an analysis of the definitions which made use of them.

It is understandable that in recent times, when translating the data of revelation into a language corresponding to new philosophical or scientific concepts, some should have experienced difficulty in using and accepting that ancient terminology. This especially concerns the distinction between nature and person which is fundamental in the Christological tradition as also in the theology of the Trinity. Some adopt the positions of various modern schools which insist on a philosophy of language and on a hermeneutics dependent on the premises of relativism, subjectivism, existentialism, structuralism, etc. These people in particular are led to undervalue or even to reject the ancient concepts and terms, as influenced by scholasticism, formalism, staticism, non-historicity, etc., in such a way as to deem them unsuitable to express and communicate today the mystery of the living Christ.

What happened then? First of all, some became prisoners of a new form of scholasticism, persuaded by notions and terminologies linked to the new currents of philosophical and scientific thought, without bothering to compare them with the form expressing the common meaning and, it may be said, the universal understanding. Even today it remains indispensable for communicating with one another in thought and in life. In the second place there has been a transition, as was foreseeable, from the crisis opened up by the question of language, to the relativization of the Nicene and Chalcedonian dogma considered as a simple attempt at an historical interpretation which is dated, superseded, and can no longer be proposed to modern intelligence. This transition has been and is very risky and can lead to results which are difficult to reconcile with the data of revelation.

In the new terminology, one has arrived at the point of speaking of the existence of a "human person" in Jesus Christ.

This is based on the phenomenological concept of personality provided by an ensemble of expressive moments of conscience and freedom, without sufficient consideration for the ontological subject which is at its origin. Or else the divine personality has been reduced to Jesus' self-awareness of the "divine" in himself, without truly understanding the Incarnation as the assuming of human nature by a transcendent and pre-existing divine "I." These concepts are reflected also in Marian dogma, and especially in that of Mary's divine motherhood, so linked by the councils to the Christological dogma. These concepts nearly always imply the negation of the distinction between nature and person, which, on the contrary, the councils had taken from the ordinary language of the people and elaborated theologically as the key to interpret the mystery of Christ.

These facts, here obviously scarcely touched upon, enable us to understand how delicate is the problem of the new language both for theology and catechesis. This is especially so when starting from the antecedent rejection of ancient categories (for example, those presented as "Hellenistic"). One ends up by being enmeshed in new categories—or in new words—in virtue of which even the substance of revealed truth is manipulated.

This is not to say that we are prohibited from continuing to investigate the mystery of the Incarnate Word, and to "seek more suitable ways to communicate Christian doctrine," according to the norms and spirit of the Second Vatican Council. Together with John XXIII, the Council strongly confirmed that "the deposit of faith or the truths are one thing, and the manner in which they are enunciated, in the same meaning and understanding, is another" (GS 62; cf. John XXIII, Discourse at the opening of the Council, October 11, 1962: AAS 54, 1962, p. 792).

An approach must be made to the modern mentality, formed according to the criteria and methods of scientific knowledge. While doing this, one must bear in mind its tendencies toward research in the various fields of knowledge; its deeper aspiration toward a "beyond" which qualitatively surpasses all the limits of experimentation and calculation; and its frequent manifestations of the needs of a wisdom far more satisfying and stimulating than science. In this way the modern mentality is by no means impenetrable to the discourse on the "ultimate reasons" of life and their basis in God. Hence arises the possibility of a well-founded and sincere discourse on the Christ of the Gospels and of history. It should be formulated in the awareness of the mystery, and therefore in a stammering way, as it were, but not without the clarity of the concepts elaborated with the help of the Spirit by the councils and the Fathers, and handed down to us by the Church.

Christological catechesis must be faithful to this revealed and transmitted deposit. By studying and presenting the figure, teaching and works of the Christ of the Gospels, it will very well be able to indicate, precisely in this sphere of truth and life, the affirmation of the eternal pre-existence of the Word, the mystery of his "self-emptying" (cf. Phil 2:7), and his predestination and exaltation. This exaltation is the true end of the entire economy of salvation, and which combines with and in Christ the God-Man the whole of humanity and in a certain way the entire creation.

Such a catechesis should present the integral truth about Christ as Son and Word of God in the intimacy of the Trinity (another fundamental Christian dogma). He became incarnate for our salvation and thereby realized the greatest union conceivable and possible between the creature and the Creator, in the human being, and in the entire universe. Besides, this catechesis must not pass over the truth that Christ has his own ontological reality of humanity belonging to the divine Person, and also an intimate awareness of his divinity, and of the salvific mission assigned to him as man.

The truth will thus become apparent that in Jesus of

Nazareth, in his interior experience and knowledge, there is the highest realization of the "personality" even in its value of *sensus sui,* of self-awareness as the basis and vital center of the entire interior and external activity, but affected within the infinitely superior sphere of the divine person of the Son.

There will likewise appear the truth about the Christ of history as a personage and particular fact *(factum ex muliere, natum sub lege:* Gal 4:4). Christ concretizes in himself the universal value of humanity conceived and created in God's "eternal counsel." The truth also appears about Christ as the total realization of the eternal plan expressed in the covenant and in the kingdom—of God and man—which we know from biblical prophecy and history. Christ is the eternal logos, the light and reason of all things (cf. Jn 1:4, 9 ff.). He became incarnate and present among men, in the midst of things, at the center of history. He did this in order to be—in accordance with the design of God the Father—the ontological head of the universe, the redeemer and savior of all humanity, who restores and sums up all things in heaven and on earth (cf. Phil 1:10).

We reflect on this mystery of God who assumed humanity in order to integrate, save and glorify it in the definitive communion of this glory. Far from temptations of every form of materialistic or panlogical monism, this new reflection loses nothing of its fascination and gives us a taste of its profound truth and beauty. But it must be enveloped and explained within the sphere of the Christology of the councils and of the Church. Thus it is given a new theological, philosophical and artistic expressions (cf. *GS* 62), in which the human spirit can acquire ever better what emerges from the infinite abyss of divine revelation.

General audience of April 13, 1988

THE MISSION OF CHRIST

Christ's Mission

Today we begin the final phase of our reflections on Jesus Christ. Until now we have sought to show who Jesus Christ is. We have done so, first in the light of Sacred Scripture, especially of the Gospels. Then, in recent reflections, we have examined and illustrated the Church's response of faith to Jesus' revelation and to the witness and preaching of the apostles in the course of the first centuries, during the elaboration of the Christological definitions of the early Councils (between the fourth and seventh centuries).

Jesus Christ is true God and true man, of one Being with the Father (and with the Holy Spirit) as regards his divinity, and of one being with us as regards his humanity: Son of God and born of the Virgin Mary. This is the central dogma of the Christian faith in which the mystery of Christ is expressed.

Jesus Christ's mission also pertains to this mystery. The creed links this mission with the truth about the being of the God-Man *(Theandrikos),* Christ, when it states concisely that "For us men and for our salvation he came down from heaven...and was made man." In our reflections we shall seek to develop the content of these words of the creed, meditating in turn on the various aspects of Jesus Christ's mission.

343

From the beginning of his messianic activity Jesus manifested first of all his prophetic mission. Jesus announced the Good News. He himself said that "he has come" from the Father (cf. Mk 1:38), "that he has been sent" to "proclaim the good news of the kingdom of God" (cf. Lk 4:43).

Jesus acted in a different way from that of his precursor John the Baptist. At the Jordan, in the desert, John taught those who came to him from various places. Instead, Jesus went out to meet those to whom he had to proclaim the Good News. This going out to the people reflects the dynamism proper to the mystery of the Incarnation: God's going toward humanity. Thus the evangelists tell us that Jesus "went around all of Galilee teaching in their synagogues" (Mt 4:23), and that "he journeyed from one town and village to another" (Lk 8:1). From the Gospel texts it is evident that Jesus' preaching took place almost exclusively in Palestine, that is, between Galilee and Judea, with visits to Samaria which links the two principal regions. However, the Gospel also mentions the "region of Tyre and Sidon," that is Phoenicia (cf. Mk 7:31; Mt 15:21), and also Decapolis, "the region of the Gerasenes on the other shore of the Sea of Galilee" (cf. Mk 5:1; also 7:31). These references prove that Jesus at times went beyond the confines of Israel (in the ethnic sense), even though he repeatedly emphasized that his mission was principally to "the house of Israel" (Mt 15:24). When he sent the disciples on a first trial journey of missionary apostolate, he explicitly enjoined: "Do not go into pagan territory or enter a Samaritan town. Go rather to the lost sheep of the house of Israel" (Mt 10:5-6). At the same time, however, one of the more important messianic conversations took place in Samaria, at the well of Sychar (cf. Jn 4:1-26).

Moreover, the evangelists themselves attest to the fact that the crowds which followed Jesus comprised people not only from Galilee, Judea and Jerusalem, but also "from Idumea and from beyond the Jordan and from the neighborhood of Tyre and Sidon" (Mk 3:7-8; cf. also Mt 4:12-15).

Even though Jesus clearly stated that his mission was restricted to the "house of Israel," at the same time he made it understood that the doctrine he preached—the Good News—is destined for the whole human race. For example, in reference to the Roman centurion's profession of faith, he foretold: "Many will come from the east and the west and will recline with Abraham, Isaac, and Jacob at the banquet in the kingdom of heaven..." (Mt 8:11). However, only after the resurrection will he command his apostles, "Go, therefore, and teach all nations" (Mt 28:19).

What is the essential content of Jesus' teaching? One can put it in a word: the Gospel, that is, the Good News. He began his preaching with the invitation: "This is the time of fulfillment. The kingdom of God is at hand. Repent, and believe in the Good News" (Mk 1:15).

The very term "Good News" indicates the fundamental character of Christ's message. God wishes to respond to the desire for good and happiness deeply rooted in the human being. It can be said that the Gospel, which is the divine response, has an optimistic character. This, however, is not a purely temporal optimism, a superficial rational happiness. It is not the announcement of an "earthly paradise." Christ's "Good News" makes essential moral demands on the hearer; it calls for self-denial and sacrifice. Ultimately it is linked to the redemptive mystery of the cross. At the heart of the "Good News" there is the program of the beatitudes (cf. Mt 5:3-11), which makes absolutely clear the kind of happiness Christ has come to announce and reveal to humanity still on its earthly journey toward its ultimate and eternal destiny. He said, "Blessed are the poor in spirit, for theirs is the kingdom of heaven." Each of the eight beatitudes has a similar structure. In the same spirit Jesus called "blessed" the servant whom the

master "will find vigilant—or busy—on his arrival" (cf. Lk
12:37). Here one can discern also the eschatological and eternal perspective of the happiness revealed and announced by
the Gospel.

The beatitude about the poor in spirit brings us back to
the beginning of Jesus' messianic activity. Speaking in the
synagogue of Nazareth he said, "The Spirit of the Lord is upon
me, because he has anointed me to bring glad tidings to the
poor" (Lk 4:18). He means not only the materially poor, but all
those who are spiritually open to God's gift of truth and grace
as the gift of his love, a gratuitous gift *(gratis datum)*, because
they are interiorly detached from material things and are willing to use and share them with others according to the
demands of justice and charity. For this condition of God's
poor *(anawim)* Jesus "gives praise to the Father," because "he
has hidden these things (that is, the great things of God) from
the wise and the learned and revealed them to the childlike"
(cf. Lk 10:21). Therefore it is not said that Jesus dismisses
from his company those who are better off financially, like the
publican Zacchaeus who climbed a tree to see him (cf. Lk
19:2-9), or those other friends of Jesus whose names we know
from the Gospels. According to Jesus' words, it is the poor in
spirit (cf. Mt 5:3) and those who hear the word of God and
observe it (cf. Lk 11:28), who are blessed.

Another characteristic of Jesus' preaching is that he
sought to convey the Gospel message in a way suited to the
mentality and culture of his hearers. He grew up and lived
among them during the years of his hidden life at Nazareth
(when "he advanced in wisdom"; Lk 2:52). He knew the mentality, culture and tradition of his people, deeply rooted in the
heritage of the Old Testament.

For this very reason he often used parables in proclaiming the truth, as is evident from the Gospels. For example,
Matthew wrote, "All these things Jesus spoke to the crowds in

parables. He spoke to them only in parables to fulfill what had been said through the prophet: 'I will open my mouth in parables, I will announce what has lain hidden from the foundation of the world'" (Mt 13:34-35).

Using images from daily life that everyone could understand, his parables made it much easier to establish contact with those who had little education (cf. *Summa Theol.,* III, q. 42, a. 2). "The mystery of God's kingdom," hidden in parables, needed further explanation, sometimes requested even by the apostles (e.g., cf. Mk 4:11-12). An adequate understanding could not be attained except with the aid of an interior light from the Holy Spirit, and Jesus promised and gave this light.

We must further note a third characteristic of Jesus' preaching, emphasized in the Apostolic Exhortation *Evangelii Nuntiandi,* published by Paul VI after the 1974 Synod on evangelization. There we read: "Jesus himself, the Good News of God, was the very first and greatest evangelizer; he was so through and through: to perfection and to the point of the sacrifice of his earthly life" *(EN* 7).

Jesus not only proclaimed the Good News, but he himself was the Good News. Those who believed in him followed what he preached, but still more they followed the preacher. They followed Jesus because he offered "words of life," as Peter confessed after the Master's discourse in the synagogue of Capernaum: "Lord, to whom shall we go? You have the words of eternal life" (Jn 6:68). This identification of word and life, of the preacher and what he preaches, is perfectly realized only in Jesus. That is why we too believe in him and follow him when he is manifested to us as the "one Master" (cf. Mt 23:8, 10).

General audience of April 20, 1988

The Kingdom of God

"This is the time of fulfillment. The kingdom of God is at hand. Repent, and believe in the Gospel" (Mk 1:15). Jesus Christ was sent by the Father "to preach good news to the poor" (Lk 4:18). He was—and remains—the first messenger of the Father, the first evangelizer, as we said in last week's reflection, quoting the words of Paul VI in *Evangelii Nuntiandi*. Rather Jesus not only announced the Gospel, the Good News, but he himself is the Gospel (cf. *EN* 7).

In the whole of his mission, by means of all that he did and taught, and finally by his cross and resurrection, he "reveals man to man" *(GS 22)*, and opens up to him the perspectives of that happiness to which God has called and destined him from the beginning. The message of the beatitudes sums up the program of life proposed to those who would follow the divine call. It is the synthesis of the whole Gospel ethos linked to the mystery of redemption.

Christ's mission consists above all in the revelation of the Good News (Gospel) addressed to humanity. It is aimed at the human person and in this sense it can be called "anthropocentric"; but at the same time it is deeply rooted in the truth of the kingdom of God, in the announcement of his kingdom which is at hand: "The kingdom of God is at hand...believe in the Good News" (Mk 1:15).

This then is "the Gospel of the kingdom." Its reference to humanity, which can be seen in the entire mission of Christ, is rooted in a "theocentric" dimension which is accordingly called the kingdom of God. Jesus announced the Gospel of this kingdom, and at the same time he made present the kingdom of God in the whole unfolding of his mission. By it, the kingdom is born and develops already in time, as a seed inserted in human history and of the world. This realization of the kingdom comes about by means of the Gospel word and the whole earthly life of the Son of Man which was crowned in the paschal mystery with the cross and resurrection. With his "obedience unto death" (Phil 2:8), Jesus began a new phase of the economy of salvation, whose process will end when God will be "all in all" (1 Cor 15:28). Therefore the kingdom of God has truly begun to be realized in the history of humanity and of the world, even though in the earthly course of human life one continually meets and comes up against another fundamental term of the historical dialectic, namely, the "disobedience of the first Adam," who subjected himself to the "ruler of the world" (cf. Rom 5:19; Jn 14:30).

Here we touch the central problem and, as it were, the critical point of the accomplishment of the mission of Christ, Son of God, in history. This is a question to which we shall have to return at a later stage of our catechesis. Whereas in Christ the kingdom of God "is at hand," and indeed present in a definitive way in the history of humanity and of the world, yet at the same time its fulfillment continues to belong to the future. This is why Jesus commanded us to pray to the Father: "Thy kingdom come" (Mt 6:10).

We must bear this question in mind while considering Christ's Gospel as the "good news" of the kingdom of God.

This was the guiding theme of the announcement of Jesus, who especially in his numerous parables spoke of God's kingdom. Particularly significant is the parable which compares the kingdom of God to a seed, which the sower plants in the earth cultivated by him (cf. Mt 13:3-9). The seed is destined "to produce fruit" by its interior power, undoubtedly, but the fruit depends also on the ground in which the seed is planted (cf. Mt 13:19-23).

On another occasion Jesus compared the kingdom of God ("the kingdom of heaven," according to Matthew) to a grain of mustard seed. This "is the least of all seeds," but when it has grown it becomes a leafy tree, and the birds of the air find refuge on its branches (cf. Mt 13:31-32). Again, he compared the growth of the kingdom of God to "leaven" which ferments the dough so that it becomes bread for human food (cf. Mt. 13:33). However, Jesus devoted another parable to the growth of the kingdom of God in this world. It is that of the good seed and the darnel weed, scattered by the enemy on the field sown with good seed (cf. Mt 13:24-30). Thus in the field of the world the good and the bad, symbolized by the good seed and the darnel, grow together "until the harvest time," that is, until the day of divine judgment. This is a further significant allusion to the eschatological perspective of human history. In any event Jesus gives us to understand that the growth of the seed which is the "word of God," is conditioned by its reception in the field of human hearts. On this depends whether it bears fruit and "yields a hundred or sixty or thirtyfold" (Mt 13:23), according to the dispositions and reactions of those who receive it.

In his announcement of the kingdom of God, Jesus informed us that it is not destined for one nation only, or merely for the "chosen people." Many will come "from the east and the west" and "recline with Abraham, Isaac and Jacob" (cf. Mt 8:11). Indeed, it is not a kingdom in the temporal and political sense. It is not "of this world" (cf. Jn 18:36), although it is found in the midst of "this world" and herein it must develop and grow. For this reason Jesus fled from the crowd that wished to make him king. ("Since Jesus knew that they were going to come and carry him off to make him king, he withdrew again to the mountain alone"; Jn 6:15.) On the eve of his passion, in the upper room, he prayed to his Father to grant his disciples to live according to that same understanding of the kingdom of God: "I do not ask that you take them out of the world, but that you keep them from the evil one. They do not belong to the world, any more than I belong to the world" (Jn 17:15-16). Again, according to Jesus' teaching and prayer, God's kingdom must grow in the hearts of the disciples "in this world"; however, it will be fulfilled in the world to come, "When the Son of Man will come in his glory...and all the nations will be assembled before him" (Mt 25:31-32). It is always in an eschatological perspective!

We can complete the notion of the kingdom of God announced by Jesus by emphasizing that it is the kingdom of the Father to whom Jesus taught us to turn in prayer in order to obtain its coming, "Thy kingdom come" (Mt 6:10; Lk 11:2). The heavenly Father in his turn offers humanity (through Christ and in Christ) the pardon of their sins and salvation. Full of love he awaits their return, as the father in the parable awaits the return of the prodigal son (cf. Lk 15:20-32), because God is truly "rich in mercy" (Eph 2:4).

The whole gospel of conversion announced by Jesus from the beginning is situated in this light. "Repent, and believe in the Good News!" (Mk 1:15). Conversion to the Father, to the God who "is love" (1 Jn 4:16), is linked to the acceptance of love as a "new" commandment: love of God, "the greatest and the first commandment" (Mt 22:38), and love of neighbor, "like to the first" (Mt 22:39). Jesus said, "I give you a new commandment: love one another. As I have loved you, so you also should love one another" (Jn 13:34). Here we are at the heart of the "kingdom of God" in humanity and in history. In this way the whole law, that is, the ethical heritage of the old covenant, must be fulfilled, and must reach its divine-human fullness. Jesus himself said so in the Sermon on the Mount: "Do not think that I have come to abolish the law or the prophets. I have come not to abolish but to fulfill" (Mt 5:17).

If anything, he frees the human person from the "letter of the Law," to introduce him into its spirit, since, as St. Paul says, "the letter brings death, but the Spirit gives life" (2 Cor 3:6). Fraternal love, as a reflection and participation of God's love, is therefore the animating principle of the New Law, which is as it were the constitutional basis of God's kingdom (cf. *Summa Theol.*, I-II, q. 106, a 1; q. 107, aa. 1-2).

Among the parables in which Jesus used similes and allegories in his preaching on God's kingdom, there is one of a king "who prepared a wedding feast for his son" (Mt 22:2). The parable tells that many of those invited declined the invitation, finding various excuses and pretexts for their absence. The king then had his servants call in people from the streets to sit at his table. However, among those who came, not all showed themselves worthy of the invitation, because they were without the prescribed "wedding garment."

This parable of the wedding feast, compared with that of the sower sowing the seed, leads us to the same conclusion: if not all the invited guests will take their place at the wedding feast, nor all the seeds produce a harvest, this depends on the dispositions with which one responds to the invitation or receives the seed of God's word in one's heart. It depends on the way we receive Christ who is the sower, and also the king's son and the bridegroom, as he frequently presented himself: "Can the wedding guests fast while the bridegroom is with them?" (Mk 2:19). He asked this on one occasion when questioned in reference to the austerity of John the Baptist. He himself supplied the answer: "As long as they have the bridegroom with them, they cannot fast" (Mk 2:19).

God's kingdom is therefore like a wedding feast, to which the heavenly Father invites all who are in communion of love and joy with his Son. All are called and invited to it, but each one is responsible for accepting or refusing the invitation, for his conformity or lack of conformity with the law regulating the feast.

This is the law of love. It derives from divine grace in those who welcome and observe it by living Christ's paschal mystery. It is a love which is realized in history, notwithstanding every refusal on the part of the invited, and notwithstanding their unworthiness. On the Christian there smiles the hope that love will triumph in all the "invited," precisely because the paschal measure of the bridegroom's love is the cross. Its eschatological perspective is opened in history by Christ's resurrection. Through him the Father "has delivered us from the power of darkness and transferred us to the kingdom of his beloved Son (cf. Col 1:13). If we yield to the call and attraction of the Father, in Christ we all have redemption and eternal life.

General audience of April 27, 1988

"I Came into the World to Testify to the Truth"

"For this I was born and for this I came into the world: to testify to the truth" (Jn 18:37). When Pilate, during the trial, asked Jesus if he were a king, Jesus answered: "My kingdom is not of this world." When the Roman governor insisted in his question, "Then you are a king?" Jesus replied, "You say I am a king" (cf. Jn 18:33-37). This dialogue during the trial, recorded in John's Gospel, links what we have to say with the previous reflection concerning Christ's message on the kingdom of God. At the same time it opens up to us a further dimension or another aspect of Christ's mission indicated by the words, "to testify to the truth." Christ is king and "he came into the world to testify to the truth." He said so himself and added, "Everyone who belongs to the truth listens to my voice" (Jn 18:37).

This reply opens before our eyes new horizons on Christ's mission, and on man's vocation, particularly on the fact that man's vocation is rooted in Christ.

Through the words addressed to Pilate, Jesus emphasized what is essential in the whole of his preaching. At the same time he anticipated in a certain way that which will always constitute the eloquent message of the paschal event, that is to say, the cross and resurrection.

Speaking of Jesus' preaching, even his opponents expressed in their own way its fundamental significance when they said to him, "Teacher, we know that you are a truthful man...you teach the way of God in accordance with the truth" (Mk 12:14). Jesus was therefore the Teacher of the "way of God"; an expression of ancient biblical and extra-biblical origin to designate a religious and salvific doctrine. As regards the ordinary hearers of Jesus they were impressed by another aspect of his teaching: "The people were astonished at his teaching, for he taught them as one having authority and not as the scribes" (Mk 1:22). "He spoke with authority" (Lk 4:32).

This authority was constituted especially by the power of the truth contained in Christ's preaching. His disciples addressed him as "Teacher," not only in the sense that he knew the law and the prophets and commented on them with acute perception, like the scribes, but for a still more compelling reason: he "spoke with authority." This was the authority of the truth whose source is God himself. Jesus himself said, "My teaching is not my own, but is from the one who sent me" (Jn 7:16).

In this sense inclusive of the reference to God, Jesus was Teacher. "You call me Teacher and Lord; and you are right for so I am" (Jn 13:13). He was Teacher of the truth which is God. He bore witness to this truth unto the end, with the authority which came to him from on high, or we could say, with the authority of one who is king in the realm of truth.

In previous reflections, we already drew attention to the Sermon on the Mount, in which Jesus revealed himself as the one who has come, not "to abolish the law or the prophets," but "to fulfill them." This fulfillment of the law was an act of kingship and authority: the kingship and authority of the truth which decides on the law, on its divine source, and its progressive manifestation to the world.

In the Sermon on the Mount (cf. Mt 5-7), one perceives

this authority with which Jesus intended to fulfill his mission. Here are some significant passages: "You have heard that it was said to your ancestors, 'You shall not kill'...but I say to you..." "'You shall not commit adultery'; but I say to you...." "It was said...'Do not take false oaths'...but I say to you...." After every "I say to you" there is an authoritative exposition of that truth of human conduct which is contained in each of God's commandments. Jesus did not comment in a human way, like a scribe, on the texts of the Old Testament. But he spoke with the authority of the lawgiver himself. This is the authority of lawmaking—kingship. At the same time it is the authority of the truth, by reason of which the new law becomes for humanity a binding principle of conduct.

When Jesus, in the Sermon on the Mount, said on various occasions, "but I say to you," his language echoed the Old Testament texts which frequently repeated, "Thus says the Lord God of Israel" (2 Sam 12:7). "O Jacob...thus says the Lord who made you" (Is 44:1-2); "Thus says the Lord, your redeemer, the Holy One of Israel" (Is 43:14). Still more directly he harked back to the reference to God which was so frequently on the lips of Moses in giving the law—the "old" law—to Israel. Much greater than that of Moses is the authority which Jesus claimed in "fulfilling the law and the prophets" by virtue of the mission received from on high: not on Sinai, but in the sublime mystery of his relationship with the Father.

Jesus was well aware of this mission which was sustained by the power of the truth drawn from his own divine source. There is a close connection between his reply to Pilate: "I have come to bear witness to the truth" (Jn 18:37), and his statement before his hearers: "My teaching is not my own, but is from the one who sent me" (Jn 7:16). The connecting and unifying thread of this and other statements of Jesus on the "authority of the truth" with which he taught is in the awareness of the mission received from on high.

Jesus knew that the eternal Wisdom was manifested to humanity in his teaching. He therefore rebuked those who refused to accept it, not hesitating to recall the "queen of the south (the Queen of Sheba), who had come "to hear the wisdom of Solomon," and added immediately, "there is something greater than Solomon here" (Mt 12:42).

He also knew and openly proclaimed that the words which flow from that divine Wisdom "will not pass away." "Heaven and earth will pass away, but my words will not pass away" (Mk 13:31). They contain the power of the truth which is indestructible and eternal. They are therefore "words of eternal life," as the Apostle Peter confessed at a critical moment, when many of those who had assembled to hear Jesus, began to leave him, because they could not understand and were not disposed to accept his words foretelling the mystery of the Eucharist (cf. Jn 6:66).

Here we touch on the problem of human freedom to accept or not to accept the eternal truth contained in Christ's teaching. It is certainly valid to give to people of all ages—and therefore of our time also—an adequate response to their vocation which opens on to the eternal. Confronted with this problem, having a theological as well as an anthropological dimension (the human reaction and response to a truth proposed), it will suffice for the present to refer to what the Second Vatican Council said, especially in regard to the particular sensitivity of the people of today. The Council first of all stated that "all men are bound to seek the truth, especially in what concerns God and his Church," but also that "truth cannot impose itself except by virtue of its own truth, as it makes its entrance into the mind at once quietly and with power" *(DH* 1). Moreover, the Council recalled the duty of people "to adhere to the truth once it is known and to order their whole lives in accord with the demands of truth." Then it adds: "Men cannot discharge these obligations in a manner in keeping with their own nature unless they enjoy immunity from external coercion as well as psychological freedom" *(DH* 2). Such is the mission of Christ as teacher of eternal truth. The Council recalled that "God calls men to serve him in spirit and in truth.... God has regard for the dignity of the human person whom he himself created." Then it said that "this truth appears at its height in Christ Jesus, in whom God manifested himself and his ways with men. Christ is at once our Master and our Lord and also meek and humble of heart. In attracting and inviting his disciples he used patience. He wrought miracles to illuminate his teaching and to establish its truth, but his intention was to rouse faith in his hearers and to confirm them in faith, not to exert coercion upon them" *(DH* 11).

Eventually, the Council linked this dimension of Christ's teaching with the paschal mystery: "In the end, when he completed on the cross the work of redemption whereby he achieved salvation and true freedom for men, he brought his revelation to completion. For he bore witness to the truth, but he refused to impose the truth by force on those who spoke against it. Not by force of blows does his rule assert its claims. It is established by witnessing to the truth and by hearing the truth, and it extends its dominion by the love whereby Christ, lifted up on the cross, draws all men to himself" *(DH* 11).

As of now we can conclude that he who sincerely seeks the truth will find easily enough in the teaching of Christ crucified the solution to the problem of freedom also.

General audience of May 4, 1988

Christ's Mission
Is to Reveal the Father

"In times past, God spoke in partial and various ways to our ancestors through the prophets; in these last days, he has spoken to us through his son..." (Heb 1:1-2). In these words, well known to the faithful through the Christmas liturgy, the author of the Letter to the Hebrews speaks of Jesus Christ's mission, presenting it against the background of the history of the old covenant. There is a continuity between the mission of the prophets and Christ's mission, but also a very clear difference. Jesus is not merely the last or the greatest of the prophets—the eschatological prophet as he was called and awaited by some. He is essentially distinguished from all the ancient prophets and infinitely surpasses the level of their personality and mission. He is the Son of the Father, the Word-Son, of one being with the Father.

This is the key truth for understanding Christ's mission. He was sent to announce the Good News (the Gospel) to the poor. Together with him God's kingdom has come to us, entering definitively into human history. Christ bore witness to the truth drawn from his own divine source, as we have seen in the previous reflections. Now we can deduce from the above-quoted text of the Letter to the Hebrews the truth that unifies all aspects of Christ's mission: Jesus reveals God in the most authentic way, because this revelation is based on the one absolutely sure and unquestionable source, the very essence of God. Therefore, Christ's testimony has the value of absolute truth.

In John's Gospel we find a statement similar to that of the Letter to the Hebrews, but expressed more concisely. At the end of the prologue we read: "No one has ever seen God; the only Son who is in the bosom of the Father has made him known" (Jn 1:18).

This is the essential difference between the revelation of God in the prophets and in the whole of the Old Testament, and that brought by Christ who said of himself, "Behold, something greater than Jonah is here" (Mk 12:41). Here it is God himself, "the Word made flesh" (cf. Jn 1:14), who speaks to us of God. That Word who "is in the bosom of the Father" (Jn 1:18), becomes "the true light" (Jn 1:9), "the light of the world" (Jn 8:12). He said of himself, "I am the way, the truth and the life" (Jn 14:6).

Christ knows God as the Son who knows the Father and at the same time is known by him. "As the Father knows me and I know the Father..." we read in John's Gospel, and almost in identical terms in the Synoptics: "No one knows the Son except the Father, and no one knows the Father except the Son and anyone to whom the Son wishes to reveal him" (Mt 11:37; cf. Lk 10:22). Therefore Christ, the Son who knows the Father, reveals the Father. At the same time the Son is revealed by the Father. Jesus himself, after the confession of Caesarea Philippi, made that known to Peter who recognized him as "the Christ, the Son of the living God" (Mt 16:16). "Flesh and blood has not revealed this to you," Jesus said, "but my Father who is in heaven" (Mt 16:17).

If Christ's essential mission is to reveal the Father, who is "our God" (cf. Jn 20:17), at the same time he himself is revealed by the Father as the Son. This Son, "being one with the Father" (Jn 10:30), can therefore say, "He who has seen me has seen the Father" (Jn 14:9). In Christ God has become "visible"; God's "visibility" is realized in Christ. St. Irenaeus expressed it concisely: "The invisible reality of the Son was the Father, and the visible reality of the Father was the Son" (*Adv. Haer.* IV, 6, 6).

Therefore God's self-revelation is realized to the full in Jesus Christ. The revelation of the Spirit will come at the appropriate moment. The Spirit will be revealed as the one who proceeds from the Father (cf. Jn 15:26), and whom the Father will send in the Son's name (cf. Jn 14:26).

In the light of these mysteries of the Trinity and Incarnation, due significance is acquired by the blessedness proclaimed by Jesus for his disciples: "Blessed are the eyes that see what you see. For I say to you, many prophets and kings desired to see what you see, but did not see it, and to hear what you heard, but did not hear it" (Lk 10:23-24).

A living echo of these words of the Master seems to resound in the First Letter of John: "What was from the beginning, what we have heard, what we have seen with our eyes, what we looked upon and touched with our hands concerns the Word of life (for the life was made visible; we have seen it and testify to it and proclaim to you the eternal life...), what we have seen and heard we proclaim now to you, so that you too may have fellowship with us" (1 Jn 1:1-3). In the prologue of his Gospel the same apostle wrote: "We saw his glory, the glory as of the Father's only Son, full of grace and truth" (Jn 1:14).

In reference to this fundamental truth of our faith the Second Vatican Council in the *Constitution on Divine Revelation* stated: "By this revelation then, the deepest truth about God and the salvation of man shines out for our sake in Christ, who is both the mediator and the fullness of all revelation"

(DV 2). Here we have the full dimension of Christ, the revelation of God, because this revelation of God is at the same time the revelation of God's salvific economy in regard to humanity and the world. As St. Paul says in regard to the apostles' preaching, it brings "to light the plan of the mystery hidden from ages past in God who created all things" (Eph 3:9). It is the mystery of the plan of salvation which God conceived from eternity in the intimacy of the Trinitarian life, wherein he contemplated, loved, willed, created and "re-created" the things of heaven and of earth by linking them to the Incarnation and therefore to Christ.

Let us return once again to the Second Vatican Council where we read: "Jesus Christ...the Word made flesh, was sent as 'a man to men.' He 'speaks the words of God' (Jn 3:34), and completes the work of salvation which his Father gave him to do (cf. Jn 5:36; 17:4)." He "perfected revelation by fulfilling it through his whole work of making himself present and manifesting himself: through his words and deeds, his signs and wonders, but especially through his death and glorious resurrection from the dead and final sending of the Spirit of truth. Moreover he confirmed with divine testimony what revelation proclaimed, that God is with us to free us from the darkness of sin and death, and to raise us up to life eternal.

"The Christian dispensation, therefore, as the new and definitive covenant, will never pass away and we now await no further new public revelation before the glorious manifestation of our Lord Jesus Christ (cf. 1 Tim 6:14 and Titus 2:13)" *(DV* 4).

General audience of June 1, 1988

Jesus Christ, "the Faithful Witness"

Regarding Jesus Christ's earthly mission, we read in the Constitution *Lumen Gentium* of the Second Vatican Council: "The Son, therefore, came, sent by the Father. It was in him, before the foundation of the world, that the Father chose us and predestined us to become adopted sons, for in him it pleased the Father to re-establish all things (cf. Eph 1:4-5 and 10). To carry out the will of the Father Christ inaugurated the kingdom of heaven on earth and revealed to us the mystery of that kingdom. By his obedience he brought about our redemption" *(LG* 3).

This text summarizes all that we have been speaking about in the recent reflections in which we sought to emphasize the essential aspects of Christ's messianic mission. The Council's text again proposes to us the truth of the close and deep connection between this mission and the envoy himself, Christ, who in the fulfillment of the mission manifested his personal dispositions and talents. Certain fundamental characteristics can be noted in Jesus' entire demeanor. They are expressed in his preaching, and they make his messianic mission completely credible.

In his preaching and in his comportment Jesus showed, above all, his deep union with the Father in his thought and in his words. What he wished to convey to his hearers (and to all humanity) comes from the Father who "sent him into the world" (Jn 10:36). "I did not speak on my own, but the Father who sent me commanded me what to say and speak. And I know that his commandment is eternal life. So what I say, I say as the Father told me" (Jn 12:49-50). "I say only what the Father taught me" (Jn 8:28). Thus we read in John's Gospel. The Synoptics also record a similar statement of Jesus: "All things have been handed over to me by my Father" (Mt 11:27). In the words, "all things," Jesus referred expressly to the content of the revelation which he brought to humanity (cf. Mt 11:24-27; similarly Lk 10:21-22).These words of Jesus manifest the spirit in which he carried out his preaching. He is and remains the "faithful witness" (Rev 1:5). This witnessing includes that particular "obedience" of the Son to the Father, which in the final moment will be shown as "obedience to death" (cf. Phil 2:8).

In his preaching Jesus also showed that his absolute fidelity to the Father as the first and ultimate source of all that was to be revealed, is the essential foundation of his veracity and credibility. "My teaching is not my own but is from the one who sent me," Jesus said, and he added, "Whoever speaks on his own seeks his own glory, but whoever seeks the glory of the one who sent him is truthful, and there is no wrong in him" (Jn 7:16, 18).

These words may appear surprising on the lips of the Son of God, spoken as they are by him who is "of one Being with the Father." However, we must not forget that he spoke also as man. It was important for him to ensure that his hearers should not be in any doubt on a fundamental point, namely, that the truth transmitted by him is divine and comes from God. It was important for him to ensure that his hearers find in his words access to the same divine source of revealed truth: they must not dwell on the one who teaches, nor let themselves be fascinated by the originality and extraordinary character of that which in this doctrine comes from the Master himself. The Master "does not seek his own glory"; he seeks solely and exclusively "the glory of him who sent him." He does not speak "in his own name," but in the name of the Father.

This, too, is an aspect of the "self-emptying" *(kenosis)* which, according to St. Paul (cf. Phil 2:7), will reach its peak in the mystery of the cross.

Christ is the "faithful witness." This fidelity—in seeking exclusively the Father's glory and not his own—is a result of the love which he intends to prove. "The world must know that I love the Father" (Jn 14:31). However, his revelation of his love for the Father also includes his love for humanity. "He went about doing good" (cf. Acts 10:38). His whole earthly mission was full of acts of love for people, especially for the little ones and those most in need. "Come to me," he said, "all you who labor and are burdened and I will give you rest" (Mt 11:28). "Come"; this exhortation is not limited to his contemporaries whom Jesus met during the days of his life and suffering on earth. It is a call for the poor of all times, ever relevant even today, always being renewed on the lips and in the heart of the Church.

Parallel to this exhortation there is another: "Learn from me, for I am meek and humble of heart, and you will find rest for yourselves" (Mt 11:29). Jesus' meekness and humility attract those called to his school: "Learn from me." Jesus is the faithful witness of God's love for humanity. In his testimony divine truth and divine love are united. Therefore, there is a profound conformity, one might almost say an identity, between word and action, between his deeds and his teaching. Jesus not only taught that love is the supreme commandment, but he himself fulfilled it in the most perfect manner. The

Beatitudes that he taught in the Sermon on the Mount were incarnated in all that he did. Not only did he teach us to love our enemies, but he himself lived out that teaching to the full, especially at the hour of his death on the cross when he said, "Father, forgive them, for they know not what they do" (Lk 23:34).

However, that meekness and humility of heart in no way implied weakness. On the contrary, Jesus is demanding; his is a demanding Gospel. Is it not he who admonishes: "Whoever does not take up his cross and follow me is not worthy of me"? And a little later: "Whoever finds his life will lose it, and whoever loses his life for my sake will find it" (Mt 10:38-39). The Gospel language is radical, and so, too, are the actual demands of the following of Christ. He did not hesitate to frequently confirm their full extent: "Do not think that I have come to bring peace upon the earth. I have come to bring not peace but the sword" (Mt 10:34). It is a forceful way of saying that the Gospel is also a source of unease for people. Jesus wishes to make us understand that the Gospel is demanding. This means shaking up consciences, not allowing them to sink into a false "peace" in which they become ever more insensitive and dulled, with the result that spiritual realities would be emptied of value and lose all interest. Jesus said to Pilate, "I came into the world to bear witness to the truth" (Jn 18:37). Those words refer also to the light which he sheds over the entire field of human actions, putting to flight obscurity of thought and especially of conscience in order to secure the triumph of truth in everyone. It is a question, however, of placing oneself on the side of truth. "Everyone who belongs to the truth listens to my voice," Jesus will say (Jn 18:37). Hence Jesus is demanding. He is not harsh or inexorably severe, but firm and unambiguous in calling everyone to live in the truth.

Thus the demands of Christ's Gospel enter into the sphere of law and morality. He who is the "faithful witness"

(Rev 1:5) of the divine truth, of the Father's truth, said from the beginning of the Sermon on the Mount, "Therefore, whoever breaks one of the least of these commandments and teaches others to do so will be called least in the kingdom of heaven" (Mt 5:19). In calling for conversion he did not hesitate to rebuke those very towns where the people refused to believe, "Woe to you, Chorazin! Woe to you, Bethsaida!" (Lk 10:13), while he warned each and every one: "If you do not repent you will all perish" (Lk 13:3).

Thus the Gospel of meekness and humility goes step by step with the Gospel of moral imperatives, and even of severe threats against those who do not wish to be converted. There is no contradiction between the one and the other. Jesus lived by the truth which he announced and by the love he revealed. This is an exacting love, like the truth from which it derives. Love imposed the greatest demands on Jesus himself in Gethsemane, on Calvary and on the cross. Jesus accepted and complied with these demands to the very depths, because, as the evangelist tells us, he "loved to the end" (Jn 13:1). It was a faithful love, so that he could say to the Father on the day before he died, "The words you gave to me I have given to them" (Jn 17:8).

As faithful witness, Jesus fulfilled the mission received from the Father in the depths of the trinitarian mystery. It was an eternal mission, included in the thought of the Father who generated him and predestined him to fulfill it "in the fullness of time" for the salvation of every man and woman and for the perfect good of all creation. Jesus was conscious of this mission of his at the center of the creative and redemptive plan of the Father. Therefore, with all the realism of the truth and love brought into the world he could say, "When I am lifted up from the earth, I will draw all people to myself" (Jn 12:32).

General audience of June 8, 1988

Jesus, Founder of His Church

"The time is fulfilled, and the kingdom of God is at hand; repent, and believe in the Gospel" (Mk 1:15). These words at the beginning of Mark's Gospel are recorded as though to sum up briefly the mission of Jesus of Nazareth, who "came to announce the Good News." At the center of his announcement is the revelation of the kingdom of God, which has drawn near and indeed has entered human history. "The time is fulfilled."

By proclaiming the truth concerning the kingdom of God, Jesus at the same time announced the fulfillment of the promises contained in the Old Testament. The Psalms frequently speak of the kingdom of God (cf. Ps 103:19; Ps 93:1). Psalm 145 sings of the glory and majesty of this kingdom, and at the same time indicates its eternal duration: "Your kingdom is an everlasting kingdom, and your dominion endures through all generations" (v. 13). Subsequent books of the Old Testament again take up this theme, especially the particularly eloquent prophecy of the Book of Daniel: "The God of heaven will set up a kingdom that shall never be destroyed or delivered up to another people: rather it shall break in pieces all these kingdoms and put an end to them, and it shall stand forever" (Dan 2:44).

Referring to these announcements and promises of the Old Testament, the Second Vatican Council noted and affirmed: "To carry out the will of the Father Christ inaugurated the kingdom of heaven on earth" *(LG* 3). At the same time the Council pointed out that "by preaching the Good News, that is, the coming of the kingdom of God, which for centuries had been promised in the Scriptures...the Lord Jesus inaugurated his Church" *(LG* 5). The inauguration of the Church, its institution by Christ, is inscribed in the Gospel of the kingdom of God, in the announcement of his coming and of his presence in humanity. If the kingdom of God is present among men by the coming of Christ, by his words and works, it is also true that, by his express will, "The Church, or in other words, the kingdom of God now present in mystery, grows visibly through the power of God in the world" *(LG* 3).

In many ways, Jesus made known to his hearers the coming of the kingdom of God. Indicative of this are his words about "casting out the devil" from persons and from the world: "If it is by the finger of God that I cast out demons, then the kingdom of God has come upon you" (Lk 11:20). Indeed, the kingdom of God means the victory over the power of evil and of him who is its principal and mysterious author. It is the spirit of darkness, the lord of this world. It is a question of every sin born in the human heart, as a result of man's evil will and under the influence of that mysterious and baleful presence. Jesus came to forgive sins. Even when he healed various illnesses, he observed that the liberation from physical evil is the sign of the liberation from a much greater evil which weighs on the human soul. This was explained at length in the previous reflections.

The various signs of God's saving power offered by Jesus in his miracles, together with his preaching, open the way to an understanding of the truth about the kingdom of God in the midst of humanity. He explained this truth especially by using parables, among which is that of the sower and the seed. The seed is the word of God which can be received in such a way as to take root in the soil of human hearts. Alternatively, for different reasons, it may not be received, or not in such a way as to mature and bear fruit in due course (cf. Mk 4:14-20). Yet another parable confronts us with the mystery of the seed developing through the work of God: "The kingdom of God is as if a man were to scatter seed on the land and would sleep and rise night and day. The seed would sprout and grow, but he knows not how. Of its own accord the land yields fruit, first the blade, then the ear, then the full grain in the ear" (Mk 4:26-28). It is God's power that "gives the growth," as St. Paul would say (cf. 1 Cor 3:6 f.), and indeed, as the same apostle wrote, it is God who "works in you both to desire and to work" (Phil 2:13).

The kingdom of God or the "kingdom of heaven," as Matthew calls it (cf. 3:2), entered human history through Christ. Even during his passion and when his death on the cross was close at hand, Jesus spoke of himself as a king and at the same time explained the nature of the kingdom he had come to inaugurate upon the earth. His replies to Pilate, recorded by the fourth Gospel (cf. Jn 18:33 ff.), are a key text for understanding this point. Jesus was before the Roman governor, to whom he had been brought by the Sanhedrin on the charge of having claimed to be "king of the Jews." When Pilate questioned him on the matter, Jesus replied, "My kingship is not of this world; if my kingship were of this world, my servants would fight, that I might not be handed over to the Jews" (Jn 18:36). However, the fact that Christ is not a king in the earthly sense of the word does not cancel the other meaning of his kingdom, which he explained in reply to a further question of his judge: "So you are a king?" Pilate asked. Jesus replied firmly, "You say that I am a king. For this I was born, and for this I have come into the world, to bear witness to the truth. Every one who is of the truth hears my voice" (Jn 18:37).

It is the most clear and unambiguous proclamation of his kingship, and also of his transcendent character, which confirms the deepest value of the human spirit and the principal basis of human relationships, "the truth."

The kingdom which Jesus, as incarnate Son of God, inaugurated in human history, is the kingdom of God. As such it is established and grows in the human spirit by the power of truth and grace which come from God. This we learned from the parables of the sower and the seed which we have summarized. Christ is the sower of this truth. However, in the last analysis, it will be by means of the cross that he will achieve his kingship and fulfill his work of salvation in human history. "When I am lifted up from the earth, I will draw everyone to myself" (Jn 12:32).

All this is evident likewise from Jesus' teaching on the good shepherd who "offers his life for the sheep" (Jn 10:11). This image of the shepherd is closely connected with that of the sheepfold and of the sheep who hear the shepherd's voice. Jesus said that he is the good shepherd who "knows his sheep and they know him" (cf. Jn 10:14). As a good shepherd, he seeks the sheep that has gone astray (cf. Mt 18:12; Lk 15:4). He thinks also of the "other sheep that are not of this fold"; those also he "must bring," so that "they will hear his voice and there shall be one flock, one shepherd" (Jn 10:16). It is a universal kingship exercised in the spirit and manner of a shepherd, which leads all to live in the truth of God.

As is evident, all of Christ's preaching and his entire messianic mission was directed to gathering the flock. It is not merely a case of so many individual hearers, followers, and imitators. It is rather an assembly, which is expressed in Aramaic as *kehala,* and in Hebrew *gahal,* corresponding to the Greek *ekklesia.* The Greek word derives from a verb meaning "to call" (the Greek translation of "a call" is *klesis*). This etymological derivation gives us to understand that, as in the old covenant God had "called" his people Israel, so Christ calls the new People of God, choosing and seeking its members from among all peoples. He draws them to himself and gathers them around him by means of the word of the Gospel and by the redemptive power of the paschal mystery. This divine power, manifested definitively in Christ's resurrection, will confirm the words once spoken to Peter: "Upon this rock I will build my Church" (Mt 16:18), that is, the new assembly of the kingdom of God.

The Church-ecclesia-assembly receives from Christ the new commandment. "I give you a new commandment, that you love one another, as I have loved you.... By this all will know that you are my disciples..." (Jn 13:34; cf. Jn 15:12). It is certain that the "assembly-Church" receives from Christ also its external structure (of which we shall treat in the near future). But its essential value is the communion with Christ himself. It is he who gathers together the Church; it is he who builds it constantly as his Body (cf. Eph 4:12), as the kingdom of God on the universal level. "They will come from east and west and sit at table (with Abraham, Isaac and Jacob) in the kingdom of God" (cf. Lk 13:28-29).

General audience of June 15, 1988

Jesus, Founder of the
Ministerial Structure of the Church

In the previous reflection, we said that the whole mission of Jesus of Nazareth, his teaching, the miracles he wrought, up to the supreme miracle of the resurrection (the sign of Jonah the prophet), were aimed at "gathering" people together. This "assembly" of the new People of God constitutes the first outline of the Church. By the will and institution of Christ, the kingdom of God, initiated with the coming and with the messianic mission of Christ, is brought into being and continues throughout human history in the Church. Jesus of Nazareth announced the Gospel to all those who followed and listened to him. But at the same time he called some in a special way to follow him in order to be prepared by him for a future mission. Such was the calling of Philip (cf. Jn 1:43), of Simon (cf. Lk 5:10), and also of Levi, the publican. Even to the latter Christ addressed "follow me" (cf. Lk 5:27-28).

Of particular importance for us is the fact that among his disciples Jesus chose the Twelve, a choice that had also the character of an "institution." In this regard Mark's Gospel used the term "appointed" (in Greek πεποιησεν), a verb that the Greek text of the Septuagint used also for the work of creation.

For this the original Hebrew text uses the word *bara,* which has no exact equivalent in Greek. *Bara* expresses what only God himself "does," by creating from nothing. In any case the Greek expression εποιησεν is sufficiently eloquent in reference to the Twelve. It speaks of their institution as a decisive act of Christ who had produced a new reality. The functions or tasks which the Twelve received are a consequence of what they became by virtue of Christ's institution (instituted—made).

The way in which Jesus chose the Twelve is also significant. "Jesus went out into the hills to pray; and all night he continued in prayer to God. And when it was day, he called his disciples, and chose from them twelve, whom he named apostles" (Lk 6:12-13). Then follow the names of those chosen: Simon, to whom Jesus gave the name Peter, James and John (Mark specifies that they were sons of Zebedee and that Jesus surnamed them *Boanerges,* which means "sons of thunder"), Philip, Bartholomew, Matthew, Thomas, James the son of Alphaeus, Simon who was called the Zealot, Judas the son of James, and Judas Iscariot, "who became the traitor" (Lk 6:16). The lists of the Twelve found in the Synoptic Gospels and in the Acts of the Apostles agree, notwithstanding some slight differences.

Jesus himself will speak one day of this choice of the Twelve, emphasizing what moved him to do so: "You have not chosen me, but I have chosen you..." (Jn 15:16); and then he will add, "If you were of the world, the world would love its own; but because you are not of the world, but I chose you out of the world, therefore the world hates you" (Jn 15:19).

Jesus appointed the Twelve "that they might be with him," and "to send them to preach and to have authority to cast out demons" (Mk 3:14-15). They were chosen and appointed for a precise mission. They are people who are sent (apostles). In John's test we read further: "You did not choose me, but I chose you and appointed you that you should go and bear fruit, and that your fruit should abide" (Jn 15:16). This fruit is designated in another place by the image of fishing, when Jesus, after the miraculous catch of fish, said to Peter who was excited by the miraculous event, "Do not be afraid; henceforth you will be catching men" (Lk 5:10).

Jesus set the mission of the apostles in a line of continuity with his own mission when, in his priestly prayer at the Last Supper, he said to the Father, "As you sent me into the world, so I sent them into the world" (Jn 17:18). In this context we can understand those other words of Jesus: "I confer a kingdom on you, just as my Father has conferred one on me" (Lk 22:29). Jesus did not simply say to the apostles, "The mystery of the kingdom of God has been granted to you" (Mk 4:11), as though it were granted merely by way of cognition. But he "handed over" to the apostles the kingdom which he himself had initiated with his messianic mission on earth. This kingdom conferred on the Son by the Father is the fulfillment of the promises already given in the old covenant. The very number of twelve apostles corresponds in Christ's words to the twelve tribes of Israel. "You who have followed me, in the new age, when the Son of Man is seated on his throne of glory, will yourselves sit on twelve thrones, judging the twelve tribes of Israel" (Mt 19:28; cf. also Lk 22:30). The apostles, "the Twelve," as the beginning of the new Israel, are at the same time "placed" in the eschatological perspective of the call of the whole people of God.

After the resurrection, before definitively sending out the apostles into the whole world, Christ linked to their service the administration of the sacraments of Baptism (cf. Mt 28:18-20), of the Eucharist (cf. Mk 14:22-24 and parallel passages), and Reconciliation (cf. Jn 20:22-23), instituted by him as salvific signs of grace. The apostles are therefore endowed with priestly and pastoral authority in the Church.

In the next reflection we shall speak of the sacramental structure of the Church. Here we wish to point out the institution of the ministerial structure, linked to the apostles and later to the apostolic succession in the Church. In this regard we must also recall the words in which Jesus described and later instituted the particular ministry of Peter: "And I tell you, you are Peter, and on this rock I will build my church, and the powers of death shall not prevail against it. I will give you the keys of the kingdom of heaven, and whatever you bind on earth shall be bound in heaven, and whatever you loose on earth shall be loosed in heaven" (Mt 16:18-19). These images reflect and indicate the idea of the Church-kingdom of God endowed with a ministerial structure, such as it was in the mind of Jesus.

The questions of ministry and at the same time of the hierarchical system of the Church will be examined in greater detail in the following series of ecclesiological reflections. Here it is fitting to point out merely a significant detail regarding the sad experience of Christ's passion and death on the cross. Foreseeing Peter's denial, Jesus said to him, "But I have prayed for you that your faith may not fail; and when you have turned again, strengthen your brethren" (Lk 22:32). Later, after the resurrection, having obtained from Peter the threefold confession of love ("Lord, you know that I love you"), Jesus definitively confirmed Peter's universal pastoral mission: "Feed my sheep..." (cf. Jn 21:15-17).

We can therefore say that the respective Gospel passages clearly indicate that Jesus Christ handed over to the apostles the kingdom and the mission which he himself had received from the Father. At the same time he instituted the fundamental structure of his Church in which this kingdom of God, through the continuation of Christ's messianic mission, must be realized among all the nations of the earth as the messianic and eschatological fulfillment of God's eternal promises.

Jesus' last words to the apostles before his return to the Father express in a definitive manner the reality and dimensions of that institution: "All authority in heaven and on earth has been given to me. Go therefore and make disciples of all nations, baptizing them in the name of the Father and of the Son and of the Holy Spirit, teaching them to observe all that I have commanded you; and behold, I am with you always, to the end of the world" (Mt 28:18-20; also Lk 24:47-48).

General audience of June 22, 1988

Jesus, Founder of the Sacramental Structure in the Life of the Church

"I am with you always, to the end of the world" (Mt 28:20). Those words of the risen Christ when sending the apostles out into the whole world, attest that the Son of God, who, on coming into the world, began the kingdom of God in the history of humanity, transmitted it to the apostles in close connection with the continuation of his messianic mission. "As my father appointed a kingdom for me, so do I appoint for you" (Lk 22:29). To achieve this kingdom and the fulfillment of his own mission, he instituted in the church a visible ministerial structure. This was to last "to the end of the world," according to the principle of apostolic succession suggested by these very words of the risen Christ. It is a ministry linked to the mystery. Consequently the apostles regarded themselves and wished to be regarded as "servants of Christ and stewards of the mysteries of God," as St. Paul says (1 Cor 4:1). The Church's ministerial structure supposes and includes a sacramental structure and it is one of service (*ministerium*).

This relationship between *ministerium* and *mysterium* recalls a fundamental theological truth. It is Christ's promise not only to be with the apostles, that is, with the Church, until the end of the world, but to be himself *in* the Church, as the source and principle of divine life. That divine life belongs to him who confirmed, by means of the paschal mystery, his victorious power over sin and death. Through the Church's apostolic service Christ wishes to transmit this divine life, so that they may "remain in him and he in them." He expressed this in the parable of the vine and the branches which was part of his farewell discourse narrated in John's Gospel (cf. 15:5 ff.): "I am the vine and you are the branches. He who abides in me, and I in him, bears much fruit, for apart from me you can do nothing" (Jn 15:5).

Therefore, by Christ's institution, the Church possesses not only its ministerial structure, visible and external, but simultaneously (and above all) an interior capacity belonging to an invisible, but real sphere, where there is the source of every bestowal of divine life, of the sharing in God's trinitarian life. That life is in Christ and is communicated from Christ to humanity through the action of the Holy Spirit for the fulfillment of God's salvific plan. Instituted by Christ, the sacraments are visible signs of this capacity to transmit the new life, the new gift of self which God himself has made to man, namely, grace. They signify grace and at the same time communicate it. Later we shall devote a special series of reflections to the Church's sacraments. What we are interested in at the moment is to point out first of all the essential union of the sacraments with Christ's mission. In founding the Church, Christ endowed it with a sacramental structure. The sacraments, as signs, belong to the Church's visible order. Simultaneously, they signify and communicate the divine life, which pertains to the invisible mystery from which the supernatural vitality of the People of God in the Church derives. This is the invisible dimension of the life of the Church, which in participating in Christ's mystery, draws this life from him, as an undepleted and inexhaustible source, and identifies herself to an ever greater extent with him as the sole "vine" (cf. Jn 15:1).

At this point we must at least mention the specific insertion of the sacraments in the ministerial structure of the Church.

We know that during Jesus' public activity, he performed signs (cf. e.g., Jn 2:23; 6:2 ff.). Each one of them manifested God's salvific power (omnipotence), with the freeing of human beings from physical evil. At the same time, however, these signs, that is, miracles, precisely as "signs," indicated the overcoming of moral evil, the transformation and renewal of man in the Holy Spirit. The sacramental signs, with which Christ has endowed his Church, must serve the same purpose. That is clearly evident from the Gospel.

As regards Baptism, this sign of spiritual purification was already used by John the Baptist. Jesus had received from him "the baptism of repentance" at the Jordan (cf. Mk 1:9; and parallel places). However, John himself clearly distinguished his baptism from that which would be administered by Christ: "He who is coming after me...will baptize you with the Holy Spirit" (Mt 3:11). Moreover, in the fourth Gospel we find an interesting reference to the baptism administered by Jesus, and more precisely by his disciples "in the land of Judea," separately from John (cf. Jn 3:22, 26; 4:2).

In his turn Jesus speaks of the baptism which he himself must receive, thereby indicating his future passion and death on the cross: "There is a baptism with which I must be baptized, and how great is my anguish until it is accomplished!" (Lk 12:50). He asked the two brothers, John and James, "Are you able to drink the cup that I drink, or to be baptized with the baptism with which I am baptized?" (Mk 10:38).

If we wish to refer, strictly speaking, to the sacrament which will be transmitted to the Church, we find it specially indicated in Jesus' words to Nicodemus: "Truly, truly, I say to you, unless one is born of water and the spirit, he cannot enter the kingdom of God" (Jn 3:5).

In sending the apostles to preach the Gospel in the whole world, Jesus commanded them to administer precisely this baptism: the baptism "in the name of the Father and of the Son and of the Holy Spirit" (Mt 28:19). He made clear that "He who believes and is baptized will be saved" (Mk 16:16). "To be saved," "to enter the kingdom of God," means to have the divine life, which Christ gives as "the vine to the branches" (Jn 15:1). He gives it by means of his baptism wherewith he himself was baptized in the paschal mystery of his death and resurrection. St. Paul magnificently presents the Christian baptism as "burial in the death of Christ," to remain united with him in the resurrection and to live a new life (cf. Rom 6:3, 11).

Baptism is the sacramental beginning of this new life of man. The fundamental importance of baptism for sharing in the divine life is emphasized by the words with which Christ sent forth the apostles to preach the Gospel to the whole world (cf. Mt 28:19).

The apostles themselves—closely united with Christ's Pasch—are endowed with authority to forgive sins. Naturally, Christ also possessed that authority: "The Son of Man has power on earth to forgive sins" (Mt 9:6). He transmitted that same power to the apostles after the resurrection, when he breathed on them and said, "Receive the Holy Spirit. If you forgive the sins of any, they are forgiven; if you retain the sins of any, they are retained" (Jn 20:22-23). To forgive sins means, in effect, to restore to man the sharing in the life which is in Christ. The sacrament of Penance (or Reconciliation) is therefore essentially connected with the mystery "of the vine and the branches."

However, it is the Eucharist which is the full expression of this communion of life with Christ. Jesus instituted this sacrament on the eve of his redemptive death on the cross, during the Last Supper (the paschal meal) in the upper room of Jerusalem (cf. Mk 14:22-24; Mt 26:26-30; Lk 22:19-20; 1 Cor

11:23-26). The sacrament is the lasting sign of the presence of his body given up to death and of his blood poured out "for the remission of sins." Likewise, every time it is celebrated, it makes present the salvific sacrifice of the world's Redeemer. All this takes place beneath the sacramental sign of bread and wine, and therefore of the paschal banquet, connected by Jesus himself with the mystery of the cross. We are reminded of this by the words of institution repeated in the sacramental formula: "This is my body which will be given up for you; this is the cup of my blood...shed for you and for all, so that sins may be forgiven."

The food and drink, which in the temporal order serve to sustain human life, in their sacramental significance indicate and effect participation in the divine life, which is in Christ, "the vine." At the cost of his redemptive sacrifice, he communicates this life to the "branches," his disciples and followers. This is made evident by the words of the announcement of the Eucharist spoken in the synagogue of Capernaum: "I am the living bread which came down from heaven; if any one eats of this bread, he will live for ever; and the bread which I shall give is my flesh for the life of the world" (Jn 6:51). "He who eats my flesh and drinks my blood has eternal life, and I will raise him up at the last day" (Jn 6:54).

The Eucharist as a sign of the fraternal meal is closely connected with the promulgation of the commandment of mutual love (cf. Jn 13:34; 15:12). According to Pauline teaching this love intimately unites all members of the ecclesial community: "Because there is one bread, we who are many are one body" (1 Cor 10:17). This union, the fruit of fraternal love, in some way reflects the trinitarian unity formed by the Son with the Father as is evident from Jesus' prayer: "That they all may be one, as you, Father, are in me and I in you" (Jn 17:21). It is the Eucharist that makes us partakers in the unity of God's life according to the words of Jesus himself: "As the living Father sent me, and I live because of the Father, so he who eats me will live because of me" (Jn 6:57).

Precisely for this reason the Eucharist is the sacrament which in a very special way "builds up the Church" as a community participating in the life of God through Christ, the one vine.

General audience of July 13, 1988

The Church's Holiness
Comes From Christ

"Abide in me and I in you..." (Jn 15:4). These words from the parable of the vine and the branches reveal what the Church's internal structure was to be according to the will of Christ. "To abide" in Christ implies a living bond with him as the source of divine life. Granted that Christ calls the Church into existence and that he endowed it with an external ministerial structure, built on the apostles, it is certain that the *ministerium* of the apostles and their successors, and indeed of the whole Church, must be at the service of the mystery. This is the mystery of the participation in the life of God which makes the Church a community of living people. For this reason the Church receives from Christ a sacramental structure, of which we spoke in the previous reflection. The sacraments are the signs of Christ's saving action which overcomes the power of sin and death, implanting and strengthening in people the power of grace and of life, whose fullness is in Christ.

This fullness of grace (cf. Jn 1:14) and this superabundance of life (cf. Jn 10:10) are identified with holiness. Holiness is in God, and only from God can it pass to the creature, especially to man. It is a truth that pervades the whole of the old covenant: God is holy and calls to holiness. The

Mosaic Law exhorted: "You shall be holy; for I the Lord your God am holy" (Lev 19:2). "Keep my statutes, and do them; I am the Lord who sanctifies you" (Lev 20:8). Even though these citations come from Leviticus, which was like a code of worship in Israel, the holiness commanded and recommended by God is not to be understood merely in a ritual sense, but also in a moral sense. It is that which renders man, in the most essential way, like to God and worthy to approach God in worship: interior rectitude and purity.

Jesus Christ is the living incarnation of this holiness. He himself is presented as "he whom the Father consecrated and sent into the world" (Jn 10:36). The messenger of his earthly birth said to Mary about him: "He who will be born will be called holy, the Son of God" (Lk 1:35). The apostles were witnesses of this holiness, as Peter in the name of all proclaimed: "We have believed, and have come to know that you are the Holy One of God" (Jn 6:69). It is a holiness which is manifested more and more in Jesus' life, beginning with the year of his infancy, and reaching its peak in the sacrifice offered "for the brethren" according to the words of Jesus himself: "For their sake I consecrate myself, that they also may be consecrated in truth" (Jn 17:19). This is in harmony with his other statement: "Greater love has no man than this, that a man lay down his life for his friends" (Jn 15:13).

Christ's holiness must become the living patrimony of the Church. This is the purpose of Jesus' salvific work which he announced: "That they also may be consecrated in truth" (Jn 17:19). St. Paul understood this, for he writes in the Letter to the Ephesians that Christ "loved the Church and gave himself up for her, that he might sanctify her" (Eph 5:25-26), "holy and without blemish" (Eph 5:27).

Jesus made his own the call to holiness already addressed by God to the people of the old covenant: "You shall be holy; for I the Lord your God am holy." He emphatically repeated it continually by word and by the example of his life. Especially in the Sermon on the Mount he left to the Church a code of Christian holiness. There we read that, after having said that "he had not come to abolish the law or the prophets, but to fulfill them" (cf. Mt 5:17), Jesus exhorted his followers to a perfection modeled on that of God himself: "You, therefore, must be perfect, as your heavenly Father is perfect" (Mt 5:48). Since the Son reflects most fully this perfection of the Father, Jesus can say on another occasion, "He who has seen me has seen the Father" (Jn 14:9).

In the light of this exhortation of Jesus, one can better understand why Vatican Council II desired to emphasize the universal call to holiness. It is a question to which we shall return in due course in the appropriate series of reflections on the Church. Here at present it is well to draw attention to some of its essential points, where one discerns better the link of the call to holiness with Christ's mission, and especially with his living example.

The Council said: "In the Church, everyone is called to holiness, according to the saying of the Apostle: 'For this is the will of God, your sanctification' (1 Thess 4:3; cf. Eph 1:4)" *(LG* 39). The apostle's words echo faithfully the teaching of Christ the Master who, according to the Council, "sent the Holy Spirit upon all men that he might move them inwardly to love God with their whole heart and their whole soul, with all their mind and all their strength and that they might love each other as Christ loves them (cf. Jn 13:34; 15:12)" *(LG* 40).

The call to holiness therefore is for everyone, "whether belonging to the hierarchy or being cared for by it" *(LG* 39). "All Christians in any state or walk of life are called to the fullness of the Christian life and to the perfection of charity" *(LG* 40).

The Council also notes that the holiness of Christians flows from that of the Church and manifests it. It says that holiness "is expressed in many ways by the individuals who, each in his own state of life, tend to the perfection of love, thus sanctifying others" *(LG 39)*. In this variety "one and the same holiness is cultivated by all, who are moved by the Spirit of God...and follow the poor Christ, the humble and cross-bearing Christ in order to be worthy of being sharers in his glory" *(LG 41)*.

Those whom Jesus exhorted "to follow him," beginning with the apostles, were ready to leave everything for him, as Peter declared to him: "We have left everything and followed you" (Mt 19:27). In this case "everything" includes not only "temporal goods" ("house...land"), but also persons who are dear to one: "brothers, sisters, father, mother, children" (cf. Mt 19:29) and therefore the family. Jesus himself was the most perfect example of such renunciation. For this reason he could exhort his disciples to similar renunciations, including "celibacy for the sake of the kingdom of heaven" (cf. Mt 19:12).

Christ's program of holiness, addressed to both the men and women who followed him (cf. e.g., Lk 8:1-3) is expressed particularly in the evangelical counsels. As the Council recalls: "The evangelical counsels of chastity dedicated to God, poverty and obedience are based upon the words and example of the Lord.... The counsels are a divine gift, which the Church received from its Lord and which it always safeguards with the help of his grace" *(LG 43)*.

However we must at once add that the vocation to holiness in its universality includes also those who are married (and likewise the widowed). It includes those who retain the possession and administration of their property, who are engaged in worldly affairs, and who follow their professions, missions and trades according to their own free disposition, following their consciences and in freedom. Jesus indicated the path to sanctity appropriate to them, for he began his messianic activity by taking part in the marriage at Cana (cf. Jn

2:1-11). Later he recalled the eternal principles of the divine law which are valid for men and women of every condition, and especially those concerning the love, unity and indissolubility of marriage (cf. Mk 10:1-2; Mt 19:1-9), and chastity (cf. Mt 5:28-30). Hence the Council also, when speaking of the universal vocation to holiness, devotes a special place to those united by the sacrament of Marriage: "Married couples and Christian parents should follow their own proper path (to holiness) by faithful love. They should sustain one another in grace throughout the entire length of their lives. They should imbue their offspring, lovingly welcomed as God's gift, with Christian doctrine and the evangelical virtues. In this manner, they offer all men the example of unwearying and generous love" *(LG* 41).

In all the commandments and exhortations of Jesus and of the Church the primacy of charity stands out. In the words of St. Paul, charity is "the bond of perfection" (Col 3:14). It is Jesus' will that "we love one another as he has loved us" (Jn 15:12). That means with a love like his, "unto the end" (Jn 13:1). This is the patrimony of holiness bequeathed by Jesus to his Church. We are all called to partake in it, and thus to draw on the fullness of grace and life which is in Christ. The history of Christian holiness is the proof that by living in the spirit of the evangelical Beatitudes proclaimed in the Sermon on the Mount (cf. Mt 5:3-12), Christ's exhortation in the parable of the vine and the branches is realized: "Abide in me, and I in you.... He who abides in me, and I in him, bears much fruit" (Jn 15:4, 5). These words are verified in many ways in the lives of individual Christians, thereby showing, down the centuries, the manifold riches and beauty of the holiness of the Church, the "king's daughter" robed in embroidered apparel (cf. Ps 45:14).

General audience of July 23, 1988

Jesus Frees Us
from the Slavery of Sin

"The time is fulfilled, and the kingdom of God is at hand. Repent, and believe in the Gospel" (Mk 1:15). These words recorded by Mark at the beginning of his Gospel summarize and stamp on the memory what we have been explaining in the current series of Christological reflections on Jesus Christ's messianic mission. According to these words, Jesus of Nazareth is the one who announced the "approach of the kingdom of God" in human history. The kingdom of God has entered definitively and irrevocably into human history through Jesus, and this kingdom moves through the fullness of time to its eschatological fulfillment in the eternity of God himself.

Jesus Christ transmitted the kingdom of God to the apostles. On them he based the building of his Church which, after his departure, must continue his mission: "As the Father has sent me, so I send you.... Receive the Holy Spirit" (Jn 20:21, 22).

In this context one must consider what is essential for Jesus' messianic mission. The Nicene-Constantinopolitan Creed expresses it as follows: "For us men and for our salvation he came down from heaven." The essential thing in

Christ's entire mission is the work of salvation, which is indicated by his very name "Jesus" *(Ye-shûa*—God saves). That name was given together with the announcement of the birth of the Son of God, when the angel said to Joseph, "She [Mary] will bear a son, and you shall call his name Jesus, for he will save his people from their sins" (Mt 1:21). Heard by Joseph in a dream, these words repeat what Mary had heard at the annunciation: "You shall call him Jesus" (Lk 1:31). Soon after, the angels announced to the shepherds at Bethlehem the coming into the world of the Messiah (Christ) as Savior: "To you is born this day in the city of David a Savior, who is Christ the Lord" (Lk 2:11). "He will save his people from their sins" (Mt 1:21).

"To save" means "to free from evil." Jesus Christ is the Savior of the world, since he came to free the human person from that fundamental evil which has invaded man's inner being throughout the whole course of history, after the first breach of the covenant with the Creator. The evil of sin is precisely this fundamental evil which comes between humanity and the realization of the kingdom of God. Jesus of Nazareth came as Savior. From the very beginning of his mission he announced the "approach of the kingdom of God." He not only announced the kingdom of God, but he eliminated the essential obstacle to its realization, which is sin. Sin is rooted in humanity according to the law of original heredity, and which is an incentive in man to the commission of personal sins *(fomes peccati).* Jesus Christ is the Savior in this fundamental sense of the word. He gets to the root of the evil that is in man. That root consists in turning one's back on God, by accepting the dominion of the "father of lies" (cf. Jn 8:44) who as the "prince of darkness" (cf. Col 1:13) has become through sin (and ever continues to become so from the beginning) the "prince of this world" (Jn 12:13; 14:30; 16:11).

Salvation through Christ's passion and death

The most immediate significance of the work of salvation, already revealed with the birth of Jesus, was expressed by John the Baptist at the Jordan. When indicating Jesus of Nazareth as the one who "was to come," John said, "Behold the Lamb of God, who takes away the sin of the world" (Jn 1:29). These words clearly refer to Isaiah's image of the suffering servant of the Lord. The prophet spoke of him as "a lamb" that is led to the slaughter, and in silence, like a "dumb sheep" (Is 53:7), he accepts death, by means of which "he shall make many to be accounted righteous, and he shall bear their iniquities" (Is 53:11). Thus the definition, "lamb of God who takes away the sin of the world," rooted in the Old Testament, indicates that the work of salvation, that is, liberation from sins, will be carried out at the cost of Christ's passion and death. The Savior is at the same time the Redeemer of man. His work of salvation is at the price of the salvific sacrifice of himself.

All this, still prior to the events of the Pasch of Jerusalem, is expressed step by step in the preaching of Jesus of Nazareth, as we read in the Gospels: "The Son of Man came to seek and to save the lost" (Lk 19:10). "The Son of Man...did not come to be served but to serve, and to give his life as a ransom for many" (Mk 10:45; Mt 20:28). Here one easily sees the reference to Isaiah's image of the servant of Yahweh. If the Son of Man, in his whole way of acting, showed himself as the "friend of tax collectors and sinners" (Mt 11:19), he thereby emphasized the fundamental characteristic of his saving mission. "God sent the Son into the world, not to condemn the world, but that the world might be saved through him" (Jn 3:17).

These words of John's Gospel, the last to be written, reflect all that appeared in the unfolding of Jesus' mission

which was eventually confirmed in his passion, death and resurrection. In the prism of this definitive event, the paschal
mystery, the New Testament authors acutely see the truth of
Christ who accomplished man's liberation from the principal
evil, sin, by means of the redemption. He who had come to
"save his people" (cf. Mt 1:21), "the man Christ Jesus...gave
himself as a ransom for all" (1 Tim 2:5-6). "When the time had
fully come, God sent forth his Son...to redeem those who were
under the law, so that we might receive adoption as sons" (cf.
Gal 4:4-5). "In him we have redemption through his blood, the
forgiveness of our trespasses" (Eph 1:7).

     This testimony of Paul is completed by the Letter to the
Hebrews: "Christ...entered once for all into the holy place
taking his own blood, thus securing an eternal redemption...";
"through the eternal Spirit he offered himself without blemish
to God" (Heb 9:11, 12, 14).

     Peter's letters are as unambiguous as those of Paul: "You
know that you were ransomed...not with perishable things such
as silver or gold, but with the precious blood of Christ, like that
of a lamb without blemish or spot" (1 Pet 1:18-19). "He bore
our sins in his body on the tree, that we might die to sin
and live to righteousness. By his wounds you have been
healed" (1 Pet 2:24-25).

     The ransom for all; the infinite price of the blood of the
Lamb; the eternal redemption: this succession of concepts in
the writings of the New Testament reveals to us at its very
roots the truth about Jesus (God saves). As Christ (Messiah,
Anointed), he frees humanity from the evil of sin, rooted by
heredity in humanity and ever being committed anew. Christ is
the liberator: he who frees before God. The work of redemption is also the justification accomplished by the Son of Man,
as "mediator between God and men" (1 Tim 2:5) by the sacrifice of himself, on behalf of all humanity.

     The New Testament witness is particularly strong. It

contains not only a clear image of the revealed truth on "redemptive liberation," but it goes back to its ultimate source in God himself, whose name is *Love*.

Hear what John says: "In this is love, not that we loved God but that he loved us and sent his Son to be the expiation for our sins" (1 Jn 4:10), since "the blood of Jesus his Son cleanses us from all sin" (1 Jn 1:7). "He is the expiation for our sins, and not for ours only but also for the sins of the whole world" (1 Jn 2:2). "He appeared to take away sins, and in him there is no sin" (1 Jn 3:5). Here we see the most complete revelation of the love with which God loved humanity. This revelation is fulfilled in Christ and through him. "By this we know love, that he laid down his life for us..." (1 Jn 3:16).

In all this we find a surprising consistency, a profound logic of the revelation which unites the two Testaments—from Isaiah to the preaching of John at the Jordan. It comes to us through the Gospels and the testimony of the apostolic letters. The Apostle Paul expresses in his own way the same things contained in John's letters. After observing that "one will hardly die for a righteous man," he declared: "God shows his love for us in that while we were yet sinners Christ died for us" (Rom 5:7-8).

Therefore the redemption is the gift of love on the part of God in Christ. The Apostle is aware that his "life in the flesh" is the life "by faith in the Son of God, who loved me and gave himself for me" (Gal 2:20). In the same way the author of the Book of Revelation sees the ranks of the future Jerusalem as those who have come out of the "great tribulation; they have washed their robes and made them white in the blood of the Lamb" (Rev 7:14).

The blood of the Lamb: from this gift of the love of God in Christ, completely gratuitous, the work of salvation takes its beginning, that is, the liberation from the evil of sin. In that liberation the kingdom of God has definitively "come nearer";

it has found a new basis, and has begun its realization in human history.

Thus the Incarnation of the Son of God has its fruit in the redemption. On the night of Bethlehem, the Savior of the world was born (Lk 2:11).

General audience of July 27, 1988

Jesus Frees Us to Seek the Good in Truth

Christ the Savior came into the world to free humanity from the slavery of sin, at the price of his paschal sacrifice. If the concept of liberation refers on the one hand to evil, freed from which we find salvation, on the other hand it refers to the good, for the attainment of which we have been liberated by Christ, Redeemer of man, and of the world with man and in man. "You will know the truth, and the truth will make you free" (Jn 8:32). These words of Jesus indicate in a concise way the *good,* for which man has been liberated by the Gospel in the sphere of Christ's redemption. It is freedom in the truth. It constitutes the essential good of the salvation effected by Christ. By means of this good the kingdom of God is really near to man and to his earthly history.

The salvific liberation effected by Christ in regard to man contains in itself, in a certain sense, two dimensions: liberation *from* (evil) and liberation *for the* (good), which are intimately united, and mutually condition and complete each other.

Referring again to the evil of sin from which Christ freed man, one must add that by means of the extraordinary "sign" of his salvific power (the miracles) worked by him in healing

395

the sick from various infirmities, he always indicated, at least indirectly, this essential liberation, which is liberation from sin, its remission. This clearly appears in the healing of the paralytic to whom Jesus first said, "Your sins are forgiven," and only later, "Rise, take up your pallet and go home" (Mk 2:5, 11). In carrying out this miracle Jesus said to those around him (especially to those who accused him of blasphemy on the ground that only God can forgive sins), "that you may know that the Son of Man has authority on earth to forgive sins" (Mk 2:10).

In the Acts of the Apostles we read that Jesus "went about doing good and healing all who were oppressed by the devil, for God was with him" (Acts 10:38). Indeed, it appears from the Gospels that Jesus healed the sick from many infirmities, for example, the crippled woman who "could not fully straighten herself" (cf. Lk 13:10-16). When he "cast out the evil spirits," if his opponents accused him of doing this with the help of the evil one, he replied by showing the nonsense of such an accusation and said, "But if it is by the Spirit of God that I cast out demons, then the kingdom of God has come upon you" (Mt 12:28; cf. Lk 11:20). In freeing the human family from sin, Jesus unmasked the one who is the father of lies. Precisely from him, the evil spirit, the slavery of sin in which humanity finds itself had begun. "Truly, truly, I say to you, everyone who commits sin is a slave of sin. The slave does not continue in the house for ever; the son continues for ever. So if the Son makes you free, you will be free indeed" (Jn 8:34-36).

Faced with the opposition of his hearers Jesus added, "For I proceeded and came forth from God; I came not of my own accord, but he sent me. Why do you not understand what I say? It is because you cannot bear to hear my word. You are of your father the devil, and your will is to do your father's desires. He was a murderer from the beginning, and has nothing to do with the truth, because there is no truth in him. When he lies, he speaks according to his nature, for he is a liar and the father of lies" (Jn 8:42-44). It is difficult to find a text in which the evil of sin is so forcefully shown in its root of demonic falsity.

Let us hear once again Jesus' words, "If the Son makes you free, you will be free indeed" (Jn 8:36). "If you continue in my word, you are truly my disciples, and you will know the truth, and the truth will make you free" (Jn 8:31-32). Jesus Christ came to free man from the evil of sin. This fundamental evil has its origin in the father of lies (as is evident in the Book of Genesis; cf. Gen 3:4). Therefore the liberation from the evil of sin, effected to its very roots, must be liberation for the truth, and by means of the truth. Jesus Christ reveals this truth. He himself is the truth (cf. Jn 14:6). This truth brings with it true liberty. It is freedom from sin and from lies. Those who were "slaves of sin" because they were under the influence of the "father of lies," are liberated through participation in the truth, which is Christ, and in the liberty of the Son of God they themselves reach "the freedom of the children of God" (cf. Rom 8:21). St. Paul can assure us, "The law of the spirit of life in Christ Jesus has set me free from the law of sin and death" (Rom 8:2).

In the same Letter to the Romans, the Apostle eloquently presents the human decadence involved in sin. Surveying the moral evil of his time, he writes that men, having forgotten God, "became futile in their thinking and their senseless minds were darkened" (Rom 1:21). "They exchanged the truth about God for a lie and worshipped and served the creature rather than the Creator" (Rom 1:25). "And since they did not see fit to acknowledge God, God gave them up to a base mind and to improper conduct" (Rom 1:28).

In other passages of his letter, the Apostle passes from the external description to the analysis of the inner man where

good and evil are locked in combat. "I do not understand my
own actions. For I do not do what I want, but I do the very
thing I hate. Now if I do what I do not want, I agree that the
law is good. So then it is no longer I that do it, but sin which
dwells within me" (Rom 7:15-17). "I see in my members another law at war with the law of my mind and making me
captive to the law of sin.... Wretched man that I am! Who will
deliver me from this body of death? Thanks be to God through
Jesus Christ our Lord!" (Rom 7:23-25). From this Pauline
analysis it results that sin is a profound alienation; in a certain
sense it renders man an outsider to himself in his intimate
identity. Liberation comes with the grace and truth (cf. Jn
1:17) brought by Christ.

One sees clearly in what the liberation effected by Christ
consists, in regard to which liberty he has made us free. The
liberation effected by Christ differed from that which his contemporaries in Israel expected. Before going definitively to the
Father, Christ was questioned by his most intimate friends:
"Lord will you at this time restore the kingdom to Israel?"
(Acts 1:6). Therefore, even then, after the experience of the
paschal events, they continued to think of liberation in a political sense; under this aspect they expected the Messiah, the
descendant of David.

However, the liberation effected by Christ at the cost of
his passion and death on the cross had an essentially different
meaning. It was liberation from that which in the innermost
depths of man is an obstacle to his relationship with God. At
that level sin implies slavery. Christ has overcome sin in order
to confer once more on man the grace of divine sonship, the
grace that frees. "You did not receive the Spirit of slavery to
fall back into fear, but you have received the spirit of sonship
through which we cry 'Abba! Father!'" (Rom 8:15).

This spiritual liberation, that is, "liberty in the Holy
Spirit," is therefore the fruit of Christ's salvific mission.

"Where the Spirit of the Lord is, there is freedom" (2 Cor 3:17). In this sense, we "were called to freedom" (Gal 5:13) in Christ and through Christ. "The faith that works through love" (Gal 5:6) is the expression of this freedom.

It is a question of the freedom of the inner man, of the "freedom of the heart." Liberation in the social and political sense is not the true messianic work of Christ. On the other hand it must be noted that without the liberation effected by him, without man's liberation from sin, and therefore from every kind of egoism, there cannot even be any real liberation in the socio-political sense. Not merely external change of structures brings about a true liberation of society, as long as man is subject to sin and lies, as long as the passions hold sway, and with them exploitation and the various forms of oppression.

Moreover, that which could be called liberation in the psychological sense cannot be fully achieved, except through the liberating power which comes from Christ. It is part of his work of redemption. Only in Christ is "our peace" (Eph 2:14). His grace and his love free man from existential fear when confronted with a lack of meaning in life, and from that gnawing of conscience which is the inheritance of fallen man in the slavery of sin.

The liberation effected by Christ with the truth of his Gospel, and definitively with the Gospel of his cross and resurrection, by preserving its particularly spiritual and interior character, can have a universal range of action, and is destined for all humanity. The words, "by grace you have been saved" (Eph 2:5) refer to every person. At the same time, however, this liberation, which is "a grace," that is, a gift, cannot be achieved without human participation. Man must receive it with faith, hope and charity. He must "work out his salvation with fear and trembling" (cf. Phil 2:12). "God is at work in you, both to will and to work for his good pleasure" (Phil

2:13). Conscious of this supernatural gift, we ourselves must collaborate with the liberating power of God, who with the redemptive sacrifice of Christ has entered the world as the eternal source of salvation.

General audience of August 3, 1988

Jesus Frees Humanity
for a New Life

It is worth repeating what we have said in recent catecheses when considering Christ's salvific mission as liberation and Jesus as liberator. What is involved is liberation from sin. Sin is the fundamental evil which imprisons man from within and subjects him to the slavery of the one whom Christ called "the father of lies" (Jn 8:44). At the same time, it involves liberation for the truth, which gives us a share in "the freedom of the children of God" (Rom 8:21). Jesus said, "If the Son makes you free, you will be free indeed" (Jn 8:36). The freedom of the children of God derives from the gift of Christ; it endows us with a share in the divine sonship. It confers a share in the life of God.

Consequently, whoever has been set free by Christ not only has his sins forgiven but is raised to a new life. Christ—the author of human liberation—is the creator of a new humanity. In him we become "a new creation" (cf. 2 Cor 5:17).

In today's catechesis, we clarify further this aspect of salvific liberation which is the work of Christ. It belongs to the very essence of his messianic mission. Jesus spoke of it himself. In the parable of the Good Shepherd, for example, he said, "I have come that they (the sheep) may have life and have it to the full" (Jn 10:10). He is referring to the abundance of new life which is a sharing in the life of God himself. Again in this way the newness of the humanity of Christ is realized in man as being a new creation.

That is what Jesus says in figurative but evocative language in his conversation with the Samaritan woman at the well in Sychar. "'If you only knew the gift of God and who it is who is saying to you "Give me to drink," you would have been the one to ask and he would have given you living water.' The woman said to him, 'Sir, you have no means of reaching down and the well is deep, how could you get this living water?' Jesus replied: 'Whoever drinks this water will get thirsty again; but anyone who drinks the water that I shall give, will never be thirsty again. The water that I shall give will turn into a spring inside him welling up to eternal life'" (Jn 4:10-14).

Jesus also repeated this truth in similar words to the crowd, when he was teaching them during the feast of Tabernacles. "Whoever is thirsty, let him come to me and let whoever believes in me come and drink. As Scripture says, from his breast shall flow a river of living water" (Jn 7:37-38). Rivers of living water are an image of the new life in which men share by virtue of the death of Christ on the cross. The tradition of the Fathers and the liturgy understand in the same sense the text of John which stated that from the side (the heart) of Christ, after his death on the cross there came forth blood and water when a Roman soldier struck his side (cf. Jn 19:34).

According to an interpretation which is dear to many of the oriental Fathers and now accepted by different exegetes, rivers of living water shall also flow from the breast of the man who drinks the water of the truth and grace of Christ. "From the breast" means from the heart. A new heart is created within man as the prophets announced very clearly, especially Jeremiah and Ezekiel.

In Jeremiah we read: "This will be the covenant that I will make with the house of Israel when those days arrive, says the Lord. I will plant my law and write it in their hearts. Then I will be their God and they shall be my people" (Jer 31:33). Ezekiel states even more explicitly: "I shall give you a new heart and put a new spirit in you; I shall remove the heart of stone from you and give you a heart of flesh instead. I shall put my spirit in you and make you live according to my precepts and make you observe and keep my laws" (Ez 36:26-27).

It is a question therefore of a profound spiritual transformation which God himself works within man by means of "the breath of his Spirit" (cf. Ez 36:26). The rivers of living water of which Jesus spoke mean the source of a new life which is life in the spirit and in truth, a life worthy of "true adorers of the Father" (Jn 4:23-24).

The writings of the apostles, and in particular the letters of St. Paul, abound in texts on this subject. "If anyone is in Christ, he is a new creation; the old creation has passed away, behold the new has come" (2 Cor 5:17). The fruit of the redemption wrought by Christ is precisely this newness of life. "You have put off the old nature with its practices and you have put on the new nature which is being renewed in knowledge of God after the image of its Creator" (cf. Col 3:9-10). The old nature is the one subjected to sin while the new nature is the one which, thanks to Christ, recovers its original dignity of being made in the image and likeness of its creator (Col 3:9-10). Hence this energetic exhortation of the Apostle to overcome everything in each one of us which is sin and the inheritance of sin: "But now you, of all people, must give up all these things: getting angry, being bad-tempered, spitefulness, abusive language and dirty talk, and never tell each other lies..." (Col 3:8-9).

A similar exhortation is found in the Letter to the Ephesians: "You must give up your old way of life, you must put aside your old self which gets corrupted by following illusory desires. Your mind must be renewed by a spiritual revolution so that you can put on the new self that has been created in God's way in the goodness and holiness of the truth" (Eph 4:22-24). "We are in fact his work, created in Christ Jesus to live a holy life as from the beginning he had meant us to live it" (Eph 2:10).

Redemption is therefore the new creation in Christ. It is a gift of God—grace—and at the same time it implies a call directed to man. Man must cooperate with the work of spiritual liberation accomplished in him by God by means of Christ. It is true that "through this grace you have been saved through faith, not by anything of your own but by a gift from God; not by anything that you have done, so that nobody can claim the credit" (Eph 2:8). Certainly man cannot attribute to himself salvation, that saving liberation which is a gift of God in Christ. Yet at the same time one must see in these gifts the origin of a constant exhortation to act in such a way as to be worthy of such a gift. The full picture of the saving liberation of man involves a profound awareness of the gift of God contained in the cross of Christ and in his redeeming resurrection. At the same time, it involves an awareness of one's own responsibility for that gift: an awareness of the moral and spiritual commitments involved. Here we touch upon the roots of what we can call "the ethos of redemption."

The redemption accomplished by Christ, which acts with the power of his Spirit of Truth (the Spirit of the Father and of the Son) has a personal dimension which is directed to each individual. At the same time, it has an inter-human and social, a communitarian and universal dimension.

This is a subject which we see developed in the Letter to the Ephesians where the reconciliation of the two "parts" of humanity in Christ is described: that is, of Israel, the chosen people of the old covenant, and of all the other peoples of the earth: "He [Christ] is the peace between us and has made the two into one and broken down the barriers which used to keep them apart, actually destroying in his own person the hostility caused by the rules and decrees of the law. This was to create one single new man in himself out of the two [races of men] and by restoring peace through the cross, to unite them both in a single body and reconcile them with God. In his own person he destroyed hostility" (Eph 2:14-16).

That, then, is the definitive dimension of the new creation and of the newness of life in Christ: liberation from division, the breaking down of barriers which separate Israel from the others. In Christ, all people are the chosen people, because in Christ man is chosen. Everyone without exception or difference is reconciled with God and, as a consequence, called to share in the eternal promise of salvation and of life. The whole of humanity is created anew as a "new man" in God's way in the goodness and "holiness of the truth" (Eph 4:24). Reconciliation of all with God through Christ must become the reconciliation of all among themselves as a communitarian and universal dimension of redemption, the full expression of the "ethos of redemption."

General audience of August 10, 1988

Jesus Is Our Model

In the gradual development of the catechesis on the theme of Jesus Christ's mission, we have seen that he is the one who effected man's liberation through the truth of the Gospel, of which the ultimate, definitive word is the cross and resurrection. Christ frees man from the slavery of sin and gives new life by means of his paschal sacrifice. The redemption has become a new creation. A new humanity begins from the redemptive sacrifice and the resurrection of the Redeemer. In accepting Christ's sacrifice, God "creates" the new man "in true righteousness and holiness" (Eph 4:24), the man who becomes an adorer of God "in spirit and truth" (Jn 4:23).

As an historical figure, Jesus Christ signifies a perfect model, the ideal, for this "new man." He who in his own humanity was the perfect "image of the invisible God" (Col 1:15), became a visible model. He was the most perfect model for humanity, through his earthly life, through all that he "did and taught" (Acts 1:1), and especially through his sacrifice.

Here we enter into the ambit of the theme of the imitation of Christ, which is clearly present in the Gospel texts and in other apostolic writings, even if the word "imitation" does not appear in the Gospels. Jesus exhorted his disciples to "follow him." "If any one would come after me, let him deny himself and take up his cross and follow me" (cf. Mt 16:24; Jn 12:26).

Only in Paul do we find this word "imitate," when the Apostle writes, "Be imitators of me, as I am of Christ" (1 Cor 11:1). And again, "You became imitators of us and of the Lord, for you received the word in much affliction" (1 Thess 1:6).

However, it is necessary to observe that the word "imitation" is not the most important thing here. Most important is the fact which underlies it; that is, that Christ's entire life and work, crowned by the sacrifice of the cross, accomplished through love for the brethren, remains a lasting model and ideal. It induces and exhorts us not only to know, but also, and especially, to imitate. Besides, Jesus himself said in the upper room when he had washed the apostles' feet, "I have given you an example, that you also should do as I have done to you" (Jn 13:15).

Jesus' words do not refer solely to the act of washing the feet, but, through that action, to the whole of his life, considered as a humble service. Each disciple is invited to walk in the footsteps of the "Son of Man," who "came not to be served but to serve and give his life as a ransom for many" (Mt 20:28). It is precisely in the light of this life, of this love, of this poverty, of this sacrifice, that the "imitation" of Christ becomes a requirement for all his disciples and followers. In a certain sense it becomes the framework of the evangelical Christian ethos.

That liberation for the new life, about which we have spoken during the previous catecheses, consists precisely in this. Christ has not transmitted merely a magnificent theory to humanity. He has revealed in what sense and in what way the salvific transformation of the "old" man, the man of sin, into the "new" man must be achieved. This existential and therefore moral transformation must succeed in conforming man to that most original model according to which he was created.

Only to a being created "in God's image and likeness" could the words which we read in the Letter to the Ephesians be applied: "Therefore be imitators of God, as beloved children, and walk in love, as Christ loved us and gave himself up for us, a fragrant offering and sacrifice to God" (Eph 5:1-2).

Christ is the model on the way of this "imitation of God." At the same time, he alone makes this imitation realizable, when, through the redemption, he offers us a participation in God's life. At this point, Christ becomes not only the perfect model, but the efficacious model. The gift, that is, the grace of the divine life, by the action of the paschal mystery of the redemption, becomes the very source of the new likeness to God in Christ. Therefore it is also the source of the imitation of Christ as a perfect model.

From this fact, exhortations like that of St. Paul to the Philippians get their force and effectiveness: "If there is any encouragement in Christ, any incentive of love, any participation in the Spirit, any affection and sympathy, complete my joy by being of the same mind, having the same love, being in full accord and of one mind. Do nothing from selfishness or conceit, but in humility count others better than yourselves. Let each of you look not only to his own interests, but also the interests of others" (Phil 2:1-4).

To what does such a "parenthesis" refer? To what purpose are these exhortations and demands addressed to the Philippians? The answer is contained in the following verses of the letter: "this mind...was in Christ Jesus...and have this mind among yourselves" (cf. Phil 2:5). Christ took "the form of a servant...humbled himself and became obedient unto death, even death on a cross" (Phil 2:7-8).

The Apostle touches on what is the central and crucial point of the whole work of redemption accomplished by Christ. Here is also found the fullness of the salvific model for each one of the redeemed. Here is the culminating point of the imitation of the Master. We find the same principle of imitation also expressed in the Letter of St. Peter: "If you do right and suffer for it you take it patiently, you have God's approval. For to this you have been called, because Christ also suffered for you, leaving you an example, that you should follow in his steps" (1 Pet 2:20-21).

In human life, suffering signifies a test of the human spirit's strength. Such a test has a "liberating" significance: it liberates the spirit's hidden strengths and allows them to appear. At the same time it becomes an occasion of interior purification. The words of the parable of the vine and the branches told by Jesus are relevant here, when he presents the Father as he who cultivates the vineyard: "Every branch of mine that does bear fruit he prunes that it may bear more fruit" (Jn 15:2). That fruit depends on remaining (like a branch) in Christ the vine, in his redemptive sacrifice, because "apart from him we can do nothing" (cf. Jn 15:5). On the contrary, as the Apostle Paul states, "I can do all things in him who strengthens me" (Phil 4:13). Jesus himself said, "He who believes in me will also do the works that I do" (Jn 14:12).

Faith in this transforming power of Christ as regards man has its deepest roots in God's eternal design regarding human salvation. "Those who he [God] foreknew he also predestined to be conformed to the image of his Son, in order that he might be the first-born among many brethren" (Rom 8:29). In this way the Father prunes every branch, as we read in the parable (Jn 15:2). In this way the Christian's gradual transformation according to the model of Christ is accomplished, to the extent that in him "all of us, gazing with unveiled face on the glory of the Lord, are being transformed into the same image from glory to glory, as from the Lord who is the Spirit." Thus says the Apostle in the Second Letter to the Corinthians (3:18).

It is a question of a spiritual process from which life flows. In that process it is Christ's generous death which bears fruit, leading into the paschal dimension of his resurrection. It is begun in each of us by baptism, the sacrament of Christ's death and resurrection, as we read in the Letter to the Romans: "We are buried therefore with him by baptism into death, so that as Christ was raised from the dead by the glory of the Father, we too might walk in newness of life" (Rom 6:4). From that moment, the process of this salvific transformation in Christ develops in us "until we all attain...to mature manhood, to the extent of the full stature of Christ" (Eph 4:13).

General audience of August 17, 1988

THE MYSTERY
OF REDEMPTION

Jesus Is the Model of Prayer

Jesus Christ is the Redeemer. The center and summit of his mission, that is, the work of the redemption, includes also this aspect: he became the perfect model of man's salvific transformation. Indeed, all the preceding catecheses in this series have been developed from the perspective of the redemption. We have seen that Jesus announced the Gospel of God's kingdom. But we have also learned from him that the kingdom definitively enters human history only in the redemption through the cross and resurrection. Now he "will hand over" this kingdom to the apostles, so that it may last and be developed in the world's history by means of the Church. The redemption carries in itself the messianic liberation of man, who passes from the slavery of sin to life in the freedom of God's children.

Jesus Christ is the perfect model of this life, as we have learned from the apostolic writings quoted in the previous catechesis. He is the Son who is consubstantial with the Father, united with him in the divinity ("I and the Father are one"; Jn 10:31). By means of all which "he did and taught" (cf. Acts 1:1), Jesus is the only model of filial life directed toward, and united with, the Father. Referring to this model, and reflecting him in our conscience and conduct, we can develop in ourselves a similar form and direction of a "Christlike" life, in which the true "freedom of God's children" (cf. Rom 8:21) is expressed and realized.

Actually, the whole life of Jesus of Nazareth was directed toward the Father, as we have noted many times. This already appears in the answer given by the twelve-year-old Jesus to his parents on the occasion of the finding in the Temple: "Did you not know that I must be busy with my Father's affairs?" (Lk 2:49). Toward the end of his life, on the first day of the passion, "when he knew that his hour had come to depart out of this world to the Father" (Jn 13:1), that same Jesus was to say to the apostles, "I go to prepare a place for you; and when I go and prepare a place for you, I will come again and will take you to myself, that where I am you may be also.... In my Father's house are many rooms" (Jn 14:2-3).

From beginning to end this theocentric direction in Jesus' life and action was clear and univocal. He led his followers to the Father, creating a clear model of life oriented toward the Father. "I have kept my Father's commandments and abide in his love." Jesus considers abiding in the Father's love, that is, fulfilling his will, to be his food: "My food is to do the will of him who sent me, and to accomplish his work" (Jn 4:34). Thus does he speak to his disciples at Jacob's well at Sychar. Before that, in the course of his conversation with the Samaritan woman, he had indicated that this "food" should become the spiritual heritage of his disciples and followers: "But the hour is coming, and now is, when the true worshippers will worship the Father in spirit and in truth, for such the Father seeks to worship him" (Jn 4:23).

The true adorers are, first of all, those who imitate Christ in what he does, and he does everything in imitation of the Father: "The works which the Father has granted me to accomplish, these very works which I am doing, bear me witness that the Father has sent me" (Jn 5:36). Also, "The Son can do nothing of his own accord, but only what he sees the Father doing; for whatever he does, that the Son does likewise" (Jn 5:19).

In this way we find a perfect basis for the Apostle's words, according to which we are called to imitate Christ (cf. 1 Cor 11:1; 1 Thess 1:6), and consequently, God himself: "Therefore be imitators of God, as beloved children" (Eph 5:1). The "Christlike" life is at the same time a life like that of God, in the fullest sense of the word.

The concept of Christ's "food," which throughout his life was to fulfill the Father's will, introduces us to the mystery of his obedience which went as far as death on a cross. Indeed, it was a bitter food, as appears especially during the prayer in Gethsemane, and afterward during the course of his whole passion and agony on the cross: "Abba, Father, all things are possible to you; remove this cup from me; yet not what I will, but what you will" (Mk 14:36). To understand this obedience and why this "food" had to be so bitter, it is necessary to look at the whole story of man on earth, marked by sin, or rather by disobedience toward God, Creator and Father. Therefore, "the Son who makes us free" (cf. Jn 8:36), makes us free by means of his obedience unto death. He did it, showing to the very end his submission full of love: "Father, into your hands I commit my spirit" (Lk 23:46). In this self-offering, in this total "self-abandonment" to the Father, the simultaneous divine union of the Son with the Father ("I and the Father are one"; Jn 10:31) is affirmed above the whole story of human disobedience. This expresses what we can describe as the central outline of the imitation to which man is called in Christ: "Whoever does the will of my Father in heaven is my brother, and sister, and mother" (Mt 12:50; cf. Mk 3:35).

In his life, totally oriented "toward the Father" and deeply united to him, Jesus Christ is the model also of our prayer, of our life of mental and vocal prayer. He not only taught us to pray, principally in the Our Father (cf. Mt 6:9 f.), but the example of his prayer offers us an essential occasion to reveal his bond and union with the Father. One can say that in his prayer the fact that "no one knows the Son except the Father" and "no one knows the Father except the Son" (cf. Mt 11:27; Lk 10:22) is confirmed in a very special way.

Let us recall the more important occasions in his life of prayer. Jesus spent much time in prayer (cf. Lk 6:12; 11:1), especially during the night, seeking places suitable for this (cf. Mk 1:35; Mt 14:23; Lk 6:12). By prayer he prepared himself for baptism in the Jordan (Lk 3:21), and to appoint the twelve apostles (cf. Lk 6:12-13). Through the prayer in Gethsemane he prepared himself to face the passion and death on the cross (cf. Lk 22:42). The agony on Calvary was borne completely through prayer: from Psalm 22:1, "My God, why have you forsaken me?" to "Father, forgive them, for they know not what they do" (Lk 23:34), to the final act of abandonment: "Father, into your hands I commit my spirit" (Lk 23:46). Yes, in life and in death, Jesus was a model of prayer.

Concerning Christ's prayer, we read in the Letter to the Hebrews that "in the days of his flesh, Jesus offered up prayers and supplications, with loud cries and tears, to him who was able to save him from death, and he was heard for his godly fear. Although he was a Son, he learned obedience through what he suffered" (Heb 5:7-8). This statement signifies that Jesus Christ perfectly fulfilled the Father's will, God's eternal design concerning the world's redemption at the price of the supreme sacrifice for love. According to John's Gospel this sacrifice was not only a glorification of the Father by the Son. It was also a glorification of the Son, in accordance with the words of the priestly prayer of the upper room: "Father, the hour has come; glorify your Son that the Son may glorify you, since you have given him power over all flesh to give eternal life to all whom you have given him" (Jn 17:1-2). This is what was fulfilled on the cross. The resurrection after three days confirmed and expressed the glory with which "the Father glorified the Son" (cf. Jn 17:1). Christ's whole life of obedience and filial devotion was based on his prayer, which therefore gained for him the final glorification.

This spirit of a loving, obedient, and devoted child stands out also from the episode already recalled, when the disciples requested Jesus "to teach them to pray" (cf. Lk 11:1-2). He passed on to them, and to all the generations of their followers, a prayer which commences with that verbal and conceptual synthesis which is so expressive: "Our Father." These words manifest Christ's spirit directed as a Son toward the Father and engaged to the very end with "the Father's affairs" (Lk 2:49). In giving us this prayer for all times, Jesus has passed on to us, in and with it, a model of life united in a filial way to the Father. If we are to make our own this model for our life, in particular, if we are to participate in the mystery of the redemption by imitating Christ, it is necessary that we do not cease to pray to the Father as Jesus has taught us.

General audience of August 24, 1988

Jesus Christ Is a
Model of Perfect Love

The filial union of Jesus with the Father is expressed in the perfect love which he also made the principal commandment of the Gospel: "You shall love the Lord your God with all your heart, and with all your soul, and with all your mind. This is the great and first commandment" (Mt 22:37-38). As we know, to this commandment Jesus attached a second, "like the first," that of love of one's neighbor (cf. Mt 22:39). He proposed himself as a model of this love: "A new commandment I give to you, that you love one another, even as I have loved you" (Jn 13:34). He taught and gave his followers a love patterned on his own model.

The qualities of charity listed by St. Paul can truly be applied to this love: "Charity is patient...kind...it is not jealous or boastful or arrogant...it does not insist on its own way...it does not rejoice at wrong...it rejoices in the truth...it bears all things...endures all things" (1 Cor 13:4-7). When the Apostle in his letter presented such an image of evangelical charity to the Corinthians, his mind and heart were certainly filled with the thought of Christ's love. Therefore his hymn to charity may be regarded as a commentary on the commandment of love after the model of Christ who is Love (as St. Catherine of Siena was to say many centuries later), "as I have loved you" (Jn 13:34).

In other texts St. Paul emphasizes that the summit of this love is the sacrifice of the cross: "Christ loved us and gave himself up for us, a fragrant offering and sacrifice to God.... Therefore be imitators of God, as beloved children" (Eph 5:1-2). It is instructive, constructive, and consoling for us to consider these qualities of Christ's love.

Christ's love for us was humble and characterized by service. "For the Son of Man also came not to be served, but to serve, and to give his life as a ransom for many" (Mk 10:45). On the eve of the passion, before instituting the Eucharist, Jesus washed the apostles' feet and said to them, "I have given you an example, that you also should do as I have done to you" (Jn 13:15). On another occasion he admonished them, "Whoever would be great among you must be your servant, and whoever would be first among you must be the slave of all" (Mk 11:43-44).

In the light of this model of humble availability which extends as far as the final "service" of the cross, Jesus can invite the disciples: "Take my yoke upon you, and learn of me; for I am gentle and lowly in heart" (Mt 11:29). The love taught by Christ is expressed in mutual service which includes self-sacrifice for others; its final proof consists in offering one's own life "for the brethren" (1 Jn 3:16). This is what St. Paul highlights when he writes that "Christ loved the Church and gave himself up for her" (Eph 5:25).

Another quality extolled in the Pauline hymn to charity is that true love "does not insist on its own way" (1 Cor 13:5). We know that Jesus has left us the most perfect model of such disinterested love. St. Paul says it clearly in another passage: "Let each of us please his neighbor for his good, to edify him. For Christ did not please himself..." (Rom 15:2-3). In Jesus' love the Gospel radicalism of the eight Beatitudes proclaimed by him is realized and reaches its summit. Christ's heroism will always be the model for the heroic virtues of the saints.

We know that John the evangelist, when he presents Jesus to us at the beginning of the passion, writes of him that "Having loved his own who were in the world, he loved them to the end" (Jn 13:1). That "to the end" seems to prove here the definitive and indomitable character of Christ's love. Jesus himself said in the discourse recounted by his beloved disciple, "Greater love has no man than this, that a man lay down his life for his friends" (Jn 15:13).

The same evangelist writes in his letter: "By this we know love, that he laid down his life for us; and we ought to lay down our lives for the brethren" (1 Jn 3:16). Christ's love, which was definitively manifested in the sacrifice of the cross—rather, "in laying down his life for the brethren"—is the definitive model for all genuine human love. If in many followers of Jesus crucified it takes the form of heroic sacrifice, as we sometimes see in the story of Christian holiness, this measure of the imitation of the master is explained by the power of the Spirit of Christ, obtained by him and sent from the Father also for the disciples (cf. Jn 15:26).

Christ's sacrifice has become the price and the indemnity for man's liberation: liberation from the "slavery of sin" (cf. Rom 6:6, 17), and the passage to the "liberty of the children of God" (cf. Rom 8:21). With this sacrifice, derived from his love for us, Jesus Christ completed his salvific mission. The announcement of the whole New Testament has its most concise expression in that passage of Marks' Gospel: "The Son of Man...came not to be served, but to serve, and to give his life as a ransom for many" (Mk 10:45).

This word "ransom" has encouraged the formation of the concept and expression "redemption." This central truth of the new covenant is at the same time the fulfillment of Isaiah's prophetic announcement regarding the servant of the Lord: "He was wounded for our sins...with his stripes we are healed" (Is 53:5); "He bore the sins of many" (Is 53:12). We can say that the redemption was the goal of the whole old covenant.

Therefore, "having loved to the end" (cf. Jn 13:1) those whom the Father "had given" him (cf. Jn 17:6), Christ offered his life on the cross as "a sacrifice for sin" (according to the words of Isaiah). The awareness of this task, of this supreme mission, was ever present in the thought and will of Jesus. His words about the "good shepherd" who "offers his life for the sheep" (Jn 10:11) tell us this; so does his mysterious though clear desire: "I have a baptism to be baptized with; and how am I constrained until it is accomplished!" (Lk 12:50); and that supreme statement over the chalice of wine during the Last Supper: "This is my blood of the covenant, which is poured out for many for the forgiveness of sin" (Mt 26:28).

From the beginning, the apostolic preaching inculcated the truth that "Christ died for our sins in accordance with the Scriptures" (1 Cor 15:3). Paul said firmly to the Corinthians: "So we preach and so you have believed" (1 Cor 15:11). He preached to the elders at Ephesus: "The Holy Spirit has made you guardians, to feed the church of the Lord which he obtained with his own blood" (Acts 2:28). Paul's preaching fully agrees with what Peter says: "Christ also died for sins once for all, the righteous for the unrighteous, that he might bring us to God" (1 Pet 3:18). Paul repeats the same idea, namely, that in Christ "we have redemption through his blood, the forgiveness of our trespasses, according to the riches of his grace" (Eph 1:7).

To systematize and continue this teaching, the Apostle resolutely states: "We preach Christ crucified, a stumbling block to Jews and folly to Gentiles" (1 Cor 1:23). "For the foolishness of God is wiser than men, and the weakness of God is stronger than men" (1 Cor 1:25). The Apostle is aware of the contradiction revealed in Christ's cross. Why, then, is this cross the supreme power and wisdom of God? There is only one answer—love is manifested in the cross: "God shows his love for us in that while we were yet sinners Christ died for us" (Rom 5:8); "Christ loved us and gave himself up for us" (Eph 5:2). Paul's words re-echo those of Christ himself: "Greater love has no man than this, that a man lay down his life for his friends" (Jn 15:13), for the sins of the world.

The truth about the redemptive sacrifice of Christ who is Love forms part of the doctrine contained in the Letter to the Hebrews. Christ is portrayed as "a high priest of the good things that have come," who "entered once for all into the Holy Place, taking...his own blood, thus securing an eternal redemption" (Heb 9:11-12). He did not offer that merely ritual sacrifice of animals' blood which used to be offered in the old covenant in the sanctuary "made with hands." He offered himself, transforming his own violent death into a means of communion with God. In this way, through "what he suffered" (Heb 5:8), Christ became "the source of eternal salvation to all who obey him" (Heb 5:9). This single sacrifice has the power to "purify our conscience from dead works" (cf. Heb 9:14). Only this offering "makes perfect once for all those who are sanctified" (cf. Heb 10:14).

In this sacrifice, in which Christ "through the eternal Spirit offered himself...to God" (Heb 9:14), he found the definitive expression of his love: the love with which "he loved to the end" (Jn 13:1), the love which required him to become obedient "unto death, even death on a cross" (Phil 2:8).

General audience of August 31, 1988

Christ's Sacrifice Fulfills God's Design of Love

In the messianic mission of Jesus, the climax which we have been gradually approaching in the previous catecheses is that Christ was sent into the world by God to accomplish humanity's redemption through the sacrifice of his own life. This sacrifice had to take the form of self-abasement in obedience even to death, a death which at that time bore a particularly shameful stigma.

In all his preaching, in all his actions, Jesus was guided by the deep awareness which he had concerning God's designs for his life and death in the economy of the messianic mission, with the certainty that they flowed from the Father's eternal love for the world, and in particular for humanity.

If we consider his adolescent years, those words of the twelve-year-old Jesus spoken to Mary and Joseph at the moment of his finding in the Temple of Jerusalem, are very thought-provoking: "Did you not know that I must be in my Father's house?" (Lk 2:49). What had he in his mind and heart? We can deduce it from other such expressions of his thought throughout the whole of his public life. From the beginning of his messianic activity, Jesus insistently impressed upon his disciples the concept that the "Son of Man...must suffer many things" (Lk 9:22). He must be "rejected by the elders and the chief priests and the scribes, and be killed (and after three days rise again)" (Mk 8:31). Yet all this did not originate merely with people, with their hostility toward his person and teaching. Rather it was the fulfillment of God's eternal design, as announced in the Scriptures containing the divine revelation: "How is it written of the Son of Man, that he should suffer many things and be treated with contempt?" (Mk 9:12).

When Peter tried to deny this eventuality ("This shall never happen to you"; Mt 16:22), Jesus reproved him in words of particular severity: "Get behind me, Satan! For you are not on the side of God, but of men" (Mk 8:33). The eloquence of these words is impressive. Jesus wished to make Peter understand that to be opposed to the way of the cross was to reject the designs of God himself. "Satan" is indeed he who "from the beginning" is opposed to that "which is of God."

Jesus was aware both of man's responsibilities for Jesus' death on the cross, which he would have to face because of a sentence by an earthly tribunal, and of the fact that through this human condemnation the divine eternal design would be fulfilled: that "which is of God," that is, the sacrifice offered on the cross for the world's redemption. Even if Jesus (as God himself) did not wish the evil of the "deicide" committed by man, nevertheless he accepted this evil, to obtain the good of the world's salvation.

After the resurrection, while walking unrecognized with two of his disciples toward Emmaus, he explained to them the Scriptures of the Old Testament in these terms: "Was it not necessary that the Christ should suffer these things and enter into his glory?" (Lk 24:26). On the occasion of his final meeting with his apostles he declared: "These are my words which I spoke to you, while I was still with you, that everything written about me in the law of Moses and the prophets and the psalms must be fulfilled" (Lk 24:44).

In the light of the paschal events, the apostles understood what Jesus had said to them in anticipation. Through love for the Master but also through lack of understanding, Peter had seemed to be particularly opposed to his cruel destiny. But he would say to his hearers in Jerusalem on the day of Pentecost, speaking about Christ: "The man...delivered up according to the definite plan and foreknowledge of God, you crucified and killed by the hands of lawless men" (Acts 2:22-23). On another occasion he added, "What God foretold by the mouth of all the prophets, that his Christ should suffer, he thus fulfilled" (Acts 3:18).

Christ's passion and death were announced in the Old Testament not as the end of his mission, but as the indispensable passage required in order to be raised up by God. In particular, the song of Isaiah about the servant of Yahweh as the man of sorrows says, "Behold, my servant shall prosper, he shall be exalted and lifted up...and shall be very high" (Is 52:13). Jesus himself, when he pointed out that the "Son of Man...must be killed," also added that "after three days he will rise again" (cf. Mk 8:31).

We find ourselves, then, in the presence of a divine design which, even if it appears so obvious when considered in the course of the events described by the Gospels, yet always remains a mystery which cannot be explained fully by human reason. In this spirit the Apostle Paul explains himself with the magnificent paradox: "For the foolishness of God is wiser than men, and the weakness of God is stronger than men" (1 Cor 1:25). These words of Paul concerning Christ's cross are invaluable. It is difficult for man to find a rationally satisfying answer to the question "Why Christ's cross?" Nevertheless the answer comes to us yet again from God's word.

Jesus himself formulated such an answer: "For God so loved the world that he gave his only Son, that whoever believes in him should not perish but have eternal life" (Jn 3:16). When Jesus said these words during his nighttime conversation with Nicodemus, probably the latter could not imagine that the phrase "gave his Son" would mean "give him up to death on the cross." However, John, who narrates it in his Gospel, well understood the meaning. The course of events has shown that that was the precise meaning of the answer to Nicodemus: God "gave" his only Son for the salvation of the world, giving him up to the death of the cross for the sins of the world, giving him out of love: "God...so loved the world," creation, humanity! Love remains the definitive explanation of the redemption through the cross. It is the only answer to the question "Why?" with regard to Christ's death being part of God's eternal design.

The author of the Fourth Gospel, in which we find the text of Christ's answer to Nicodemus, returns to the same idea in one of his letters: "In this is love, not that we loved God but that he loved us and sent his Son to be the expiation for our sins" (1 Jn 4:10).

It is a question of a love which surpasses justice. Justice can investigate and catch up with the transgressor. If an innocent person who is holy, like Christ, is sentenced to suffering and death on a cross to fulfill the Father's eternal design, it means that, in sacrificing his Son, God goes in a certain sense beyond the order of justice. He reveals himself in this Son, and, through him, all the riches of his mercy—*dives in misericordia* (cf. Eph 2:4)—as if to introduce, together with his crucified and risen Son, his mercy, his merciful love, in the story of the relations between man and God.

Precisely through his merciful love, man is called to conquer evil and sin in himself and with regard to others. "Blessed are the merciful, for they shall obtain mercy" (Mt 5:7). "God shows his love for us in that while we were yet sinners Christ died for us" (Rom 5:8).

The Apostle comes back to this subject in various places in his letters, in which there often recur the three words: redemption, justice and love. "Since all have sinned and fallen short of the glory of God, they are justified by his grace as a gift, through the redemption which is in Christ Jesus...by his blood..." (Rom 3:23-25). In this way God shows that he does not wish to be satisfied with the rigor of justice which, on seeing evil, punishes it. He wishes to triumph otherwise over sin, that is, by giving the possibility to be free of it. God wishes to appear just in a positive way, by giving sinners the possibility to become just through adhering to faith in Christ the Redeemer. Thus God "is righteous and he justifies" (Rom 3:26). This happens in a disquieting way since, "For our sake he made him to be sin who knew no sin, so that in him we might become the righteousness of God" (2 Cor 5:21).

He who "knew no sin"—the Son, consubstantial with the Father—took upon himself the terrible burden of the sin of all humanity, in order to obtain our justification and sanctification. Here is God's love revealed in the Son. The love of the Father "who did not spare his own Son but gave him up for us all" (Rom 8:32) is manifested through the Son. To understand the significance of these words, "he did not spare," the account of Abraham's sacrifice can be useful. He showed himself ready "not to spare his beloved son" (Gen 22:16), but God spared him (22:12). On the other hand, God "did not spare" his own only Son, "but gave him up" to death for our salvation.

The Apostle's certainty that no one and nothing, "neither death nor life, nor angels...nor anything else in all creation, will be able to separate us from the love of God in Christ Jesus our Lord" (Rom 8:38-39) has its origin here. Together with Paul, the entire Church is certain of this love of God which conquers everything, the ultimate word of God' self-revelation in the history of humanity and of the world, the supreme self-communication which comes through the cross, at the center of Jesus Christ's paschal mystery.

General audience of September 7, 1988

The Death of Christ
As an Historical Event

We profess our belief in the central truth of Jesus Christ's messianic mission: he is the Redeemer of the world through his death on the cross. We profess it in the words of the Nicene-Constantinopolitan Creed, according to which Jesus Christ "for our sake was crucified under Pontius Pilate, suffered death and was buried." In professing this faith we commemorate Christ's death as an historical event, which, like his life, is made known to us by sure and authoritative historical sources. On the basis of these sources we can and we desire to know and understand the historical circumstances of that death, which we believe to have been "the price" of human redemption in all ages.

First of all, what were the circumstances that led to the death of Jesus of Nazareth? How does one explain the fact that he was handed over to death by the representatives of his nation, who delivered him to the Roman procurator, whose name, recorded by the Gospels, is mentioned in the creeds of the faith? For the present let us seek to recall the circumstances which, humanly speaking, explain the death of Jesus. The evangelist Mark, describing Jesus' trial before Pontius Pilate, notes that he was delivered by the chief priests "out of envy," and that Pilate was aware of the fact: "For he perceived that it was out of envy that the chief priests had delivered him up" (Mk 15:10). We may ask: why this envy? We can find its roots in their resentment not only for what Jesus taught, but also for the manner in which he did so. If as Mark says, he taught "as one having authority, and not as the scribes" (Mk 1:22), this must have made him appear to the latter as a threat to their prestige.

We know that there was conflict already at the beginning of Jesus' teaching in his native town. Speaking in the synagogue, the thirty-year-old Nazarene indicated that he was the one in whom Isaiah's announcement of the Messiah was fulfilled. This caused a sense of wonder in his hearers, and later provoked them to wrath. They wished to throw him down headlong from the brow of the hill "on which their city was built...but passing through the midst of them he went away" (Lk 4:29-30).

This incident was only the beginning; it was the first signal of subsequent hostility. Let us recall the principal examples. When Jesus claimed to have the power to forgive sins, the scribes regarded this as blasphemy, because only God has such power (cf. Mk 2:6). When he worked miracles on the sabbath day, asserting that "the Son of Man is lord of the sabbath" (Mt 12:8), the reaction was similar. Already from that time their intention to kill Jesus was evident (cf. Mk 3:6). "They sought to kill him...because he not only broke the sabbath, but also called God his Father, making himself equal with God" (Jn 5:18). What else could be the meaning of the words, "Truly, truly, I say to you, before Abraham was, *I Am*" (Jn 8:58)? His hearers knew very well the meaning of that "I Am." Therefore Jesus again ran the risk of being stoned. This time, however, Jesus "hid himself, and went out of the temple" (Jn 8:59).

The fact that eventually brought things to a head and led to the decision to kill Jesus was the raising of Lazarus from the dead in Bethany. John's Gospel informs us that at the subsequent meeting of the Sanhedrin it was stated: "This man performs many signs. If we let him go on thus, every one will believe in him, and the Romans will come and destroy both our holy place and our nation." In view of these forecasts and fears Caiaphas, the high priest, said to them, "It is evident that one man should die for the people and that the whole nation should not perish" (Jn 11:47-50). The evangelist adds, "He did not say this of his own accord, but being high priest that year he prophesied that Jesus should die for the nation, and not for the nation only, but to gather into one the children of God, who are scattered abroad." And he concludes, "So from that day on they took counsel how to put him to death" (Jn 11:51-53).

In this way John informs us of the twofold aspect of the position adopted by Caiaphas. From the human point of view, which could be more accurately described as opportunist, it was an attempt to justify the elimination of a man regarded as politically dangerous, without caring about his innocence. From a higher point of view, made his own and noted by the evangelist, Caiaphas' words, independently of his intention, had a truly prophetic content regarding the mystery of Christ's death according to God's salvific plan.

Here let us consider the human development of the events. In that meeting of the Sanhedrin a decision was taken to kill Jesus of Nazareth. They took advantage of his presence in Jerusalem during the paschal feasts. One of the Twelve, Judas, betrayed Jesus for thirty pieces of silver, by indicating the place where he could be arrested. They seized Jesus and brought him before the Sanhedrin. To the vital question of the high priest, "I adjure you by the living God, tell us if you are the Christ, the Son of God." Jesus replied, "You have said so" (Mt 25:63-64; cf. Mk 14:62; Lk 22:70). In this statement the

Sanhedrin saw an evident blasphemy, and decreed that Jesus was "guilty of death" (Mk 14:64).

The Sanhedrin, however, could not carry out the sentence without the consent of the Roman procurator. Pilate was personally convinced that Jesus was innocent, and indicated that several times. After having opposed an uncertain resistance to the pressures of the Sanhedrin, he at last gave in for fear of risking the disapproval of Caesar. He did this all the more so because the crowd also, urged on by those in favor of Jesus' elimination, now cried out for his crucifixion. "Crucify him!" Thus Jesus was condemned to death by crucifixion.

Historical responsibility for Christ's crucifixion rests with those mentioned in the Gospels, at least in part, by name. Jesus himself said so when he told Pilate during the trial, "He who delivered me to you has the greater sin" (Jn 19:11). Another passage also says, "The Son of Man goes as it is written of him, but woe to that man by whom the Son of Man is betrayed! It would have been better for that man if he had not been born" (Mk 14:21; Mt 26:24; Lk 22:22). Jesus alluded to various persons who, in different ways would be responsible for his death: Judas, the representatives of the Sanhedrin, Pilate and the others. In his discourse after Pentecost, Simon Peter will also charge the leaders of the Sanhedrin with the killing of Jesus: "You crucified and killed him by the hands of lawless men" (Acts 2:23).

However, this accusation cannot be extended beyond the circle of people really responsible. We read in a document of the Second Vatican Council: "True, the Jewish authorities and those who followed their lead pressed for the death of Christ; still, what happened in his passion cannot be charged against all Jews without distinction, then alive, nor against the Jews of today" (*NA* 4).

As for the consciences of those individuals who were responsible, we must remember Christ's words on the cross:

"Father, forgive them; for they know not what they do" (Lk 23:34). There is an echo of these words in another of Peter's discourses after Pentecost: "And now, brethren, I know that you acted in ignorance, as did also your rulers" (Acts 3:17). What a sense of reserve before the mystery of the human conscience, even in the case of the greatest crime committed in history, the killing of Christ!

Following the example of Jesus and Peter, even though it is difficult to deny the responsibility of those who deliberately brought about the death of Christ, we too shall view things in the light of God's eternal plan. God asked from his beloved Son the offering of himself as a victim for the sins of all humanity. In this higher perspective we realize that, because of our sins, we are all responsible for Christ's death on the cross: all of us, to the extent that through sin we have contributed to causing Christ's death for us as a victim of expiation. In this sense also we can understand Jesus' words, "The Son of Man is to be delivered into the hands of men, and they will kill him, and he will be raised on the third day" (Mt 17:22).

Christ's cross is for all, therefore, a realistic reminder of the fact expressed by the Apostle John in the words: "The blood of Jesus, his Son, cleanses us from all sin. If we say we have no sin, we deceive ourselves, and the truth is not in us." (1 Jn 1:7-8). Christ's cross is a call to each one of us that is both merciful and demanding. It is a call to recognize and confess our guilt and to live in the truth.

General audience of September 28, 1988

Christ's Awareness of His Vocation to Redemptive Sacrifice

"For our sake he was crucified under Pontius Pilate; he suffered death and was buried." In the previous reflection, when referring to these words of the creed, we considered Christ's death as an event with its own historical dimension, and which is explained in the light of the historical circumstances in which it occurred. The creed gives us indications in this regard, echoing the fuller information to be found in the Gospels. The creed also emphasizes the fact that Christ's death on the cross was a sacrifice for sins and was therefore the "price" of human redemption: "He was crucified for our sake," "for us men and for our salvation."

One spontaneously asks: to what extent was Jesus aware of this purpose of his mission? When and how did he perceive his vocation to offer himself in sacrifice for the sins of the world?

In this regard, one must point out in advance that it is not easy to penetrate the historical evolution of Jesus' consciousness. The Gospel refers to it (cf. Lk 2:52), but without offering precise data to determine its stages. Many Gospel texts quoted in the previous reflection testify to Jesus' already clear awareness about his mission. So deeply felt was that awareness that he reacted vigorously and even brusquely against those who, because of their affection for him, tried to dissuade him from that path. A case in point is Peter whom Jesus did not hesitate to rebuke with the words, "Get behind me, Satan!" (Mk 8:33).

Even before his preaching and manner of acting met with opposition and aroused the enmity of those who had the power to decide his fate, Jesus was conscious of the "baptism" of blood (cf. Lk 12:50) that awaited him. He was aware that over his head there hung that "it is expedient," corresponding to the Father's eternal plan (cf. Mk 8:31), long before the historical circumstances were to lead to the fulfillment of what had been preordained. Doubtlessly Jesus abstained for some time from announcing his death, though from the beginning he was aware of his messianic mission, as is evident from his self-manifestation in the synagogue of Nazareth (cf. Lk 4:16-21). He knew that the *raison d'être* of the Incarnation, the purpose of his life, is that which is contemplated in God's eternal plan of salvation. "The Son of Man has not come to be served but to serve and to give his life in ransom for many" (Mk 10:45).

In the Gospels we can find not a few other proofs of Jesus' awareness of his future destiny in accordance with the divine plan of salvation. Already when he was twelve years old, Jesus' reply on the occasion when he was found in the Temple is in a certain way the first expression of this awareness. In explaining to Mary and Joseph that he "must be about his Father's business" (cf. Lk 2:49), the youth let it be understood that he was interiorly oriented to the events of the future. Though barely twelve years old, he seemed to desire to prepare for the future those dearest to him, especially his mother.

When the time arrived to begin his messianic activity, Jesus was among those receiving the baptism of repentance from John in the Jordan. He tried to make it understood, despite the protest of the Baptist, that he felt called to express his solidarity with sinners, to take upon himself the yoke of the sins of humanity, as was indicated by John's presentation of him: "Behold the Lamb of God...who takes away the sin of the world" (Jn 1:29). These words echo and in a certain sense contain a synthesis of what Isaiah announced about the servant of the Lord: "...wounded for our transgressions, bruised for our iniquities.... The Lord has laid on him the iniquity of us all.... Like a lamb that is led to the slaughter, my servant shall make many to be accounted righteous, and he shall bear their iniquities" (Is 53:5-7, 11). Undoubtedly there is a harmony between Jesus' messianic awareness and those words of the Baptist, which expressed the prophecy and expectation of the Old Testament.

Later, the Gospels present us with further information indicating Jesus' awareness of his sacrificial death. For instance, there is the case of the bridegroom's friends, his disciples, who are not expected to fast as long as the bridegroom is with them. "But the days will come when the bridegroom is taken away from them, and then they will fast in that day" (Mk 2:20). It is a significant allusion that reveals Christ's state of awareness.

Besides, it is evident from the Gospels that Jesus never accepted any thought or discourse that could hold out hope of the earthly success of his work. The divine signs he offered, the miracles he worked, could provide a basis for such hopes. But Jesus did not hesitate to deny every intention and to dissipate every illusion in that regard, because he knew that his messianic mission could not be fulfilled otherwise than through his sacrifice.

With the disciples Jesus used a pedagogy that revealed to them little by little the death that awaited him. This is seen with particular clarity at the moment when the apostles seemed to have arrived at the conviction that Jesus was the Messiah, the Christ. Simon Peter expressed this conviction when he exclaimed, "You are the Christ, the Son of the living God" (Mt

16:16). It may be regarded as the culminating point of the process of maturation of the Twelve in their already remarkable experience in following Jesus. It was precisely after this profession of faith (near Caesarea Philippi) that Christ spoke for the first time of his passion and death: "And he began to teach them that the Son of Man must suffer many things, and be rejected by the elders and the chief priests and the scribes, and be killed, and after three days rise again" (Mk 8:31, cf. Mt 16:21; Lk 9:22).

Even the words of stern rebuke addressed to Peter, who was unwilling to accept what he heard ("God forbid, Lord! This shall never happen to you"; Mt 16:22), prove how much Jesus' consciousness was identified with the certainty of the future sacrifice. Being the Messiah meant for him "giving his life in ransom for many" (Mk 10:45). From the very beginning Jesus knew that this was the definitive meaning of his mission and life. Therefore he rejected whatever could be or appear to be the negation of that salvific purpose. This can already be seen in the hour of temptation when Jesus resolutely rejected the tempter (cf. Mt 4:5-10; Lk 4:1-12).

We should note, however, that in the texts quoted, when Jesus announced his passion and death, he spoke also of his resurrection which would take place on "the third day."

This does not in any way affect the essential significance of the messianic sacrifice by death on the cross. On the contrary, it emphasizes its salvific and life-giving meaning. This pertains to the most profound essence of Christ's mission: the world's Redeemer is he who fulfills the Pasch, that is, the passage of man to a new life in God.

In this same spirit Jesus formed his apostles and outlined the perspective in which his future Church should move. The apostles, their successors and all followers of Christ, in the footsteps of the crucified Master, shall have to follow the way of the cross: "They will hand you over to the courts. You will be arraigned before governors and kings because of me, as a witness before them" (Mk 13:9). "They will hand you over to persecution, and they will kill you. You will be hated by all nations because of my name" (Mt 24:9). Jesus foretold also, both to the apostles and to the future followers who would partake in the redemptive passion and death of their Lord, "Truly, truly I say to you...you will grieve, but your grief will become joy" (Jn 16:20). Both the apostles and the Church are called, in all ages, to take part in Christ's paschal mystery in its entirety. It is a mystery in which there is born the joy of the new life in God, from the suffering and grief of those who partake in the sacrifice of the cross.

General audience of October 5, 1988

The Value of the Suffering and Death of Jesus Christ

In the previous catecheses we have summarized the biblical and historical data on the death of Christ. It has been the object of the Church's reflection in all ages, from the first Fathers and Doctors, and from the ecumenical councils, to the great theologians of the various schools that succeeded each other down the centuries to the present day.

The principal object of study and research has been and is the value of Jesus' passion and death in regard to our salvation. The results achieved on this point, besides making us better acquainted with the mystery of redemption, have served to cast a new light also on the mystery of human suffering. Of this it has been possible to discover unthought-of dimensions of greatness, finality and fruitfulness, ever since it has been possible to compare it and indeed to connect it with Christ's cross.

Let us raise our eyes first of all to him who is hanging on the cross, and let us ask ourselves: who is it that is suffering? It is the Son of God: true man, but also true God, as we know from the creeds. For example, the Creed of Nicaea proclaims him "true God from true God...who for us men and for our salvation came down from heaven, was made flesh and...suffered" *(DS* 125). The Council of Ephesus, on its part, declared that the "Word of God suffered in the flesh" *(DS* 263).

"The Word of God suffered in the flesh." This is a wonderful synthesis of the great mystery of the Incarnate Word, Jesus Christ, whose human sufferings pertain to his human nature, but must be attributed, like all his actions, to the divine Person. We have in Christ a God who suffers!

It is an overwhelming truth. Tertullian had already posed the question to Marcion: "Would it be so foolish to believe in a God who was born of a virgin, precisely in the flesh and who has undergone the humiliations of nature?... Say rather that a crucified God is wisdom" *(De carne Christi, 4, 6-5, 1).*

Theology has made clear that this which we cannot attribute to God as God—except in an anthropomorphic metaphorical way whereby we speak of his suffering, regrets, etc.—has been realized by God in his Son, the Word, who assumed human nature in Christ. Christ is God who suffers in his human nature, as a true man born of the Virgin Mary and subjected to the vicissitudes and pains and aches of every son of woman. As the Word, a divine Person, he confers an infinite value on his suffering and death, which thus falls within the mysterious ambit of the human-divine reality, and touches, without affecting, the infinite glory and bliss of the Trinity.

Undoubtedly, God in his essence remains above the horizon of human-divine suffering. But Christ's passion and death pervade, redeem and ennoble all human suffering, because through the Incarnation he desired to express his solidarity with humanity, which gradually opens to communion with him in faith and love.

The Son of God, who has assumed human suffering, is a divine model for all who suffer, especially for Christians who know and accept in faith the meaning and value of the cross.

The incarnate Word suffered according to the Father's plan so that we too "should follow in his steps" (1 Pet 2:21; cf. *Summa Theol.*, II, q. 46, a. 3). He suffered and taught us to suffer.

What stands out most in Christ's passion and death is his perfect conformity to the Father's will, with that obedience which has always been considered the most characteristic and essential disposition of sacrifice.

St. Paul says of Christ that he "became obedient unto death, even death on a cross" (Phil 2:8). He thus reached the extreme limit of self-emptying included in the Incarnation of the Son of God, in contrast with the disobedience of Adam who had desired to "grasp" equality with God (cf. Phil 2:6).

Thus the "new Adam" overturned the human condition (Saint Irenaeus called it a *recirculatio*). Christ "though he was in the form of God, did not count equality with God a thing to be grasped, but emptied himself" (Phil 2:6-7). The Letter to the Hebrews follows in the same line: "Although he was a Son, he learned obedience through what he suffered" (Heb 5:8). He himself it was who in life and in death, according to the Gospels, offered himself to the Father in the fullness of obedience: "Not what I will, but what you will" (Mk 14:36). "Father, into your hands I commit my spirit" (Lk 23:46). St. Paul summarizes all this when he says that the Son of God made man "humbled himself and became obedient unto death, even death on a cross" (Phil 2:8).

At Gethsemane we see how painful this obedience was to be: "Father, all things are possible to you; remove this cup from me; yet not what I will, but what you will" (Mk 14:36). In that moment Christ's agony of soul was much more painful than that of the body (cf. *Summa Theol.*, III, q. 46, a. 6). This was because of the interior conflict between the supreme motives of the passion in the divine plan, and the perception which Jesus, in the refined sensitivity of his soul, had of the abominable filth of sin. Sin seems to have been poured over him, who had become as it were "sin" (that is, the victim of sin) as St. Paul says (cf. 2 Cor 5:21), so that universal sin might be expiated in him. Thus Jesus arrived at death as at the supreme act of obedience: "Father, into your hands I commit my spirit" (Lk 23:46): the spirit, that is, the principle of his human life.

Suffering and death are the definitive manifestation of the Son's total obedience to the Father. The incarnate Word's homage and sacrifice of obedience are a marvelous demonstration of filial availability, which in the mystery of the Incarnation rises up and in a certain way penetrates the mystery of the Trinity! With the perfect homage of his obedience Jesus Christ obtained a complete victory over the disobedience of Adam and over all the rebellions which can arise in human hearts, more especially because of suffering and death. Here also it can be said that "where sin increased, grace abounded all the more" (Rom 5:20). Jesus made up for the disobedience which is always included in human sin, by satisfying on our behalf the demands of divine justice. Many saints are "heroes of the cross."

In the work of salvation accomplished in the passion and death on the cross, Jesus pushed to the very limit the manifestation of the divine love for humanity, which is at the origin of his oblation and of the Father's plan.

"Despised and rejected by men, a man of sorrows and acquainted with grief" (Is 53:3), Jesus demonstrated the truth of those prophetic words: "Greater love has no man than this, that a man lay down his life for his friends" (Jn 15:13). Becoming a "man of sorrows," he established a new solidarity of God with human suffering. The Eternal Son of the Father, in communion with him in his eternal glory, in becoming man was careful not to claim privileges of earthly glory or at least exemption from pain. Instead, he entered on the way of the cross. He chose as his part both the physical and moral sufferings which accompanied him unto death. All this was for love of us, to give us the decisive proof of his love, to make reparation for our sins, and to lead into unity those who had been scattered abroad (cf. Jn 11:52). All this was because Christ's love reflects God's love for humanity.

St. Thomas can therefore state that the first reason indicating the appropriateness of human liberation through the passion and death of Christ is that "in this way man knows how much God loves him, and man on his part is induced to love him in return; in this love consists the perfection of human salvation" *(Summa Theol.,* III, q. 46, a. 3). Here the holy Doctor quotes the Apostle Paul who writes, "God shows his love for us in that while we were yet sinners Christ died for us" (Rom 5:8).

Before this mystery we can say that without Christ's suffering and death, God's love for humanity would not have been manifested in all its depth and immensity. Suffering and death have become, with Christ, an invitation, a stimulus, a call to a more generous love, as has happened in the case of so many saints who can rightly be called "heroes of the cross." This always happens in so many people, known and unknown, who are able to sanctify suffering by mirroring in themselves the lacerated face of Christ. In this way they associate themselves with his redemptive oblation.

It remains to be said that, in his humanity united to the divinity, and made capable, by virtue of the abundance of charity and of obedience, of reconciling man with God (cf. 2 Cor 5:19), Christ has been established as the sole mediator between humanity and God. This is at a level far superior to that of the saints of the Old and New Testaments and even of the Virgin Mary, when we speak of their mediation or invoke their intercession.

Here we are then before our Redeemer, Jesus Christ crucified, who died for love of us and has thereby become the author of our salvation. With one of her striking and expressive images, St. Catherine of Siena compared him to a "bridge on the world." Yes, he is truly the bridge and the mediator, because through him we receive every heavenly gift and through him there rises up to God our every yearning and invocation for salvation (cf. *Summa Theol.*, III, q. 26, a. 2). With Catherine and so many other saints of the cross, let us hold on tightly to this our most sweet and most merciful Redeemer, whom Catherine called Christ-Love. In his pierced heart is our hope, and our peace.

General audience of October 19, 1988

The Redemptive Value of Christ's Sacrifice

We consider again some concepts which patristic tradition took from biblical sources in an attempt to explain the "unsearchable riches" (Eph 3:8) of the redemption. We have already referred to them in the preceding reflections, but they deserve to be explained in greater detail because of their theological and spiritual importance.

When Jesus said, "The Son of Man came not to be served but to serve, and to give his life as a ransom for many" (Mk 10:45), he summed up in these words the essential purpose of his messianic mission: "to give his life as a ransom." It is a redemptive mission for all humanity, because the expression, "as a ransom for many," according to the Semitic mode of thought, does not exclude anyone. The Messiah's mission had already been seen in the light of this redemptive value in the book of the prophet Isaiah, and particularly in the servant of the Lord oracles: "Yet it was our infirmities that he bore, our sufferings that he endured, while we thought of him as stricken, as one smitten by God and afflicted. But he was pierced for our offenses, crushed for our sins, upon him was the chastisement that makes us whole, by his stripes we were healed" (Is 53:4-5).

These prophetic words make us understand better what Jesus meant when he spoke of the Son of Man who had come "to give his life as a ransom for many." He meant that he gave his life "in the name of" and in substitution for all humanity, to free all from sin. This "substitution" excludes any participation whatsoever in sin on the part of the Redeemer. He was absolutely innocent and holy. You alone are the Holy One! To say that a person was chastised in place of another implies obviously that he did not commit the fault. In his redemptive substitution *(substitutio)*, Christ, precisely because of his innocence and holiness, "is certainly equal to all," as St. Cyril of Alexandria writes *(In Isaiam* 5, 1; PG 70, 1176; *In 2 Cor* 5:21: PG 74, 945). Precisely because "he committed no sin" (1 Pet 2:22), he could take upon himself that which is the effect of sin, namely, suffering and death, giving to the sacrifice of his life a real value and a perfect redemptive meaning.

What confers on substitution its redemptive value is not the material fact that an innocent person has suffered the chastisement deserved by the guilty and that justice has thus been in some way satisfied (in such a case one should speak rather of a grave injustice). The redemptive value comes instead from the fact that the innocent Jesus, out of pure love, entered into solidarity with the guilty and thus transformed their situation from within. When a catastrophic situation such as that caused by sin is taken upon oneself on behalf of sinners out of pure love, then that situation is no longer under the sign of opposition to God. On the contrary, it is under the sign of docility to the love which comes from God (cf. Gal 1:4), and therefore becomes a source of blessing (Gal 3:13-14). Christ, by offering himself "as a ransom for many," put into effect to the very ultimate his solidarity with man, with every man and with every sinner. The Apostle Paul indicates this when he writes, "The love of Christ impels us, once we have come to the conviction that one died for all; therefore, all have died" (2 Cor 5:14). Christ therefore is in solidarity with everyone in

death, which is an effect of sin. But in him this solidarity was
in no way the effect of sin; instead, it was a gratuitous act of
the purest love. Love induced Christ to give his life, by accepting death on the cross. His solidarity with man in death
consists in the fact that he not only died as every man dies, but
that he died for every one. Thus this "substitution" signified
the superabundance of love which overcomes every deficiency
and insufficiency of human love, every negation and contrari-
ety linked with human sin in every dimension—interior and
historical—in which this sin has weighed on the relationship
of man with God.

The sacrifice of Christ's human life
had an infinite value

At this point, however, we go beyond the purely human
measure of the "ransom" which Christ offered "for all." No
one, not even the greatest saint, was in a position to take upon
himself the sins of all humanity and to offer himself in sacrifice "for all." Only Jesus Christ was capable of that, because,
though true man, he was the Son of God, of the same being
with the Father. For this reason the sacrifice of his human life
had an infinite value. The subsistence in Christ of the divine
Person of the Son, who transcends and at the same time embraces all human persons, makes possible his redemptive
sacrifice "for all." "Jesus Christ was worth all of us" writes St.
Cyril of Alexandria (cf. *In Isaiam* 5, 1: PG 70, 1176). The
same divine transcendence of the person of Christ enables him
"to represent" all humanity before the Father. This explains the
"substitutive" character of Christ's redemption in the name of
all and for all. "He won for us justification by his most holy
passion on the wood of the cross," the Council of Trent taught
(Decree on Justification, ch. 7: *DS* 1529), underlining the
meritorious value of Christ's sacrifice.

Here it is to be noted that the merit of Christ's sacrifice is universal, that is to say, it is efficacious for each and every one. This is because it is based on a universal representativeness, made evident by the texts which we have seen on Christ's substitution for all humanity in his sacrifice. He who "was equal to all of us," as St. Cyril of Alexandria said, could very well by himself alone suffer for all (cf. *In Isaiam* 5.1: PG 70, 1176; *In 2 Cor* 5, 21: PG 74, 945). All this was included in God's salvific plan and in Christ's messianic vocation.

This is a truth of faith, based on Jesus' clear and unambiguous words, repeated by him also at the moment of the institution of the Eucharist. St. Paul transmits them to us in a text that is considered the most ancient on this point: "This is my body which is (given) for you.... This cup is the new covenant in my blood" (1 Cor 11:24-25). The Synoptics are in agreement with this text, when they speak of the body which "is given" and of the blood which will be "poured out...for the remission of sins" (cf. Mk 14:22-24; Mt 26:26-28; Lk 22:19-20). Moreover, in the priestly prayer at the Last Supper, Jesus said, "For their sake I consecrate myself, that they also may be consecrated in truth" (Jn 17:19). An echo and in a certain way a clarification of the meaning of these words of Jesus is found in the First Letter of St. John: "He is the expiation for our sins, and not for ours only but also for the sins of the whole world" (1 Jn 2:2). As can be seen, St. John offers us the authentic interpretation of the other texts on the substitutive value of Christ's sacrifice, in the sense of the universality of redemption.

This truth of our faith does not exclude but demands the participation of each and every human being in Christ's sacrifice in collaboration with the Redeemer. As we said above, no human being could carry out the work of redemption by offering a substitutive sacrifice "for the sins of the whole world" (cf. 1 Jn 2:2). But it is also true that each one is called upon to participate in Christ's sacrifice and to collaborate with him in the work of redemption carried out by him. The Apostle Paul says so explicitly when he writes to the Colossians: "Now I rejoice in my sufferings for your sake, and in my flesh I complete what is lacking in Christ's afflictions for the sake of his body, that is, the Church" (Col 1:24). The same Apostle also writes, "I have been crucified with Christ" (Gal 2:20). These statements do not derive merely from Paul's personal experience and interpretation. They express the truth about man, redeemed certainly at the price of Christ's cross, and yet at the same time called to "complete in his flesh" what is lacking in Christ's suffering for the redemption of the world. All this is situated in the logic of the covenant between God and man. In human beings it presupposes faith as the fundamental way of participation in the salvation deriving from Jesus' sacrifice on the cross.

Christ himself has called and constantly calls his disciples to this participation: "If any man would come after me, let him deny himself and take up his cross and follow me" (Mk 8:34). More than once he spoke of the persecutions which await his disciples: "A servant is not greater than his master. If they persecuted me, they will persecute you" (Jn 15:20). "You will weep and lament, but the world will rejoice; you will be sorrowful, but your sorrow will turn into joy" (Jn 16:20). These and other New Testament texts have rightly provided the basis for the theological, spiritual and ascetical tradition which from the earliest times has maintained the necessity and shown the ways of the following of Christ in his passion. This is done not only as an imitation of his virtues, but also as a cooperation in the universal redemption by participating in his sacrifice.

Here we have one of the cornerstones of the specific Christian spirituality that we are called upon to reactivate in our life by virtue of Baptism itself which, as St. Paul says (cf. Rom 6:3-4) brings about sacramentally our death and burial by immersing us in Christ's salvific sacrifice. If Christ has redeemed humanity by accepting the cross and death "for all," the solidarity of Christ with every human being contains in itself the call to cooperate in solidarity with him in the work of redemption. This is the eloquence of the Gospel. This is especially the eloquence of the cross. This is the importance of Baptism, which, as we shall see in due course, already effects in itself the participation of every person in the salvific work, in which he is associated with Christ by the same divine vocation.

General audience of October 26, 1988

Christ Made His Death
an Act of Offering and of Love

Today's liturgical feast of November 2 directs our thoughts to eternity. It opens up before us the perspective of that "new heaven" and that "new earth" (Rev 22:1) which will be "the dwelling of God with men" (v. 3). Then God "will wipe away every tear from their eyes, and death shall be no more, neither shall there be mourning nor crying nor pain any more, for the former things have passed away" (v. 4).

Already this vision has become a reality for the immense number of saints in heaven who now enjoy the beatific vision of God. Today we pause to contemplate their glory, rejoicing in the hope of one day sharing in it, mindful of Jesus' promise: "In my Father's house are many rooms...I go to prepare a place for you" (Jn 14:2).

The serenity of the Christian when faced with death is rooted in this certainty. It does not derive from a kind of insensitivity or indifferent resignation to the fact of death, but from the conviction that—contrary to appearances—death does not have the last word in human destiny. Death can and must be conquered by life. The final perspective and the hope of the Christian who lives in God's grace is not death but life: eternal life, as Scripture tells us. This is a full and unending sharing—beyond the confines of the present life and beyond death—in God's infinite life itself.

Today's commemoration of all the faithful departed leads us logically to meditate on death, on this mysterious and disturbing fact well known to all of us. But at times we endeavor to remove it from our consciousness as an irksome and troublesome thought, believing thereby to lead a more serene life. Thus it happens that even on certain occasions—for example, certain serious illnesses—when the thought of death arises spontaneously, one seeks instead to banish it from ourselves or from others, thinking by doing so to be compassionate and delicate. We should ask ourselves, we Christians also, if and how and to what extent we can think about death and how to speak about death.

Nevertheless, is not one of the fundamental truths of our creed a certain concept of death? Does not our faith perhaps offer us a decisive light—and an extremely consoling one—about the meaning and, we might add, the value of death? Indeed, dear brothers and sisters, it is exactly so; for us Christians death is a value. Yes, it is true that for us Christians, death is and remains a negative fact against which our nature rebels. And yet we know that Christ was able to make of death an act of offering, an act of love, an act of ransom and of liberation from sin and from death itself. By accepting death in a Christian way we conquer death forever.

What do we seek, then, for our departed brothers and sisters? What do we hope for? We pray that they may be freed from all evil and suffering. It is the hope inspired by the abiding word of Christ and by the transcendent message of Sacred Scripture. Christianity is the final and certain victory over every kind of evil: over sin, especially, and on the last day, over death and all suffering.

Here on earth our liberation begins with freedom from sin, which is the fundamental thing and the condition for all the rest. Suffering remains as a means of expiation and ransom. But if we die in the grace of God, we know with certainty that we shall enter into life and eternal happiness. Our soul shall one day reassume that body destroyed by death, so that it also may participate in a certain way in the blessed vision of paradise.

> "The Lord is my light and my salvation;
> whom shall I fear?
> The Lord is the stronghold of my life;
> of whom shall I be afraid?
> One thing have I asked of the Lord,
> that will I seek after;
> that I may dwell in the house of the Lord
> all the days of my life"
> (Ps 27:1, 4).

Life on earth is not a journey toward death, but a journey toward life and light, toward the Lord. Death, beginning with that of sin, can and must be overcome.

Let us pray for our brothers and sisters who have preceded us on the path of life here below, fighting the good fight of faith, and let us intercede for them.

> "Eternal rest grant unto them, O Lord,
> and let perpetual light shine upon them."

Thus let us remember them so that they may be at rest in peace; that they may enjoy the fruits of their labors and sacrifice; that their sufferings may not have been in vain; and that they may enjoy what they desired: "To dwell in the house of the Lord forever."

General audience of November 2, 1988

The Meaning of Suffering
in the Light of Christ's Passion

"If a grain of wheat...dies, it bears much fruit" (Jn 12:24).

The redemption carried out by Christ at the price of his passion and death on the cross is a decisive event in human history, not only because it fulfills the supreme divine plan of justice and mercy, but also because it gave new meaning to the problem of suffering. No problem has weighed more heavily on the human family, especially in its relationship with God. We know that the value of human existence is conditioned by the solution of the problem of suffering. To a certain extent it coincides with the problem of evil, whose presence in the world is so difficult to accept.

Christ's cross—the passion—throws a completely new light on this problem by conferring another meaning on human suffering in general.

In the Old Testament suffering was considered as a penalty inflicted on man for his sins by a just God. However, within this perspective, based on an initial divine revelation, it was difficult to explain the suffering of the innocent. This is an acute problem, the classic example of which is found in the case of Job. It must be added, however, that already in the

Book of Isaiah the problem is seen in a new light. The figure of the servant of Yahweh seems to constitute a particularly significant and effective preparation in relation to the paschal mystery, in the center of which those who suffer in all times and peoples find their place alongside the "man of sorrows"— Christ.

Christ who suffers is, in the words of a modern poet, "the Holy One who suffers," the innocent one who suffers. This is so because his suffering has a much greater intensity compared with that of all other human beings, even of all the Jobs, that is to say, of all those who suffer without fault of their own. Christ is the only one truly without sin, and who, moreover, could not sin. He is therefore the only one who absolutely did not deserve to suffer. Yet he is the one who accepted suffering in the fullest and most resolute manner, and who accepted it voluntarily and with love. This indicates his desire, his interior urge, as it were, to drink to the dregs the cup of suffering (cf. Jn 18:11), and this "for our sins, and not for ours only, but also for the sins of the whole world," as the Apostle John explains (1 Jn 2:2). In this desire, communicated to a soul without guilt, is found the essence of the redemption of the world by means of the cross. The redemptive power of suffering is in love.

Thanks to Christ, the meaning of suffering changes radically. It no longer suffices to see in it a punishment for sin. One must discern in it the redemptive, salvific power of love. The evil of suffering, in the mystery of Christ's redemption, is overcome and in every case transformed. It becomes a force of liberation from evil, for the victory of the good. All human sufferings, united to that of Christ, complete "what is lacking in Christ's afflictions for the sake of his body" (cf. Col 1:24). The body is the Church as the universal community of salvation.

In what is known as his pre-paschal teaching, Jesus made it known on more than one occasion that the concept of suffering, understood exclusively as a punishment for sin, is insufficient and even incorrect. Thus when some told him of the Galileans "whose blood Pilate had mingled with their sacrifices," Jesus inquired, "Do you think that these Galileans were worse sinners than all the other Galileans, because they suffered thus?... Or those eighteen upon whom the tower of Siloam fell and killed them, do you think that they were worse offenders than all the others who dwelt in Jerusalem?" (Lk 13:1-2, 4). Here Jesus clearly called in question a view that was widely and commonly accepted at the time. He made it understood that the misfortune that brings the suffering cannot be understood exclusively as a punishment for personal sins. "No, I tell you," Jesus declared, and then added, "But unless you repent, you will all likewise perish" (Lk 13:3-4). In the context, a comparison of these words with those that went before makes it evident that Jesus intended to emphasize the necessity of avoiding sin, because that is the real evil, the evil in itself. Given the solidarity that binds human beings among themselves, sin is the ultimate root of all suffering. It does not suffice to avoid sin merely through fear of the punishment that the sinner may incur. One must truly be converted to the good, so that the law of solidarity can reverse its effectiveness and develop, through communion with Christ's suffering, a positive influence on the other members of the human family.

This is the meaning of Jesus' words when he healed the man born blind. The disciples asked him: "Rabbi, who sinned, this man or his parents, that he was born blind?" Jesus answered: "It was not that this man sinned, or his parents, but that the works of God might be made manifest in him" (Jn 9:1-3). By giving sight to the blind man, Jesus made known the works of God which were to be revealed in that disabled man, to the advantage of himself and of all those who should come to know of the event. The miraculous healing of the blind man was a sign which led him to believe in Christ and introduced into the mind of others a seed of disquiet (cf. Jn 9:16). The profession of faith of the blind man who had received his sight manifested the essential "work of God," the gift of salvation which he received together with the gift of sight. "Do you believe in the Son of Man?... Who is he, sir, that I may believe in him?...You have seen him, and it is he who speaks to you.... Lord, I believe" (Jn 9:35-38).

Against the background of this event we perceive in the light of the cross some aspects of the truth about suffering. A judgment that views suffering exclusively as a punishment of sin runs counter to love for man. This had appeared already in the case of Job's "comforters" who accuse him with arguments based on a conception of justice devoid of any opening to love (cf. Job 4 ff.). One sees it still better in the case of the man born blind: "Who sinned, this man or his parents, that he was born blind?" (Jn 9:2). It is like pointing a finger at someone. It is a judgment which passes from suffering seen as a physical torment, to that understood as a punishment for sin. Someone must have sinned, either the man in question or his parents. It is a moral imputation: he suffers, therefore he must have been guilty.

To put an end to this petty and unjust way of thinking, it was necessary to reveal in its essential profundity the mystery of the suffering of the innocent one, the holy one, the man of sorrows! Ever since Christ chose the cross and died on Golgotha, all who suffer, especially those who suffer without fault, can come face to face with the "holy one who suffers." They can find in his passion the complete truth about suffering, its full meaning and its importance.

In the light of this truth, all those who suffer can feel called to share in the work of redemption accomplished by means of the cross. To share in the cross of Christ means to believe in the saving power of the sacrifice which every believer can offer together with the Redeemer. Suffering then casts off the mantle of absurdity which seems to cover it. It acquires a profound dimension and reveals its creative meaning and value. It could then be said that it changes the scenario of existence, from which the destructive power of evil is ever farther removed, precisely because suffering bears its copious fruits. Jesus himself revealed and promised that to us when he said, "The hour has come for the Son of Man to be glorified. Truly, truly, I say to you, unless a grain of wheat falls into the earth and dies, it remains alone; but if it dies, it bears much fruit" (Jn 12:24). From the cross to glory!

It is necessary with the help of the Gospel to make evident another aspect of the truth about suffering. Matthew tells us that "Jesus went about...preaching the Gospel of the kingdom, and healing every disease and every infirmity" (Mt 9:35). Luke in his turn tells us that when Jesus was questioned about the true meaning of the commandment of love, he replied with the parable of the good Samaritan (cf. Lk 10:30-37). From these texts it follows that, according to Jesus, suffering should impel in a special way to love of neighbor and to the commitment of rendering him all necessary services. Such a love and such services, carried out in every way possible, constitute a fundamental moral value which accompanies suffering. When speaking of the last judgment, Jesus set out with particular clarity the idea that every work of love performed on behalf of a suffering person is directed to the Redeemer himself: "I was hungry and you gave me food; I was thirsty and you gave me drink; I was a stranger and you welcomed me; I was naked and you clothed me; I was sick and you visited me; I was in prison and you came to me" (Mt 25:35-36). The whole Christian ethic of service, even social service, is based on these words, as well as the definitive turning to account of suffering accepted in the light of the cross.

Could not one find here the answer which humanity awaits today? It can be received only from Christ crucified, the holy one who suffers. He can penetrate the heart of the most painful human problems, because he already stands beside all who suffer and who ask him for an awakening of new hope.

General audience of November 9, 1988

"Father, Forgive Them..."

All that Jesus taught and did during his earthly life reached the peak of truth and holiness on the cross. The words which Jesus then uttered are his supreme and definitive message and, at the same time, the confirmation of a holy life which ended with the total gift of himself, in obedience to the Father, for the salvation of the world. Those words, heard by his mother and by the disciples present on Calvary, were consigned to the first Christian communities and to all future generations, so that they might illumine the meaning of Jesus' redemptive work and inspire his followers during their life and at the moment of death. Let us also meditate on those words, as countless Christians have done in all ages.

The first thing we discover on reading them is that they contain a message of pardon. "Father, forgive them; for they know not what they do" (Lk 23:43). According to Luke's account this was the first word uttered by Jesus on the cross. We ask ourselves right away: was not this the word we needed to hear in our regard?

But in that situation, after what had taken place, in the presence of those people who had asked for his condemnation and had treated him with such ferocity, who would have thought that Jesus would have said that? And yet the Gospel gives us this certainty. From the height of the cross there sounded forth the word, "forgive"!

Let us take up the fundamental aspects of that message of forgiveness.

Jesus not only forgave, but he asked the Father's forgiveness for those who had put him to death, and therefore for us also. It is the sign of the total sincerity of Christ's forgiveness and of the love that derives from it. It is a new fact of history, even in that of the covenant. In the Old Testament we read so many texts of the psalmists who had asked for the vengeance or punishment of the Lord on their enemies. These texts are repeated in Christian prayer, even in liturgical prayer, but not without our feeling the need of interpreting them and bringing them into line with the teaching and example of Jesus, who loved even his enemies. The same can be said of certain expressions of the prophet Jeremiah (cf. 11:20; 20:12; 15:15) and of the Jewish martyrs in the Book of the Maccabees (cf. 2 Mac 7:9, 14, 17, 19). Jesus confirmed this position in the sight of God and spoke words that are quite different. He had reminded those who had rebuked him for associating with sinners, that already in the Old Testament, according to the inspired word, God "desires mercy" (cf. Mt 9:13).

It is also to be noted that Jesus forgave immediately, even though the hostility of his enemies continued to manifest itself. Forgiveness is his only response to their hostility. Moreover, his forgiveness was addressed to all those who, humanly speaking, were responsible for his death. This included not merely the soldiers who were carrying out the execution, but all those, near or distant, manifest or hidden, who had played a part in the process that led to his condemnation and crucifixion. For all of them he asked forgiveness. He so defended them before the Father that the apostle John, after enjoining on Christians that they should not sin, can add: "But if any one does sin, we have an advocate with the Father, Jesus Christ the righteous; and he is the expiation for our sins, and not for ours only but also the sins of the whole world" (1 Jn 2:1-2). The same line is followed also by the Apostle Peter who, in his discourse to the people of Jerusalem, extends to all the excuse of "ignorance" (cf. Acts 3:17; cf. Lk 23, 34) and the offer of forgiveness (cf. Acts 3:19). It is consoling for all of us to know that, according to the Letter to the Hebrews, Christ crucified, the eternal priest, remains for all time the one who makes intercession for sinners who draw near to God through him (cf. Heb 7:25).

He is the intercessor and also the advocate, the "Paraclete" (cf. 1 Jn 2:1) who, on the cross, instead of accusing his crucifiers of their guilt, mitigated it by saying that they know not what they do. His judgment is marked by indulgence. But it also conforms with the real truth that only he can see in those enemies of his and in all sinners, namely, that many may be less guilty than what may appear or what one may think, and therefore Jesus taught us "not to judge" (cf. Mt 7:11). Now, on Calvary, he became the intercessor and advocate of sinners before the Father.

This forgiveness from the cross is the image and principle of that forgiveness that Jesus wishes to convey to all humanity through his sacrifice. To merit this forgiveness and, in the concrete, the grace that purifies and confers divine life, Jesus made the heroic offering of himself for all humanity. All men, each in the individuality of his own personal "I," of his good and evil, are therefore potentially and, indeed, one could say, intentionally included in Jesus' prayer to the Father, "Forgive them." That request for clemency and for heavenly understanding is certainly valid also for us, "because they know not what they do." Perhaps no sinner completely escapes that ignorance and is therefore beyond the range of that intercession for forgiveness which issues from the most tender heart of Christ dying on the cross. However, this should not impel anyone to impose on the richness of God's goodness, tolerance and patience, to the point of not recognizing that this goodness invites him to conversion (cf. Rom 2:4). Because of the hardness of his impenitent heart he would heap anger on his head against the day of wrath and of the revelation of God's just judgment (cf. Rom 2:5). And yet even for him the dying Christ asked the Father's forgiveness, even though a miracle were necessary for his conversion.

Already in the early Christian communities, the message of forgiveness was received and followed by the first martyrs for the faith, who repeated almost literally Jesus' prayer to the Father. We find this in the case of the protomartyr Stephen who, at the moment of his death—as recounted by the Acts of the Apostles—asked, "Lord, do not hold this sin against them" (Acts 7:10). According to Eusebius of Caesarea, St. James also repeated the words of Jesus as a request for forgiveness during his martyrdom (Eusebius, *Historia Eccles.* II, 23, 16). In any event, this was an application of the Master's teaching which recommended, "Pray for your persecutors" (Mt 5:44). Jesus joined example to teaching in the supreme moment of his life and his first followers did likewise in forgiving and in asking God to forgive their persecutors.

However, they also bore in mind another concrete fact that took place on Calvary and which constituted an integral part of the message of the cross as a message of forgiveness. Jesus said to the criminal crucified with him, "Truly, I say to you, today you will be with me in Paradise" (Lk 23:43). It is a striking fact which reveals in action all the dimensions of the work of salvation which finds expression in forgiveness. That criminal had acknowledged his guilt, rebuking his accomplice and companion in punishment who mocked Jesus, "We are condemned justly, for we are receiving the due reward for our deeds." He had asked Jesus to remember him when he came into the kingdom proclaimed by him: "Jesus, remember me when you come in your kingly power" (Lk 23:42). He regarded Jesus' condemnation as unjust: "This man has done nothing wrong." He did not join in the railing of his fellow criminal ("Save yourself and us!"; Lk 23:39), and of the others who, like the rulers, said, "He saved others: let him save himself, if he is the Christ of God, his chosen one!" (Lk 23:35). He did not join in the mockery of the soldiers: "If you are the king of the Jews, save yourself!" (Lk 23:37).

The criminal, therefore, by asking Jesus to remember him, professed his faith in the Redeemer. At the moment of his death, he not only accepted death as the just penalty for the evil he had done, but he turned to Jesus to tell him that he placed all his hope in him.

This is the most obvious explanation of that episode narrated by Luke, in which the psychological element, the criminal's change of attitude—while having as its immediate cause the impression received from the example of the innocent Jesus who suffered and died and at the same time forgave—has, however, its real mysterious root in the grace of the Redeemer, who converted this man and granted him divine forgiveness. Jesus' response was immediate. To the penitent and converted criminal, Jesus promised paradise in his company on that very day. It was a case of complete forgiveness. He who had committed crimes and robberies—and therefore sins—became a saint in the final moment of his life.

One could say that in this text of Luke we have the first canonization in history, performed by Jesus in favor of a criminal who turned to him in that dramatic moment. This shows that people can obtain, through Christ's cross, forgiveness of all their offenses, even of an entire evil life, if they surrender to the grace of the Redeemer who converts and saves them.

Jesus' words to the repentant criminal contain also the promise of perfect happiness: "Today you will be with me in

paradise." The sacrifice of redemption obtains eternal beatitude for humanity. It is a gift of salvation certainly proportionate
to the value of the sacrifice, notwithstanding the lack of pro-
portion that seems to exist between the criminal's simple
request and the greatness of the reward. This disproportion is
overcome by Christ's sacrifice which, through the infinite
value of his life and death, merited the happiness of heaven.

The episode narrated by Luke reminds us that paradise is
offered to all humanity and to each and every human being
who, like the penitent criminal, yields to grace and places all
his hope in Christ. A moment of real conversion, a "moment of
grace," which we can say with St. Thomas, "is worth more
than the whole universe" *(Summa Theol.,* I-II, q. 113, a. 9, ad
2), can square the accounts of a whole life. It can bring about
in anyone what Jesus promised to his companion in torment:
"This day you will be with me in paradise."

General audience of November 16, 1988

"Behold Your Mother!"

The message of the cross includes some sublime words of love, which Jesus addressed to his mother and to the beloved disciple John, present on Calvary during his agony.

St. John recounts in his Gospel that "standing by the cross of Jesus was his Mother" (Jn 19:25). There was the presence of a woman—already widowed for years, as everything suggests—who was about to lose her son also. Every fiber of her being was shaken by what she had seen during the final days of the passion, by what she felt and offered now, beside the cross of execution. How could one prevent her from suffering and weeping? Christian tradition has perceived the dramatic experience of that woman full of dignity and decorum, but with a broken heart, and has paused to contemplate her while participating intimately in her sorrow:

> *"Stabat Mater dolorosa*
> *iuxta crucem lacrimosa*
> *dum pendebat filius."*

It is not merely a question of flesh and blood, nor of an affection undoubtedly most noble, but simply human. Mary's presence beside the cross indicates her commitment of total sharing in her Son's redemptive sacrifice. Mary had willed to participate to the very depth in the sufferings of Jesus because she did not reject the sword foretold to her by Simeon (cf. Lk 2:35). Instead, she accepted with Christ the mysterious plan of the Father. She was the first to partake in that sacrifice, and she would forever remain the perfect model of all those who would agree to associate themselves unreservedly with the redemptive offering.

The maternal compassion expressed by her presence helped to make the drama of the death on the cross more intense and profound. Mary is so close to the drama of so many families, of so many mothers and children, reunited by death after long periods of separation for reasons of work, illness or violence at the hands of individuals or groups.

On seeing his mother beside the cross, Jesus recalled the memories of Nazareth, Cana and Jerusalem. Perhaps he reviewed in memory the moments of Joseph's death, and then of his own separation from her, and of the solitude in which she lived during the last years, a solitude which will now be increased. For her part, Mary considered all the things which for years and years "she had kept in her heart" (cf. Lk 2:19, 51). Then more than ever she understood them in connection with the cross. Sorrow and faith were united in her heart. And then, at a certain point, she became aware that Jesus was looking at her and speaking to her from the cross.

"When Jesus saw his mother, and the disciple whom he loved standing near, he said to his mother, 'Woman, behold, your son!'" (Jn 19:26). It was an act of tenderness and filial love. Jesus did not want his mother to remain alone. In place of himself he left to her as a son the disciple whom Mary knew as the beloved one. Thus Jesus entrusted to Mary a new motherhood, asking her to treat John as her son. But the solemnity of that act of entrustment ("Woman, behold, your son!"), its situation at the heart of the drama of the cross, the sobriety and pithiness of the words which could be described as proper to an almost sacramental formula, suggest that over and above family relationships, the fact should be considered in the perspective of the work of salvation. The woman Mary was engaged with the Son of Man in the mission of redemption. At the conclusion of this work, Jesus asked Mary to accept definitively the offering which he made of himself as the victim of expiation, by now considering John as her son. It is at the price of her maternal sacrifice that she received that new motherhood.

However, that filial gesture, full of messianic meaning, went far beyond the person of the beloved disciple, designated as the son of Mary. Jesus wished to give Mary the mission of accepting all his followers of every age as her own sons and daughters. Jesus' gesture has a symbolic value.

It is not merely a gesture of a family nature, as of a son making provision for his mother. But it is a gesture of the world's Redeemer who assigns to Mary, as "woman," a role of new motherhood in relation to all those who are called to membership of the Church. In that moment, Mary was constituted—one might almost say consecrated—Mother of the Church by her Son on the cross.

In this gift made to John and, through him, to Christ's followers and to all humanity, there is a completion of the gift which Jesus made of himself to humanity by his death on the cross. Mary is "all one" with him, not only because they are mother and son "according to the flesh," but because in God's eternal plan they were contemplated, predestined and situated together at the center of the history of salvation. Thus Jesus thought that he should involve his mother not only in his own oblation to the Father, but also in the gift of himself to humanity. Mary, on her part, was in perfect harmony with her Son in this act of oblation and of giving, as a prolongation of her fiat at the annunciation.

On the other hand Jesus was despoiled of everything in his passion. On Calvary his mother was still with him. With a gesture of supreme detachment he gave her also to the entire world, before ending his mission with the sacrifice of his life. Jesus was aware that the final moment had arrived, for the evangelist says, "After this Jesus, knowing that all was now finished..." (Jn 19:28). He wished to include also among the things accomplished this gift of his mother to the Church and to the world.

It is certainly a case of spiritual motherhood, which is realized, according to Christian tradition and the Church's teaching, in the order of grace. "Mother in the order of grace," the Second Vatican Council calls her (LG 61). It is therefore an essentially supernatural motherhood in the sphere of grace which generates divine life in man. It is an object of faith, as is also grace itself to which it is related. It does not exclude but rather implies a whole flowering of thoughts, of tender and delicate affections, and of intense sentiments of hope, trust and love, which form part of Christ's gift.

Jesus had experienced and appreciated Mary's maternal love in his own life. He wished that his disciples also in their turn should enjoy this maternal love as an element of their relationship with him in the development of their spiritual life. It is a question of regarding Mary as mother and of treating her as mother, allowing her to form us to true docility to God, to true union with Christ and to real charity in regard to our neighbor.

It can be said that this aspect also of the relationship with Mary is included in the message of the cross. Indeed the evangelist says that Jesus "then said to the disciple, 'Behold, your mother!'" (Jn 19:27). Jesus expressly asked the disciple to behave toward Mary as a son toward his mother. To Mary's maternal love there should correspond a filial love. Since the disciple takes the place of Jesus in regard to Mary, he is invited to love her truly as if she were his own mother. It is as if Jesus were to say to him, "Love her as I have loved her." Since Jesus saw in the disciple all human beings to whom he leaves that testament of love, the request to love Mary as one's own mother is valid for all. With these words Jesus laid the foundation of Marian devotion in the Church. Through John, he made known his will that Mary should receive a sincere filial love from every disciple whose mother she is by the decision of Jesus himself. The importance of Marian devotion, always desired by the Church, is deduced from Jesus' words at the hour of his death.

The evangelist concludes with the words that "from that hour the disciple took her to his own home" (Jn 19:27). This indicates that the disciple immediately responded to the will of Jesus. From that moment, by taking Mary into his own home, he showed her his filial affection. He surrounded her with every care and ensured that she could enjoy recollection and peace while waiting to be reunited with her Son, and carry out her role in the newborn Church both at Pentecost and in the subsequent years.

John's action was the execution of Jesus' testament in regard to Mary. But it had a symbolic value for each one of Christ's disciples, who are asked to make room for Mary in their lives, to take her into their own homes. By virtue of these words of the dying Christ, every Christian life must offer a space to Mary and provide for her presence.

We can then conclude this reflection on the message of the cross with an invitation which I address to each one, namely, to ask how one accepts Mary into one's home and into one's life. May everyone appreciate to an ever greater extent the gift which Christ crucified made to us by leaving us his own mother as our mother.

General audience of November 23, 1988

"My God, My God, Why Have You Forsaken Me?"

According to the Synoptics, Jesus on the cross cried out aloud twice (cf. Mt 27:46, 50; Mk 15:34, 37); but only Luke tells us what he said when he cried out the second time (cf. 23:46). The first cry expresses the depth and intensity of Jesus' suffering, his interior participation, his spirit of oblation, and perhaps also his prophetic-messianic understanding of his drama in the terms of a biblical psalm. Certainly the first cry manifests Jesus' feelings of desolation and abandonment with the first words of Psalm 2: "And at the ninth hour Jesus cried with a loud voice, *'Eloi, Eloi, lema sabachthani?'* which means, 'My God, my God, why have you forsaken me?'" (Mk 15:34; cf. Mt 27:46).

Mark quotes the words in Aramaic. One may suppose that the cry appeared so characteristic that the witnesses who heard it, when later recounting the drama of Calvary, deemed it opportune to repeat the very words of Jesus in Aramaic. It was the language spoken by him and by the majority of his contemporary Israelites. They could have been relayed to Mark by Peter, as happened in the case of the word "Abba" (cf. Mk 14:36) in the prayer of Gethsemane.

The fact that Jesus, in his first cry, used the initial words of Psalm 22 is significant for various reasons. Jesus was accustomed to pray following the sacred texts of his people. There must have remained in his mind many of those words and phrases which particularly impressed him, because they expressed better man's need and anguish before God. In a certain way they alluded to the condition of the one who would have taken upon himself all our iniquity (cf. Is 53:11).

Therefore on Calvary it came natural to Jesus to make use of the psalmist's question to God when he felt completely worn out by suffering. But on Jesus' lips the "why" addressed to God was also more effective in expressing a pained bewilderment at that suffering which had no merely human explanation, but which was a mystery of which the Father alone possessed the key. Therefore, though arising from the memory of the Psalm read or recited in the synagogue, the question contained a theological significance in regard to the sacrifice whereby Christ, in full solidarity with sinful humanity, had to experience in himself abandonment by God. Under the influence of this tremendous interior experience, the dying Jesus found the energy to utter that cry!

In that experience, in that cry, in that "why" addressed to heaven, Jesus also established a new manner of solidarity with us who are so often moved to raise our eyes and words to heaven to express our complaint and even desperation.

In hearing Jesus crying out his "why," we learn indeed that those who suffer can utter this same cry, but with those same dispositions of filial trust and abandonment of which Jesus is the teacher and model. In the "why" of Jesus there is no feeling or resentment leading to rebellion or desperation. There is no semblance of a reproach to the Father, but the expression of the experience of weakness, of solitude, of abandonment to himself, made by Jesus in our place. Jesus thus became the first of the "smitten and afflicted," the first of the abandoned, the first of the *desamparados* (as the Spanish call

them). At the same time, however, he tells us that the benign
eye of Providence watches over all these poor children of Eve.

If Jesus felt abandoned by the Father, he knew however
that that was not really so. He himself said, "I and the Father
are one" (Jn 10:30). Speaking of his future passion he said, "I
am not alone, for the Father is with me" (Jn 16:32). Jesus had
the clear vision of God and the certainty of his union with the
Father dominant in his mind. But in the sphere bordering on
the senses, and therefore more subject to the impressions, emo-
tions and influences of the internal and external experiences of
pain, Jesus' human soul was reduced to a wasteland. He no
longer felt the presence of the Father, but he underwent the
tragic experience of the most complete desolation.

Here one can sketch a summary of Jesus' psychological
situation in relationship to God. The external events seemed to
manifest the absence of the Father who permitted the crucifixion of his Son, though having at his disposal "legions of
angels" (cf. Mt 26:53), without intervening to prevent his condemnation to death and execution. In Gethsemane Simon Peter
had drawn a sword in Jesus' defense, but was immediately
blocked by Jesus himself (cf. Jn 18:10 f.). In the praetorium
Pilate had repeatedly tried wily maneuvers to save him (cf. Jn
18:31, 38 f.; 19:4-6, 12-15); but the Father was silent. That
silence of God weighed on the dying Jesus as the heaviest pain
of all, so much so that his enemies interpreted that silence as a
sign of his reprobation: "He trusted in God; let God deliver
him now, if he desires him; for he said, 'I am the Son of God'"
(Mt 27:43).

In the sphere of feelings and affection this sense of the
absence and abandonment by God was the most acute pain for
the soul of Jesus who drew his strength and joy from union
with the Father. This pain rendered all the other sufferings
more intense. That lack of interior consolation was Jesus'
greatest agony.

However, Jesus knew that by this ultimate phase of his sacrifice, reaching the intimate core of his being, he completed the work of reparation which was the purpose of his sacrifice for the expiation of sins. If sin is separation from God, Jesus had to experience in the crisis of his union with the Father a suffering proportionate to that separation.

On the other hand in quoting the beginning of Psalm 22, which he perhaps continued to recite mentally during the passion, Jesus did not forget the conclusion which becomes a hymn of liberation and an announcement of salvation granted to all by God. The experience of abandonment is therefore a passing pain which gives way to personal liberation and universal salvation. In Jesus' afflicted soul this perspective certainly nourished hope, all the more so since he had always presented his death as a passage to the resurrection as his true glorification. From this thought his soul took strength and joy in the knowledge that at the very height of the drama of the cross, the hour of victory was at hand.

A little later, however, perhaps under the influence of Psalm 22, which again came to the surface in his memory, Jesus uttered the words, "I thirst" (Jn 19:28).

It is easy to understand that these words of Jesus refer to physical thirst, to the great agony which is part of the pain of crucifixion, as the experts in these matters tells us. One may also add that in manifesting his thirst Jesus gave proof of humility, by expressing an elementary need, as anyone would have done. Also in this Jesus expressed his solidarity with all those, living or dying, healthy or sick, great or small, who are in need and ask at least for a cup of water (cf. Mt 10:42). For us it is good to think that any help given to one who is dying, is given to Jesus crucified!

However, we cannot ignore the evangelist's remark that Jesus uttered the words, "I thirst," "to fulfill the Scripture" (Jn 19:28). These words of Jesus have another dimension beyond the physico-psychological. Once again the reference is to Psalm 22: "My throat is dried up like baked clay, my tongue cleaves to my jaws; to the dust of death you have brought me down" (v. 16). Also in Psalm 69:22 we read: "In my thirst they gave me vinegar to drink."

The Psalmist's words treat of physical thirst, but on the lips of Jesus they enter into the messianic perspective of the suffering of the cross. In his thirst the dying Christ sought a drink quite different from water or vinegar, as when he asked the Samaritan woman at the well of Sychar: "Give me to drink" (Jn 4:7). Physical thirst on that occasion was the symbol and the path to another thirst, that of the conversion of the Samaritan woman. On the cross, Jesus thirsted for a new humanity which should arise from his sacrifice in fulfillment of the Scriptures. For this reason the evangelist links Jesus' "cry of thirst" to the Scriptures. The thirst of the cross, on the lips of the dying Christ, is the ultimate expression of that desire of baptism to be received and of fire to be kindled on the earth, which had been manifested by him during his life. "I came to cast fire upon the earth and would that it were already kindled! I have a baptism to be baptized with; and how I am constrained until it is accomplished!" (Lk 12:49-50). Now that desire is about to be fulfilled. With those words Jesus confirmed the ardent love with which he desired to receive that supreme "baptism" to open to all of us the fountain of water which really quenches the thirst and saves (cf. Jn 4:13-14).

General audience of November 30, 1988

Christ's Last Words on the Cross

"It is finished" (Jn 19:30). According to John's Gospel Jesus spoke these words just before expiring. They were his last words. They express his awareness of having fully accomplished the work for which he had been sent into this world (cf. Jn 17:4). Note that is was not so much the awareness of having realized his own plans as having accomplished his Father's will in obedience even to the complete immolation of himself on the cross. Openly in this way does the dying Jesus appear as the model of the death of every human being, namely, the conclusion of the work assigned to each one in fulfillment of the divine plan. According to the Christian view of life and death, every person up to the moment of death is called to fulfill the Father's will. Death is the final act, that definitive and decisive act of the fulfillment of his will. Jesus teaches us this truth from the cross.

"Father, into your hands I commit my spirit" (Lk 23:46). With these words Luke makes explicit the content of Jesus' second cry shortly before he died (cf. Mk 13:37; Mt 27:50). In his first cry he exclaimed, "My God, my God, why have you forsaken me?" (Mk 15:34; cf. Mt 27:46). These words are completed by those others which are the fruit of interior reflection matured in prayer. If for a moment Jesus had experienced the terrible sensation of being abandoned by the Father, his soul reacted in the only way which, as he well knew, befits a man who at the same time is also the "beloved Son" of God, namely, by total abandonment into his hands.

Jesus expressed his feeling with words taken from Psalm 31, the Psalm of a suffering man who foresees his liberation and gives thanks to God for accomplishing it: "Into your hands I commit my spirit; you have redeemed me, O Lord, faithful God" (Ps 31:6). Lucid in his agony, Jesus recalled and also muttered some verses of that psalm recited often during his life. But according to the Gospel narrative those words take on a new value on the lips of Jesus.

Jesus calls God "Father" (Abba), thus showing his filial trust when abandoning himself into the Father's hands. Jesus died as Son. He died in perfect harmony with the Father's will, for the purpose of the Father's love which had been assigned to him and which the Son well knew.

In the Psalmist's perspective, the man, stricken by misfortune and afflicted with suffering, surrenders his spirit into the hands of God in order to escape death which threatens him. Jesus, however, accepted death and yielded up his spirit into the Father's hands to attest his obedience and to manifest to him his trust for a new life. His abandonment was therefore more complete and radical, more daring and definitive, more fraught with a sacrificial will.

Besides, this last cry was a completion of the first, as we noted right from the beginning. Let us take up again the two texts and see what results from a comparison between the two, first of all from the merely linguistic or, as it were, semantic aspect.

The term "God" of Psalm 22 is used, in the first cry, as an invocation which can signify the dismay of a man in his own nothingness before the experience of abandonment on the part of God, considered in his transcendence and almost experienced in a state of separation (the Holy One, the Eternal, the Immutable). In the following cry Jesus had recourse to Psalm 31, inserting into it the invocation of God as Father (Abba), a name which is habitual to him and which well expresses the familiarity of an exchange of paternal warmth and filial attitude.

Moreover, in the first cry Jesus also asked God the question "why," certainly with profound respect for his will, for his power and infinite greatness, but without concealing a sense of human dismay which such a death must certainly arouse. Now, instead, the second cry expresses trusting abandonment in the arms of the wise and kind Father who disposes and upholds everything with love. There was a moment of desolation when Jesus felt without support and defense on the part of everyone, even of God. It was a dreadful moment; but Jesus soon overcame it by entrusting himself into the hands of the Father. Jesus realized in the depths of his being the loving and immediate presence of the Father, since Jesus is in the Father as the Father is in him (cf. Jn 10:38; 14:10 f.), even on the cross!

In order to understand Jesus' words and cries on the cross, one must consider them in relation to what Jesus himself had announced beforehand in the prophecies of his death and in his teaching on man's destiny in a new life. For all, death is a passage to existence beyond the grave. For Jesus it was, rather, the preliminary of the resurrection which would take place on the third day. Death, therefore, always has the character of the dissolution of the human composite, which arouses revulsion. But after the first cry, Jesus with great serenity yielded his spirit into the hands of the Father, in view of the new life and indeed of the resurrection from the dead, which would be the crowning point of the paschal mystery. Thus, after all the agonies of his physical and moral sufferings, Jesus embraced death as an entrance into the immutable peace of the "Father's bosom" to which his whole life had been ordered.

By his death Jesus reveals that at the end of life man is not doomed to immersion in obscurity, in the existential void, in the abyss of nothingness. But man is invited to meet the Father toward whom he moved in the journey of faith and love during life, and into whose arms he threw himself with holy abandonment at the hour of death. It is an abandonment which, like that of Jesus, implies a total gift of self on the part of a soul which accepts to be despoiled of the body and of earthly life, but in the knowledge that it will find in the arms and heart of the Father the new life, a participation in the very life of God in the trinitarian mystery.

Through the ineffable mystery of death the soul of the Son came to enjoy the glory of the Father in the communion of the Spirit (the Love of the Father and of the Son). This is "eternal life," made up of knowledge, love, joy and infinite peace.

The evangelist John says that Jesus "gave up his spirit" (Jn 19:30). Matthew says "he gave up the spirit" (Mt 27:50). Mark and Luke say that "he breathed his last" (Mk 15:37; Lk 23:46). Jesus' soul entered into the beatific vision in the bosom of the Trinity.

In this light of eternity one can grasp something of the mysterious relationship between Christ's humanity and the Trinity. The Letter to the Hebrews touches on this when, speaking of the salvific efficacy of the blood of Christ, far superior to that of the blood of animals offered in the sacrifices of the old covenant, it states that in his death Christ "through the eternal spirit offered himself without blemish to God" (Heb 9:14).

General audience of December 7, 1988

The Fruitfulness of Christ's Redemptive Death

The evangelist Mark writes that when Jesus died, the centurion who stood facing him, on seeing that he thus breathed his last, said, "Truly this man was the Son of God" (Mk 14:39). This implies that in that moment the Roman centurion had a clear intuition about the reality of Christ, an initial perception of the fundamental truth of faith.

The centurion had heard the reproaches and insults addressed to Jesus by his enemies. In particular, they derided Jesus about the title Son of God claimed by him who could not now come down from the cross, nor do anything to save himself.

Looking at the crucified, perhaps earlier during his agony but more intensely and searchingly at the moment of his death, (and perhaps, who knows, their eyes may have met), he felt that Jesus was right. Yes, Jesus is a man, and in fact he died; but in him there is more than a man. He is a man who, as he himself said, is truly the Son of God. That manner of suffering and dying, that yielding up of his spirit into the hands of the Father, the evident sacrifice of himself for a supreme cause to which he had dedicated his whole life, exercised a mysterious power on that soldier. Perhaps the centurion had arrived at Calvary after a long military and spiritual adventure, as a certain writer has imagined, and who in a certain sense can represent every pagan in search of some evidence and revelation of God.

The fact is remarkable, also because at that time the disciples were bewildered and shaken in their faith (cf. Mk 14:50; Jn 16:32). The centurion, on the contrary, at that very hour, heads the line of pagans who, very soon, will seek to be admitted among the disciples of that man in whom, especially after his resurrection, they will acknowledge the Son of God, as attested to by the Acts of the Apostles.

The centurion of Calvary did not wait for the resurrection. That death, those words and that look of the dying man sufficed to lead him to his act of faith. How can we fail to see in this the fruit of an impulse of divine grace, obtained by that soldier from Christ the Savior through his sacrifice?

On his part, the centurion had placed the indispensable condition to receive the gift of faith: objectivity, which is the primary form of sincerity. He looked, he saw and he believed in the reality of the facts, and for this he was granted the gift of faith. He did not speculate on the advantages of siding with the Sanhedrin, nor did he let himself be intimidated like Pilate (cf. Jn 19:8). He looked at the persons and the facts, and he was present as an impartial witness at Jesus' death. He was therefore struck by the force of the truth and believed. Nor did he hesitate to proclaim that that man was the Son of God. It was the first sign of redemption accomplished.

Another sign is recorded by John when he writes: "One of the soldiers pierced his side with a spear, and at once there came out blood and water" (Jn 19:34).

Jesus was already dead. He died before the two criminals who had been crucified with him. This is a proof of the intensity of his sufferings.

The thrust of the spear, therefore, was not a new suffering inflicted on Jesus. It served rather as a sign of the total gift which he had made of himself. It was a sign marked in his very flesh by the piercing of his side. It may be said that with the opening of his heart, it was a symbolic representation of that love through which Jesus had given everything and would continue to give everything to humanity.

From that opening of his heart there flow blood and water. It is a fact that can be explained physiologically. However, the evangelist mentions it for its symbolic value. It is a sign and announcement of the fruitfulness of the sacrifice. So great is the importance attributed to it by the evangelist that, immediately after narrating the episode, he adds: "He who saw it has borne witness, and his testimony is true; he knows that he is speaking the truth, so that you also may believe" (Jn 19:35). He appealed to direct observation, made by himself to emphasize that it is a fact full of great significance concerning the motives and effects of Christ's sacrifice.

Indeed the evangelist perceived in the event the fulfillment of two prophecies. The first concerns the paschal lamb of the Jews, of which "not a bone shall be broken" (Ex 12:46; Num 9:12; cf. Ps 34:21). For the evangelist, Christ crucified is therefore the paschal lamb and the "lamb bled dry," as St. Catherine of Siena says. Jesus is the lamb of the new covenant, prefigured in the pasch of the old law, and the effective sign of the new liberation not only of Israel but of all humanity from the slavery of sin.

John's other biblical citation is an obscure text attributed to the prophet Zechariah who says: "They shall look on him whom they have pierced" (Zech 12:10). The prophecy concerns the liberation of Jerusalem and Judah by a king, for whose coming the nation acknowledges its guilt and mourns over him whom it has pierced as one mourns the loss of an only son. The evangelist applies this text to Jesus pierced and crucified, now contemplated with love. The hostile glances of his enemies were followed by the loving gaze of those converted. This possible interpretation helps us to understand the theological-prophetical perspective in which the evangelist considered the history which he saw developing from the open heart of Jesus.

The symbolic meaning of the blood and water has been given various interpretations.

In John's Gospel it is possible to note a relationship between the water that flows from the pierced side and Jesus' invitation on the Feast of Tabernacles: "If any one thirst, let him come to me and drink. He who believes in me, as the Scripture has said, 'Out of his heart shall flow rivers of living water'" (Jn 7:37-38; cf. Jn 4:10-14; Rev 22:1). The evangelist then makes clear that Jesus was speaking of the Spirit which those who believed in him were to receive (cf. Jn 7:39).

Some have interpreted the blood as the symbol of the forgiveness of sins through the sacrifice of expiation, and the water as the symbol of purification. Others relate the blood and water to the Eucharist and Baptism.

The evangelist has not provided sufficient grounds for precise interpretations. However, we seem to have an indication from the text on the pierced side from which flow blood and water, namely, the outpouring of grace flowing from the sacrifice, as John himself, from the very beginning of his Gospel, says of the Word Incarnate: "From his fullness we have all received, grace upon grace" (Jn 1:16).

We wish to conclude by observing that the testimony of the beloved disciple acquires its full meaning if we recall that this disciple had rested his head on Jesus' breast during the Last Supper. Now he beheld this breast torn open. Hence he felt the need to emphasize the symbol of infinite charity which he had discovered in that heart. He invited the readers of his Gospel and all Christians to contemplate that heart "that had so loved men" as to give himself in sacrifice for them.

General audience of December 14, 1988

"He Descended into Hell"

In the most recent reflections we have explained with the help of biblical texts, the article of the Apostles' Creed which says of Jesus: "He suffered under Pontius Pilate, was crucified...and was buried." It was not merely a case of narrating the history of the passion, but of penetrating the truth of faith contained in it and which we profess in the creed: human redemption effected by Christ with his sacrifice. We dwelt particularly on his death and on his words during the agony on the cross as recorded by the evangelists. These words help us to discover and understand more profoundly the spirit wherewith Jesus immolated himself for us.

That article of faith ends, as we have just noted, with the words: "...and was buried." It might appear a mere factual statement; on the contrary, it is a fact whose significance enters the wider sphere of the whole of Christology. Jesus Christ is the Word made flesh in order to assume the human condition and to be like us in everything except sin (cf. Heb 4:15). He truly became "one of us" (cf. *GS* 22), to be able to redeem us, thanks to the profound solidarity established with every member of the human family. In that condition of true man he experienced completely the lot of man, even to death, which is usually followed by burial, at least in the religious and cultural world in which Jesus lived. Christ's burial is therefore an object of our faith inasmuch as it reproposes for us his mystery as the Son of God who became man and ventured to the limit of human experience.

The following article which says: "He descended into hell," is linked in a certain way to these final words of the article on the passion and death of Christ. This article about the descent into hell reflects some texts of the New Testament which we shall see shortly. It is well to mention, however, that although in the time of the Arian controversies the same formula was found in the writings of those heretics, it was nevertheless introduced also into the so-called Creed of Aquileia, one of the professions of the Catholic faith then in use, which was drawn up at the end of the fourth century (cf. *DS* 16). It entered definitively into the teaching of the councils with the Fourth Lateran (1215) and the Second Council of Lyons in the profession of faith of Michael Paleologus (1274).

It should also be mentioned that the word "hell" does not mean the hell of eternal damnation, but the abode of the dead which is *sheol* in Hebrew and *hades* in Greek (cf. Acts 2:31).

The formula is derived from numerous New Testament texts. The first is found in the Apostle Peter's discourse on Pentecost. Referring to Psalm 16 to confirm the announcement of Christ's resurrection which it contains, Peter stated that the prophet David "foresaw and spoke of the resurrection of the Christ, that he was not abandoned to Hades, nor did his flesh see corruption" (Acts 2:31). The Apostle Paul's question in the Letter to the Romans has a similar meaning: "'Who will descend into the abyss?' (that is, to bring Christ up from the dead)" (Rom 10:7).

Also in the Letter to the Ephesians there is a text which asks a significant question in reference to a verse of Psalm 68: "When he ascended on high he led a host of captives, and he gave gifts to men" (Ps 68:19). "In saying, 'he ascended,' what does it mean but that he had also descended into the lower parts of the earth? He who descended is he who also ascended far above all the heavens, so that he might fill all things" (Eph 4:8-10). In this way Paul seems to link Christ's "descent" into the abyss (among the dead, of which he speaks in the Letter to the Romans), with his ascension to the Father, which begins the eschatological "fulfillment" of all things in God.

In line with this are the words placed in Christ's mouth: "I am the First and the Last, and the Living One. I died, and behold I am alive for evermore, and I have the keys of death and Hades" (Rev 1:17-18).

As is evident from the texts quoted, the article of the Apostles' Creed: "He descended into hell," is based on the New Testament statements on the descent of Christ, after his death on the cross, into the "region of death," into the "abode of the dead," which in Old Testament language was called the "abyss." If the Letter to the Ephesians speaks of "the lower parts of the earth," it is because the earth receives the human body after death, and so it received also the body of Christ who expired on Calvary, as described by the evangelists (cf. Mt 27:59 f., and parallel passages; Jn 19:40-42). Christ passed through a real experience of death, including the final moment which is generally a part of the whole process: he was placed in the tomb.

It is a confirmation that this was a real and not merely an apparent death. His soul, separated from the body, was glorified in God, but his body lay in the tomb as a corpse.

During the three (incomplete) days between the moment when he "expired" (cf. Mk 15:37) and the resurrection, Jesus experienced the "state of death," that is, the separation of body and soul, as in the case of all people. This is the primary meaning of the words "he descended into hell"; they are linked to what Jesus himself had foretold when, in reference to the story of Jonah, he had said, "For as Jonah was three days and three nights in the belly of the whale, so will the Son of Man be three days and three nights in the heart of the earth" (Mt 12:40).

This is precisely what the words about the descent into hell mean: the heart or the womb of the earth. By dying on the cross, Jesus had delivered his spirit into the Father's hands: "Father, into your hands I commit my spirit!" (Lk 23:46). If death implies the separation of the soul from the body, it follows that in Christ's case also there was, on the one hand, the body in the state of a corpse, and on the other, the heavenly glorification of his soul from the very moment of his death. The First Letter of Peter speaks of this duality when, in reference to Christ's death for sins, it says of him: "Being put to death in the flesh but made alive in the spirit" (1 Pet 3:18). Soul and body are therefore in the final condition corresponding to their nature, although on the ontological plane the soul has a relationship to be reunited with its own body. However, the letter adds: "In spirit he [Christ] went and preached to the spirits in prison" (1 Pet 3:19). This seems to indicate metaphorically the extension of Christ's salvation to the just men and women who had died before him.

Obscure as it is, the Petrine text confirms the others concerning the concept of the "descent into hell" as the complete fulfillment of the gospel message of salvation. It is Christ—buried in the tomb as regards the body, but glorified in his soul, which had been admitted to the fullness of the beatific vision of God—who communicates his state of beatitude to all the just whose state of death he shares in regard to the body.

The Letter to the Hebrews describes his freeing of the souls of the just: "Since...the children share in flesh and blood, he himself likewise partook of the same nature, that through death he might destroy him who has the power of death, that is, the devil, and deliver all those who through fear of death were subject to lifelong bondage" (Heb 2:14-15). As dead—and at the same time as alive "forevermore"—Christ has "the keys of death and Hades" (cf. Rev 1:17-18). This manifests and puts into effect the salvific power of Christ's sacrificial death which brought redemption to all, even to those who died before his coming and his "descent into hell," but who were contacted by his justifying grace.

In the First Letter of Peter we read further: "The reason the gospel was preached even to the dead was that though judged in the flesh like men, they might live in the spirit like God" (1 Pet 4:6). This verse also, though not easy to interpret, confirms the concept of the "descent into hell" as the ultimate phase of the Messiah's mission. It is a phase condensed into a few days by the texts which try to present in a comprehensible way to those accustomed to reason and to speak in metaphors of space and time, but immensely vast in its real meaning of the extension of redemption to all people of all times and places, even to those who in the days of Christ's death and burial were already in the "realm of the dead." The word of the Gospel and of the cross reaches all, even those belonging to the most distant generations of the past, because all who have been saved have been made partakers in the redemption, even before the historical event of Christ's sacrificial death on Calvary took place. The concentration of their evangelization and redemption into the days of the burial emphasizes that the historical fact of Christ's death contains the super-historical mystery of the redemptive causality of Christ's humanity, the "instrument" of the omnipotent divinity. With the entrance of Christ's soul into the beatific vision in the bosom of the Trinity, the "freeing from imprisonment" of the just who had descended to the realm of the dead before Christ, finds its point of reference and explanation. Through Christ and in Christ there opens up before them the definitive freedom of the life of the Spirit, as a participation in the life of God (cf.

Summa Theol., III, q. 52, a. 6). This is the truth that can be drawn from the biblical texts quoted and which is expressed in the article of the creed which speaks of the "descent into hell."

We can therefore say that the truth expressed by the Apostles' Creed in the words: "he descended into hell," confirms the reality of Christ's death. At the same time it proclaims the beginning of his glorification, and not only of Christ's glorification, but of all those who, by means of his redemptive sacrifice, have been prepared for sharing in his glory in the happiness of God's kingdom.

General audience of January 11, 1989

The Resurrection: A Historical Event and an Affirmation of Faith

Today we reflect on the crowning truth of our faith in Jesus Christ. It is a truth documented by the New Testament, and was a matter of supreme importance in the faith and life of the first Christian communities. It was transmitted by tradition as a fundamental element of the faith. It was never neglected by true Christians, and today it is examined in depth, studied and preached as an essential part of the paschal mystery, together with the cross. It is, in short, the truth of Christ's resurrection. The Apostle's Creed tells us: "The third day he rose again from the dead." The Nicene-Constantinopolitan Creed adds: "On the third day he rose again in accordance with the Scriptures."

It is a dogma of the Christian faith, based upon a fact that historically took place and was verified. We shall seek to investigate "with minds bowed down," the mystery expressed by the dogma and contained in the fact, by beginning with an examination of the biblical texts which attest it.

The oldest written testimony to Christ's resurrection is in the First Letter of St. Paul to the Corinthians (about Easter, AD 57). Paul writes: "I delivered to you as of first importance what I also received, that Christ died for our sins in accordance with the Scriptures, that he was buried, that he was raised on the third day in accordance with the Scriptures, and that he appeared to Cephas, then to the twelve. Then he appeared to more than five hundred brethren at one time, most of whom are still alive, though some have fallen asleep. Then he appeared to James, and then to all the apostles. Last of all, as to one untimely born, he appeared also to me" (1 Cor 15:3-8).

As is obvious, the Apostle speaks here of the living tradition of the resurrection, which had come to his knowledge after his conversion on the road to Damascus (cf. Acts 9:3-18). When he went to Jerusalem he met the Apostle Peter and also James, as Paul states in the Letter to the Galatians (1:18 f.). Now he mentions them as the two principal witnesses of the risen Christ.

In the text cited, St. Paul not only speaks of the resurrection as having taken place on the third day "in accordance with the Scriptures" (a biblical reference which already touches the theological dimension of the fact), but at the same time he has recourse to eye-witnesses, to those to whom Christ appeared personally. It is a sign, among others, that the faith of the first community of believers, expressed by Paul in the Letter to the Corinthians, was based on the testimony of specific individuals, known to the Christians, and most of them still living in their midst. These "witnesses to Christ's resurrection" (cf. Acts 1:22) are first of all the twelve apostles, but not only those. Paul speaks even of more than five hundred persons to whom Jesus appeared at one time, besides appearing to Peter, James, and all the apostles.

In the face of this Pauline text, those hypotheses are untenable which seek in different ways to interpret Christ's resurrection by abstracting it from the physical order in such a way as not to recognize it as a historical fact. Such, for example, is the hypothesis that the resurrection was merely a kind of interpretation of Christ's state after his death (a state of life, and not of death). Again, another interpretation reduces the resurrection to the influence which Christ, after his death, did not cease to exercise on his disciples and indeed resumed with new and irresistible power. These hypotheses seem to imply a prejudicial opposition to the reality of the resurrection, which was considered solely as the "product" of the situation, that is to say, of the Jerusalem community. Neither the interpretation nor the prejudice is supported by the facts. St. Paul, on the contrary, in the text quoted has recourse to eyewitnesses of the fact. His conviction about Christ's resurrection is therefore based on a fact of experience. It is linked to that argument from the facts which was chosen and followed by the apostles precisely in that first community of Jerusalem. The apostles chose Matthias, one of Jesus' most constant disciples, to make up the number of the "Twelve" which had remained incomplete because of the betrayal and death of Judas Iscariot. They required as a condition that the candidate to be chosen should not only have accompanied them during the time of Jesus' teaching and activity, but above all, that he should be a "witness to his resurrection" through the experience of the events during the days preceding the moment when Christ—as they say—"was taken up from us" (Acts 1:22).

The resurrection cannot therefore be presented as a "product" of the first Christian community, that of Jerusalem, as is done by a certain brand of New Testament criticism which has scant respect for historical data. The truth about the resurrection is not a product of the faith of the apostles or of the other disciples before or after the Pasch. Rather, the texts show that the "prepaschal" faith of Christ's followers was subjected to the extreme test of their Master's passion and death on the cross. He himself had foretold this test, especially in his words to Simon Peter on the threshold of the tragic events of Jerusalem: "Simon, Simon, behold, Satan demanded to have you, that he might sift you all like wheat, but I have prayed for you that your faith may not fail" (Lk 22:31-32). The shock occasioned by Christ's passion and death was so great that the disciples (at least some of them) did not initially believe the news of his resurrection. The proof of that is found in each Gospel. In particular Luke informs us that when the women "on returning from the tomb, told all this (about the empty tomb) to the eleven and to all the rest...these words seemed to them an idle tale; and they did not believe them" (Lk 24:9-11).

After all, the hypothesis that the resurrection is a "product" of the apostles' faith is refuted by what happened when the risen Christ stood in their midst and said to them, "Peace to you!" In fact, "they supposed that they saw a spirit." On that occasion Jesus himself had to overcome their doubts and fear and convince them that "it was really he." "Touch me and see, for a spirit has not flesh and bones as you see that I have." Since they were "still incredulous and were amazed," Jesus asked them to give him something to eat and "he ate it in front of them" (cf. Lk 24:36-43).

Moreover, the episode of Thomas is well known. He was not with the other apostles when Jesus came to them the first time, entering the upper room through the closed doors (cf. Jn 20:19). When the other disciples told Thomas, "We have seen the Lord," he was amazed and incredulous and replied, "Unless I see in his hand the print of the nails, and place my finger in the mark of the nails, and place my hand in his side, I will not believe." After eight days Jesus came again to the upper room, to satisfy the demand of "doubting" Thomas and said to him, "Put your finger here, and see my hands; put out your hand, and place it in my side. Do not be faithless, but believing." When Thomas professed his faith with the words, "My Lord and my God!" Jesus said to him, "Have you believed because you have seen me? Blessed are those who have not seen and yet believe" (Jn 20:24-29).

The exhortation to believe without demanding to see what is hidden in the mystery of God and of Christ is always valid. However, Thomas's difficulty in admitting the resurrection without having personally experienced the presence of the living Jesus, and then his yielding in the presence of the proofs offered to him by Jesus himself, confirm the evidence of the Gospels concerning the reluctance of the apostles and disciples to admit the resurrection. The hypothesis that the resurrection is a "product" of the faith (or of the credulity) of the apostles is therefore illogical. On the contrary, their faith in the resurrection comes—under the action of divine grace—from the direct experience of the reality of the risen Christ.

It is Jesus himself who, after the resurrection, got in contact with the disciples in order to give them a sense of the reality and to dispel the opinion (or fear) that it was a question of a "ghost" and that they were therefore victims of an illusion. Jesus established direct relations with them, precisely through touch. Thus it was in the case of Thomas, which we have just mentioned, and also in the meeting described in Luke's Gospel, when Jesus said to the startled disciples: "Touch me and see, because a ghost does not have flesh and bones as you can see I have" (24:39). He invited them to verify that the risen body in which he came to them was the very same that was tortured and crucified. At the same time, however, that body possessed new properties. It had "become spiritual" and "glorified," and therefore no longer subject to the usual limitations of material beings and of a human body. Jesus entered the upper room despite the fact that the doors were shut; he appeared and disappeared, etc. At the same time, however, that body was authentic and real. The proof of Christ's resurrection is in his material identity.

The meeting on the road to Emmaus, recorded in Luke's Gospel, is an event which shows in a particularly evident way that the conviction about the resurrection matured in the disciples' awareness precisely through contact with the risen Christ (cf. Lk 24:15-21). At the beginning of the journey, those two followers of Jesus were "sad and downcast" by the memory of what had happened to their Master on the day of the crucifixion. They did not conceal their disappointment on seeing the collapse of their hope in him as the liberating Messiah. ("We had hoped that he was the one to redeem Israel.") Yet they later experienced a total transformation when it became clear to them that the stranger with whom they had been speaking was the very same Christ as before, and they realized that he was therefore risen. From the whole narrative it is clear that the certainty of Jesus' resurrection had made them, as it were, new men. Not only had they reacquired faith in Christ, but they were also ready to bear witness to the truth about his resurrection.

All these converging elements of the Gospel text prove the fact of the resurrection which was the foundation of the apostles' faith, and of the witness which, as we shall see in the coming reflections, was at the center of their preaching.

General audience of January 25, 1989

From the Empty Tomb to the Meeting with the Risen Christ

The profession of faith which we make in the creed when we proclaim that Jesus Christ "on the third day rose again from the dead," is based on the Gospel texts which, in their turn, transmit and make known to us the early preaching of the apostles. From these it is clear that faith in the resurrection is, from the very beginning, a conviction based on a fact, a real event. It is not based on a myth or on a conception. It is not an idea thought up by the apostles or invented by the post-paschal community gathered around the apostles at Jerusalem in order to overcome together with them the disappointment following upon Christ's death on the cross. The texts show quite the contrary, and therefore, as I said, the hypothesis put forward is also critically and historically untenable. The apostles and disciples did not invent the resurrection. It is easy to understand that they were quite incapable of doing so. There is no trace of their being in a state of exaltation, either individually or as a group, which would have led them to imagine an event desired and expected, and to pass it off on public opinion and belief as real, as though to make up for their disappointment. There is no trace of a creative process of the psychological, sociologi-

cal or literary order, not even in the primitive community or in
the authors of the early centuries. The apostles were the first to
believe, not without reluctance, that Christ had risen, simply
because they had experienced the resurrection as a real event.
They were personally convinced of it by having, on several
occasions, met Christ newly alive, during the course of forty
days. Succeeding Christian generations accepted that testimony, trusting the apostles and the other disciples as credible
witnesses. The Christian faith in Christ's resurrection is linked
to a fact which has a precise historical dimension.

However, the resurrection is a truth which, in its deepest
dimension, pertains to divine revelation. It had gradually been
foretold by Christ in the course of his messianic activity during
the prepaschal period. Several times Jesus had explicitly foretold that, after having suffered much and being put to death, he
would rise again. Thus it is stated in Mark's Gospel that, after
Peter's profession of faith near Caesarea Philippi, Jesus "began to teach them that the Son of Man must suffer many
things, and be rejected by the elders and the chief priests and
the scribes, and be killed, and after three days rise again. And
he said this plainly" (Mk 8:31-32). Mark also says that after
the transfiguration, "as they were coming down the mountain,
he charged them to tell no one what they had seen, until the
Son of Man should have risen from the dead" (Mk 9:9). The
disciples were puzzled about the meaning of "resurrection"
and they raised the question, already discussed in the Jewish
world, about the return of Elijah (cf. Mk 9:11). But Jesus
confirmed the idea that the Son of Man must "suffer many
things and be treated with contempt" (Mk 9:12).

After the cure of the epileptic possessed of a dumb spirit,
and while passing through Galilee in secret, Jesus resumed the
instruction of his disciples: "'The Son of Man will be delivered into the hands of men, and they will kill him. When he is
killed, after three days he will rise.' But they did not under-

stand the saying, and they were afraid to ask him" (Mk 9:31-32). It was the second announcement of his passion and resurrection, and it would be followed by a third one when they were already on the road to Jerusalem: "Behold, we are going up to Jerusalem; and the Son of Man will be delivered to the chief priests and the scribes, and they will condemn him to death, and deliver him to the Gentiles; and they will mock him, and spit upon him, and scourge him, and kill him; and after three days he will rise" (Mk 10:33-34).

Jesus' power over life and death

Here we have a prophetic vision and prediction of events in which Jesus acted as revealer, by unifying his death and resurrection in the redemptive purpose of these events, and by referring to the divine plan, according to which all that he foresaw and foretold "must" happen. Therefore, Jesus made known to the astonished and even appalled disciples something of the theological mystery underlying the proximate events, and indeed the whole of his life. Other flashes of light on this mystery occur in the allusion to the "sign of Jonah" (cf. Mt 12:40), which Jesus made his own and applied to the days of his death and resurrection, and likewise in the challenge to the Jews: "Destroy this temple, and in three days I will raise it up" (Jn 2:19). John notes that Jesus "was speaking of the temple of his body. When, therefore, he was raised from the dead, his disciples remembered that he had said this; and they believed the Scripture and the word which Jesus had spoken" (Jn 2:20-21). Once again we are confronted with the relation between Christ's resurrection and his word, with his announcements linked "to the Scriptures."

Over and above Jesus' words, his messianic activity in the prepaschal period shows his power over life and death, and his awareness of this power. We see this clearly in the raising to life of the daughter of Jairus (cf. Mk 5:39-42), and likewise of the son of the widow of Naim (cf. Lk 7:12-15). We see it, above all, in the raising to life of Lazarus (cf. Jn 11:42-44), which is presented in John's Gospel as an announcement and foreshadowing of Jesus' resurrection. In the words addressed to Martha during this last episode, there is a clear manifestation of his self-knowledge about his identity as the Lord of life and death, and that he held the keys of the mystery of resurrection: "I am the resurrection and the life; he who believes in me, though he die, yet shall he live, and whoever lives and believes in me shall never die" (Jn 11:25-26).

They are all words and events which contain in different ways the revelation of the truth about the resurrection in the prepaschal period.

Among the events connected with the resurrection, the first is the discovery of the empty tomb. Needless to say, this in itself is not a direct proof of the resurrection. The absence of Christ's body from the tomb in which it had been buried could be explained differently. On seeing the empty tomb, Mary Magdalen presumed that someone had taken away the body of Jesus (cf. Jn 20:13). Indeed, the Sanhedrin tried to spread the story that, while the soldiers were asleep, the disciples had stolen the body. "This story," Matthew notes, "has been spread among the Jews to this day" (Mt 28:12-15).

Nonetheless, the empty tomb was for all, friend and foe alike, an impressive sign. For those of good will it was a first step toward recognizing the "fact" of the resurrection as a truth which could not be denied.

So it was first of all for the women who went early in the morning to the tomb to anoint Christ's body. They were the first to receive the news: "He has risen, he is not here.... Go, tell his disciples and Peter..." (Mk 16:7-8). "'Remember how he told you, while he was still in Galilee, that the Son of Man must be delivered into the hands of sinful men, and be crucified, and on the third day rise.' And they remembered his words" (Lk 24:6-7).

Certainly the women were upset and frightened (cf. Mk 16:8; Lk 24:5). Not even they were inclined to accept too readily a fact which, though foretold by Jesus, effectively surpassed all power of imagination and invention. In their intuitive sensitivity and refinement they, and especially Mary Magdalen, grasped the truth and ran to the apostles to tell them the good news.

Matthew's Gospel (cf. 28:8-10) tells us that along the way Jesus himself met them. He greeted them and repeated the command to tell the news to his brethren. Thus the women were the first messengers of Christ's resurrection, even for the apostles themselves (cf. Lk 24:10)—an eloquent testimony of woman's importance even in the days of the paschal event!

Peter and John were among those who received the news from Mary Magdalen (cf. Jn 20:3-8). They went to the tomb with a certain hesitancy, all the more so since Mary had told them that Jesus' body was missing from the tomb (cf. Jn 20:2). On arriving at the tomb, they too found it empty. They ended by believing, after quite some hesitation, because as John says, "they did not yet understand the Scriptures, that he had to rise from the dead" (Jn 20:9).

Truth to tell, the fact was dumbfounding for those men who were confronted by a situation which was far beyond them. The same difficulty which the traditions of the event show in giving a fully consistent account of it, confirms its extraordinary character and the upsetting effect it had on the minds of the fortunate witnesses. The reference "to the Scripture" is a proof of their confused perception of finding themselves in the presence of a mystery, on which only revelation could throw light.

Here there is still another fact to be well pondered over. The empty tomb could at first sight cause upsetment and even give rise to a certain suspicion. But the gradual knowledge of this initial event, as noted by the Gospels, ended by leading to the discovery of the truth of the resurrection.

In fact, we are told that the women, and later the apostles, found themselves in the presence of a particular "sign": the sign of victory over death. If the tomb itself, closed by a heavy stone, was a witness to death, the empty tomb and the stone rolled away gave the first news that death had been overcome.

One cannot but be struck by the state of mind of the three women who, on their way to the tomb at sunrise, were saying to one another: "Who will roll away the stone for us from the door of the tomb?" (Mk 6:13). On arriving at the tomb later, they were utterly amazed to find that "the stone was rolled back, for it was very large" (Mk 16:4). According to Mark's Gospel, the women found in the tomb someone who gave them the news of the resurrection (cf. Mk 16:4). But they were afraid and, notwithstanding the reassurances of the young man dressed in a white robe, "they fled from the tomb, for trembling and astonishment had come upon them" (Mk 16:8). How can one fail to understand them? And yet a comparison with the parallel texts of the other evangelists permits us to state that, although frightened, the women brought the news of the resurrection, of which the "empty tomb" with the stone rolled back was the first sign.

For the women and for the apostles the road opened by the "sign" closes with the meeting with the risen one. Then the still timid and uncertain perception became conviction, indeed faith in him who "is truly risen." Thus it was for the women who, on seeing Jesus on their path and on hearing his greeting to them, threw themselves at his feet and adored him (cf. Mt 28:9). Thus it was especially in the case of Mary Magdalen. On hearing Jesus call her by name, she addressed him at first by the customary name, *"Rabbouni,* Teacher!" (Jn 20:16). Enlightened by him about the paschal mystery, she ran full of radiance to give the news to the disciples: "I have seen the Lord" (Jn 20:18). Thus it was for the disciples assembled in the upper room, who, on the evening of that "first day after the Sabbath," when they finally saw Jesus in their midst, were happy because of the new certainty that had entered their hearts: "They were glad when they saw the Lord" (Jn 20:18-20). Direct contact with Christ releases the spark that enkindles faith!

General audience of February 1, 1989

The Apparitions of the Risen Christ

St. Paul was chronologically the first to record the truth of Christ's resurrection. We are familiar with the passage of the First Letter to the Corinthians in which he states: "I handed on to you...what I also received, that Christ died for our sins in accordance with the Scriptures, that he was buried, that he was raised on the third day in accordance with the Scriptures, and that he appeared to Cephas, then to the twelve..." (1 Cor 15:3-5). It was a question of a truth handed on, received and again handed on. It is a truth pertaining to the "deposit of revelation" which Jesus himself, through his apostles and evangelists, left to his Church.

Jesus gradually revealed this truth in his prepaschal teaching. It was realized in the concrete in the paschal events at Jerusalem. These events were historically verified, but fraught with mystery.

The announcements and the facts were confirmed especially by the meetings with the risen Christ, which the Gospels and Paul record. It must be said that the Pauline text presents the meetings—in which the risen Christ is revealed—in a global and synthetic way. He added at the end his own meeting with the risen one at the gates of Damascus (cf. Acts 9:3-6). The Gospel accounts of the meetings are rather fragmentary.

It is not difficult to gather and compare some characteristics of each of these apparitions and of all of them taken together, to arrive still closer at the discovery of the meaning of this revealed truth.

First of all, we can observe that, after the resurrection, Jesus presented himself to the women and the disciples with his body transformed, made spiritual and sharing in the glory of the soul—but in no way triumphalistic. He appeared with great simplicity. He spoke as a friend to his friends, in the ordinary circumstances of their daily lives. He did not wish to confront his adversaries, adopting a victorious attitude. He was not concerned to show them his superiority; still less did he wish to annihilate them. It does not appear that he even met them. Everything that the Gospel says leads to the conclusion that he did not appear, for example, to Pilate, who had handed him over to the high priests to be crucified (cf. Jn 19:16), or to Caiaphas who had rent his garments because Christ claimed to be God (cf. Mt 26:63-66).

To those to whom he appeared, Jesus made himself known in his physical identity: that face, those hands, those features which they knew so well, the side which had been pierced, the voice which they had heard so often. Only in the meeting with Saul near Damascus did the light which surrounds the risen one blind the rabid persecutor of the Christians and strike him to the ground (cf. Acts 9:3-8). However, it was a manifestation of the power of him who, already ascended to heaven, struck a man whom he wished to make a "chosen instrument" (Acts 9:15), a missionary of the Gospel.

It is significant that Jesus appeared first to the women, his faithful followers, before appearing to the disciples and even to the apostles whom he had chosen to preach his Gospel to the world. It was to the women that he first disclosed the mystery of his resurrection. They were the first witnesses to this truth. Perhaps he wished to reward their delicacy, their sensitiveness to his message, and their strength that drove them all the way to Calvary. Perhaps he wished to reveal an exquisite trait of his humanity, consisting in the kindness and gentleness with which he approached and rewarded those who counted less in the great world of his time. That is what seems to follow from a text of Matthew: "And behold, Jesus met them (the women who were running to give the news to the disciples) and said, 'Hail!' And they came and took hold of his feet and worshipped him. Then Jesus said to them, 'Do not be afraid; go and tell my brethren to go to Galilee, and there they will see me'" (28:9-10).

Moreover, the appearance to Mary Magdalene (cf. Jn 20:11-18) is of extraordinary delicacy. This is true both on the part of the woman who revealed all her passionate and reserved devotedness to the following of Jesus, and on the part of the Master who treated her with exquisite delicacy and kindness. This special place given to woman in the paschal events is an inspiration to the Church which, in the course of history, has been able to rely on them for her life of faith, prayer and apostolate.

Some characteristics of these postpaschal meetings are in a certain way typical examples of the spiritual situations which so often arise in personal relationships with Christ when people feel called or "visited" by him. Above all, there is an initial difficult in recognizing Christ on the part of those who meet him. This can be seen in the case of Mary Magdalene (cf. Jn 20:14-16) and of the disciples on the road to Emmaus (cf. Lk 24:16). There is a certain element of fear in his presence. He is loved and he is sought, but when found, there is a certain hesitation....

In the case of Mary Magdalene (cf. Jn 20:16), of the disciples on the road to Emmaus (cf. Lk 24:26 ff.), and similarly in the case of the other disciples (cf. Lk 24:25-48), Jesus gradually led them to recognize him and to believe in him. It is a sign of Christ's patient pedagogy in revealing himself to people, in attracting them, in converting them and in leading them to the knowledge of the riches of his heart and to salvation.

It is interesting to analyze the psychological process that the various meetings give us a glimpse of. The disciples experienced a certain difficulty not only in recognizing the truth of the resurrection, but also the identity of the one who stood before them. He appeared as the same and yet as different: a transformed Christ. It was not easy for them to identify him immediately. Yes, they perceived that it was Jesus, but at the same time they felt that he was not in the same condition as he was before. In his presence they were seized with reverence and fear.

When they realized with his help that it was not a case of someone different, but of himself transformed, a new capacity for discovery, understanding, charity and faith was released in them. It was like an awakening of faith: "Did not our hearts burn within us while he talked to us on the road, while he opened the Scriptures to us?" (Lk 24:32). "My Lord and my God!" (Jn 20:28). "I have seen the Lord!" (Jn 20:18). Then they began to understand the event of the cross in an absolutely new light. The mystery of Christ's suffering and death was seen to end in the glory of new life! This would be one of the principal elements of the announcement of salvation brought by the apostles from the very beginning to the Jewish people and gradually to all nations.

Finally, an important characteristic of the appearances of the risen Christ, especially in the last appearances, was his entrusting to the apostles (and to the Church) the mission of evangelizing the world by the announcement of his Word and the gift of his grace.

Remember the apparition to the disciples in the upper

room on the evening of the first Easter Day: "As the Father has sent me, even so I send you..." (Jn 20:21). He granted them the power to forgive sins.

Then in the apparition at the Sea of Tiberias, followed by the miraculous catch of fish which symbolized and foretold the fruitfulness of their mission, it was evident that Jesus wished to direct their attention to the work that awaited them (cf. Jn 21:1-23). This was confirmed by the definitive conferring of the special mission on Peter (Jn 21:15-18): "Do you love me?... You know that I love you.... Feed my lambs.... Feed my sheep...."

John notes that "this was the third time that Jesus was revealed to the disciples after he was raised from the dead" (Jn 21:14). This time they not only took note of his identity: "It is the Lord!" (Jn 21:7). They also understood that all that had happened and was happening during those Easter days committed each of them, and especially Peter, to building a new era of history, an era that had begun on Easter morning.

General audience of February 22, 1989

The Resurrection Is a Historical Event that Transcends History

Christ's resurrection was an event consisting essentially in a passage from death to life. It was a unique event which, like the Passover, took place in the context of the paschal feasts during which the descendants of Israel annually recalled the exodus from Egypt. They gave thanks for the freeing of their forefathers from bondage, and exalted the power of the Lord God which was clearly manifested in that ancient Passover.

Christ's resurrection is the new Passover, the new Pasch, which must be interpreted against the background of the ancient Passover which prefigured and foretold it. Thus it was considered in the Christian community according to the teaching offered to the faithful by the apostles and evangelists on the basis of Jesus' own words.

In line with what has been handed down by those ancient sources, the resurrection is, in the first place, a historical event. It took place in a precise context of time and place: "on the third day" after Jesus' crucifixion at Jerusalem and his burial in the tomb provided by Joseph of Arimathea (cf. Mk 15:46). At dawn of the third day (the day after the paschal sabbath) this same tomb was found empty.

Jesus had foretold his resurrection on the third day (cf. Mt 16:21; 17:23; 20:19). The women who went that day to the tomb found an angel who said to them: "You seek Jesus who was crucified. He is not here. He has risen as he said" (Mt 28:5-6).

In the Gospel account the circumstance of the "third day" is related to the Jewish celebration of the sabbath, which forbade work and movement beyond a certain distance from the evening of the vigil. Therefore the embalming of the body according to the Jewish practice had to be postponed until the first day after the sabbath.

While the resurrection is an event that is determined according to time and place, nevertheless it transcends and stands above history. No one beheld the event in itself. No one could have been an eyewitness of the event. Several people had seen the agony and death of Christ on Calvary. Some had taken part in placing Jesus' body in the tomb, well sealed and presided over by the guards whom the "high priests and Pharisees" had made it their business to obtain from Pilate. They remembered that Jesus had said that after three days he would rise again. "Therefore, order the sepulcher to be made secure until the third day, lest his disciples go and steal him away and tell the people, 'He has risen from the dead'" (Mt 27:63-64). But the disciples had not thought of such a thing. It was the women coming with spices on the morning of the third day who discovered the tomb empty, with the stone rolled away. They saw a young man dressed in a white robe who spoke to them of Jesus' resurrection (cf. Mk 16:6). Certainly Christ's body was no longer there. However, no one was an eyewitness of the resurrection. No one could say how it had happened in its physical reality. Still less could the senses perceive the most interior essence of his passage to another life.

It is this transhistorical feature of the resurrection that must be especially considered if we are to understand to some extent the mystery of that historical, but also transhistorical event, as we shall see immediately.

Indeed, Christ's resurrection was not simply a return to earthly life, like those whom he had raised from the dead during his public ministry: the daughter of Jairus, Lazarus and the young man of Naim. These facts were miraculous events (and therefore extraordinary), but these persons reacquired through the power of Jesus "ordinary" earthly life. At a later time they again died, as St. Augustine frequently observes.

In the case of Christ's resurrection the situation was essentially different. In his risen body he passed from death to another life beyond time and space. This risen body of Jesus was filled with the power of the Holy Spirit and shared in the divine life of glory. So it can be said of Christ, in the words of St. Paul, that he is the "heavenly man" (cf. 1 Cor 15:47 f.).

In this sense Christ's resurrection is beyond the purely historical dimension. It is an event pertaining to the transhistorical sphere, and therefore eludes the criteria of simple human empirical observation. It is true that Jesus, after the resurrection, appeared to his disciples. He spoke to them, had dealings with them, and even ate with them. He invited Thomas to touch him in order to be sure of his identity. However, this real dimension of his entire humanity concealed another life which was now his, and which withdrew him from the normality of ordinary earthly life and plunged him in mystery.

Another mysterious element of Christ's resurrection is the fact that the passage from death to new life took place through the power of the Father. He "had raised" (cf. Acts 2:32) Christ, his Son, and thus perfectly introduced Jesus' humanity—even his body—into the communion of the Trinity, so that Jesus is definitively revealed as "designated Son of God in power according to the Spirit...by his resurrection from the dead" (Rom 1:3-4). St. Paul insists on presenting Christ's resurrection as a manifestation of the power of God (cf. Rom 6:4;

2 Cor 13:4; Phil 3:10; Col 2:12; Eph 1:19 f.; cf. also Heb 7:16) through the work of the Spirit. In restoring Jesus to life, the Spirit placed him in the glorious state of Lord *(kyrios)* in which he definitively merits, even as man, that name of Son of God which belonged to him from eternity (cf. Rom 8:11; 9:5; 14:9; Phil 2:9-11; cf. also Heb 1:1-5; 5:5, etc.).

It is significant that many New Testament texts speak of Christ's resurrection as a "resurrection from the dead" accomplished by the power of the Holy Spirit. Others speak of it as taking place through Christ's own power, as indeed is indicated in many languages by the word "resurrection." This active meaning of the word (noun and verb) is also found in Christ's prepaschal discourses, e.g., in foretelling the passion when he says that the Son of Man must suffer many things, die, and then rise again (cf. Mk 8:31; 9:9, 31; 10:34). In John's Gospel Jesus explicitly states: "I lay down my life, that I may take it again...I have power to lay it down, and I have power to take it again" (10:17-18). In the First Letter to the Thessalonians, St. Paul writes: "We believe...that Jesus died and rose again" (4:14).

The Acts of the Apostles frequently states that "God raised up Jesus..." (2:24, 32; 3:15, 26 etc.), but there we also find Jesus' resurrection spoken of in the active sense (cf. 10:41). From this point of view Acts sums up Paul's preaching in the synagogue of Thessalonica, where "on the basis of the Scriptures he showed that it was necessary for the Christ to suffer and to rise from the dead" (Acts 17:3).

From all these texts taken as a whole, there emerges the trinitarian nature of Christ's resurrection. It is the joint work of the Father, Son and Holy Spirit, and thus reflects the very mystery of God.

The expression "according to the Scriptures" which we find in the First Letter to the Corinthians (15:3-4) and in the Nicene-Constantinopolitan Creed, emphasizes the eschato-

logical nature of Christ's resurrection. We find in it the fulfillment of the Old Testament prophecies. When speaking of his
passion and glory with the two disciples on the road to
Emmaus, Jesus himself, according to Luke, rebuked them for
their slowness of heart "to believe all that the prophets had
spoken." Then "beginning with Moses and all the prophets he
interpreted for them in all the Scriptures the things concerning
himself" (Lk 24:2-27). Likewise in his last meeting with the
apostles he said, "'These are my words which I spoke to you,
while I was still with you, that everything written about me in
the law of Moses and the prophets and the psalms must be
fulfilled.' Then he opened their minds to understand the Scriptures, and said to them, 'Thus it is written, that the Christ
should suffer and on the third day rise from the dead, and that
repentance and forgiveness of sins should be preached in his
name to all nations, beginning from Jerusalem'" (Lk 24:44-48).

This was the messianic interpretation, given by Jesus
himself to the whole of the Old Testament and especially to the
texts that more directly concerned the paschal mystery, such as
those of Isaiah on the humiliations and the exaltation of the
servant of the Lord (Is 52:13-53:12), and Psalm 110. On the
basis of this eschatological interpretation given by Jesus,
which linked the paschal mystery to the Old Testament and
projected its light on the future (the preaching to all nations),
the apostles and evangelists also spoke of the resurrection
"according to the Scriptures," and subsequently the formula of
the creed was fixed. It was another dimension of the event as
mystery.

From what we have said it is clearly evident that Christ's
resurrection is the greatest event in the history of salvation,
and indeed, we can say in the history of humanity, since it
gives definitive meaning to the world. The whole world re-
volves around the cross, but only in the resurrection does the
cross reach its full significance of salvific event. The cross and

resurrection constitute the one paschal mystery in which the history of the world is centered. Therefore Easter is the Church's greatest solemnity. Every year she celebrates and renews this event. It is fraught with all the prophecies of the Old Testament, beginning with the "protoevangelium" of the redemption, and of all the eschatological hopes and expectations projected toward the "fullness of time," which was realized when the kingdom of God definitively entered human history and the universal order of salvation.

General audience of March 1, 1989

The Resurrection Is
the High Point of Revelation

In St. Paul's Letter to the Corinthians, several times quoted during the course of these reflections on Christ's resurrection, we read: "If Christ has not been raised, then our preaching is in vain and your faith is in vain" (1 Cor 15:14). Evidently St. Paul saw the resurrection as the basis of the Christian faith. He saw it as the keystone of the entire edifice of doctrine and life built up on revelation, inasmuch as it is the definitive confirmation of the whole ensemble of truth taught by Christ. Hence all the Church's preaching, from apostolic times down the centuries and spanning the generations even to the present day, makes its appeal to the resurrection. It draws from it its driving and persuasive force and its vigor. It is easy to understand why.

The resurrection was first of all the confirmation of all that Christ had "done and taught." It was the divine seal stamped on his words and life. He himself had indicated to his disciples and adversaries this definitive sign of his truth. On the first Easter the angel told the women at the empty tomb: "He has risen as he said" (Mt 28:6). If this word and promise of his are revealed as true, then all his other words and prom-

513

ises possess the power of truth that does not pass away, as he himself had proclaimed: "Heaven and earth will pass away, but my words will not pass away" (Mt 24:35; cf. Mk 13:31; Lk 21:33). No stronger, more decisive and more authoritative proof than the resurrection from the dead could have been imagined or asked for. All the truths, including those most impenetrable to the human mind, find their justification, even from the rational point of view, in the fact that the risen Christ gave the definitive proof, promised beforehand, of his divine authority.

Thus the truth of Christ's divinity itself is confirmed by the resurrection. Jesus had said: "When you have lifted up the Son of Man, then you will realize that I Am" (Jn 8:28). Those who heard these words wanted to stone Jesus, because for the Jews the words "I Am" were the equivalent of the unspeakable name of God. In fact, when asking Pilate to condemn Jesus to death, they presented as the principal charge that he had "made himself the Son of God" (Jn 19:7). For this reason the Sanhedrin had condemned him as guilty of blasphemy. In reply to the high priest's question, Jesus had declared that he was the Christ, the Son of God (cf. Mt 26:63-65; Mk 14:62; Lk 22:70), that is to say, not merely the earthly Messiah as understood and awaited by Jewish tradition, but the Messiah-Lord announced by Psalm 110 (cf. Mt 22:41 ff.), the mysterious personage perceived by Daniel (cf. 7:13-14). This was the great blasphemy and the charge for the death sentence: that he had proclaimed himself the Son of God! Jesus' resurrection confirms the truth of his divine identity, and justifies the self-attribution of the "name" of God which he made before the Pasch: "Truly, truly, I say to you, before Abraham was, I Am" (Jn 8:58). For the Jews this was a claim punishable by stoning (cf. Lev 24:16). "They took up stones to throw at him; but Jesus hid himself and went out of the temple" (Jn 8:59). If they had not then been able to stone him, they later succeeded in "lifting him up" on the cross. The resurrection of the crucified proved that he was really *I Am,* the Son of God.

In actual fact, Jesus, while calling himself Son of Man, had not only asserted that he was truly the Son of God. But in the upper room, before the passion, he had also prayed the Father to reveal that the Christ-Son of Man was his eternal Son: "Father, the hour has come; glorify your Son that the Son may glorify you" (Jn 17:1). "Glorify me in your own presence with the glory which I had with you before the world was made" (Jn 17:5). The paschal mystery was the answer to this prayer, the confirmation of Christ's divine sonship, and indeed his glorification with that glory which he "had with the Father before the world was made": the glory of the Son of God.

According to John's Gospel Jesus, in the prepashcal period, had on several occasions alluded to this future glory which would be manifested in his death and resurrection. Only after the event did the disciples understand the meaning of those words of his.

Thus we read that during his first Pasch at Jerusalem, after having driven the merchants and money-changers out of the temple, Jesus replied to the Jews who had asked him for a sign of his authority for doing as he had done: "'Destroy this temple, and in three days I will raise it up....' But he spoke of the temple of his body. When therefore he was raised from the dead, his disciples remembered that he had said this, and they believed the Scripture and the word which Jesus had spoken" (Jn 2:19-22).

Moreover, Jesus' reply to those sent by the sisters of Lazarus who besought him to come to visit their brother who was ill, referred to the paschal events: "This illness is not unto death; it is for the glory of God, so that the Son of God may be glorified by means of it" (Jn 11:4).

It was not merely the glory which he could acquire from the miracle, all the more so since it would have been a con-

tributory cause of his death (cf. Jn 11:46-54). His real glorification would have come precisely from his being raised up on
the cross (cf. Jn 12:32). The disciples had a clear understanding of all this after the resurrection.

Particularly interesting is St. Paul's teaching on the value
of the resurrection as the determinant element of his
Christological concept, linked also to his personal experience
of the risen one. Thus at the beginning of his Letter to the
Romans he writes: "Paul, a servant of Jesus Christ, called to be
an apostle, set apart for the Gospel of God which he promised
beforehand through his prophets in the holy Scriptures, the
Gospel concerning his Son, who was descended from David
according to the flesh, and designated Son of God in power
according to the Spirit of holiness by his resurrection from the
dead, Jesus Christ our Lord" (1:1-4).

This means that from the very first moment of his human
conception and birth (descended from David), Jesus was the
eternal Son of God become Son of Man. In the resurrection
this divine sonship was manifested in all its fullness through
the power of God. God restored Jesus to life by the work of the
Holy Spirit (cf. Rom 8:11) and constituted him in the glorious
state of *kyrios* (cf. Phil 2:9-11; Rom 14:9; Acts 2:36). Jesus
merited under a new, messianic title the recognition, worship
and glory of the eternal name of Son of God (cf. Acts 13:33;
Heb 1:1-5; 5:5).

Paul had expounded this same doctrine in the synagogue
of Antioch in Pisidia on the sabbath day. At the invitation of
the leaders of the synagogue, he spoke to announce that as the
high point of the economy of salvation, effected between the
lights and shadows of the history of Israel, God had raised up
Jesus from the dead. For many days Jesus had appeared to
those who came up with him from Galilee to Jerusalem and
these were now his witnesses to the people. "And we," the
Apostle concluded, "bring you the good news that what God

promised to our fathers, he has fulfilled to us their children by raising Jesus; as also it is written in the second psalm: 'You are my Son, today I have begotten you'" (Acts 13:32-34: cf. Ps 2:7).

For Paul there is an assimilation of ideas between the glory of Christ's resurrection and Christ's eternal divine sonship, which is fully revealed in that victorious conclusion of his messianic mission.

Paul's personal experience of the Lord

This glory of *kyrios* manifests that power of the risen one (Man-God) whom Paul had known by personal experience at the moment of his conversion on the road to Damascus. Then he too heard himself called to be an apostle (though not one of the Twelve), inasmuch as he was an eye-witness of the living Christ. Paul received from him the power to face all the toil and bear all the suffering of his mission. Paul's spirit was so marked by that experience that in his teaching and witness he gave precedence to the idea of the power of the risen one over that of sharing in Christ's sufferings, which was also dear to him. That which he had verified in his personal experience he proposed to the faithful as a rule of thought and a norm of life: "Indeed I count everything as loss because of the surpassing worth of knowing Christ Jesus my Lord...in order that I may gain Christ and be found in him...so that I may know him and the power of his resurrection, and may share his sufferings, becoming like him in his death, that if possible I may attain the resurrection from the dead" (Phil 3:8-11). At this point his thought turned to his experience on the road to Damascus: "...because Christ Jesus has made me his own" (Phil 3:12).

As appears from the texts quoted, Christ's resurrection is closely connected with the mystery of the Incarnation of the Son of God. It is its fulfillment, according to God's eternal plan. Rather, it is the supreme crowning of all that Jesus had revealed and wrought throughout his whole life, from his birth to his passion and death, by his deeds, miracles, teaching, example of perfect holiness and above all by his transfiguration. He had never revealed directly the glory which he had with the Father "before the world was made" (Jn 17:5), but he concealed this glory in his humanity until the definitive emptying of himself (cf. Phil 2:7-8) through his death on the cross.

The resurrection reveals the fact that "in Christ the whole fullness of the deity dwells bodily" (Col 1:19). Thus the resurrection completes the manifestation of the content of the Incarnation. It can therefore be said that it is also the fullness of revelation. It stands therefore, as we have said, at the center of the Christian faith and of the Church's preaching.

General audience of March 8, 1989

The Saving Power
of the Resurrection

The Christian faith and the Church's preaching are rooted in Christ's resurrection because it is the definitive confirmation and culmination of revelation. One must also add that as the completion of the paschal mystery, it is the source of the saving power of the Gospel and of the Church. According to St. Paul, "by his resurrection from the dead" Jesus Christ is revealed as "Son of God in power according to the Spirit of holiness" (cf. Rom 1:4). He conveys this holiness to mankind, because "he was put to death for our trespasses and raised for our justification" (Rom 4:25). There is a twofold aspect of the paschal mystery: death for liberation from sin, and resurrection to open the way to a new life.

Certainly the paschal mystery, like the whole of Christ's life and work, has a deep internal unity in its redemptive function and efficacy. This does not prevent us from distinguishing various aspects in relation to its effects for us. Hence the specific effect of "new life" is attributed to the resurrection, as St. Paul says.

In this teaching some points must be indicated which, in reference to New Testament texts, enable us to perceive all its truth and beauty. First of all, it can well be said that the risen

Christ is the principle and source of new life for everyone. This appears also from Jesus' marvelous prayer on the eve of his passion, which John records in the following words: "Father...glorify your Son that the Son may glorify you, since you have given him power over all flesh, to give eternal life to all whom you have given him" (Jn 17:1-2). In his prayer Jesus sees and embraces especially his disciples whom he had informed of his proximate painful separation through his passion and death, but to whom he had promised: "I live and you will live" (Jn 14:19). That is to say, you will share in my life which will be revealed after the resurrection. However, Jesus' glance has a universal range: "I do not pray for these only," he said, "but also for those who believe in me through their word" (Jn 17:20). All must become one by sharing in God's glory in Christ.

The new life granted to believers by virtue of Christ's resurrection consists in victory over the death caused by sin, and a sharing in the divine life of grace. St. Paul states it in a striking manner: "God, who is rich in mercy...even when we were dead through our trespasses, made us alive with Christ" (Eph 2:4-5). Similarly St. Peter wrote: "Praised be the God and Father of our Lord Jesus Christ...by his great mercy we have been born anew to a living hope through the resurrection of Jesus Christ from the dead" (1 Pet 1:3).

This new life—life according to the spirit—manifests our adoption as sons, another Pauline concept of fundamental importance. The classic passage on this point is from the Letter to the Galatians: "God sent forth his Son...to redeem those who were under the law, so that we might receive adoption as sons" (Gal 4:4-5). This divine adoption through the Holy Spirit makes man like to the only-begotten Son: "...all who are led by the Spirit of God are sons of God" (Rom 8:14). In the Letter to the Galatians St. Paul appeals to the believers' experience of the new condition in which they find themselves: "...and because you are sons, God has sent the spirit of his Son into our hearts, crying, 'Abba! Father!' So through God you are no longer a slave but a son, and if a son then an heir" (Gal 4:6-7). There is then in the new man a first effect of redemption: freedom from slavery. But freedom is acquired by becoming an adopted son, not merely on a level of legal access to the inheritance, but with the real gift of divine life which the three Persons of the Trinity infuse into man (cf. Gal 4:6; 2 Cor 13:13). The source of this new life of man in God is Christ's resurrection.

Participation in the new life enables men to become brethren of Christ, as Jesus himself called the disciples after the resurrection: "Go and tell my brethren..." (Mt 28:10; cf. Jn 20:17). This means brothers not by nature, but by the gift of grace, since this adoptive sonship gives a true and real participation in the life of the only-begotten Son, who is revealed fully in his resurrection.

Finally, Christ's resurrection—rather, the risen Christ— is the principle and source of our future resurrection. When he foretold the institution of the Eucharist, Jesus referred to himself as the sacrament of eternal life and of the future resurrection: "He who eats my flesh and drinks my blood has eternal life, and I will raise him up at the last day" (Jn 6:54). Since his hearers murmured, Jesus said to them: "Do you take offense at this? Then what if you were to see the Son of Man ascending where he was before?" (Jn 6:61-62). In this way he indirectly indicated that under the sacramental species of the Eucharist, those who receive it are granted to partake of the Body and Blood of the glorified Christ.

St. Paul, too, emphasizes the connection between Christ's resurrection and ours, especially in his First Letter to the Corinthians where he writes: "Christ has been raised from the dead, the first fruits of those who have fallen asleep...for as in Adam all die, so also in Christ shall all be made alive"

(1 Cor 15:20-22). "For this perishable nature must put on the imperishable, and this mortal nature must put on immortality. When the perishable puts on the imperishable, and the mortal puts on immortality, then shall come to pass the saying that is written: 'Death is swallowed up in victory'" (1 Cor 15:53-54). "Thanks be to God, who gives us the victory through our Lord Jesus Christ" (1 Cor 15:57).

The definitive victory over death, already won by Christ, is shared by him with humanity in the measure in which it receives the fruits of redemption. It is a process of admission to the new life, to the eternal life which will last until the end of time. Thanks to this process there is being formed down the centuries a new humanity, the people of the redeemed, gathered in the Church, the true community of the resurrection. At the final moment of history all shall rise again, and those who belong to Christ will have the fullness of life in glory, in the definitive realization of the community of those redeemed by Christ, "so that God may be everything to every one" (1 Cor 15:28).

The Apostle also teaches that the redemptive process, concluding with the resurrection of the dead, will take place in a sphere of indescribable spirituality which transcends the power of human comprehension and operation. On the one hand he writes: "Flesh and blood cannot inherit the kingdom of God, nor does the perishable inherit the imperishable" (1 Cor 15:50). This recognizes our natural incapacity for the new life. On the other hand, in the Letter to the Romans he thus reassures the believers: "If the Spirit of him who raised Jesus from the dead dwells in you, he who raised Christ Jesus from the dead will give life to your mortal bodies also through his Spirit who dwells in you" (Rom 8:11). It is a mysterious process of spiritualization which at the moment of the resurrection will affect also the bodies, through the power of that same Holy Spirit who brought about Christ's resurrection.

Undoubtedly it is a reality which escapes our capacity of rational understanding and demonstration. Therefore it is an object of our faith based on the word of God which, through St. Paul's teaching, enables us to penetrate the mystery which transcends all limits of space and time: "The first man Adam became a living being; the last Adam became a life-giving spirit" (1 Cor 15:45). "Just as we have borne the image of the man of dust, we shall also bear the image of the man of heaven" (1 Cor 15:49).

In expectation of that final transcendent fulfillment, the risen Christ dwells in the hearts of his disciples and followers as a source of sanctification in the Holy Spirit. He is a source of divine life and divine sonship, a source of future resurrection.

This certainly leads St. Paul to say in the Letter to the Galatians: "I have been crucified with Christ; it is no longer I who live, but Christ who lives in me. The life I now live in the flesh I live by faith in the Son of God, who loved me and gave himself for me" (Gal 2:20). Every Christian also, like the Apostle, while still living in the flesh (cf. Rom 7:5) lives a life already spiritualized through faith (cf. 2 Cor 10:3). The living Christ, the risen Christ, has become as it were the subject of all his actions: Christ lives in me (cf. Rom 8:2, 10-11; Phil 1:21; Col 3:3). It is life in the Holy Spirit.

This certainly sustained the Apostle, as it can and should sustain every Christian amid the toils and sufferings of the present life. So too Paul recommended to his disciple Timothy in a passage of one of his letters with which we wish to put the seal—for our instruction and consolation—on our reflection on Christ's resurrection: "Remember that Jesus Christ," he writes, "descended from David, was raised from the dead, as preached in my Gospel.... Therefore I endure everything for the sake of the elect, that they may obtain the salvation which in Christ Jesus goes with eternal glory. The saying is sure [perhaps it was a part of a hymn of the early Christians]: If we have died with him, we shall also live with him; if we endure, we shall also reign with him; if we deny him, he also will deny us; if we are faithless, he remains faithful—for he cannot deny himself..." (2 Tim 2:8-13).

"Remember that Jesus Christ is risen from the dead": these words of the Apostle are the key of our hope for the true life in time and in eternity.

General audience of March 15, 1989

Every Christian Is Called
to be a Witness to the Risen Christ

Christ, our paschal sacrifice, offered himself on the cross for our sins and has risen in glory: let us rejoice in the Lord!

This is the thought which runs through the liturgy of these days after the celebration of Easter. During Mass we repeat with joy the words of the sequence: *Mors et vita duello conflixere mirando—dux vitae mortuus regnat vivus!* "Death and life have contended in that combat stupendous; the prince of life, who died, reigns immortal!"

Christ, victorious over death, is actively present also in the world today. Christianity continues its course, because it can count on the action of the Word Incarnate who was made man, died on a cross, was buried and rose again, as he had foretold. "The Christian faith," wrote the well-known theologian Romano Guardini, "stands or falls according to whether or not one believes in the Lord's resurrection. The resurrection is not a marginal phenomenon of this faith, nor is it a mythological development which the faith has drawn from history and which could later be discarded without harm to its content. The resurrection is the very heart of the faith" *(Il Signore,* Part 6, Resurrection and Transfiguration).

Thus the Church, beside the empty tomb, always reminds

humanity: "Seek not the living one among the dead! He is not here, but has risen!" The Church says in the words of the angels to the terrified women before the stone rolled back from the tomb: "Remember how he told you while he was still in Galilee, that the Son of Man must be delivered into the hands of sinful men, and be crucified, and rise on the third day" (Lk 24:6-7).

On Easter morning the Apostle Peter entered the empty tomb. There he saw the linen cloths lying, and the piece of cloth which had been on Jesus' head, not lying with the linen cloths but rolled up in a place by itself (cf. Jn 20:6-7). Later, together with the other apostles and disciples Peter met the risen Lord and conversed with him, as he stated in his discourse in the house of the centurion Cornelius: "The Jews put him to death by hanging him on a tree; but God raised him up on the third day and made him manifest; not to all the people but to us who were chosen by God as witnesses, who ate and drank with him after he rose from the dead. And he commanded us to preach to the people, and to testify that he is the one ordained by God to be judge of the living and the dead" (Acts 10:39-42).

Peter, the apostles and the disciples understood perfectly that their principal mission was to be witnesses to the Lord's resurrection. Faith in Christ and the acceptance of his saving message depends upon this unique and amazing event.

Every Christian, in every age and place, is a witness to the risen Christ. He sees with the eyes of Peter and the apostles. He is convinced of the glorious resurrection of Christ crucified and therefore believes completely in him who is the Way, the Truth, the Life and the Light of the world. He proclaims Jesus with a serene courage. The paschal witness is thus the specific characteristic of the Christian.

St. Paul therefore writes to the Colossians: "If you have been raised with Christ, seek the things that are above, where

Christ is seated at the right hand of God. Set your minds on things that are above, not on things that are on earth. For you have died, and your life is hidden with Christ in God" (Col 3:1-3).

Rightly then does St. Ambrose observe in a discourse on the sacraments: "God has anointed you; Christ has marked you with his seal. In what way? Because you have been marked to receive the imprint of his cross, to conform you to his passion. You have received the seal that makes you like to him, so that you may be able to rise to his image, to live by imitating him who was crucified to sin and lives for God. Your old self has been immersed in the font and has been crucified in sin, but is risen for God" *(Discourse VI, 2, 7).*

When treating of the universal call to holiness, the Second Vatican Council taught in the *Constitution on the Church:* "All the faithful of Christ are invited to strive for the holiness and perfection of their own proper state. Indeed they have an obligation to so strive. Let all then have care that they guide aright their own deepest sentiments of soul. Let neither the use of the things of this world nor attachment to riches, which is against the spirit of evangelical poverty, hinder them in their quest for perfect love" *(LG 42).*

The obligation to paschal witness undoubtedly implies for the Christian a great dignity, but also a grave responsibility. Indeed, he must always be a credible witness by clarity of doctrine and consistency of life.

Paschal witness is expressed first of all by spiritual asceticism, and thus through a constant and decisive striving toward perfection in conformity with the demands of Baptism and Confirmation. Further, it is also expressed through apostolic commitment by accepting with a healthy realism tribulations and persecutions, ever mindful of what Jesus said: "If the world hates you, know that it has hated me before it hated you.... In the world you will have tribulations; but be of good cheer, I have overcome the world" (Jn 15:18; 16:33). Finally, it is expressed in the "ideal of charity," whereby the Christian, while suffering because of the many sad situations in which humanity finds itself, is always engaged, like the Good Samaritan, in the temporal and spiritual works of mercy. He constantly breaks down the walls of selfishness and shows others in practical ways the love of God.

The whole life of a Christian must be paschal! I invite you all to bring to your families, your work, your daily concerns, your schools, your professions, your free time and also to your suffering, the serenity and peace, the joy and trust that come from the certainty of Christ's resurrection! May Mary Most Holy accompany you and strengthen you in your paschal witness!

Scimus Christum surrexisse a mortuis vere: tu nobis, victor rex, miserere! "Christ indeed from death is risen, our new life obtaining. Have mercy, victor king, ever reigning!"

General audience of March 29, 1989

The Ascension:
A Mystery Announced Beforehand

In the most ancient creeds the article on Christ's resurrection is followed by that on his ascension. The Gospels tell us that the risen Christ appeared to his disciples on several occasions and in different places for forty days before withdrawing himself fully and definitively from the laws of space and time in order to ascend into heaven. Thus he completed the "return to the Father" already begun with the resurrection from the dead.

In the present reflection we shall see that Jesus foretold his ascension (or return to the Father) by speaking of it to Mary Magdalene and the disciples during the paschal and pre-paschal days.

On meeting Mary Magdalene after the resurrection Jesus said to her: "Do not hold me, for I have not yet ascended to the Father; go to my brethren and say to them, I am ascending to my Father and your Father, to my God and your God" (Jn 20:17).

On several occasions during the paschal period Jesus made that same announcement to his disciples. He did so especially at the Last Supper: "When Jesus knew that his hour had come to depart from this world to the Father...knowing that the Father had given all things into his hands, and that he had come from God and was going to God..." (Jn 13:1-3). Jesus

certainly had in mind his death which was already near, and
yet he was looking beyond that and spoke those words in the
perspective of his proximate departure, of his return to the
Father through the ascension into heaven: "Now I am going to
him who sent me" (Jn 16:5); "I go to the Father, and you will
see me no more" (Jn 16:10). At that time the disciples had no
clear understanding of what Jesus had in mind, all the more so
since he spoke in a mysterious way: "I go away and I will come
to you," and then he added: "If you loved me, you would have
rejoiced because I go to the Father; for the Father is greater
than I" (Jn 14:28). After his resurrection the disciples would
understand these words as a prophecy of his ascension into
heaven.

If we examine briefly the content of the announcements
quoted, we note especially that the ascension into heaven was
the final stage of the earthly pilgrimage of Christ, Son of God,
of one being with the Father, who had become man for our
salvation. However, this final stage remains closely linked
with the first, namely, the "descent from heaven" in the Incarnation. Christ "came from the Father" (Jn 16:28) into the
world through the Incarnation. Now, after the conclusion of his
mission, "he leaves the world and goes to the Father" (cf. Jn
16:28). His "ascent" is as unique as his "descent." Only he
who came from the Father in the manner of Christ can return to
the Father in like manner. Jesus himself makes that clear in his
conversation with Nicodemus: "No one has ascended into
heaven but he who descended from heaven, the Son of Man"
(Jn 3:13). Only he and no one else has the divine power and
the right "to ascend into heaven." Left to ourselves and our
own resources we cannot gain access to the "Father's house"
(Jn 14:2), to a sharing in the life and happiness of God. Only
Christ can open the way to the Father: he, the Son who "descended from heaven," who "came from the Father" for this
very purpose. Here we have a first result of our analysis: the

ascension is included in the mystery of the Incarnation as its concluding moment.

The ascension into heaven is therefore closely connected with the economy of salvation which is expressed in the mystery of the Incarnation, and especially in Christ's redemptive death on the cross. In the conversation with Nicodemus mentioned above, Jesus himself, in referring to a symbolic and figurative event in the Book of Numbers (cf. 21:4-9) states: "As Moses lifted up the serpent in the wilderness, so must the Son of Man be lifted up [that is, crucified], that whoever believes in him may have eternal life" (Jn 3:14).

Near the end of his ministry, shortly before the Pasch, Jesus clearly repeats that it is he who will open to humanity access to the "Father's house" by means of his cross: "And I, when I am lifted up from the earth, will draw all men to myself" (Jn 12:32). The "lifting up" on the cross is the special sign and definitive foretelling of the other "lifting up" by his ascension into heaven. John's Gospel sees this exaltation of the Redeemer already on Golgotha. The cross is the beginning of the ascension into heaven.

Redemptive value of the ascension

We find the same truth in the Letter to the Hebrews where we read that Jesus Christ, the unique priest of the new and eternal covenant, "entered not into a sanctuary made with hands...but into heaven itself, now to appear in the presence of God on our behalf" (Heb 9:24). He entered "through his own blood, thus securing an eternal redemption"; "He entered once for all" (Heb 9:12). He entered as the Son "who reflects the glory [of the Father] and bears the very stamp of his nature, upholding the universe by his word of power. When he had made purification for sins, he sat down at the right hand of the Majesty on high" (Heb 1:3).

This text of the Letter to the Hebrews and that of the conversation with Nicodemus (Jn 3:13) coincide substantially in affirming the redemptive value of the ascension into heaven as the culmination of the economy of salvation. This is in accordance with Jesus' own fundamental principle: "No one has ascended into heaven but he who descended from heaven, the Son of Man" (Jn 3:13).

Other words of Jesus at the Last Supper refer to his death, but in the perspective of the ascension: "Little children, yet a little while I am with you. You will seek me, but...where I am going you cannot come [now] (Jn 13:33). Later, however, he said: "In my Father's house there are many rooms. If it were not so, would I have told you that I go to prepare a place for you?" (Jn 14:2).

The discourse is addressed to the apostles, but is directed well beyond their circle. Jesus Christ goes to the Father—to the Father's house—to lead us there, because without him we could not enter it. Only he can open access to all: he who "descended from heaven" (Jn 3:13), who "came from the Father" (Jn 16:28) and now returns to the Father "through his own blood, thus securing an eternal redemption" (Heb 9:12). He himself stated: "I am the way...no one comes to the Father except through me" (Jn 14:6).

For this reason Jesus also said on the eve of his passion: "It is to your advantage that I go away." It is to your advantage, it is necessary and it is indispensable from the point of view of the eternal salvific economy. Jesus explained this fully to the apostles: "It is to your advantage that I go away, for if I do not go away, the Counselor will not come to you: but if I go, I will send him to you" (Jn 16:7). Yes, Christ must end his earthly presence, the visible presence in the world of the Son of God made man, so that he may remain in an invisible way, by virtue of the Spirit of truth, of the Counselor-Paraclete. He therefore promised repeatedly: "I go away, and I will come to you" (Jn 14:1-3, 28).

Here we are in the presence of a twofold mystery: that of the eternal divine predestination, which determines the ways, the times and the harmonious flow of the history of salvation according to a marvelous plan which is unfathomable to us; and that of Christ's presence in the human world through the Holy Spirit who sanctifies and vivifies. It is the mystery of the Son's humanity acting through the Holy Spirit in souls and in the Church—a truth clearly taught by Jesus—which remains shrouded in the translucent obscurity of the trinitarian and Christological mystery, and demands our humble and wise act of faith.

Christ is visibly present in the Church also in a sacramental manner. The Eucharist is at the heart of the Church. When Jesus for the first time announced its institution, many "took offense" (cf Jn 6:61) because he spoke of "eating his body and drinking his blood." It was then that Jesus retorted: "Do you take offense at this? Then what if you were to see the Son of Man ascending where he was before? It is the Spirit that gives life; the flesh is of no avail" (Jn 6:62-63).

Jesus is speaking here of his ascension into heaven. When his earthly body is put to death on the cross, the Spirit "which gives life" will be manifested. Christ will ascend to the Father so that the Spirit may come. On Easter day the Spirit will glorify Christ's body in the resurrection. On the day of Pentecost the Spirit will descend on the apostles and on the Church. By renewing in the Eucharist the memorial of Christ's death, we may participate in the new life of his body glorified by the Spirit, and in this way prepare ourselves to enter the "eternal dwellings" where our Redeemer has preceded us to prepare a place for us in the "Father's house" (Jn 14:2).

General audience of April 5, 1989

The Ascension Is the Fulfillment of the Mystery of the Incarnation

The "announcements" of the ascension examined in the previous catechesis shed light on the truth expressed by the earliest creeds in the concise words: "He ascended into heaven." We have already observed that we are dealing with a mystery which is an object of faith. It completes the mystery of the Incarnation. It is the ultimate fulfillment of the messianic mission of the Son of God who had come on earth to redeem us.

Nonetheless, it is also a fact which can be known from the biographical and historical data concerning Jesus, which are contained in the Gospels.

Let us refer to the texts of Luke, and first of all to the last verses of his Gospel: "Then he led them out as far as Bethany, and lifting up his hands he blessed them. While he blessed them, he parted from them, and was carried up into heaven" (Lk 24:50-51). This means that the apostles had a sensation of "movement" of the whole figure of Jesus, and of an action of "separation" from the earth. The fact that Jesus blessed the apostles at that moment indicates the salvific meaning of his departure. As in the whole of his redemptive mission, his departure included and gave to the world every spiritual good.

This text of Luke, considered in isolation from the others, would seem to suggest that Jesus ascended into heaven on the very day of the resurrection, after his apparition to the apostles (cf. Lk 24:36-49). However, if we read the entire account, we see that the evangelist wishes to synthesize the final events of Christ's life, for he is anxious to describe Jesus' salvific mission which ended with his glorification. Luke records further details of those final events in the Acts of the Apostles, which completes his Gospel. In it he resumes the narrative contained in the Gospel, in order to continue the history of the origins of the Church.

Time and place of the ascension

We read at the beginning of Acts a passage in which Luke presents the apparitions and the ascension in greater detail: "To them [the apostles] he presented himself alive after his passion by many proofs, appearing to them during forty days, and speaking of the kingdom of God" (Acts 1:3). This gives us an indication about the date of the ascension: forty days after the resurrection. We shall see shortly that it also informs us about the place.

As regards the question of time, one does not see why it should be denied that Jesus appeared repeatedly to his disciples during forty days, as stated in Acts. The biblical symbolism of the number forty, understood as indicating a period of time completely sufficient for the attainment of the desired purpose, is accepted by Jesus. He had previously withdrawn for forty days into the desert before beginning his ministry, and now appeared for forty days on earth before ascending definitively into heaven. Undoubtedly time in relation to the risen Jesus is a different standard of measure from ours. The risen one is already in the eternal *now* which is without succession or variation. However, inasmuch as he still operates in the world, instructing the apostles and establishing the Church, the transcendent *now* is inserted into the time of the human world, by once again adapting himself to it through love. Thus the mystery of the eternity-time relationship is heightened by the permanence of the risen Christ on earth. Nevertheless, the mystery does not cancel his presence in space and time. Rather it exalts and raises to the level of eternal values what he does, says, touches, institutes and determines: in a word, the Church. Therefore, we say once again: I believe, but without in the least glossing over the reality of what Luke has told us.

Certainly, when Christ ascended into heaven, this coexistence and nexus between the eternal *now* and earthly time is dissolved, and there remains the time of the pilgrim Church in history. Christ's presence is now invisible and beyond time, like the action of the Holy Spirit in souls.

According to the Acts of the Apostles, Jesus "was taken up into heaven" (1:2) on the Mount of Olives (cf. 1:12). It was from there that the apostles returned to Jerusalem after the ascension. Before this happened, Jesus gave them their final instructions. For example, "He charged them not to depart from Jerusalem, but to wait for the promise of the Father" (Acts 1:4). This promise of the Father was the coming of the Holy Spirit: "You shall be baptized with the Holy Spirit" (Acts 1:5); "You shall receive power when the Holy Spirit has come upon you..." (Acts 1:8). Then it was that "when he had said this, as they were looking on, he was lifted up, and a cloud took him out of their sight" (Acts 1:9).

The Mount of Olives had been the place of Jesus' agony in Gethsemane, and it was the last point of contact between the risen one and the small group of his disciples at the moment of his ascension. This happened after Jesus has repeated the announcement of the sending of the Spirit, by whose action that small group would be transformed into the Church and launched on the pathway of history. The ascension is therefore the final event of Christ's life and earthly mission. Pentecost will be the first day of the life and history "of his body which is the Church" (Col 1:24). This is the fundamental meaning of the fact of the ascension, beyond the particular circumstances in which it took place and the context of the biblical symbolism in which it can be considered.

According to Luke, Jesus "was lifted up, and a cloud took him out of their sight" (Acts 1:9). In this text two essential points are to be noted: "he was lifted up" (elevation-exaltation) and "a cloud took him" (entrance into the *chiaroscuro* of mystery).

"He was lifted up": this expression corresponds to the sensible and spiritual experience of the apostles. It refers to an upward movement, to a passage from earth to heaven, especially as a sign of another "passage": Christ passes to the glorified state in God. The first meaning of the ascension is precisely this: a revelation that the risen one has entered the heavenly intimacy of God. That is proved by "the cloud," a biblical sign of the divine presence. Christ disappears from the eyes of his disciples by entering the transcendent sphere of the invisible God.

This last consideration is a further confirmation of the meaning of the mystery which is Jesus Christ's ascension into heaven. The Son who "came forth from the Father and came into the world, now leaves the world and goes to the Father" (cf. Jn 16:28). This return to the Father, the elevation "to the right hand of the Father," concretely realizes a messianic truth foretold in the Old Testament. When the evangelist Mark tells us that "the Lord Jesus...was taken up into heaven" (Mk 16:19), his words echo the "prophecy of the Lord" recorded in Psalm 110:1: "The Lord said to my lord, 'Sit at my right hand, till I make your enemies your footstool.'" "To sit at the right hand of God" means to share in his kingly power and divine dignity.

Jesus had foretold it: "You will see the Son of Man sitting at the right hand of the Power, and coming with the clouds of heaven," as we read in Mark's Gospel (Mk 14:62). Luke in his turn writes: "The Son of Man shall be seated at the right hand of the power of God" (Lk 22:69). Likewise the deacon Stephen, the first martyr at Jerusalem, at the time of his death will see Christ: "I see the heavens opened, and the Son of Man standing at the right hand of God" (Acts 7:56). The idea was therefore rooted and widespread in the early Christian communities, as an expression of the kingship attained by Jesus by his ascension into heaven.

Likewise the Apostle Paul, when writing to the Romans, expresses the same truth about Christ Jesus, "who died, yes, who was raised from the dead, who is at the right hand of God, who intercedes for us" (Rom 8:34). In the Letter to the Colossians Paul writes: "If, then, you have been raised with Christ, seek the things which are above, where Christ is seated at the right hand of God" (Col 3:1; cf. Eph 1:20). We read in the Letter to the Hebrews: "We have such a high priest, one who is seated at the right hand of the throne of the Majesty in heaven" (Heb 1:3; 8:1); and again: "...who endured the cross, despising the shame, and is seated at the right hand of the throne of God" (Heb 10:12 and 12:2).

Peter, in his turn, proclaims that Christ "has gone into heaven, and is at the right hand of God, with angels, authorities, and powers subject to him" (1 Pet 3:22).

In his first discourse on Pentecost Day, Peter will say of Christ that "being exalted at the right hand of God, and having received from the Father the promise of the Holy Spirit, he has poured out this which you see and hear" (Acts 2:33; cf. also 5:31). Here a new element referring to the Holy Spirit is inserted into the truth of the ascension and kingship of Christ.

Let us reflect on it for a moment. In the Apostles' Creed the ascension into heaven is associated with the Messiah's elevation into the Father's kingdom: "He ascended into heaven and is seated at the right hand of the Father." This signifies the inauguration of the kingdom of the Messiah, which fulfills the prophetic vision of the Book of Daniel on the Son of Man: "To him was given dominion and glory and kingdom, that all peoples, nations, and languages should serve him; his dominion is an everlasting dominion, which shall not pass away, and his kingdom one that shall not be destroyed" (Dan 7:13-14).

Peter's Pentecost discourse makes known to us that to the eyes of the apostles, in the context of the New Testament, Christ's elevation to the right hand of the Father is linked especially to the descent of the Holy Spirit. Peter's words witness to the apostles' conviction that only by the ascension did Jesus "receive the Holy Spirit from the Father," to pour it out as he had promised.

Peter's discourse likewise testifies that with the descent of the Holy Spirit the apostles definitively became aware of the vision of that kingdom which Christ had announced from the very beginning and of which he had spoken also after the resurrection (cf. Acts 1:3). Even then his hearers had asked him about the restoration of the kingdom of Israel (cf. Acts 1:6), so deeply imbedded in their minds was the temporalistic interpretation of the messianic mission. Only after having received "the power" of the Spirit of truth, "did they become witnesses to Christ" and to his messianic kingdom, which was definitively brought into being when the glorified Christ "was seated at the right hand of the Father." In God's economy of salvation there is therefore a close connection between Christ's elevation and the descent of the Holy Spirit upon the apostles. From that moment the apostles became witnesses to the kingdom that will have no end. In this perspective the words which they heard after Christ's ascension acquire a fullness of meaning, namely, "This Jesus who was taken up from you into heaven, will come in the same way as you saw him go into heaven" (Acts 1:11). This is a prophecy of a final and definitive fullness which will be had when, in the power of the Spirit of Christ, the whole divine plan in history will attain its fulfillment.

General audience of April 12, 1989

Jesus Is Lord

There is a solemn eloquence about Peter's announcement in his first discourse on the day of Pentecost at Jerusalem: "This Jesus God raised up, and of that we all are witnesses. Being therefore exalted at the right hand of God, and having received from the Father the promises of the Holy Spirit, he has poured out this which you see and hear" (Acts 2:32-33). "Let all the house of Israel therefore know assuredly that God has made him both Lord and Christ, this Jesus whom you crucified" (Acts 2:36). These words, addressed to the multitude comprising the inhabitants of Jerusalem and the pilgrims who had come there from various parts for the celebration of the feast, proclaim the lifting up of Christ—crucified and risen—"to the right hand of God." The "lifting up," that is, the ascension into heaven, signified the sharing of Christ as man in the power and authority of God himself. This sharing in the power and authority of the Triune God is manifested in the sending of the Counselor, the Spirit of truth who, "taking" (Jn 16:14) from the redemption effected by Christ, brings about the conversion of human hearts. So true is this, indeed, that on

that very day at Jerusalem "when they heard this they were cut
to the heart" (Acts 2:37). It is well known that there were
thousands of conversions within a few days.

The ensemble of the paschal events mentioned by the
Apostle Peter in his Pentecost discourse definitively reveals
Jesus as sent by the Father as Messiah and Lord.

The awareness that he was "the Lord" had already in
some way entered the minds of the apostles during Christ's
prepaschal activity. He himself referred to this fact at the Last
Supper: "You call me Teacher and Lord; and you are right, for
so I am" (Jn 13:13). This explains why the evangelists speak of
Christ as "Lord" as something generally accepted in the Christian communities. In particular, Luke has the angel announcing
to the shepherds the birth of Christ in the words: "There is
born to you...a Savior, who is Christ the Lord" (Lk 2:11). In
many other places Luke uses the same term (cf. Lk 7:13; 10:1;
10:41; 11:39; 12:42; 13:15; 17:6; 22:61). It is certain, however, that the ensemble of the paschal events finally
consolidated this awareness. It is in the light of these events
that one must understand the word "Lord" also in reference to
the previous life and activity of the Messiah. Nevertheless, one
must examine in depth the import and meaning of the word
particularly in the context of the taking up and glorification of
the risen Christ in his ascension into heaven.

One of the most frequently repeated statements in the
Pauline letters is that Christ is Lord. There is the well-known
passage of the First Letter to the Corinthians: "For us there is
one God, the Father, from whom are all things and for whom
we exist, and one Lord, Jesus Christ, through whom are all
things and through whom we exist" (1 Cor 8:6; cf. 16:22; Rom
10:9; Col 2:6). Again, in the Letter to the Philippians Paul
presents as Lord, the Christ who humbled himself unto death
and was exalted so "that at the name of Jesus every knee
should bow, in heaven and on earth and under the earth, and

every tongue confess that Jesus Christ is Lord, to the glory of God the Father" (Phil 2:10-11). However, Paul emphasizes that "no one can say that 'Jesus is Lord' except by the Holy Spirit" (1 Cor 12:3). Therefore, it is "through the power of the Holy Spirit" that the Apostle Thomas said to Christ who appeared to him after the resurrection: "My Lord and my God!" (Jn 20:28). The same is true for the deacon Stephen who, while being stoned, prayed: "Lord Jesus, receive my spirit...do not hold this sin against them" (Acts 7:59-60).

Finally, the Book of Revelation concludes the cycle of sacred history and of revelation with the invocation of the Bride and of the Spirit: "Come, Lord Jesus" (Rev 22:20).

It is the mystery of the action of the "enlivening" Holy Spirit who continually infuses into our souls the light to recognize Christ, the grace to root his life more deeply within us and the power to proclaim that he—and he alone—is Lord.

Jesus Christ is Lord because he possesses the fullness of power "in heaven and on earth." It is kingly power "far above all rule and authority and power and dominion.... He has put all things under his feet" (Eph 1:21-22). At the same time it is priestly power of which the Letter to the Hebrews speaks at length in reference to Psalm 110:4: "You are a priest for ever, according to the order of Melchizedek" (Heb 5:6). Christ's eternal priesthood implies the power to sanctify so that Christ "becomes the source of eternal salvation to all who obey him" (Heb 5:9). "Consequently he is able for all time to save those who draw near to God through him, since he always lives to make intercession for them" (Heb 7:25). Likewise in the Letter to the Romans we read that Christ "is at the right hand of God and intercedes for us" (Rom 8:34). Finally, St. John assures us: "If any one does sin, we have an advocate with the Father, Jesus Christ the righteous" (1 Jn 2:1).

As Lord, Christ is the Head of the Church, his Body. It is the central idea of St. Paul's great cosmic-historical-soteriological "fresco" describing the content of God's eternal plan in the first chapters of the letters to the Ephesians and to the Colossians: "He has put all things under his feet and has made him the head over all things for the Church, which is his body, the fullness of him who fills all in all" (Eph 1:22). "For in him all the fullness of God was pleased to dwell" (Col 1:19), in him in whom "the whole fullness of deity dwells bodily" (Col 2:9).

The Book of Acts tell us that Christ "acquired" the Church "with his own blood" (Acts 20:28; cf. 1 Cor 6:20). Moreover, Jesus, when going to the Father, said to his disciples: "I am with you all days, to the close of the age"; in this he was really announcing the mystery of this Mystical Body which continually draws from him the life-giving powers of the redemption. The redemption continues its work as the effect of Christ's glorification.

It is true that Christ has always been "Lord" from the first moment of the Incarnation, for he is the Son of God, one in being with the Father, who became man for us. Undoubtedly, he became Lord in the fullest sense by the fact that "he humbled himself ('he emptied himself') and became obedient unto death, even death on a cross" (Phil 2:8). Lifted up, assumed into heaven and glorified, having thus completely fulfilled his mission, he remains in the Body of his Church on earth by means of the redemption effected in individuals and in the whole of society through the Holy Spirit. The redemption is the source of the authority which Christ, through the Holy Spirit, exercises over the Church, as we read in the Letter to the Ephesians: "And his gifts were that some should be apostles, some prophets, some evangelists, some pastors and teachers, for the equipment of the saints, for the work of the ministry, for building up the body of Christ...to the measure of the stature of the fullness of Christ" (Eph 4:11-13).

By an extension of the kingship conferred on him over the whole economy of salvation, Christ is Lord of the entire universe. We learn this from the other great "fresco" of the Letter to the Ephesians: "He who descended is he who also ascended far above all the heavens, that he might fill all things" (Eph 4:10). In the First Letter to the Corinthians St. Paul adds that everything has been subjected to him: "For God has put all things in subjection under his feet" (referring to Psalm 8:5). "When it says 'All things are put in subjection under him,' it is plain that he is excepted who put all things under him" (1 Cor 15:27). The Apostle further develops this thought when he writes: "When all things are subjected to him, then the Son himself will also be subjected to him who put all things under him. that God may be everything to every one" (1 Cor 15:28). "Then comes the end, when he delivers the kingdom to God the Father after destroying every rule and every authority and power" (1 Cor 15:24).

The Constitution *Gaudium et Spes* of the Second Vatican Council has taken up this fascinating. theme by stating that: "The Lord is the goal of human history, the focal point of the longings of history and civilization, the center of the human race, the joy of every heart and the answer to all its yearnings" *(GS* 45). We can summarize this by saying that Christ is the Lord of history. In him the history of man, and it may be said of all creation, finds its transcendent fulfillment. This is what was called in tradition the recapitulation, that is, the uniting or summing up *(re-capitulatio)*. This concept is based on the Letter to the Ephesians which describes God's eternal design "to unite all things in Christ, things in heaven and things on earth...as a plan for the fullness of time" (Eph 1:10).

Finally, we must add that Christ is Lord of eternal life. It is he who shall come to judge the living and the dead in the last judgment of which Matthew's Gospel speaks: "When the Son of Man comes in his glory, and all the angels with him, then he will sit on his glorious throne...Then the king will say to those at his right hand, 'Come, O blessed of my Father, inherit the

kingdom prepared for you from the foundation of the world'"
(Mt 25:31, 34).

The full right to judge definitively human actions and
consciences belongs to Christ as Redeemer of the world. He
"acquired" this right through the cross. Therefore the Father
"has given all judgment to the Son" (Jn 5:22). The Son, however, did not come precisely to judge, but to save; to bestow
the divine life that is in him. "For as the Father has life in
himself, so he has granted the Son also to have life in himself,
and has given him authority to execute judgment, because he is
the Son of Man" (Jn 5:26-27).

It is therefore a power that coincides with the mercy that
flows into his heart from the bosom of the Father, from whom
the Son proceeds and becomes man "for us men and for our
salvation." Christ crucified and risen, Christ who "ascended to
heaven and sits at the right hand of the Father," Christ who is
therefore the Lord of eternal life, towers above the world and
above history as a sign of infinite love surrounded with glory,
but desirous to receive from every man a reply of love in order
to grant him eternal life.

General audience of April 19, 1989

Index

S

auline BOOKS & MEDIA

ALASKA
750 West 5th Ave., Anchorage, AK 99501; 907-272-8183

CALIFORNIA
3908 Sepulveda Blvd., Culver City, CA 90230; 310-397-8676
5945 Balboa Ave., San Diego, CA 92111; 619-565-9181
46 Geary Street, San Francisco, CA 94108; 415-781-5180

FLORIDA
145 S.W. 107th Ave., Miami, FL 33174; 305-559-6715

HAWAII
1143 Bishop Street, Honolulu, HI 96813; 808-521-2731

ILLINOIS
172 North Michigan Ave., Chicago, IL 60601; 312-346-4228

LOUISIANA
4403 Veterans Memorial Blvd., Metairie, LA 70006; 504-887-7631

MASSACHUSETTS
50 St. Paul's Ave., Jamaica Plain, Boston, MA 02130; 617-522-8911
Rte. 1, 885 Providence Hwy., Dedham, MA 02026; 617-326-5385

MISSOURI
9804 Watson Rd., St. Louis, MO 63126; 314-965-3512

NEW JERSEY
561 U.S. Route 1, Wick Plaza, Edison, NJ 08817; 908-572-1200

NEW YORK
150 East 52nd Street, New York, NY 10022; 212-754-1110
78 Fort Place, Staten Island, NY 10301; 718-447-5071

OHIO
2105 Ontario Street, Cleveland, OH 44115; 216-621-9427

PENNSYLVANIA
Northeast Shopping Center, 9171-A Roosevelt Blvd., Philadelphia, PA
19114; 215-676-9494

SOUTH CAROLINA
243 King Street, Charleston, SC 29401; 803-577-0175

TENNESSEE
4811 Poplar Ave., Memphis, TN 38117; 901-761-2987

TEXAS
114 Main Plaza, San Antonio, TX 78205; 210-224-8101

VIRGINIA
1025 King Street, Alexandria, VA 22314; 703-549-3806

CANADA
3022 Dufferin Street, Toronto, Ontario, Canada M6B 3T5; 416-781-9131